# Crime Fiction and National Identities
## in the Global Age

# Crime Fiction and National Identities in the Global Age

## Critical Essays

*Edited by* JULIE H. KIM

McFarland & Company, Inc., Publishers
*Jefferson, North Carolina*

Library of Congress Cataloguing-in-Publication Data

Names: Kim, Julie H., editor.
Title: Crime fiction and national identities in the global age : critical essays /
    edited by Julie H. Kim.
Description: Jefferson, North Carolina : McFarland & Company, Inc.,
    Publishers, 2020 | Includes bibliographical references and index.
Identifiers: LCCN 2020012653 | ISBN 9781476677156 (paperback : acid free paper) ∞
    ISBN 9781476640426 (ebook)
Subjects: LCSH: Detective and mystery stories—History and criticism. |
    National characteristics in literature.
Classification: LCC PN3448.D4 C734 2020 | DDC 809.3/872—dc23
LC record available at https://lccn.loc.gov/2020012653

British Library Cataloguing data are available

ISBN 978-1-4766-7715-6 (print)
ISBN 978-1-4766-4042-6 (ebook)

Front cover photograph by Igor Stevanovic/Shutterstock

Printed in the United States of America

*McFarland & Company, Inc., Publishers*
    *Box 611, Jefferson, North Carolina 28640*
    *www.mcfarlandpub.com*

For my family

# Table of Contents

# Introduction

## National Identity and International Crime Fiction in the Age of Populism and Globalization

### Julie H. Kim

In the opening chapters of *Blood from a Stone* (2005), the fourteenth installment of American novelist Donna Leon's police procedural set in Venice, the detective's professor wife Paola is appalled that their teenaged daughter regarded the murder of a Senegalese street vendor an insufficient justification for her father being late for dinner. In young Chiara's assessment, "it was only a *vu cumprà*"[1] and not "one of us." When pressed by her mother, Chiara defines "us" as "Europeans." Later, after Paola recounts the episode to her husband, readers are treated to one of Commissario Guido Brunetti's ruminations: "He liked to think he was a moderate person, but he was honest enough to accept that this belief was probably yet another national myth. It is easy to grow up without racial prejudice in a society in which there is only one race."[2] Brunetti's reflections here invite further examination: What does it mean to be a "moderate" person these days? What sorts of "national" myths do we carry about our countries? Is "racial prejudice" typically more present in societies composed of many different races? Then, a corollary to these questions emerges: What happens to a possibly self-congratulatory "national myth" when natives of a country are placed in reluctant contact with national others, forced to confront different ethnicities, races, or religions?

Perhaps one answer to this last question can be found in *The Body in the Castle Well* (2019), the twelfth entry in British reporter-turned-novelist Martin Walker's Chief Bruno Courrèges series set in the Dordogne region of France. The liberal-minded Bruno is perturbed when a local laborer rails against what he characterizes as the deteriorating state of the country: "Even the cops are going soft. Arab immigrants everywhere, calling themselves refugees. The Muslims are taking the country over, terrorists half of them, and you guys are doing nothing to stop 'em. It makes me sick." Bruno is neither the first nor the last sympathetic detective who recognizes, in the process of policing, that "there was an ugly mood building in the country."[3] Recent decades of crime fiction provide plenty of evidence that the clash of cultures brought about by immigration, recession, and wars has resulted in—or perhaps merely uncovered—resentments and hostilities flaring up in pockets of almost every country. Against the backdrop of widespread globalization, the allure of a more exclusive national identity (or "myth") sets up an ideological struggle that has been playing out in various geo-political contestations, and which are represented in popular culture.

Genres like detective and crime fiction[4] share some important advantages in tackling thorny contemporary issues. Despite early popularity at the micro level with locked room mysteries and village whodunits of the British Golden Age, the mystery story has smoothly morphed to engage with macro-level concerns in this age of globalization and multi-national crime scenes. Unlike news reporting or editorials, the same geo-political conflicts can perhaps be scrutinized with less tension in deceptively innocuous genres such as detective or crime fiction, reducing the stakes for writers and readers alike. And, of course, there are surprisingly high numbers of writers and readers. While "mystery" was always a popular genre, the 21st century witnessed an unprecedented growth. In 2010, a *Forbes* piece exclaims, "Mystery and crime publishing is bloody blooming!" and then details how "there are more debut authors, more acquisitions by editors, higher sales and greater dominance on the bestseller lists."[5]

Moreover, with the speed and frequency at which today's best-selling authors churn out series titles numbering in the teens and twenties, their works are able to mirror and dissect nearly contemporaneous socio-political events. There is such a "ripped from the headlines" quality about these genres that to read a work of murder mystery or a crime novel largely simulates the exercise of reading or watching the news—a startling array of competing nationalisms; Indian secularism versus Hindu communalism; populist rhetoric tinged with misogyny or homophobia; racial or religious or ethnic others increasingly sidelined in craven political appeals to dominant native voices; global capitalism's rampant money grab creating an economic chasm between a nation's rich and poor. All found in crime fiction. All in this collection.

## National Identity and International Crime Fiction

Australian scholar Stephen Knight has written that crime fiction "is a more interwoven and international body of writing than has often been recognized."[6] In part, this internationalization of detective fiction is owing to the pursuit of the novelty factor. As Eva Erdmann argues, the requisite "suspense" for murder mysteries is "created when the foreseeable riddle of the whodunit is replaced by mysterious surroundings that the investigative troops explore."[7] It also follows that once cities like New York, San Francisco, Chicago, Los Angeles, London, and the like are claimed by series detectives already synonymous with these towns, even American and British writers might send their new creations abroad to offer venues that are fresh and original to their readers, whether that be France (Cara Black's Aimée Leduc), Japan (Sujata Massey's Rei Shimura), Italy (Michael Dibdin's Aurelio Zen), Thailand (John Burdett's Sonchai Jitpleecheep), or Turkey (Jason Goodwin's Yashim Togalu).

In a genre where its practitioners seek to distinguish themselves amid fierce competition in a crowded field, new sites are conscripted into service to seduce loyal readers. Extreme winter weather conditions and mouthwatering bistro specials receive plenty of attention in Louise Penny's Inspector Armand Gamache series set in Québec, while digressions on the natural beauty of the Périgord and lengthy descriptions of *foie gras* preparations sometimes threaten to overwhelm murder mystery plots in Martin Walker's Chief Bruno Courrèges novels. In both series, we become familiar with habits, prejudices, foods, and idiosyncrasies of the locals in such a way that "the reading of crime novels becomes an ethnographic reading; the scene of the crime becomes the *locus genius* of the cultural tragedy."[8] Yet, as Andrew Pepper and David Schmid urge readers and scholars of contemporary crime fiction, "we need to do more than focus on the proliferation of crime fiction cultures in an ever-expanding list of countries and regions." They themselves focus on the "key tension" between "the state and globalization," and the essays in this collection share their belief about the need to study the "move between the national and the international."[9] Specifically, these essays inquire into the role of national *identity* in international crime fiction.

Cultural geographer Tim Edensor submits that "the nation persists as a pre-eminent constituent of identity and society at theoretical and popular levels. Despite the globalisation of economies, cultures and social processes, the scalar model of identity is believed to be primarily anchored in national space."[10] That is, readers in Toulouse would likely consider themselves French first, before European. People in the U.S. rarely—if ever—identify more broadly as North American. If anything, it appears that the rapid pace of globalization and expanding multiculturalism have crystallized for some individuals the necessity of fashioning a specifically *national* identity. Erdmann points to a returning interest in the status of nationality in "societies that regard multiculturalism as part of their political self-understanding and their national identity, like the USA and Israel." And, "in Europe, where the historical formation of nineteenth-century nation building is itself becoming history, there is growing affirmation, even a sort of reanimation of the culture of nationality." Writing before the second decade of 21st century, she argued that "the pursuit of the criminal was displaced by the search for cultural identity" in the crime fiction of the second half of the 20th century.[11] One can imagine that after the global economic collapse of 2008–09 and especially after the upsurge in populist rhetoric with the Brexit referendum and the American presidential election of 2016, the quest for national identity in international crime fiction has picked up even greater urgency.

## Nationalisms and Masculinities

In *The Atlantic* article "The New Authoritarians Are Waging War on Women," Peter Beinart traces a point of commonality between Donald Trump, Brazil's Jair Bolsonaro, the Philippines' Rodrigo Duterte and other authoritarian rulers. Beinart notes significant cultural and economic disparities in this "diverse set of countries": "Some are mired in recession; others are booming. Some are consumed by fears of immigration; others are not." He then goes on to argue that "besides their hostility to liberal democracy, the right-wing autocrats taking power across the world share one big thing, which often goes unrecognized in the U.S.: They all want to subordinate women."[12] Others would add, in addition to a hatred of immigrants and contempt for women, a loathing for gays and lesbians is also on the rise in many authoritarian-leaning countries.[13] Populism and especially misogyny and homophobia might accompany what some would label "toxic masculinity"; in other cases, attempts to promote or recover a sense of national pride and solidarity can align with idealized notions of masculinity associated with a country's romanticized past. In the first four essays of this collection, the authors approach the topic of national identity and masculinity in crime stories with varied perspectives and nuanced conclusions.

Tim Libretti starts the collection with an analysis of Spike Lee's *Summer of Sam* by offering a wide-ranging study on American populism and what he locates as the origins of hate. In an essay that traverses many periods, he first places the film's subject in its true-crime contexts of David Berkowitz's serial killings in 1976 and 1977 in New York City. The essay then moves both forward and far backward in time. As he writes early in the essay, "For those of us currently living in the United States under the regime of the authoritarian-minded President Donald Trump, coming to terms with and understanding the current political buzzwords of 'populism,' 'nationalism,' and 'globalism' has taken on an intellectual urgency." For Libretti, studying Spike Lee's 1999 film can be instructive for an audience grappling with our current socio-cultural moment. What might be more surprising, however, is how far back he takes this study. Ultimately revisiting the American Revolutionary period, this essay contends that "instead of achieving liberation, the processes of nation-formation and so-called revolution throughout U.S. history have only consolidated class power in the hands of the elite and sustained that class hierarchy through repressive mobilizations of racism, sexism, and homophobia—in short, through mobilizing the vast menu of hate, the varieties of which we see animating what we have come to call contemporary right-wing populism."

Offering a different type of origin narrative, Janice Shaw's essay on Australian crime fiction treats several different—including some positive—iterations of masculinity. She writes about how 19th-century Australian crime fiction situated the "hero within a harsh yet idealized vision of the Australian bush, one that fostered a protagonist both independent and disdainful of authority, while also being resilient enough to cope with the demands of an isolating and unforgiving landscape." In a study that includes works about real-world bushrangers like Ned Kelly and contemporary Australian reboots of 1930s American hard-boiled crime fiction by Raymond Chandler and Dashiell Hammett, the second essay of our collection presents Australian crime writing—true, quasi-historical, and fictional—as largely embracing several types of masculinity. The essay's title specifically references hard-boiled "larrikins" ("hero and the powerful cultural stereotype of the bush myth"), and we come to understand that readers adopt a fairly benign and perhaps even admiring attitude towards the masculine figure who flouts authority. Like Libretti, Shaw explores early nationalist roots while also analyzing trends in contemporary crime writing. She argues that Australian crime writers are "interweaving and challenging the notion of truth and historical anecdote" as well as "exploring the boundaries between literary and expository writing and engaging with the notion of what constitutes a crime."

In the next essay, Heath A. Diehl moves us to Europe and concentrates on Spanish writer Domingo Villar's Inspector Caldas novels. In the end, this essay finds that Villar "celebrates his picturesque settings of Vigo and Panxón parish as sites at which progress and tradition can co-exist." Along the way, however, "Villar's novels indict the conservatism that characterizes rural Spain, identifying his perpetrators with anti-progressive ideological formations (like heterosexism, homophobia, misogyny) that must be excised from the narrative/nation." I juxtapose this essay by Diehl with Shaw's essay on Australian crime fiction since it seems useful for us to consider when rascally law-and-order-defying masculinity is celebrated and when a version of masculinity verges too close to a harmful "machismo" that must be eradicated in order for a nation to progress. Diehl defines machismo in this essay as referring "to a form of toxic masculinity that structures self-identities and power relationships among men, women, and children in Iberian and Iberian-descended cultures. Within this ideological framework, LGBTQ+ individuals stand as non-entities not only because their identities cannot be codified or explained through the 'logic' of machismo, but also because their identities threaten the very foundations of the ideology by pointing up its gaps and omissions."

Jean Gregorek's study of Icelandic financial crime fiction delivers us two contrasting types of Icelandic masculinity. The essay demonstrates how, on one hand, a "new class of financiers gained popular support in part through casting themselves as hypermasculine 'Business Vikings,' boldly circling the globe in search of fortune, tapping into nationalistic sentiments of Icelanders as 'a special breed of people.'" On the other hand, "critical Icelandic fictions reconfigure this image of Icelanders as a 'special breed' by challenging the cosmopolitan 'New Viking' and replacing him with older versions of masculinity that retain contact with land and sea." In crime novels and films where "banking and speculative finance are portrayed as parasitic, unproductive, and ultimately un–Icelandic," a glorified national image of masculinity (re-)emerges as one in pursuit of "real work" and "real trade" like "farming, fishing, and manual work." This two-pronged focus on Icelandic financial crimes and Icelandic masculinity determines that "borders still matter, cultures are still fundamentally distinguishable, and finance capital can be brought to heel."

## Insider/Outsider: The Marginal Within

In their introduction to *Detective Fiction in a Postcolonial and Transnational World,* Nels Pearson and Marc Singer maintain that "from its inception, the detective genre has been intrinsically engaged with epistemological formations that are not simply those of 'society' in the abstract—that is, dominant cultural groups and their hegemonic discourse—but those produced in encounters between nations, between races and cultures, and especially between imperial powers and their colonial territories."[14] Increasingly, crime fiction reproduces such interactions between natives and migrant others—like that between Donna Leon's Venetian policeman and Senegalese street peddler community mentioned at the beginning of this introduction—as well as perhaps more contested confrontations between dominant cultures and their marginalized or colonized others. These encounters are the subjects of the next four essays in this collection.

Somdatta Bhattacharya's essay on Danish writer Peter Høeg's 1992 novel *Miss Smilla's Feeling for Snow*[15] concentrates on the marginalized status of Smilla Qaaviqaaq Jaspersen, daughter of a Greenlandic Inuit mother and a

Danish doctor father, living in Copenhagen since the death of her mother. As the essay explains, the Danish state imposes such a "startling array of restrictions and rules and regulations" over its colonized Greenlanders that they even require a visa to visit her own homeland, and "the paternalist state often bares its fangs in the narrative, and all pretences of being a benevolent benefactor of colonial subjects are shed in moments when the state suspects Smilla of rebellion." Smilla, with her "hybrid identity" as a Greenlander in Denmark, is a physical "exile" from her beloved birthplace yet is also a cultural "outsider" in Danish society. Bhattacharya asserts that Smilla's "affirmation of a Greenlandic identity and refusal to forget that what binds her to the Danish society is a history of colonialism is also a refusal to be interpellated into a homogenous Nordic identity. The colonial metropolis and its state apparatus, with their barely disguised suspicion of the Inuit, underline the Otherness that underscores Smilla's responses to Denmark."

Our next essay, by Colette Guldimann, starts by evaluating South African literary scholar Leon de Kock's claim that "in postapartheid South Africa crime thrillers have emerged as the new form of the political novel or politically engaged fiction." Paralleling the trajectory of Deon Meyer's writing career with different stages in South Africa's recent history, this essay traces the country's postapartheid transition from the period when the country initially grappled with the construction of a new national identity to much later in the post-transition period where Meyer might be presenting a "re-enactment of the new start promised by South Africa's transition." Like Janice Shaw's earlier essay in this collection, Guldimann demonstrates how the global engages with and perhaps even facilitates the national in the way "these narratives target a South African readership using the global framework of the hardboiled detective." She reads "the personal transition Meyer's white male protagonists undergo" as providing "models of new forms of white, and Afrikaner, masculinity in postapartheid South Africa," and she also casts a spotlight on lesser-known black protagonists of Deon Meyer in two of the essay's three sections. Highlighting the cultural prominence of detective fiction, Guldimann frames the individual sections on different works by Deon Meyer—spanning 2003 to 2017—within a broader critical debate surrounding the role of global crime fiction in shaping national identity.

In the next essay, Somali Saren writes, "Contemporary authors, by introducing detectives from minority groups—be it in terms of race, gender, class or sexual orientation—have repeatedly proven that the structure of crime narrative is favorable for the discourse of identity politics." In addition to a focus on "identity politics," Saren's entry in this collection provides further support for Leon de Kock's claim about crime novels having emerged as "politically engaged fiction." As described by Joanna Slater in *The Washington Post*, Narendra Modi, re-elected in 2019 as prime minister of India, "has long embraced a brand of nationalism that views India as a fundamentally Hindu country rather than a secular republic, wooing voters with a mixture of hope and fear common to right-leaning populist leaders around the globe—a group that includes President Trump."[16] Readers of Vikram Chandra's *Sacred Games* (2006) would not be surprised to hear about the geo-political apprehension in Muslim Kashmir that followed Modi's 2019 landslide victory since, as illustrated by Saren, the crime story recreates conflicts between India's secular and Hindu nationalisms. Add to the mix the Sikh identity of Chandra's police detective Sartaj Singh, and we have an eerily timely crime novel in which its fictional plot appears to replicate some of the same tensions—between Hindu, Muslim, and Sikh—found within contemporary India.

The final essay addressing the insider/outsider is Alexandra Hauke's study which reads Native American crime fiction—concentrating on Gerald Vizenor's *The Heirs of Columbus* (1991)—through the interdisciplinary framework of law and literature, which allows for nuanced discussions of the suffering and disenfranchisement of tribal peoples. As with other essays, this entry explores marginalized others who are both insider and outsider in countries that have failed to properly protect, recognize, and affirm their status. Focusing particularly on the role of political representation, Hauke reminds us that individuals from minority communities are "statistically subjected to higher rates of victimization, incarceration, and inequalities by primarily white legal institutions and thus rely heavily on representatives working against ethnic disadvantage and white privilege in the government's highest branches." She demonstrates that "the literary and political imperatives of Native American detective writing culminate in revisionist versions of federal-tribal legal history, signifying on the inextricable link between fiction and law and thus on the power of narrative to reshape the American imaginary of 'Indians' as both constituting and challenging factors for the myth of national-legal unity."

## Crossing Cultural and Generic Borders

In an overview of central issues and perspectives involving postcolonial detective fiction, Christine Matzke and Susanne Mühleisen point out that "while cosy mysteries continue to be associated with the 'English,' or the 'hardboiled' is seen as a particular 'American' variety, regional boundaries of the classic crime novel no longer hold—and probably never did in the first place.... [N]owadays we increasingly encounter investigators with a migrant or transcultural background operating across countries and continents."[17] As we saw above, Australians and South Africans adopted the hard-boiled in the fictional world while, in real life, Icelanders made the mistake of embracing Wall Street–type financialization. Generic and cultural boundaries are repeatedly crossed in literature and in real life, and the final three essays in this collection offer examples of both types of hybridity.

Andrew Hock Soon Ng analyzes Rick Moody's "The Albertine Notes" against the "framework of the metaphysical detective fiction to reflect on … an epistemological inquiry into the nature of memory and forgetting, and whether effecting the latter serves salvific ends or renders the subject's being (*Dasein*) inauthentic." In this collection which treats mostly "realistic" narratives in recognizable socio-cultural milieus often defined by national borders, Ng's essay encourages us to take our deliberations to a "meta" level and re-calibrate our understanding of what constitutes a crime, who can bear witness, and how we recognize truthful testimony. In addition to evaluating "The Albertine Notes" as an example of "metaphysical detective fiction," Ng ponders the ambiguous treatment of "race matters" in a work where the New Yorker protagonist Kevin Lee's Asian "ethnicity is consistently made into an issue" even while this same identity does not figure significantly into the narrative's conclusion. In a haunting image from the novel, Kevin's memory of Manhattan is "fused" with the image of immigrants to New York City from places like Italy, Ireland, and Puerto Rico. This most iconic American city is also one of the most international, and it is telling that Kevin memorializes how "all those voices layered over one another, in their hundred and fifty languages, can't hear anything distinct about what they are saying, except that they're saying, *hey, time for us to be heard.*"[18]

Then, in our final two essays of the collection, we literally cross geographic boundaries and national borders. In the first of the pair, Peter Clandfield takes us from Istanbul to London's East End with Barbara Nadel who sets her novels in both Turkey and England. In one of the Istanbul-based works considered in depth, Nadel's Inspector Çetin İkmen actually migrates—undercover, through criminal traffickers—from Istanbul to London. Clandfield asserts that, in Nadel's novels, "clashes between global economics and local concerns can fuel forms of populism that are overtly intolerant or—more insidiously—that promote consumerist individualism as the sovereign good." In works which reference—without actually naming—political leaders like Britain's Boris Johnson and Turkey's Recep Tayyip Erdoğan, Nadel challenges "neat oppositions between globalized elitism and localized populism, pointing, particularly, to alliances between international finance and property industries and leading populist politicians." Positively depicting hard-working and open-minded policemen like Inspector İkmen as someone "who possesses both broad cosmopolitan views and strong local loyalties, representing a fusion of globalism and populism," Nadel's works appear to model how we might successfully support populist perspectives in this age of globalization.

Our final essay brings us back almost to the very beginning of detective fiction with its focus on Sherlock Holmes, even as author Neil McCaw ushers us well into the 21st century. Directing our attention to some of the most contemporary works in the entire collection, this essay on the "global hybridity of Sherlock Holmes" introduces us to two TV shows, Russia's *Sherlock Holmes* (2013) and Japan's *Miss Sherlock* (2018–). McCaw points out that the "pliability" of the crime fiction genre allowed it to gain "wider, *global* popularity" while, simultaneously, writers were able to "chime with—and crucially more likely to appeal to—the characteristics of a range of native audiences." As we recognize, "crime texts of all kinds became particular manifestations of cultural hybridity," and the inherent intermingling of nationalities and ethnicities was central to "how the genre was able to address both international and local audiences in parallel, responding implicitly to global and regional sensibilities." Accordingly, Holmes has evolved into "a repeatedly exchanged cultural currency, traded between nations, ethnicities, and languages, and yet always seemingly *owned* by each of them." Like Clandfield's essay which precedes it, this final essay by McCaw identifies ways in which crime fiction complicates the ostensible dichotomy between national and international, bridging populist impulses and global appeals.

## NOTES

1. Donna Leon, in an interview, describes a *vu cumprà* as an "African street peddler," http://italian-mysteries.com/leon-MacActivity.html?q=interviews/2005/donnaleon. Accessed September 9, 2019.

2. Donna Leon, *Blood from a Stone* (New York: Atlantic Monthly Press, 2005), 26, 30.

3. Martin Walker, *The Body in the Castle Well* (New York: Alfred A. Knopf, 2019), 228–29.

4. Some works in this collection treat more narrowly defined "detective" fiction (with series detectives, police affiliation, or identifiable investigative processes), while others focus on the broader category of "crime" stories (whether they be in short stories, books, movies, or on TV).

5. Alan Rinzler, "Mystery and Crime Publishing Is Bloody Blooming!" *Forbes* (October 28, 2010), https://www.forbes.com/sites/booked/2010/10/28/mystery-and-crime-publishing-is-bloody-booming/#73d8ee254c42. Accessed September 16, 2019.

6. Quoted in Christine Matzke and Susanne Mühleisen, *Postcolonial Postmortems: Crime Fiction from a Transcultural Perspective* (Amsterdam: Rodopi Press, 2006), 2–3.

7. Eva Erdmann, "Nationality International: Detective Fiction in the Late Twentieth Century," in *Investigating Identities: Questions of Identity in Contemporary International Crime Fiction,* Marieke Krajenbrink and Kate M. Quinn, eds. (Amsterdam: Rodopi Press, 2009), 18–19.

8. *Ibid.*, 19.

9. Andrew Pepper and David Schmid, *Globalization and the State in Contemporary Crime Fiction: A World of Crime* (London: Palgrave Macmillan, 2016), 1–2.

10. Tim Edensor, *National Identity, Popular Culture and Everyday Life* (Oxford: Berg, 2002), 1.

11. Erdmann, 19.

12. Peter Beinart, "The New Authoritarians Are Waging War on Women," *The Atlantic* (January/February 2019), https://www.theatlantic.com/magazine/archive/2019/01/authoritarian-sexism-trump-duterte/576382/. Accessed September 14, 2019.

13. For example, "like many right-wing populists around the world, Bolsonaro

embraced racist, homophobic, and misogynist rhetoric, achieving a level of provocation so incendiary that the country's attorney general charged then-candidate Bolsonaro 'with inciting hatred and discrimination against blacks, indigenous communities, women and gays.'" Max Bergmann, Carolyn Kenney, and Trevor Sutton, "The Rise of Far-Right Populism Threatens Global Democracy and Security," *The Center for American Progress* (November 2, 2018), https://www.americanprogress.org/issues/security/news/2018/11/02/460498/rise-far-right-populism-threatens-global-democracy-security/. Accessed September 14, 2019.

14. Nels Pearson and Marc Singer, *Detective Fiction in a Postcolonial and Transnational World* (Surrey: Ashgate, 2009), 3.

15. In the U.S., the novel's title is *Smilla's Sense of Snow.*

16. Joanna Slater, "In Modi's move on Kashmir, a road map for his 'new India,'" *The Washington Post* (August 15, 2019), https://beta.washingtonpost.com/world/asia_pacific/in-modis-move-on-kashmir-a-road-map-for-his-new-india/2019/08/15/1fff923a-beab-11e9-a8b0–7ed8a0d5dc5d_story.html?noredirect=on. Accessed September 15, 2019.

17. Matzke and Muhleisen, 3.

18. Rick Moody, "Albertine Notes," in *McSweeney's Mammoth Treasure of Thrilling Tales,* Michal Chabon, ed. (Harmondsworth: Penguin, 2004), 463.

## BIBLIOGRAPHY

Beinart, Peter. "The New Authoritarians Are Waging War on Women." *The Atlantic,* January/February 2019. https://www.theatlantic.com/magazine/archive/2019/01/authoritarian-sexism-trump-duterte/576382/.

Bergmann, Max, Carolyn Kenney, and Trevor Sutton. "The Rise of Far-Right Populism Threatens Global Democracy and Security." *The Center for American Progress,* November 2, 2018. https://www.americanprogress.org/issues/security/news/2018/11/02/460498/rise-far-right-populism-threatens-global-democracy-security/.

Edensor, Tim. *National Identity, Popular Culture and Everyday Life.* Oxford: Berg, 2002.

Erdmann, Eva. "Nationality International: Detective Fiction in the Late Twentieth Century," in *Investigating Identities: Questions of Identity in Contemporary International Crime Fiction.* Marieke Krajenbrink and Kate M. Quinn, eds. 11–26. Amsterdam: Rodopi Press, 2009.

Leon, Donna. *Blood from a Stone.* New York: Atlantic Monthly Press, 2005.

Leon, Donna. Interview accessed at http://italian-mysteries.com/leon-MacActivity.html?q=interviews/2005/donnaleon.

Matzke, Christine, and Susanne Mühleisen, eds. *Postcolonial Postmortems: Crime Fiction from a Transcultural Perspective.* Amsterdam: Rodopi Press, 2006.

Moody, Rick. "Albertine Notes," in *McSweeney's Mammoth Treasure of Thrilling Tales.* Michael Chabon, ed. Harmondsworth: Penguin, 2004.

Pearson, Nels, and Marc Singer. *Detective Fiction in a Postcolonial and Transnational World.* Surrey: Ashgate, 2009.

Pepper, Andrew, and David Schmid, eds. *Globalization and the State in Contemporary Crime Fiction: A World of Crime.* London: Palgrave Macmillan, 2016.

Rinzler, Alan. "Mystery and Crime Publishing Is Bloody Blooming!" *Forbes,* October 28, 2010. https://www.forbes.com/sites/booked/2010/10/28/mystery-and-crime-publishing-is-bloody-booming/#532007dc4c42.

Slater, Joanna. "In Modi's move on Kashmir, a road map for his 'new India,'" *Washington Post,* August 15, 2019. https://beta.washingtonpost.com/world/asia_pacific/in-modis-move-on-kashmir-a-road-map-for-his-new-india/2019/08/15/1fff923a-beab-11e9-a8b0–7ed8a0d5dc5d_story.html?noredirect=on.

Walker, Martin. *The Body in the Castle Well.* New York: Alfred A. Knopf, 2019.

# Getting Fooled Again by Populism

## Detecting the Origins of American Hate in Spike Lee's Summer of Sam

### TIM LIBRETTI

At a climactic moment in Spike Lee's 1999 film *Summer of Sam*,[1] the self-authorized vigilante squad of Italian-American characters from the Bronx head to the home of Richie Trangali (Adrien Brody), having, they believe, sleuthed him out as the Son of Sam serial killer. The scene is thick with dramatic yet tragic irony. Viewers know full well that Richie Trangali is not the murderer, as the film takes as its setting and informing historical narrative David Berkowitz's serial killing spree that stretched from 1976 through the summer of 1977 in New York City, actually featuring scenes dramatizing Berkowitz's shootings of women and young lovers. Indeed, Lee even simultaneously represents the police apprehension of Berkowitz just before he represents the vigilantes mercilessly beating Richie. What accounted, in Lee's narrative of detection, for the vigilantes' erroneous crime-solving? Their sleuthing was informed by a set of cultural attitudes, which we might now term "hate" or "right-wing populism," that made them see Richie, an old friend of theirs from the neighborhood, as a "freak," an ultimate "other," causing them anxiety and arousing suspicion and terror on their part.

Early in the movie, after being away from the neighborhood for some time, Richie returns to the waterfront hangout in front of the "Dead End" sign where his neighborhood friends congregate. He has re-fashioned himself in punk rock style, featuring spiked hair, wearing a British flag muscle shirt and a spiked collar, and speaking with a British accent. His friend Joey (Michael Rispoli), from whom Richie has come to buy drugs, derides him, saying, "You come back to neighborhood lookin' like a fuckin' freak, talkin' like a British fag. And we're supposed to be okay with that?" As the city's hysteria over the murders swells to a tumult, Joey and his gang also learn that Richie has been dancing for money at Male World, a gay male erotic dance club, where he also lets men perform oral sex on him for pay. This discovery is the tipping point. They conclude he must be the killer because he is not what he says he is and has disturbed the cultural order by defying the safe and familiar identity categories of heterosexist white America, by being, in Joey's words, "a fuckin' freak." Luring Richie from his mother's garage where he lives, Joey and the other neighborhood men, including Anthony (Al Palagonia) dressed prominently in a t-shirt with an American flag design, surround Richie—associated with Britain in his punk attitude even if he is not wearing the shirt in this scene—attacking him with baseball bats while he swings back, fending them off with his electric guitar. The scene is a brilliant one for the way Lee over-determines the dense symbolism. Clearly, Lee analogizes this misguided attack, a hateful scapegoating, to the American Revolution, when America birthed itself as a nation freeing itself from British rule. Here, though, Richie is the national "other," seen as the enemy of America, and his enemy status is arrived at through the homophobia of the men in the neighborhood. Lee effectively links American national identity as connected to and even borne out of a heterosexist and homophobic cultural ethos, or, more to the point, a repressive—especially sexually repressive— and patriarchal, cultural system.

Looking back from our present moment, Lee seems to have diagnosed somewhat presciently the defining ethos of right-wing populism that engendered American culture and identity at its "revolutionary" inception and, arguably, has animated the development of national identity and culture to the present, such that this violent climactic scene, more than simply an analogue of the revolution, is seen as a repetition of it. Chip Berlet and Matthew Lyons, for example, in their impressive historical study *Right-Wing Populism in America: Too Close for Comfort*, chart what they refer to as "repressive populist politics" from early America to the present. Their description of its manifestations in the 1980s resonates strongly with the historical analysis *Summer of Sam* unfolds and provides a useful kind of definition to talk about "populism" in America, particularly as we see Lee address and represent it in the film. Looking at the 1980s, for example, Berlet and Lyons write:

> Economic dislocations ... increased scapegoating's appeal among sections of the population. The erosion of traditional hierarchies fueled demands to reassert White male heterosexual privilege and power. Newly visible social groups—such as lesbians and gay men, or millions of recent immigrants from Asia, Latin America, and elsewhere—became handy targets for old bigotries.[2]

This repeated pattern of so-called populist movements, fascist in nature—acting out of resentment and real misery and disfranchisement, and hoping to challenge power structures by targeting minority groups—characterizes for Berlet and Lyons the trajectory of right-wing populism, often masquerading as radical revolutionism, from early America to the present, as I will explore in this essay.

This climactic moment in *Summer of Sam* really dramatizes in an encapsulated way what Berlet and Lyons identify in U.S. history as "a pattern of repressive populist politics that would be repeated again and again." The wonder of *Summer of Sam*, in fact, particularly in its focus on sexuality and sexual repression in American culture, is its analysis of hate in American culture as a function of repression and its diagnosis of the failure of actual revolutionary liberation in the U.S. as a function of our repeated cultural confusing of repression as freedom. Lee's focus on sexuality and sexual repression and more broadly on the category-defying "freak," in fact, I will argue, enables an analysis of U.S. history and culture that encompasses the intertwined dynamics of race, class, gender, and sexuality within the context of economic development. As I develop this reading of how *Summer of Sam* analyzes U.S. history and culture, I will draw on James Baldwin's 1985 essay "Freaks and the American Ideal of Manhood," which gives us a language to unlock and discuss the multiple and mutually informing dimensions of repression—and hence of repressive and hateful populism—in U.S. culture in historical and deeply human ways. The "freak," for Baldwin—and Lee as well—defies categories by overtly expressing the multiplicity (racial, gender, sexual, etc.) we all contain but are taught and encouraged to repress or otherwise risk great danger. As Baldwin explains,

> Freaks are called freaks and are treated as they are treated—in the main, abominably—because they are human beings who cause to echo, deep within us, our most profound terrors and desires.
>
> Most of us, however, do not appear to be freaks—though we are rarely what we appear to be. We are, for the most part, visibly male or female, our social roles defined by our sexual equipment.
>
> But we are all androgynous, not only because we are all born of a woman impregnated by the seed of a man but because each of us, helplessly and forever, contains the other—male in female, female in male, white in black and black in white. We are part of each other. Many of our countrymen appear to find this fact exceedingly inconvenient and even unfair, and so, very often, do I. But none of us can do anything about it.[3]

The freak, then, is an over-determined figure, much like Richie Trangali in *Summer of Sam*, containing and hence exploding all the dichotomies organizing U.S. culture and society—racial, sexual, and otherwise—highlighting the "otherness" that is part of each of us but which we repress, individually and collectively on the social level, to our great detriment. Baldwin, as we will see, analyzes this repression as an informing and deleterious dynamic in the historical development of the U.S. nation and economy, as does Lee in *Summer of Sam*, diagnosing the deadly hate of right-wing populism as rooted in racial, economic, and sexual repression. Both Baldwin and Lee pose the embracing of the freak, of our freakish selves and of a freakish cultural logic, as a solution to the inhumanity of our social and economic systems. While *Summer of Sam* was released in a context of rising hate crimes, the complex of populist hate did not manifest itself with the same intensity, overtness or cultural and political sanction as it does in our contemporary moment. Yet, looking back to Lee's film helps us understand the production of hate and right-wing populism in fuller and more deeply historical ways—and, in fact, in more deeply human ways.

## Narrating the Process of Detection

For those of us currently living in the United States under the regime of the authoritarian-minded President Donald Trump, coming to terms with and understanding the current political buzzwords of "populism," "nationalism," and "globalism" has taken on an intellectual urgency. As many have argued, Trump's ascension to the Presidency of the United States is perhaps best understood as a symptom, rather than a cause, of the historical hotbed of racism, nativism, misogyny, homophobia, and every other form of the varieties of hateful repression and violence his presidency has encouraged and exemplified. So, we have to ask, what are the historical and cultural currents that have motivated this surge or intensification of this always-already existing condition in the United States? Do the cultural and political forms, narratives, and mentalities that grew out of this history, charged with comprehending and addressing the frustrations and challenges people experienced in that history, effectively help us to do that, directing us in healthy social directions rooted in a full, comprehensive, and reasoned understanding of the history and reality of the power dynamics that have created our present?

Such questions have, not surprisingly, come front and center in intellectual discourse and inquiry since the 2016 elections in the United States and recent anti-elite uprisings in Emmanuel Macron's France and elsewhere across Europe, although the historical insight, appropriate diagnosis, and forward-thinking direction have been less than satisfactory. Steven Hahn, for example, writing for *The Nation* in a recent piece titled "The Populist Specter: Is the groundswell of popular discontent in Europe and America what's really threatening democracy?" in which he reviews a spate of the literature addressing the "populist" wave, opens by addressing the nebulousness of both the term and actual manifestation: "There is, many believe, a specter haunting the Euro-American world. It is not, as Marx and Engels once exulted, the specter of communism. Nor is it the specter of fascism.... Rather, it is what journalists, scholars, and other political observers now routinely call 'populism.'" He argues, interestingly, that despite the widespread deployment of the term in our current political lexicon, one does not really find political movements afoot adopting the moniker of "populist," nor parties identifying themselves as such; and, unlike the late-19th-century United States, there are not even populist platforms or sustained political critiques of the status quo employing the language of populism. In "the current parlance," Hahn observes, "populism is less a movement than a menace." He expatiates,

> "Populism" is instead a term meant to encapsulate the rage often found among white and native-born voters across Europe and other parts of the Western Hemisphere, who regard themselves as victimized by established political institutions, the corrupt practices of politicians, and the influx of migrants from afar. Indeed, these "populists" appear to be united both by shared grievances and by a disposition to place the blame not on the workings of the economic system or the excesses of economic elites (though anti–Semitic currents suggest some of this), but on the threats posed by immigrants to the national culture and economic well-being.

While Hahn derives this meaning of "populism" from both observation of the dynamics of our current political moment and from the literature he is reviewing, he nonetheless finds a dearth of adequate historical understanding in the approaches he analyzes, finding the recent literature largely does not offer "a compelling definition of populism" and does not explain "why the term is a useful rubric for the political discontent that has grown so powerful in recent years" or "give us much of a definition of where populism comes from, whether it has a meaningful history, or whether a deeper historical perspective would serve our understanding better."[4] Turkish economist Dani Rodrik, in his paper "Populism and the Economics of Globalization," has raised similar concerns about the lack of historical understanding informing studies of populism, particularly as it occurs as a response to economic globalization. He asserts in his review of the scholarship, "A number of empirical papers have linked the rise of populist movements—Trump and the right-wing Republicans in the U.S., Brexit in Britain, far-right groups in Europe—to forces associated with globalization, such as the China trade shock, rising import penetration levels, de-industrialization, and immigration." But, he continues, "A question that has attracted little interest to date is why the backlash has taken the particular form it has in different countries."[5] In short, while there are attempts to analyze contemporary manifestations of right-wing populism, in particular, a proper historical understanding of precisely how populism has developed as a political form or outlet over time is missing.

In other words, the history of right-wing, politically and humanly regressive "populisms" and "nationalisms," rooted in hatred and realized in violence against "others" and understood as responses to globalization, or really any kind of economic or political crisis that threatens people's social and individual well-being, remains a mystery to be solved. In this sense, *Summer of Sam* stands as an illuminating and instructive analysis of the cultural and historical dynamics productive of the hateful nationalism, in this case "Americanism," characterized by homophobia, working-class exploitation, racism, misogyny, and, in short, overall repression, particularly sexual repression.

Part of the reason Lee's film provides a rather perfect cultural artifact for exploring and seeking to understand right-wing populisms and nationalisms from a historical perspective is precisely because Lee tells the story of right-wing populism by using and expansively innovating on the traditional detective or crime fiction genre. He treats this history, indeed, as a mystery to be solved. Certainly, traditionally, the detective or crime genre has been viewed as a conservative political form, devoted not to social change or amelioration but to the status quo, featuring narratives that restore and affirm social innocence and the existing law and order by tracking down and locking up the guilty individual. Nonetheless, the detective genre also has the ability, inherent in its form, to enable profound historical thinking and investigation. Think about it: the process or narrative of detection is one that by the necessity of its internal dynamics drives us back into a history and requires, in narrative terms, a reconstruction of history. Crime narratives typically open with a murder in the present, and the ensuing narrative reconstructs the past to understand the present. It isn't just a "who done it?"; it is also a "how did this happen?" In this sense, the genre of detection pushes us to think historically. So, Lee taking up the issue of hate in this generic form lends itself to thinking about these issues of right-wing nationalism and populism historically.

Lee orchestrates this historical analysis of repressive and hateful "Americanism"—that is, its right-wing "populist" rendering of American national identity and cultural values—through a brilliant innovation of the crime genre that expands our understanding of criminality beyond individual behaviors to include—and indict—the larger processes of U.S. historical development and the ingrained behaviors, habits, and values that both emerged from as well as conditioned and directed those processes of development, such as the racist values underwriting the genocide, colonization, and enslavement of people of color as well as misogynist and patriarchal values ratifying the oppression of women and their exploitation as unpaid labor, both so central to the development of the U.S. political economy, in domestic and global contexts.

In *Summer of Sam*, of course, Lee takes as his focus, and also substantially and artfully elaborates, the serial killings of David Berkowitz, most famously called the Son of Sam. Yet, as I have been suggesting, the crime story Lee unfolds narrates and reveals far more than Berkowitz's murderous spree and his eventual capture by the police. Lee's representation of the detection process itself, by both the police and vigilante groups, offers a piercing analysis of the cultural values and worldviews at work in the dominant American culture framing the very way we produce knowledge about people, define deviancy and criminality, and participate in and endorse the mechanisms of repression that alienate us from the most essentially human parts of ourselves and hence also from others. Thus, Lee, working within the genre of detection, in narrating the process of detection, is also able to critique that process as well, highlighting how the very means by which we decipher and make meaning of our world are informed by deeply ingrained prejudices. This prejudicial value system, characterized by homophobia, misogyny, nativism, and racism, I will argue, Lee figures in *Summer of Sam* as definitive of, as profoundly informing, the cultural complex of nation- and identity-formation Lee identifies as "Americanism."

Indeed, the film's title *Summer of Sam* already lets us know that the story Lee is telling is larger than Berkowitz. Lee, in fact, approaches the story of these murders in terms of the way the New York City residents, media, and larger police and cultural apparatus respond to the murders. Lee's story tells the Son of Sam murders as an episode that indexes and encapsulates the trajectory and cultural and economic dynamics of U.S. history itself, exploring the various strains of hate at work in U.S. culture and history which account for the political phenomena of right-wing populism and nationalism which emerge as responses to the long-standing injustices and inequities of class society, particularly in times of economic downturns that tend to be seen, or scapegoated as, effects of globalization. *Summer of Sam* reveals the deep structure, the underlying racism, misogyny, and homophobia, with all of their accompanying violence and repression, that define for Lee the fundamental grammar of "Americanism" as an ideology, national identity, and informing set of dominant national values.

Lee elaborates the meaning of terror in United States in relation to a complex of American values as well as the economic context and history that the episode of the Son of Sam serial murders telescope and reveal in an intense concentrated way, detecting the whole of American history itself as a history of terror. In a way, this film prefigures his more recent production *BlacKkKlansman* (2018) but also in some sense outdistances that story. For sure, *BlacKkKlansman* connects the history of white supremacist thought and hate groups to the present, ending the film with clips of the Charlottesville riot of the summer of 2017 that featured white nationalists chanting "Jews will not replace us," highlighting the fatal intertwinement of economic anxiety, anti-semitism and racism, and white supremacy. In *Summer of Sam*, Lee layers this analysis and roots it most fundamentally in an exploration of sexuality and sexual repression in order to diagnose the story of U.S. history and its serial violence as a result of the racism, misogyny, nativism, and homophobia that sustain a repressive class society, alienating the inhabitants of America from what makes them most human. It is through narrating the process of detection, of solving the serial murders of Son of Sam, that Lee solves as well the larger crimes of serial violence that offer insight into the right-wing populism and nationalism thriving in our contemporary moment.

## Revolution and Repression in American Capitalist History

*Summer of Sam* opens with celebrity New York columnist Jimmy Breslin standing in the midst of a rambunctious Times Square, with the flurry of lights, advertising, and the big jumbotron in the background. He introduces the story to us: "Today things are much different. Business is booming up, up, and up. Crime is down, down, down. Homicides are the lowest it's been since 1961. Well, it wasn't always like this. This film is about a different time, a different place—the good old days. The hot, blistering summer of 1977."

Already we see that the story Breslin introduces and Lee wants to tell is much larger than the story of Berkowitz and the serial murders themselves. Lee opens with a brief and telescoped history, comparing and charting the transition or trajectory from the 1970s to the 1990s, casting that history in terms of the performance of the U.S. economy and also the relative decline in crime rates. And yet Breslin's words introduce, even in their brevity, a set of complicated attitudes toward history. He at once suggests that conditions in the '90s are thriving, "business is booming … crime is down," and yet at the same time drifts into an easy, conventional, and certainly recognizable nostalgia for an earlier time—"the good old days"—which the story that is about to follow represents not just as the wonderful age of disco but also as characterized by terror, violence, mass unemployment, racism, and homophobia. Indeed, while some look to this past to "make America great again," Michael Tomasky, in his book *If We Can Keep It: How the Republic Collapsed and How It Might Be Saved,* looks back to the 1970s as a period when a long and protracted history of economic dislocation began. He writes, encapsulating the moment,

> A final bleak development began to catch observers' attention in the mid-to-late 1970s. The vast steel mills and other factories that had won the war and built the middle class started to shrink, or close, or move to nonunion states in the South and

West (in many cases on their way, eventually, to Mexico and China). Union membership, which had peaked in the 1950s, began declining around this time: from 24 percent in 1973 to 20.1 percent in 1983 to 15.8 percent in 1993. The phrase "Rust Belt" entered the lexicon in 1982. The Homestead Steel Works, the great plant just south of Pittsburgh that had employed 15,000 men during the war, the one plant that symbolized the city's dominance of American and indeed global steel production, that epitomized the industry that gave the city's beloved football team its name, started downsizing in the early 1980s. Wrote Jefferson Cowie and Joseph Heathcott of Homestead in 2003, "on that once world-famous bend in the Monongahela River are now a Loew's Cineplex; a McDonald's; a Target; a Bed, Bath, and Beyond; and other national chains displaying wares produced in an immense global network of production." And, they might have added, stocked and sold by clerks making a fraction (in inflation-adjusted terms) of what men at the Homestead Works had been paid.[6]

With this longer history in mind, from one perspective, we can be tempted to read Breslin's expression of nostalgia for "the good old days" as ironic, but such a reading erases the complexity of this opening as well as the critical analysis of U.S. history—and tellings of U.S. history—Lee develops in the film. If we interpret the nostalgia as ironic, we perhaps implicitly endorse the present as indeed better, when Lee actually turns to the 1970s to debunk any reading of history forwarding a myth of progress and to highlight and analyze a moment—Berkowitz's serial murders and the cultural response—that provides insights into the historical development of the present in the 1990s.

To gain insight into the attitudes toward history, indeed the historiography, *Summer of Sam* critiques and revises, let us jump ahead six months from the release of *Summer of Sam* in 1999 to President Bill Clinton's State of the Union address on January 27, 2000. In this address, Clinton, with the U.S. flag as his backdrop, rallied the nation with stirring rhetorical flourishes, cajoling us that we should be "filled with awe and humility at our progress and prosperity," assuring us that "this is our moment." He highlights the fastest economic growth in more than thirty years and the lowest poverty rates in twenty years. "We have built a new economy," he declares, and this "economic revolution," he asserts, "has been matched by a revival of the American spirit: crime down by 20 percent to its lowest level in twenty-five years."[7] It is almost as if Clinton took his line from Jimmy Breslin's opening, echoing his sentiments about the thriving economy and reduction in crime, underscoring the dominant currency of the political narrative to which Lee is responding in *Summer of Sam*.

Indeed, *Summer of Sam* constitutes Lee's State of the Union address in the summer of 1999. While Breslin's encomium of the current state of the U.S. economy and society is an eerily anticipatory echo of Clinton's canned rhetoric, Lee embeds this rhetorical narrative of progress, newness, and social advancement in a critical and ironic context. The story about to unfold before us, that of the Son of Sam murders, is not the "good old days"; but, by the same token, the present Breslin celebrates may not be so halcyon. At the end of film, for example, the tawdry, glittery back-drop of Times Square is traded for a "Dead End" sign, one of the most recognizable and densely signifying images in the film, such that the visual image undermines the verbal optimism of Breslin's putative narrative of progress, whereas President Clinton's narrative of progress wishfully invests his back-drop, the United States flag, with meaning. He means to define Americanism and its historical legacy back to the framers of the Constitution. Lee means to expose the content of Americanism as rooted in the racism, genocide, misogyny, and labor exploitation upon which the nation's development depended.

In his address, Clinton connects the nation's achievement of putative prosperity and progress with the original revolutionaries, arguing, "After 224 years the American Revolution continues. We are the new nation." He insists proudly, "We have built a new economy."[8] At the same time as he invokes the U.S.'s revolutionary past, he insists upon newness, upon a break from the past. Even as he speaks about "a new economy," he dissociates it from an historical mode of production and does not name it "global capitalism," divorcing this "economy" from the economic development and history of the United States rooted in genocide, slavery, and patriarchal oppression—even divorcing it from the mid–1970s that Tomasky represents as the dislocating transition that spurred the evolution towards this "new economy" Clinton hails.

Clinton's address does have a darker side, though, invoking the context surrounding the release of *Summer of Sam* which conditioned my own approach to this film when I saw the film on July 4, 1999. In the Summer of 1999, on the night of July 3 and the morning of July 4, Benjamin Smith, in the Chicago area, took deadly aim at African Americans, Asian Americans, and Jewish Americans, proclaiming his actions as linked to the original fight for independence that, in his view, the nation had been losing. For Ben Smith, too, after 224 years, the revolution continued.[9]

Here we see Smith's actions as validating Berlet's and Lyons's readings of U.S. history, as one that mistakes repressive populism for genuine revolutionary liberation. Berlet and Lyons trace the origins of contemporary right-wing populism to dynamics present in Bacon's Rebellion in 1676 and in the American Revolution, dynamics which they present as paradigmatically informing U.S. history and culture. They present Bacon's Rebellion as emblematic of those movements in America that manipulate the resentments of the exploited and oppressed and pretend to represent them while in reality working in the end only to consolidate class hierarchy and foster racial and other divisions. Nathaniel Bacon in July 1676, issued a manifesto titled "Declaration of the People," railing against Virginia's Governor Berkeley for what he viewed as unjust taxation, political cronyism, monopolization of the beaver trade, and supporting Indians, despite their attacks on colonists, in order to protect his own trade interests. To be sure, Bacon, of the planter class himself but outside the elite inner circle of planters, did mobilize and unite in the struggle white European and African bond laborers, who worked side by side in a world that did not yet make racial distinctions as we know them. In addition to taking on Berkeley's regime, Bacon's rebellion also engaged in massacres against Indians to secure land and further their economic interests. The participation in genocide was no small part of the movement, which promised laborers a remedy for their economic misery and political disfranchisement. When Bacon died suddenly because of illness, the movement collapsed. What is important to note from this historical episode, according to Berlet and Lyons, is that the movement pretended to represent the laboring classes, and indeed mobilized them, but nonetheless still served the interests of the planter class and also played a role in its genocidal practices in producing white supremacy. Indeed, they note, historian Theodore Allen looks to this moment as pivotal in the development of white supremacy because the colonial elite effectively—to disarm future rebellions—drove a wedge between white and black workers by inventing categories of "black" and "white" and reserving special exploitation for black workers to give white workers a minimal sense of privilege. Berlet and Lyons, however, do not see Bacon's Rebellion itself as anti-white supremacist in the way Allen does precisely because they view genocide as central to the creation of white supremacy in America. Importantly, they conclude about Bacon's Rebellion that it "was a confused, contradictory upheaval." In the final analysis, though, they write,

> Yet the general pattern of its contradiction—plebeian resentment coupled with intra-elite conflict, and egalitarianism for a limited group of people with expansionist, murderous attacks against non–European peoples—set a pattern of repressive populist politics that would be repeated again and again.

They analyze the American Revolution, also, "as a repressive populist movement," asserting:

> First, by equating tyranny with the British crown, the struggle for U.S. independence promoted a form of antielite scapegoating that deflected discontent away from inequities within colonial society. Second, the drive for independence was also a drive to expand and intensify the system of White supremacy. People of color were not simply "left out" of the Revolution—they were among its major targets.[10]

This reading of U.S. history gives us a template for understanding the linkage between—or rather the confusion of—revolution and repression that *Summer of Sam* elaborates.

In his address, President Clinton even mentions Ben Smith as well as the shootings at a Jewish school that happened in August 1999 in a summer that witnessed a rash of violent hate crimes. Echoing the words of a Rabbi who, in a CNN report in August 1999 I remember, labeled such actions "a transgression of American values," Clinton similarly charged, "This is not the American way, and we must draw the line."[11]

I lay out this context because this discussion over the meaning and content of Americanism or American values, over the historical trajectory of national development, over American culture and tradition, puts into stark focus the critical thematic of Spike Lee's *Summer of Sam* released in Chicago in 1999 the same week as Ben Smith's shootings. As Lee looks at history in *Summer of Sam*, the racist violence of Ben Smith does indeed define "the American way" in thoroughgoing fashion and to deny that characteristic reality of American history is to engage in a counterproductive repression that keeps us, as a collective national identity, from truly understanding who we are and being accountable for what we have done so that we can, in fact, therapeutically address the traumas we have as a nation caused and experienced.

From the start, in almost comic fashion, the film is a meditation on the meaning of "America's" quest for and definition of liberty and the intimate linkage of this quest for liberty with prejudice and violence borne out of repression. After Breslin's opening panegyric, we move to a scene where we see the Son of Sam killer murder a pair of young women talking in a parked car. The soundtrack for the scene is ABBA's priceless romantic song from the 1970s "Fernando." We hear the lyrics as the song's persona recalls a starlit night ripe both with romantic passion and revolutionary fervor. The stars shone, the lyrics tells us, both for the lovers and for the quest for liberty; and the persona suggests that while the revolution apparently failed, she would happily to repeat, re-live, that history again.[12] The song here, merging romance and revolution, both complements and complicates the murderous action of the scene. In complementing the action, the song endows Berkowitz's murder with revolutionary significance, confusing the quest for liberty through revolutionary action with violent repression; or, perhaps, more aptly, elaborating Lee's analysis that in U.S. history the revolutionary energies that spawned the U.S. nation, since its inception, have been inherently repressive, even hatefully so, in ways that have hindered the U.S. from becoming truly the land of free. Instead of achieving liberation, the processes of nation-formation and so-called revolution throughout U.S. history have only consolidated class power in the hands of the elite and sustained that class hierarchy through repressive mobilizations of racism, sexism, and homophobia—in short, through mobilizing the vast menu of hate, the varieties of which we see animating what we have come to call contemporary right-wing populism. In this sense, Lee's use of ABBA's "Fernando" in this scene complicates conventional understandings of U.S. revolutionary history, underscoring how America's supposed historical quest for freedom has, sadly and perhaps even unwittingly, instead realized itself as a recursive ritual in re-affirming and enforcing violent repression of racism, heterosexism, misogyny, and labor exploitation, not liberation of the full humanity of those living in U.S. culture.

This thematic is immediately elaborated and emphasized in the next scene when we transition from Berkowitz's murders to Vinny (John Leguizamo) and his wife Dionna (Mira Sorvino) entering a discotheque and dancing to the song "There but for the Grace of God Go I" by Machine, which opens telling the story of a young couple living in Brooklyn who have just had a child and now feel the need to move to a better place to raise their daughter, a place free of African Americans, Jewish people, and LGBTQ folk. As we watch Vinny and Dionna elegantly and erotically dance in the vibrant upbeat scene to a song about racism, anti-semitism, and homophobia, the film is developing the same tension it does with "Fernando," underscoring a maladjustment, a repression, in our relationships and culture often belied in our most visible expressions. The song's narrative plays out this same theme, as it unfolds the daughter's future growing up in a repressive and hateful culture. The song even invokes Baldwin's language of the freak to characterize the daughter. She ends up turning to drugs and leaving her parents, much to the mother's pain, who wonders if she loved her daughter in the most nurturing way. The song underscores the way we confuse repression and violence for love, speaking to unhealthy love relationships, indeed unhealthy lives, that grow out of the soil of racism, homophobia, and anti-semitism—out of repression. (Interestingly, this song was produced in 1979, while the film is set in 1977, revealing Lee's careful choice of the song for this moment in the film.[13])

In developing this analysis of U.S. history, Lee's choice of Berkowitz as a kind of emblematic figure of these repressive and recursive processes characterizing the development of the U.S. nation-state is an exceedingly apt and revealing one, enabling Lee to diagnose the national dysfunctions of the U.S., particularly the prevalence of hate informing our cultural practices and institutions, as precisely rooted in the unhealthy and distorted development of the nation caused by repression—sexual, racial, class, and otherwise. First, in focusing on Berkowitz as an American emblem enables Lee to explore the psycho-social and particularly psychosexual dimensions, on both an individual and larger social and collective level, of hate and right-wing populism in the U.S. Indeed, David Abrahamsen, in his study *Confessions of Son of Sam*, links Berkowitz's killing spree to his "distorted sexual development" pointing out also that "sexual emotions are practically always involved in homicide."[14] Interestingly, Abrahamsen's psychoanalytic approach provides insight into the roots of hate in our sexual structures and drives. He writes, for example,

> Love and hate are so intimately intertwined that one does not always know where one emotion ends and the other takes over. It may surprise us to learn that our sexual drive, used most often to express loving feelings, is also intimately associated with hateful and murderous emotions. One may even go so far as to say that the sexual force, in most instances, through jealousy, envy, competition, hate, and revenge is the force that initiates, stimulates, mobilizes, and maintains murderous impulses.[15]

Berkowitz, with all of his sexual dysfunction and repression, is not an isolated or aberrant character, as we see in Lee's representation, but rather a representative figure of a larger national, social, and sexual dysfunction that manifests itself in hateful and violent repressions. Focusing on Berkowitz provides Lee a context to explore, in loving and poignant fashion, really, the way hate is generated in our repressive culture in the pain of our most intimate personal lives and, through the same dynamics, in the relationships in our larger social dynamics that also foster and condition our intimate relationships.

Again, for Lee, Berkowitz is not a social aberrant but rather a social representative. The film establishes this point clearly in the interactions between the characters at the waterfront dead end. In one moment, the men are making fun of the overtly gay character Bobby Del Fiore (Brian Tarantina), suggesting he might be the Son of Sam killer because he is a woman hater. They childishly call him a "homo-cidal maniac" and talk about putting him in the "penile system." When he teases Brian (Ken Garito) that he would like him for a cell mate, Brian violently takes his hand and burns his palm with his cigarette. Meanwhile, while we watch this scene, we can see written on the back of the "Dead End" sign, the words "Ruby Sucks the Big One" and "Yankees #1." While they accuse Bobby and the Son of Sam of being woman haters, we see their own misogyny evident on the sign; and, as the Yankees come to be a symbol of Americanism in the film, with their image being a red, white, and blue Uncle Sam hat, this misogyny and violent homophobia refer back to a dominant American value system. Lee deconstructs the difference between the criminality of Berkowitz and the everyday sanctioned violence in American life informed by the same regressive—and repressive—value system.

Additionally, we need to understand Berkowitz's compulsive serial killing as similarly emblematic of the serial violence—such as the recursive genocides, enslavement, exploitations—that characterizes the historical development of the U.S. nation-state. The earlier-referenced "Fernando" by ABBA captures the violent dynamics of America's compulsion in its lyrics promising to repeat and relive history. The song encapsulates, for Lee, this serial violence, which the film represents as a dysfunctional and hateful romance as opposed to the loving romance informing the revolutionary spirit in "Fernando."

Lee throughout the film layers this moment of the mid–1970s with historical depth, highlighting how this moment, as a recursive episode in the violent history of U.S. national development, indexes U.S. history itself. Lee develops this historical layering, this pattern of repetition, also through the way he references through literary allusion a history of working-class response to the repetitive economic dislocations of capitalism that have ravaged rather than liberated the lives of Americans. While Clinton in his State of the Union address argues that an economic revolution has occurred, that a new economy has been created with a new prosperity, *Summer of Sam*, as we see with Breslin's opening, underscores the cyclical nature of capitalism and its crises, not letting us get caught up in any singular moment of seeming prosperity.

Indeed, one of the most prevalent, pronounced, and charged images in the film is the "Dead End" sign around which his Italian American characters gather to sell and take drugs, harass and inflict violence on one another, and generally loiter, living out the experience of unemployment which marked the recessionary economy of U.S. capitalist class society in the late 1970s. The image is a powerful one for many reasons, not the least for its invocation of Sidney Kingsley's 1936 Depression era proletarian drama *Dead End*, which, to give a short hand account, thematized class difference and conflict in portraying the violent and consequential contact between street kids (as well as unemployed young adults) and the wealthier inhabitants of a dockside neighborhood along the East River in New York City.

The invocation of 1930s and the Great Depression itself[6] underscores the recursiveness or cyclical nature of economic crises that characterizes the political economy of capitalism, as Lee connects the recessionary era of the 1970s with the Great Depression, writing in an age of economic boom in the 1990s. There is nothing terribly "new" about the economy; it is simply on one of its upswings. Lee's point also is that economic prosperity is not the same thing as a humane or dis-alienating economic system; indeed, the film represents capitalism as a system that curtails and represses basic elements of the human personality and creativity, which includes our erotic dimensions, as Lee neatly weaves issues of sexual repression into his economic analysis. Lee's film, through this cultural layering and allusion, corrects the tendency to look at our history, particularly our economic history, as a "moment." Remember Clinton's phrase: "This is our moment," suggesting we have evolved into a new way of being: "We are the new nation. We have built the new economy." Lee asks us to look at the long view and see the repetitive violence, alienation, and repressiveness involved in the persecution of gays and lesbians and racial genocide that have been hallmarks of U.S. capitalist development throughout its history—indeed, that inform the ideology of "Americanism." For Lee, the murderous hate and violence of Ben Smith does not constitute a "transgression of American values," but a realization of them.

Against Clinton's insistence that such violence is not "the American way," Lee asserts it has always been.

## Embracing the Freak, Challenging Right-Wing Populism

As I have been suggesting, Lee centers and foregrounds representations of sexuality in his analysis of the economic dimensions of U.S. history, partly in order to highlight the repressive and alienating dimensions of capitalism itself even in times of prosperity and also to highlight how in times of economic dislocation resurgences of right-wing populism manifest themselves in targeting sexual and racial others. Lee's focus on sexual repression in American culture is evident from the beginning of *Summer of Sam* when the central character Vinny leaves the disco where he has been dancing with his wife Dionna to drive home her cousin. He is having anal sex with the cousin in his car when he is interrupted by another car honking, a moment when he also unwittingly encounters the Son of Sam killer—something he realizes later that evening when he drives by the same block, only to realize it is now a crime scene. The next day he reunites with Richie Trangali at the dead end, in the scene I mentioned at the beginning of this essay. Vinnie and Richie, old friends, end up engaging in a private conversation in which Vinnie expresses being shaken up by having been so close to the Son of Sam killer, and he connects this encounter, through his religious worldview, with his self-perceived sexual transgression. He tells Richie that God spared him, continuing, "God's telling me I'm gonna burn in hell if I don't stop cheating." He chastises himself for his sexual desires for "butt-fucking," "sixty-nine," and "doggie style," and insists, "God is telling me I shouldn't be doing these things with my wife" (which he does not). He expresses his anxiety to Richie, saying, "Once you're deviated, you can't go back." In short, Lee represents Vinnie as a victim of a sexually repressive culture in certain regards. His marriage suffers because he is uncomfortable sharing his desires, plagued by the traditional Madonna/whore complex. Despite his wife's efforts to experiment sexually with him, he feels ashamed of his desires and will only have "vanilla" sex with her, with the lights off. In one scene, when they wind up at a sex club after being invited to a party while waiting outside the Studio 54 discotheque, we see them, while high on cocaine, engaging in a wide range of sexual activities with multiple partners. On their way home, however, Vinnie is silent, full of shame, finally taking out his shame on her, calling her a "lesbian whore," triggering her to call him a "faggot hairdresser" and a "perverted sick fuck." Vinnie's inability to come to terms with the reality of his sexual desires, his repression of them leading to a form of self-alienation, leads to the ruin of his marriage, his unhappiness, and his inability to relate to others in a humane way.

Lee elaborates these themes of sexual repression, homophobia, and alienation in his representation of Richie's sexuality as well. As I mentioned earlier, Richie performs erotic dances for money at a gay club called Male World, where we see men from the audience pay him for performing oral sex on him. Interestingly, the homoerotic dances he performs are often sexually violent as well. In one dance routine, for example, Richie wields a knife in one hand while dancing with a stuffed human doll figure in the other. He salaciously plays with the knife with his tongue while pressing the doll's head in his crotch, and then later penetrates the doll with the knife in a kind of violent intercourse. This mixture of sex and violence, of course, mirrors the sexualized violence, or the violence borne of sexual repression that we see with David Berkowitz, underscoring the way Lee represents Berkowitz not as a criminal aberration from, but in fact as an emblematic representative of America's repressive culture which breeds violence. Richie, too, for example, is not represented as having a healthy, well-adjusted relationship to his sexuality. First, he commodifies his sexuality, not only dancing at Male World but also making pornographic movies for money with his girlfriend Ruby, with whom otherwise we see he has difficulty relating to sexually. Second, as we see in a conversation he has with Vinnie, he is conflicted about his sexuality. In this conversation, Vinnie comments on the fact that Richie wears a dog collar. Richie responds that everybody's wearing a collar. "You're on a leash to a certain way of thinking," he says. "Everybody's got two personalities—one you're born with; one the world gives you." He struggles to articulate his conflicts to Vinnie, telling him, "I got these things I like doing." But he wonders, "Is it me? Or am I pre-programmed to do it?" In this dialogue, Richie struggles to articulate the sexually repressive dynamics of American culture, embodied in the dog collar. While he symbolizes the "freak" in the film who becomes the targeted "other," we also see that he has internalized homophobia. In one scene, he is eating in a diner with Vinnie, and he calls two men sitting together "Freaks in pink shirts," identifying them as gay. When he is asked to leave the diner, by the waiter wearing an American flag shirt, Richie turns this violence on himself, busting a glass against his head. Alienated from this key creative component of himself, his sexuality, his repression engenders a violent response, although in the form of self-inflicted violence, as opposed to Berkowitz's murderous violence.

Lee's representation of sexual maladjustment and repression centers his critique of the repressiveness of U.S. racial patriarchal capitalism overall and the way it ideologically produces what is called right-wing populism these days. To explain Lee's critique, I am again going to return to James Baldwin's essay "Freaks and the Ideal of American Manhood," as I believe the dynamics and interplay of sexuality and economics Lee portrays in *Summer of Sam* really mirrors, and perhaps even draws on, the language and analysis of U.S. capitalism Baldwin develops in this essay, approaching the historical and economic development of the U.S. nation-state and culture through an analysis of sexuality and sexual repression in the U.S. As he writes about the processes of U.S. historical development which have both created and brutally stigmatized homosexuality, he continually links U.S. culture's attitudes toward sexuality with the development of racial patriarchal capitalism.

That sexuality is or needs to be part and parcel of any fully developed understanding of American racial, patriarchal, and economic systems is profoundly apparent in the necessity with which homosexuality, race, and class are linked in Baldwin's writing; in the way he narrates U.S. history; and in the constant slippage into analysis of race, class, and economics in discussions centered on sexuality and into analysis of sexuality in discussions apparently centered on race. For example, he opens his essay insisting that human beings are by nature androgynous, arguing that "the existence of the hermaphrodite reveals, in intimidating exaggeration, the truth concerning every human being—which is why the hermaphrodite is called a freak." The truth, of course, is that "there is a man in every woman and a woman in every man." After what appear to be "digressions" into discussions of slavery, poverty, the Cold War, the Civil Rights Movement, Boy George, and later Michael Jackson, he concludes by analyzing what he calls the "rage for order" in U.S. history and society, writing, "This rage for order can result in chaos, and in this country chaos connects with color." And he ends almost where he began in his treatment of androgyny, but now his conceptualization of androgyny is more layered and complex, arguing we all contain the "other": "male in female, female in male, white in black and black in white." Thus, while the original formulation of the human being's androgynous condition was limited exclusively to the dual presence of male and female characteristics in one person, by the end of the essay Baldwin's conception of androgyny has expanded to contain and harmonize the vexed divisions within the U.S. racial order.[17]

The conflicted dichotomies of hetero- and homosexual and black and white constitute, for Baldwin, not isolated or incidental divisions but rather over-determinations of an overarching contradiction that fundamentally and pervasively structures social and economic relations in the U.S., which is the logic we see in *Summer of Sam* as well. These sexual and racial contradictions are conditioned, for Baldwin, by the central contradiction between the forces and relations of production which, from a Marxist humanist perspective such as that which Baldwin adopts if not in name then in character, fetters individual human creativity, creating partialized human beings subordinated to a system geared toward creating profit rather than fully realizing its productive or creative potential. He underlines this point early in the essay, sketching a brief and fascinating historical overview of U.S. economic development and, really, class formation:

> The exigencies created by the triumph of the industrial revolution—or, in other terms, the rise of Europe to global dominance—had, among many mighty effects, that of commercializing the roles of men and women. Men became the propagators, or perpetrators, of property, and women became the means by which the property was protected and handed down. One may say this was nothing more than the ancient and universal division of labor—women nurtured the tribe, men battled for it—but the concept of property had undergone a change. This change was vast and deep and sinister.
>
> For the first time in human history, a man was reduced not merely to a thing but to a thing the value of which was determined, absolutely, by that thing's commercial value. That this pragmatic principle dictated the slaughter of the native American, the enslavement of the black, and the monumental rape of Africa—to say nothing of creating the wealth of the Western world—no one, I suppose, will now attempt to deny.
>
> But this principle ... also controlled the pens of the men who signed the declaration of independence—a document more clearly commercial than moral. This is how, and why, the American constitution was able to define the slaves as three-fifths of a man, from which legal and commercial definition it followed that a black man "had no rights a white man was bound to respect."[18]

The point that Baldwin's brief historical narrative stresses over and over again is how capitalist development limited and curtailed people's selfhood and creativity by subordinating them to a commercial instrumentality, as Richie Trangali does, for example, with his sexuality. Women and men were limited by their roles in the sexual division of labor; enslaved blacks were reduced to less than full human beings; and Native Americans were slaughtered, denied personhood altogether.

## Conclusion

The point of the essay overall, though, is that this process of capitalist development which entails genocide and slavery is part and parcel of the American idea or ideal of masculinity, ideals that bind characters like Richie and Vinny and thugs who beat up Richie. It is precisely this ideal that Baldwin identifies as underlying the contradiction in U.S. culture that stifles human development and creativity. "This ideal," he writes, "has created cowboys and Indians, good guys and bad guys, punks and studs, tough guys and softies, butch and faggot, black and white. It is an idea so paralytically infantile that it is virtually forbidden—as an unpatriotic act—that the American boy evolve into the complexity of manhood."[19] So, sexual, class, and racial contradictions in this analysis are all systematically linked in a unified narrative of economic and cultural development such that neither can be separated and receive full accounting in its own historical narrative. The masculine ideal informs, even premises, the economic development of U.S. capitalism that has entailed genocide and slavery, denied people a full human identity. It is the same logic that reduces gays and lesbians to a status as less than fully human, as Baldwin talks about being called "faggot and, later, pussy, but those epithets really had nothing to do with the question of sexual preference: You were simply being told that you had no balls."[20] In short, he was being told that he was less than fully a person. As I have discussed, we see this sexual immaturity of which Baldwin speaks, and the alienation from oneself and others it engenders, throughout the film, particularly in the scenes at Dead End, where we see the same kind of sexual violence and repression that mirrors Berkowitz, deconstructing the difference between criminality and dominant social value systems.

Again, I want to stress that *Summer of Sam*, taking a similar approach as that of Baldwin to analyzing U.S. historical dynamics and centering psychosexual analysis in understanding the larger social and historical dynamics of U.S. national development, presents an analysis of U.S. history as one of revolutionary repression rather than revolutionary liberation, providing insight into the historical development of right-wing populism, white nationalism, and fascism in the United States.

To end where we began, we can return to the climactic scene this essay opened with in which the vigilante group has mis-identified Richie Trangali as the Son of Sam killer. The musical soundtrack Lee provides for this scene is The Who's "Won't Get Fooled Again," which warns about false revolutions that merely repeat the same old repressions. The lyrics open signaling change and the promise of liberation; and then as this supposed revolution comes, accompanied by a re-written constitution, the persona realizes the hope of revolutionary transformation was nothing but an ideological mirage. The revolution was the same old war, creating the same old world with different people in power perhaps. History has repeated.[21]

The point, of course, as Lee shows us, is that the revolution is not new; it is a repetition of the same old repressive revolutions that have sustained hate and right-wing populism. And Lee's characters do get fooled, targeting the wrong murderer and taking out their vengeance on the wrong person. The point is that hateful populisms, which are really politics of scapegoating, are dead ends, leading us to no positive political destination.

*Summer of Sam*, in taking on the issue of repression more generally, moving beyond narrow treatments of racism and white supremacy which tend to miss this overarching dynamic, offers a necessary diagnosis to the intensified and overt upsurge in populist hate these days. In the end, though,

*Summer of Sam* shows us that even if the vigilante sleuths had in fact identified Berkowitz as the murderer, the violence would persist until we confront our own collective repressions.

## NOTES

1. Spike Lee, *Summer of Sam* (New York: 40 Acres and Mule Filmworks, 1999).
2. Chip Berlet and Matthew N. Lyons, *Right-Wing Populism in America: Too Close for Comfort* (New York: The Guilford Press, 2000), 266.
3. James Baldwin, "Freaks and the American Ideal of Manhood," in *James Baldwin: Collected Essays* (New York: The Library of America, 1998), 828.
4. Stephen Hahn, "The Populist Specter: Is the groundswell of popular discontent in Europe and the Americas what's really threatening democracy?" *The Nation* (January 10, 2019): 28. https://www.thenation.com/article/mounk-galston-deneen-eichengreen-the-populist-specter/.
5. Dani Rodrik, "Populism and the Economics of Globalization" (Cambridge, MA: National Bureau of Economic Research, July 2017), 22.
6. Michael Tomasky, *If We Can Keep It: How the Republic Collapsed and How It Might Be Saved* (New York: Liveright, 2019), 115.
7. William J. Clinton, State of the Union Address, January 27, 2000. https://www.infoplease.com/homework-help/us-documents/state-union-address-william-j-clinton-january-27-2000.
8. Clinton, State of the Union Address.
9. Berlet and Lyons, 335–36.
10. Berlet and Lyons, 22–23.
11. Clinton, State of the Union Address.
12. ABBA, "Fernando." https://genius.com/Abba-fernando-lyrics.
13. Machine, "There but for the Grace of God Go I." https://songmeanings.com/songs/view/3530822107858918290/.
14. David Abrahamsen, *Confessions of Son of Sam* (New York: Columbia University Press, 1985), 162.
15. Abrahamsen, 163.
16. *Summer of Sam*, with its barrage of U.S. flag imagery, particularly through the emblem of the New York Yankees which figures prominently in the film, could also be referencing Sidney Howard's 1930s play *The Ghost of Yankee Doodle*, which critiques Americanism as centrally informed by violence at the heart of its quest for economic prosperity. In this play, an old money family with liberal values is on the brink of losing its wealth in pre–World War II America. Their wealth comes from a tool and die factory, and the factory would be saved if the U.S. entered the war. With such reminders, Lee asks us to look through even those moments of economic prosperity to comprehend how they, too, are premised on violence and repression.
17. Baldwin, 815–16.
18. Baldwin, 819.
19. Baldwin, 828.
20. Baldwin, 814–15.
21. The Who, "Won't Get Fooled Again." https://www.azlyrics.com/lyrics/who/wontgetfooledagain.html.

## BIBLIOGRAPHY

Abba. "Fernando." https://genius.com/Abba-fernando-lyrics.
Abrahamsen, David. *Confessions of Son of Sam*. New York: Columbia University Press, 1985.
Baldwin, James. "Freaks and the American Ideal of Manhood," in *James Baldwin: The Collected Essays*, 814–829. New York: The Library of America, 1998.
Berlet, Chip, and Matthew N. Lyons. *Right-Wing Populism in America: Too Close for Comfort*. New York: The Guilford Press, 2000.

Clinton, William J. State of the Union Address, January 27, 2000. https://www.infoplease.com/homework-help/us-documents/state-union-address-william-j-clinton-january-27-2000.

Hahn, Stephen. "The Populist Specter: Is the groundswell of popular discontent in Europe and America what's really threatening democracy?" *The Nation* (January 10, 2019): 27–31.

Lee, Spike. *Summer of Sam*. New York: 40 Acres and a Mule Filmworks, 1999.

Machine. "There but for the Grace of God Go I." https://songmeanings.com/songs/view/3530822107858918290/.

Rodrik, Dani. "Populism and the Economics of Globalization." Cambridge, MA: National Bureau of Economic Research, July 2017.

Tomasky, Michael. *If We Can Keep It: How the Republic Collapsed and How It Might Be Saved.* New York: Liveright, 2019.

The Who. "Won't Get Fooled Again." https://www.azlyrics.com/lyrics/who/wontgetfooledagain.html.

# Australian Crime Fiction

## *Such Is Life*[1] *for Hard-Boiled Larrikins*

### JANICE SHAW

Australian literature in general is informed by the country's convict origins, and this is particularly evident in the development of its crime fiction. From Marcus Clark's convict novel *For the Term of His Natural Life,* to Henry Lawson's short stories often depicting lawlessness as a means of survival in the harsh bush landscape, and Mary Fortune's "The Detective's Album," Australian 19th-century literature involved crime informing the national identity by enshrining the "larrikin" hero and the powerful cultural stereotype of the bush myth.[2] Early fiction situated this hero within a harsh yet idealized vision of the Australian bush, one that fostered a protagonist both independent and disdainful of authority, while also being resilient enough to cope with the demands of an isolating and unforgiving landscape. Not only was this bush myth incorporated in 19th-century literature by writers such as Henry Lawson, Banjo Paterson, and Steele Rudd, but the newspapers of the time also published fictional pieces that presented as real-world tales such as the supposedly first-person accounts from police memoirs like "The Detective's Album," published serially in the *Australian Journal* in the 1860s. Such a transgression of the boundaries of real with fictional crime foreshadows the true crime genre flourishing in contemporary Australian fiction, particularly as it also invokes literary techniques in its presentation of an actual crime.

In addition, the stereotype of the Australian as anti-authoritarian is perpetuated by the eulogizing in crime fiction of real-world bushrangers, particularly Ned Kelly. Incarnations of the larrikin stereotype have infiltrated the national ideal even to contemporary Australia, fostered by a post-colonial resentment of authority. The most iconic versions of the larrikin have been created by 20th-century popular culture through characters such as Crocodile Dundee and Mad Max. Such film versions are a progression from the 19th-century fictional convict heroes that were constructed within literature detailing a harsh British penal system. As a result, the national identity is strongly related to an ideology of the typical Australian as being a rugged, egalitarian, anti-authoritarian male, and this informs the development of crime fiction through the presence of a larrikin hero who is an extension and adaptation of the bushranger, while still incorporating globalization through drawing on the American model of hard-boiled crime fiction, mainly as a result of this early hero's cynical humor associated with a complex and fraught relationship with authority.

Contemporary Australian writers Peter Temple, Peter Corris and Marele Day have developed a distinctively Australian form of crime fiction by appropriating the fiction of first-generation American hard-boiled crime writers Raymond Chandler and Dashiell Hammett as it engages with an undercurrent of criminality within society. These authors, along with Frank Moorhouse, invoke not only fictional models of crime writing but also incorporate real world events and people associated with crime through a *roman à clef* approach, and often those writing about their works do so in an introduction or foreword. At the same time, a literary model that emerged from both fictional and factual 19th-century newspaper accounts of the exploits of bushrangers and other criminal stereotypes has generated a different line in Australian crime fiction, one which is associated with the American nonfiction novel made popular by Truman Capote in the mid–20th century. Fictionalized true crime accounts, particularly those by the contemporary writers Peter Carey and Helen Garner, typically integrate real-world events with national myths and cultural icons such as Ned Kelly. Actual criminal figures are positioned within conventional crime fiction models. Therefore, a hybrid form of crime fiction has emerged that incorporates real world figures associated with crime—such as academics who interrogate and critique crime literature—as well as historical criminals and those on trial. This further extends a network of crime fiction in a manner that assumes a knowledgeable reader familiar with Australian culture and history. As a result, crime fiction and true crime offer especially appropriate genres to navigate issues of the Australian identity since both relate to the convict origins and extrapolate the early literature that is based on true accounts of real crime, extended to become part of the culture through a process of enshrining criminal figures into a national mythology.

Since Australian literature is related to the white settlement's convict origins, characteristics of the land's mysterious and strange nature emerge as it appeared to the perspective of British colonizers. Constructions of the landscape involving elements—such as "size itself, wild-life, remarkably ancient inhabitants, the absence of water, the possible presence of unlimited wealth"[3]— engage with and inform the development and popularization of crime fiction in Australia, both thematically in a depiction of an initially unknowable continent, and socially as white settlement occurred through a coming together of disparate people with often shaded or criminal pasts.

The nationalist character of Australian crime fiction, similar to the detective literature of other countries, is constructed in reaction to its historical and cultural development. Despite recent attempts to consider crime fiction as part of World Literature,[4] an approach designed to "push back against the dominant critical model of national taxonomies," according to Alastair Rolls et al,[5] Stephen Knight, the Australian academic specializing in crime fiction and continually invoked within its framework, has contrasted what he considers to be essential elements of global crime fiction where "the versions vary according to national self-concepts"[6]:

> America admires the assertive private eye, both Dashiell Hammett's late 1920s Sam Spade and the nearly as tough modern feminists, such as Sara Paretsky. Britain prefers calm mystery-solvers, amateurs like Hercule Poirot or Lord Peter Wimsey or sensitive police like Ian Rankin's Edinburgh-based John Rebus. The French seem to favour semi-professionals who are distinctly dissenting—in 1943 Léo Malet's Nestor Burma stood up to Nazi occupiers nearly as overtly as to Paris criminals.[7]

Distinct from these approaches, due to its convict background within the white settlement, Knight considers that Australian crime fiction "reveals a range of national myths, fantasies, and even elements of truth-telling about a country whose origin lay in convictions for crime."[8]

Contemporary Australian crime writers have explored and extrapolated just such nationalist characteristics by extending the notion of crime to include the injustices perpetrated upon the Indigenous population at the time of white settlement, and thereby both interweaving and challenging the notion of truth and historical anecdote. In its historical origins, this approach has connections with the flourishing true crime market in Australia, exploring the boundaries between literary and expository writing and engaging with the notion of what constitutes a crime. To do so, a range of national myths are incorporated within crime literature, using as its basis the bushranger figure as the model for a larrikin detective.

## Historical Crime Fiction

The popularization of criminals such as Ned Kelly and bushranger figures is associated with their creation as Australian cultural icons through literature, but this is mainly due to the knowledge about such figures within Australian society. Associated with what Geoffrey Blainey terms "a tyranny of distance"[9] in relation to the geographical isolation of Australia, there is also a distance of knowledge due to the ambiguous nature of the bush myth, one which presents a country at once magnificent and dangerous, with both appealing marsupials and wide settings as well as more negative and apocalyptic elements of bushfires, floods, and venomous snakes and spiders.[10] Not only does this lack of knowledge of the land impact the reception of crime fiction in Australia, but the space itself is inherently related to its nationalist identity, as evident when the difficulties of translating its crime literature reveal its integration of national allegories with their markers of local identity, since "the overvaluation of place in crime fiction makes the genre a privileged vector of a national allegory."[11] The mythic and romanticized nature of the setting in early Australian literature is associated with the criminal hero who inhabits it, both idealized as the representative of an immigrant Irish subclass, and symbolic of the anti-authoritarian nature of a nation defying its colonial British heritage. In early Australian literature, the Indigenous people are presented as equally unknowable and are therefore little represented except as one of the dangers of the bush landscape to white settlers.

Australian writer Peter Carey has appropriated and extended a metatextual awareness in the crime genre by presenting a fictional account of the bushranger, Ned Kelly, one who is an iconic figure in the national culture. Indeed, Ned Kelly is so entrenched in Australian society as the embodiment of the oppressed underclass that his figure appeared center stage in the opening ceremony of the Summer Olympic Games 2000 held in Sydney. In his *True History of the Kelly Gang* Carey engages with the mythologized and romanticized version of a larrikin-figure considered to be a forerunner of Australian nationalism by questioning the "truth" of an account based on historical records, one which is neither "The" True History or even "A" True History. Here, fictionalized documentary evidence is used to endorse a polyvocal approach that problematizes the notion of truth and historical accounts, especially by privileging the Irish-Catholic experience and perspective of Ned Kelly over the English-Protestant narrative voice that traditionally dominates Australian literature. In the process, the broader notion of the construction of Australian nationalism is addressed, along with the idea of crimes committed against portions of Australian society. In the first person narrative in the novel, Kelly relates his own criminal past with that of his forebears, and implicates the Australian society in a cycle of crime and social inequality as he characterizes the national identity being inextricably linked to a convict racial memory: "And here is the thing about them men they was Australians they knew full well the terror of the unyielding law the historic memory of UNFAIRNESS were in their blood and a man might be a bank clerk or an overseer he might never have been lagged for nothing but still he knew in his heart what it were to be forced to wear the white hood in prison he knew what it were to be lashed for looking a warder in the eye."[12] In this way, Carey comments upon the manner in which the myth of Ned

Kelly is both constructed and dominated by the discourse of white colonial Australia through introducing the subjective perspective of the marginalized Irish-Catholic subculture. The dominant culture views Kelly as a criminal, whereas his viewpoint within the text positions the English and the authorities as the true criminals, thereby inverting and challenging the nature of crime. In addition, the text addresses the wider construction of Australian nationalism by privileging an Irish-Catholic viewpoint over the dominant English-Protestant perspective, and in doing so introduces a competing narrative.

Therefore, while a number of other Australian writers have appropriated the Kelly myth and fictionalized his life and criminal career, Carey presents the "history" of Ned Kelly told through his own perspective, that of the criminal and the Irish-Catholic underclass, rather than through a narrative voice that allies with the dominant culture.[13] In addition, the fictional artefacts and letters purporting to be real documents endorsing Kelly's ill-treatment as part of an oppressed sub-culture relate to the notion of Australian history itself being based on a crime. Like Chloe Hooper's *A Child's Book of True Crime: A Novel*,[14] the subtext is of the Australian culture as one of criminal enterprise, incorporating crimes against sections of society. Similar to Carey's writing, Hooper's novel is a crossover between crime fiction and historical crime, although unlike Carey's focus on the treatment of the Irish subculture, Hooper's "true crime" is that of unacknowledged crimes against Tasmanian Indigenous Australians. Their history as it involves the genocide of the Tasmanian Indigenous people is invoked to relate to the Australian colonial past and national identity being based on crimes against the original inhabitants and sub-cultures within society.

Hooper and Carey consider Australian nationalism through the genre of crime fiction by invoking Australian history as intrinsically a crime due to its colonial origins. This develops a model established by Australian 19th-century writers engaging with newspaper accounts of the time to one similar to the American model developed by such American writers as Truman Capote and Norman Mailer. While Carey, especially, could be viewed as adopting the non-fiction novel initiated by Capote's *In Cold Blood*, the clear alteration of facts and integration of fictional elements into an account in which the main events are well-known to Australian readers, at least, means that there is a transparent departure from its purported "history." The title of the novel, *True History of the Kelly Gang*, is clearly ironic in the same manner as *A Child's Book of True Crime*, since, owing to both style and content, Hooper's novel is clearly not one intended for a child reader. Carey and Hooper are both using true historical crimes against sub-cultures and Indigenous sections of Australia to situate the typical individual murder or theft made familiar in detective fiction. To do so, the bush myth is invoked by events occurring in a setting with historical authenticity.

## True Crime and Crime Fiction in Australia

Early 19th-century Australian crime fiction has a focus on specific sub-genres linked with historical and social formations within the nation: convict writing, goldfields mysteries, and the squatter thriller.[15] Both early and contemporary constructions of Australian nationalism have a clear connection with crime.[16] Fiction is confounded with fact in Australia's 19th-century detective fiction, in particular through its presentation as police accounts and memoirs despite its fictional content. Stories of colonial life as depicted by the convicts in their diaries and correspondence, as well as criminal cases detailed within newspapers, formed the basis of literature that related to crime, extending to the confabulation of fictional tales with purportedly real anecdotes in "Memoirs of an Australian Police Officer" and "The Detective's Album: Tales of the Australian Police" in the 1860s *Australian Journal*. The integration of real with fictional events in the literature of the time has given rise to a tradition of Australian true crime that as a genre is characterized by a "dual investment in history and storytelling, information and imagination."[17] Therefore, in a literary arena that characterizes itself as being based on truth and fact, there is a clear integration of fictional elements whereby subjective re-creation and selection of events, along with editorializing through the narrative voice, blurs the demarcation between truth and fiction.

As a corollary, in the late 20th and early 21st centuries, Australian crime fiction forms emerged that question the judgmental nature of conventional crime fiction by their alliance with the New Journalism and the non-fiction novel. Capote incorporated fictional techniques into traditional journalistic practice based on interviews and reference to transcripts with crime writing about a real occurrence in his work *In Cold Blood,* based on the murder of the Clutter family in the United States in 1959. Similarly, Helen Garner, a contemporary Australian writer, adopts a blend of documentation and literary style in *The First Stone: Some Questions About Sex and Power,*[18] *Joe Cinque's Consolation: A True Story of Death, Grief and the Law,*[19] and *This House of Grief: The Story of a Murder Trial.*[20] Such texts form a divergent path from a highly stylized genre, emphasizing and exploring its stereotypical elements such as a clear moral authority and "characters" endorsed by the narrative voice. These works, by referencing actual events and real people, claim to depict no villains or heroes. There is no distinction made or moral imperative imposed to endorse one set of "characters" at the expense of another. Related to this is a lack of closure and no sense of resolution since the "characters" remain as unknowable and voiceless at the conclusion of the text as at the beginning, because those involved often refused to speak to the writer and the victims are voiceless. Despite their connection to traditional crime fiction, such texts not only deny a single detective hero, but they also lack an authorized narrative voice that guides the reader to the "true" perspective of the crime and criminal. A multi-faceted and polyvocal form is emerging in Australia today that challenges the idea of authority through the lack of an authorized and endorsed vision or version of events. As well, the idea of true crime is in the process of becoming a popularized text, one that is removed from the factual and sparse newspaper account and which draws on a literary approach that includes the descriptive and figurative style typical of fiction and the hybrid nature of the police memoir published in early broadsheets.

Australian true crime, especially as presented by Garner and Carey, has an ambiguity that is not a feature of earlier, classical fictional models such as the British "whodunit" or clue puzzle form, but does relate in some ways to the individual and eccentric morality of the hard-boiled hero and more especially the American true crime model of Capote and Norman Mailer. Like Capote especially, their approach has a complex and shifting set of moral parameters. Ned Kelly in Carey's *True History of the Kelly Gang*[21] is as much a victim of society as a perpetrator of crimes against it, and Garner's texts are even more morally ambiguous since there is a deliberate lack of authorized voice to guide the reader's perspective of events. Since Garner writes of current events, on occasion before the legal system at the time, there is an implied invitation to the reader to adopt a position, yet the book itself offers no guidance on a reading of events. Often, Garner has been accused of bias by both sides of the event, so that both supporters of the accused and of the victim of the crime claim that the writing prioritizes the other position. Such a charge of subjectivity, as well as criticism for constructing a story from real world events, can be attributed to her approach to writing about real crime. At a writers' gathering, she defended "using a broad brush to create and shape a story" in her talk where "Garner dwelt on the value of incorporating unexpected writers' tools in non-fiction, which she is celebrated for—imagery, associations, emblematic objects; analysis of the subject bordering on the psychoanalytic (or using the psychoanalyst's techniques)."[22] Garner's popularity in Australia comes as a result of this blending of topical and local content with her approach incorporating the selectivity and narrative techniques of fiction. Ironically, her limited fame overseas may be attributed to the same reasons as her local appeal.

Writers such as Carey and Garner rely upon a reader who is familiar with Australian folk tale and social history to inform the writing and thereby discern the sub-text of the work. In addition, Australian crime fiction draws on a relatively small and knowledgeable readership where there is an assumption that the reader will be aware, not only of the conventions of the American model, but also of the Australian culture. Carey's reinvention of the bushranger Ned Kelly's history assumes that the reader will recognize the fictional nature of many of the artefacts presented as documentary evidence. Like the topical nature of political satire and its embeddedness within a particular social and temporal context, the writings of Garner appropriate recent true crimes in Australia and, while not fictionalizing them through re-creation, adopt an editorializing approach in the prioritizing of those persons who agree to speak with the author, as well as selectivity in the presentation of facts and interviews. Such an approach connects with an Australian readership, according to Garner: "I understand Australia. I fit in here. My work has never, until recently, gone outside Australia. My publishers used to mind that a lot more than I did. I felt I was writing for people here. I never wanted to write about Australia as a spectacle for people elsewhere."[23] She refers to other fiction writers as writing about Australia "as if it were a phenomenon" and asserts her lack of "urge or ability" to do so. Like John Bryson's *Evil Angels*[24] about the death of Lindy Chamberlain's baby, Azaria, and Chamberlain's subsequent trial for her murder, Garner's true crime writing is as much about morality as the crime itself. In this respect, then, it is embedded in an Australian cultural framework, one that does not easily translate to an overseas market.

Garner's works are presentations of a mixture of fact and fiction about crimes that strike the national consciousness, and they often question the notion of the Australian identity. *This House of Grief* details a real case where Robert Farquarson is driving his sons back to the home of his estranged wife on Father's Day when he veered into a dam, drowning all three children while he escaped.[25] Such a crime challenges the iconic view of Australian masculinity and its associated loyalty, mateship and rugged heroism, and even the nature of crime. The situation calls into question the idea of Farquarson as "a good bloke," ironically still in keeping with the sub-text of an inherent misogyny in the Australian culture, wherein the children were a sacrifice made to inflict damage upon his ex-wife. Similarly, *The First Stone* explores the repercussions of a male academic being accused of assaulting female students, again interrogating the Australian notion of masculinity as having an entitlement to fumbling, often drunken actions against an unwilling female with the expectation that they will not be considered a crime. In the early stages of the book, just after a transcript of the police interview with Dr. Shepherd, the fictionalized name of the defendant, Garner writes of her "jolt" and the emotions of disbelief shared by her friends, all "feminists pushing fifty," who question the nature of the act as a crime in the cry, "He touched her breast and she went to the *cops*?" Further, she presents the idea of such male actions as accepted practice within the society, albeit an unwelcome and unpleasant one, when a previously unvoiced thought was stated: "And then some-one said what no doubt we had all been thinking: 'Look—if every bastard who's ever laid a hand on *us* were dragged into court, the judicial system of the state would be clogged for years."[26] The notion of what constitutes a crime is here explored in the arena of sexual harassment, all within a further environment of an Australian national identity that not only tolerates but promotes the larrikin male. Garner herself states that "the ability to discriminate must be maintained" based on the notion of what constitutes a crime in social terms, because "there is a sense that there is no *degree* of offence. But no one wants to know about that now, it is *all* a crime" (my emphasis).[27] The idea of what constitutes a crime connects with the globalization of crime fiction and whether it is based on a particular social milieu. It raises the possibility that Garner's lack of overseas recognition and popularity is as a direct result of the cultural embeddedness of her material within an Australian context.

In addition, the popularity of Garner's writing within Australia has contributed to the perception that it is cult fiction or genre literature, and thereby it has received limited critical attention, despite the fact that it "traverses popular and elite, canonical and non-canonical cultural form and disciplinary borders."[28] Originally a fiction writer, Garner adopts an academic approach to her true crime writing that crosses boundaries between fiction and nonfiction, yet continually emphasizes that she is constructing a story with the material. In this respect, her works are borderline populist literature even in Australia, because although they are based on controversial crimes, they are not high profile in the same manner as Bryson's *Evil Angels* which engaged with the Australian and even overseas culture, for example, through its adaptation into the film distributed globally as *A Cry in the Dark*. Few Australians beyond academia had heard of the accusations of misconduct against the Melbourne University Ormond College scholar that formed the basis of *The First Stone*. That it is more a study of power dynamics and what constitutes a crime within an academic context and Australian society in the late 20th century is clear from the subtitle and the change in name of the "characters" so that there is no obvious relationship with news reports. Similarly, *Joe Cinque's Consolation* is another crime that is controversial due to the curious gender inversion of the stereotypical crime, and the collusion of the academic society in which it took place. A law student declares to her friends that she intends killing her boyfriend at a dinner party, and then does so. None of the friends intervene or even explore the situation further, believing that it is not a serious threat. While the events were prominent in the news at the time in Australia, it had little of the high profile of some other murders. Similarly, *This House of Grief* is based on the events of a family murder. Again, while horrifying, the crime itself is not one that continued to resonate with the Australian public, and the focus of the true crime book is mainly the moral issue of the father's motivation within the context of Australian society and domestic power relations.

Each of the texts offers a shift in the nature of crime, rather than the solution of it as in typical crime fiction. Garner's popularity is not a product of the text—in providing a solution to the crime or its motivations—so much as from the story constructed around its situation in the national consciousness. Like writers such as Carey and Chloe Hooper who integrate real-world crimes on a national scale as the setting for their works, the emphasis in Garner's writing is on the nature of crime as it is perceived by the Australian culture, and as it engages with a concept of masculinity and its embeddedness within a literary tradition of the larrikin male.

## Hard-Boiled Australian Fiction

Academics such as Stephen Knight have associated fiction writer Peter Temple's global success, especially in his Jack Irish series, with an integration of the Australian style and setting with an American model—in this case, hard-boiled fiction. According to Knight, "Australian crime fiction has long-standing local success, but limited international impact. Temple has gone further both through his innate skills and because he has meshed Australian anti-authoritarianism and landscape-linked writing with interrogative approaches like that of James Ellroy."[29] Indeed, Knight considers Irish to be "Chandleresque." Temple's first novel, *Bad Debts*,[30] clearly engages with the larrikin model through the name of the main character, Jack Irish. Not only is Jack generic derivative of John and indicative of a working-class nickname, but his surname relates to the Irish subclass of Australia's first settlement days. Irish, previously a solicitor, is a private enquiry and general collection agent. Throughout the work, the humor is both specifically Australian in tone, but with an expectation of a globalized context, such as in the following description of a character: "Mrs. Davenport … had twenty years as the receptionist for a specialist in sexually transmitted diseases before joining Wootton. J. Edgar Hoover knew fewer secrets."[31]

Similar to a number of Australian fiction writers of the 1980s, Temple's style is an extension of the model established by the American hard-boiled crime authors, but, like his compatriot predecessors, he provides an Australian air by including national references within humorous asides within the larrikin detective's narrative. A typical exchange is one which takes place between Irish and other recurring characters in a pub, introducing the reader to both the detective's working-class origins and credentials as the child of an AFL hero:

> There are only a few dozen Fitzroy supporters left who remember my father: to them I represent a genetic melt-down. Three of these veterans were sitting at the bar nursing glasses of beer and old grievances. As I stood brushing rain off my sleeves, they

looked at me as if I were personally responsible for Fitzroy's 36-point loss to despised Carlton on Saturday.

"Three in a row, Jack," said Eric Tanner, the one nearest the door. "Played like girls. Where the hell were you?"

"Sorry, men," I said. "Business."

Three sets of eyes with a combined age of around 220 examined me. They all held the same look. It was the one the boy in the gang gets when he is the first to put talking to a girl ahead of kicking the football in the street.

"I had to go to Sydney," I said. "Work." I might as well have said I had to go to Perigord for truffles for all the exculpatory power this statement carried.

"Should've taken the team with you," said Wilbur Ong.

"What kind of work does a man have in Sydney on a Satdee arvo?" said Norm O'Neill in a tone of amazement. These men would no more consider being away from Melbourne on a Saturday in the football season than they would consider enrolling in personal development courses.[32]

In this scene, the casual misogyny reflected in the description of a team that "played like girls," the assumption of what is due to Australian masculinity—certainly not involving "personal development courses"—and the set of priorities where Australian Rules football comes before all else, speaks to a reader who is familiar with the Australian culture. Even the references to AFL, originally Victorian Football League and now Australian Football League, is itself embedded in the culture with an assumption that the reader will understand the religious fervor with which this code is embraced nationally, along with the rivalry between Fitzroy and Carlton teams.

While the scene itself conveys a set of priorities to the reader, the humor still relies upon a shared set of cultural assumptions between the reader and the narrator. As well, the dialect of working "on a Satdee arvo" is a clear indicator of the Australian discourse. This is despite its connection to the American film noir associations within hard-boiled crime fiction: rain, desperation, and a pervasive metaphor of the social body being related to that of the individual. Here the city is Melbourne, where "the room was comfortable: good furniture scuffed by life. Outside, it was raining on the big garden, the usual thin Melbourne drizzle that dampened the heart more than anything else."[33] Throughout there are metaphors of urban loneliness and desolation made familiar to the reader through a knowledge of American hard-boiled crime fiction. The relationship to the American model positions Australian crime fiction such that it can explore a globalization of the literary world it constructs. Reference to travelling to Perigord to hunt for truffles is clearly both irrelevant and unknowable to the stereotyped elderly Australian male in the fictional context of a "pub" or hotel, but the reader is able to relate the stereotypes of the American hard-boiled crime novel to the text, despite the idiosyncratic dialect and cultural associations.

## *The Body of the Detective as Metaphor for the Social Body*

The relationship of Australian crime fiction to the body politic and the national body is also clearly evident in the writings of Peter Corris, a contemporary crime writer whose popularity lies in his presentation of the detective hero, Cliff Hardy, as a typical Australian male, with the egalitarian attitude that this implies. Both Corris and Temple employ a clearly defined Australian larrikin as their detective hero, where Garner in her true crime texts includes the writer as well as having a focus on the perpetrators and victims of the crime. This approach eliminates the larrikin and produces an effect of reducing humor and light-heartedness in the narrative while still allowing an intermediary between the events of the text and the reader. In both crime forms, though, the Australian dialect and discourse is maintained through the first-person account. A further intermediary is introduced in the 2012 reprint in a Text Classics edition of Corris's first novel in which Hardy appears, *The Dying Trade*.[34] The novel has an introduction by Charles Waterstreet, a well-known Australian solicitor who is acknowledged in popular culture as the model for an equally famous Australian television crime series, *Rake*. This introduction to the novel is indicative of the nationalism inherent within Australian crime fiction in general. Waterstreet positions the reason for the popularity of Corris's writing in terms of both its embeddedness within the Australian context and its relationship to globalization. He views the detective hero of Corris's novel as being of the larrikin and ANZAC stereotype, since "Cliff Hardy represents the true Australian male at his best: a larrikin, despising greed and conservatism, living hand-to-mouth while cursing the affluence around him."[35] The irony here lies in the notion of what is "best." Clearly, for Waterstreet there is no reservation in considering the relationship between a literary model of an anti-authoritarian larrikin and the stereotype of the typical Australian male as one that needs no qualification.[36] The qualities of the ANZAC—which stands for Australian and New Zealand Army Corp—are those of the larrikin, with the added association that the ANZAC is the embodiment of mateship, courage, resilience and anti-authoritarian humor.

The connection between the egalitarianism of the national identity and body politic and Corris's crime fiction is so entrenched within his writing that Waterstreet considers it applies to the author himself. Waterstreet sees intellectualism and elitism as in opposition to the Australian spirit that it becomes a disease, one which Corris has resisted since he has "outstanding academic qualifications in history and journalism that he does not allow to infect his writing at all."[37] In a similar vein, his detective Hardy has the metaphor of the body and infection related to his cynical attitude to the hierarchy and composition of Australian life, because "he knows that crime infects all levels of society, under every rock is a paedophile spider, money is always in the wrong hands, the rich abuse their privileges and the poor, physically, sexually and socially."[38] The anti-elitism of the attitude attributed to both writer and character relates to a detective whose popularity rests on conforming to the stereotype of the Australian male and "like his creator, he comes equipped with an inbuilt bullshit detector."[39]

Not only was this book published in 1980 at the time of the surge in popularity of Australian crime fiction, but it is also viewed as instrumental in achieving a change in attitude to the national product. In its republication within the Text Classic series, *The Dying Trade* is one of selected books chosen since they are "milestones in the Australian experience."[40] In his introduction, "Brick by Brick," Waterstreet considers Corris's national consciousness to be the source of his popularity and success both in Australia and globally, since "he writes in Australia, about Australia and Australians, and by being specific he communicates something that can be read internationally."[41] At the same time, Waterstreet acknowledges the insular nature of such an approach: "He captures the permanent smirk on Australian faces and puts it into short burst of language like rapid fire from a machine-gun. Everyone is in on the joke, all coppers are crooked. It's just a matter of degree."[42] Here, again, the nature of the Australian crime fiction arena is displayed as having a connectedness and level of irony that relies on the knowledge of the reader, both of Australian society and its stereotypes and priorities.

In his commentary, Waterstreet himself has no introduction, and much of the irony of his comments rely on the reader's realization that he is the real-life model for the popular television series *Rake*. Again, no explanation to the reader is forthcoming when he refers to another popular Australian crime television series: "Without Corris, there would be no *Underbelly* series, or dare I say *Rake*, no Australian accent in our crime fighters, criminals, victims, coppers; no Australian point of view in the very stuff of our own restless history."[43] The *Underbelly* series referred to is again based on a number of true crime events within Australian history, made familiar to the viewer through numerous literary and popular cultural references. Further, like other writers, Waterstreet also refers to Stephen Knight, the Australian academic who specializes in critical commentary on crime fiction—with an expectation that the reader will be familiar with the scholar's role and body of work—as he delves, without preamble, into the Australian character of Corris's humor: "Stephen Knight talks of 'dryly aggressive wit.'"[44] Knight is invoked within the introduction due to his renown within the Australian academic arena, especially in the field of Australian crime fiction and the period in which Corris's novel was published. *The Dying Trade*, first published in 1980, emerged at a time Knight considered to be a critical point in the genre in Australia. Despite a strong historical and social association of crime fiction with the cultural stereotype of the bush myth—as a result of early publication of Australian crime writers in London combined with a later lack of interest both in academia and from reviewers—until the 1980s crime writing in Australia was what Stephen Knight termed "the missing genre."[45] This also can be attributed to Blainey's tyranny of distance since Australia is so far removed from the major London and New York publishing houses. A change effected around this decade in the 20th century was as a result of Australian crime writers being published in paperback locally, and advertising campaigns meant that emerging writers of the time such as Peter Corris were more widely recognized. But despite this growing recognition, as Knight points out in the Introduction to his seminal book on Australian Crime Fiction, *Continent of Mystery*, cultural stereotypes are still both powerful and pervasive, so that "even when Australians recognised in recent times how limited and limiting the bush myth had become, even when many aspects of the multicultural and multi-faceted national culture had been brought to light … there was still in the mid-eighties no general awareness of a common and continuously produced genre in Australian writing—crime fiction."[46]

But around the late 20th century, despite a cultural shift from a setting of the bush environment to an urban scene of Peter Temple's Melbourne and the Sydney of Peter Corris and Marele Day that engages with the typical corrupt cityscape of American crime writers, Australian crime fiction still includes a commentary on national stereotypes. Throughout, populism is promoted by the humor and commentary on Australian society by a larrikin-detective, and globalization through the clear connection to an overseas tradition of crime fiction normally situated within the American urban environment. Corris's hero who is introduced in the first book, Cliff Hardy, is according to Knight the embodiment of nationalism, being "a rugged individualist in the national self-image, who traced the hidden causes of crime among dysfunctional families and criminal connections in contemporary Sydney."[47] In the opening pages of *The Dying Trade* Hardy is depicted as fair-minded and ready to defend the vulnerable. When a client asks about his objections to the shooting of innocent wildlife, he states that it is because "they're harmless, attractive, too easy to hit. There's no sport in it."[48] Such a hero has a connection to the chivalrous detective within such texts as Chandler's *The Big Sleep*, but just as Philip Marlowe realizes that it is impossible to maintain a sense of honor in a corrupt city because "knights have no meaning in this game" and "it wasn't a game for knights,"[49] Hardy has a similar realization. He acknowledges the futility of attempting to defend a harmless bird in such a context: "I shrugged. Big men were raping little girls, fanatics were torturing each other and people were going mad in cells all over the world. A protest here and now seemed a vain and futile thing."[50] Like Marlowe, he accepts that a personal code of honor has limitations, yet Hardy maintains a less cynical perspective than his American counterpart, mainly through the ameliorating force of both his adherence to the mateship and loyalty of the ANZAC tradition, and the humorous perspective of the larrikin.

Even as he writes of the typically Australian humor in the novel, Waterstreet praises Corris's figurative approach with similar metaphors, reminiscent of the similes of American hard-boiled crime, but with an integration of Australian slang. For instance, he comments on Hardy's client Ailsa, "with whom he has more conflicts of interest than a bookie taking his own bets." Waterstreet also describes Corris's writing to be "as arresting and as easy on the eyes as a blonde tanning on Bondi Beach."[51] Both examples involve Australian setting, syntax and dialect. The acknowledgment that Corris's style is reminiscent of Chandler and Hammett is the mention of globalization in its form, that "the waters of the Mississippi and the Potomac might flow through his novels, but his work tastes definitely and defiantly of the Murray Darling, or rather the big beautiful bowl of salty blue water contained in Sydney Harbour."[52] That global recognition is important to providing the legitimacy of Corris's writing is displayed, despite Waterstreet's claim that national popularity is enough, through the inclusion of a glowing tribute to the "brilliant strangeness of Australian crime fiction" being praised in the *Atlantic.* Despite, then, Corris's writing being bathed in American waters, it is essentially an Australian model in its incorporation of Australian dialect and social relationships because, as Waterstreet writes, "in our country there is a subterranean reflexive prickliness between everyone"[53] that the *Atlantic* identified as "joshing camaraderie" based on the eccentric and peculiarly Australian mateship tradition of the ANZAC.

The use of terms such as "our country" makes a clear statement that in his introduction to *The Dying Trade* Waterstreet is addressing an assumed Australian reader, and this is especially evident when he makes a statement on the way Corris's writing appeals to the national identity: "when we read Corris, we see ourselves, we laugh at ourselves, we cringe at ourselves, and finally we understand ourselves a little better. He reflects the way in which the Australian psyche is imprisoned by its past, the way we walk as if in invisible shackles, our arms handcuffed by our sides instead of raised in outrage."[54] Such a comment has a direct relationship to the historical context of Australian crime fiction and its origins, since his opening remarks link the two in the critical commonplace that "Australia started its white life at a distinct advantage in the telling of criminal stories. Everyone was a criminal."[55]

## *The* Roman à Clef *and the Social Body*

The contemporary Australian writer Frank Moorhouse also explores the integration of the national identity and the relationship between fact and fiction within crime fiction in his book of short stories, *Lateshows,* and does so by interrogating the classical whodunit through the inclusion of the same Stephen Knight as Waterstreet invokes. Again similar to Waterstreet, Moorhouse assumes that the reader will be familiar with this scholar in his capacity as a well-known academic critic of crime fiction in general, but particularly of Australian literature. In his *roman à clef,* "Reading Detective Fiction," Moorhouse introduces a Stephen Knight character, also a literary critic, who comments that "sometimes when reading a batch of detective fiction books for review their sameness causes him to begin to think that *all* detective fiction is written by the same author."[56] Such a comment engages not only with Knight's real critical commentary, in which he defends the formulaic style of Agatha Christie by stating that it "replicates the mechanistic and simply certain view of the world held by author and also held—perhaps uncertainly—by audience,"[57] but also those such as Todorov, who asserts that "the masterpiece of popular literature is precisely the book which best fits its genre," and further that "the whodunit par excellence is not the one which transgresses the rules of the genre, but the one which conforms to them."[58] Here, crime fiction is related not only to its own generic stereotypes, but the cultural and historical context within which that model has developed. More than this, Moorhouse engages with the expectation of a small and knowledgeable readership of Australian literature, and especially crime fiction, in his expectation that the reader will be aware of the identity of Stephen Knight and other real-life characters he refers to in the fiction, such as bookshop owners and editors, and therefore be aware of the *roman à clef* nature of the story.

Like Waterstreet also, Moorhouse presents in his story how Knight relates crime fiction to the national identity through a metaphor of Australian crime fiction as a "body of writing" that is embedded in the social body when he states that it is "central to the cultural bloodstream."[59] Moorhouse introduces this metaphor of the social body when he refers not only to the globalization through borrowing the American model where Australian writers use a linguistic patterning established by writers such as Raymond Chandler, thereby in process of writing their fiction "[e]ither an FBI manual or FBI drinking buddy ... infected and informed both their stories."[60] Moorhouse acknowledges the influence of Chandler in creating the linguistic model of crime fiction, related to the social body since he acknowledges that "Raymond Chandler ... invented a criminal argot. He made up the expressions Big Sleep, meaning death; The Persuader, meaning a handgun; and other terms. Criminals sometimes took their vocabulary from crime writers. The words then found their way into other crime fiction."[61] Moorhouse presents this as a reciprocal process so that the language did not merely influence other crime fiction, but also the speech patterns of real-life detectives, and terms this process a "verbal virus" so that the inter-relatedness of crime fiction and the social condition is revealed when "to even talk of 'verbal viruses' is to borrow from the language system of immunology now in the mainstream language because of AIDS."[62] While the story is constructed in the form of crime fiction, the conclusion does not conform to the usual strong closure. Moorhouse examines the form of crime writing that integrates fact with fiction, since "where the boundaries between the real and the fictive dissolve, a space is opened up for the exploration of social and cultural anxieties, disturbances and crises that resist simple resolutions."[63] The point is made that style is not necessarily related only to the linguistic mannerisms of individual writers but that both generic influences and the cultural context are determining factors. As Knight claims in his reference to the sameness of detective writing, there are established conventions of dialogue, description and narrative realism that dictate the form of crime fiction, each of which is related to the populist environment in which these are fostered.

The conventions Knight refers to are further related to the metaphor of the body as it relates to a corrupt social body in the parody and pastiche of Australian writer Marele Day's *The Life and Crimes of Harry Lavender*.[64] Figurative language continues whereby the infected heart of the city is symbolic of social corruption, and this is related to the human body, as well as being analogous to the technological heart of contemporary Australian culture through the metaphor of a faulty pacemaker causing a "terminal illness." Symbolism of technology as it relates to the body is all-pervasive throughout the novel, but the hard-boiled novel's technology for organized crime of guns, cars and telephones has been replaced by the more modern counterparts of computers, modems and pacemakers. An urban setting of late 20th-century Sydney replaces the 1930s of Chandler's Los Angeles or Hammett's San Francisco, but the same notion of a superficially attractive cityscape with an undercurrent of corruption remains. Claudia Valentine, the main character detective, characterizes the setting of Sydney as both pure yet rotten at its heart: "My city was the most beautiful harbour in the world, a childhood of open doors, of ocean breezes on hot summer nights, of passionfruit and choko vines growing in the heart of a city without pollution, the innocence of a time past.... But the stench had always been there, I just hadn't smelled it till there was no place left that didn't reek of it."[65]

Despite such conformity to typical attributes of an urban setting, stereotypes of hard-boiled fiction that relate to the main character are challenged throughout in conjunction with a connection to the typical larrikin of

Australian fiction. The reader is invited to expect the conventional male main character by the opening scene of the novel conforming to the situation where the detective awakens to a "blond" in the bed after a sexual encounter. Here, only the spelling is a clue to the gender of this partner as male, and it is only in the next chapter that the narrator is revealed as being female. Even more, the language of the novel echoes that of the puns and wordplays of Chandler's prose, with the added inclusion of Australian slang and dialect. The novel starts with a Chandleresque simile and typical situation as the detective explains that "someone was pounding my brain like a two year old who's just discovered a hammer.... Close by the bed was a bottle of Jack Daniels: empty. And an ash tray: full.... As I got out of bed I realised I wasn't the only one in it. There was a good looking blond in there as well."[66] This establishing scene ends with an inversion of the reader's generic expectations along with, once again, an inclusion of the Australian dialect:

> I dressed and took a long hard look at myself in the mirror. As long as I didn't start haemorrhaging from the eyes things would be all right. I grabbed the dark glasses. Just in case.
> "Time to go sweetheart," I whispered into the blond's aural orifice. Not a flicker of an eyelid or a murmur. Next time I shook him. "C'mon mate, wake up. I've got to go to a funeral."[67]

Through such an exploration of gender stereotypes then current in crime fiction, Day is adapting a globalized form to an Australian setting, and specifically invoking the original as the main character puzzles, "I could never understand how Philip Marlowe and those guys, from one end of the story to the other, got shot, beaten up, and sometimes laid, without ever going to bed."[68] Clearly, there is an expectation that the reader will not only connect the style and approach of the text to the earlier American model, but realize that it challenges the male larrikin detective made familiar in Australian crime fiction.

## Conclusion

The presence of the larrikin-detective introduces a peculiarly Australian form of humor within literary forms extrapolated from those developed in a global setting, especially by a contrast with the cynicism of the American detective hero or anti-hero. That crime fiction is particularly suited both to the origins and traditional setting of Australian literature is evident by both its popularity and the development of distinctively Australian detectives as they typify such national tropes as the larrikin and the ANZAC. While Australian crime fiction draws on American models familiar to the reader through the first-generation hard-boiled fiction of Chandler and Hammett, its development has been towards a hybrid of fiction and non-fiction through the progression from 19th-century newspaper accounts of crimes, often themselves fictionalized despite being presented as police memoirs. As a result, the Australian model includes real crime, both by a fictionalization of actual events in a manner similar to the true crime fiction of Capote and Mailer, and also by a *roman à clef* inclusion of real world historical figures such as the bushranger Ned Kelly and the scholar of crime fiction, Stephen Knight. A small market for Australian crime literature creates the assumption that the reader will have a knowledge of this process of fictionalizing real Australian events and people and will recognize the real-world models even as pseudonyms are used or topical in-jokes are created.

More importantly, the hybrid form of fictional and true crime that has emerged in Australia is not only based on an assumption of globalized knowledge on the part of the reader, but it amalgamates fact and fiction to challenge the truth of history and emphasize the nationalized nature of crime. The concept of what constitutes a crime, not only in literature but in the real world, is challenged in Australian crime fiction since it incorporates historical and cultural crime as well as the individual crime presented in classical crime fiction. Because Australian society is based upon crime in its convict origins of white settlement and history of the relationship with Indigenous persons and sub-cultures, this has given rise to a flourishing crime literature with a larrikin detective, engaging with popularization and globalization.

## NOTES

1. "Such is life" are the Australian bushranger Ned Kelly's final words before being hanged at Melbourne Gaol in 1880, according to popular culture. The truth of this is contentious, but it persists in Australian folklore.
2. For Australians, the (typically male) larrikin is one who adopts a dismissively humorous and cynical approach to institutional power and so is the embodiment of the resistance to authority within the national identity.
3. Stephen Knight, *Continent of Mystery: A Thematic History of Australian Crime Fiction* (Carlton South: Melbourne University Press, 1997), 8.
4. S. King, "Crime Fiction as World Literature," *Clues: A Journal of Detection* 32:2, 8–19. Doi:10.3172/CLU.32.2.8.
5. Alistair Rolls, Marie-Laure Vuaille-Barcan and John West-Sooby, "Translating National Allegories: The Case of Crime Fiction," *The Translator* 22:2, 2016, 135–43, 13.
6. Stephen Knight, "Friday Essay: From Convicts to Contemporary Convictions—200 Years of Australian Crime Fiction." https://theconversation.com/friday-essay-from-convicts-to-contemporary-convictions-200-years-of-australian-crime-fiction-98845.
7. *Ibid.*, 1.
8. *Ibid.*
9. Geoffrey Blainey, *The Tyranny of Distance: How Distance Shaped Australia's History* (Sydney: Macmillan, 1966).
10. The most iconic story in populist literature involving such events is Henry Lawson's "The Drover's Wife."
11. Rolls et al., 136.
12. Peter Carey, *True History of the Kelly Gang* (Brisbane: University of Queensland Press, 2000), 312.

13. Such fiction spans the spectrum from Robert Drewe's *Our Sunshine* to Jean Bedford's *Sister Kate.*

14. Chloe Hooper, *A Child's Book of True Crime: A Novel* (New York: Scribner, 2002).

15. These categories are designated and explored in Knight, *Continent of Mystery,* Chapter 1, 13–49.

16. Delys Bird, ed., *Killing Women: Rewriting Detective Fiction* (Sydney: Angus and Robertson, 1993), 5.

17. Rosalind Smith, "Dark Places: True Crime Writing in Australia." *JASAL* 8 2008, 18.

18. Helen Garner, *The First Stone: Some Questions About Sex and Power* (Sydney: Pan Macmillan, 1995).

19. Helen Garner, *Joe Cinque's Consolation: A True Story of Death, Grief and the Law* (Sydney: Picador, 2004).

20. Helen Garner, *This House of Grief: The Story of a Murder Trial* (Melbourne: Text, 2014).

21. Carey, *True History.*

22. Cathy Alexander, "Garner Cheats Death, Unlike Some of her Subjects." *Crikey,* November 23, 2012. https://www.crikey.com.au/2012/11/23/helen-garner-cheats-death-unlike-some-of-her-subjects.

23. Sian Cain, "Interview. Helen Garner: I Used to Feel Spiteful Because I Never Won Prizes. Now I Can Die Happy," *The Guardian,* December 30, 2017. https://www.theguardian.com/books/2017/dec/30/helen-garner-i-used-to-feel-spiteful-because-i-never-won-prizes-now-i-can-die-happy.

24. John Bryson, *Evil Angels: The Trial of Lindy Chamberlain* (New York: Summit, 1985). This text is regarded as instrumental in establishing Australia's true crime genre.

25. Garner, *House of Grief.*

26. Garner, *The First Stone,* 15.

27. Cain, "Die Happy," 1.

28. Smith, "Dark Places," 21.

29. Stephen Knight, "Peter Temple: Australian Crime Fiction on the World Stage," *Clues* 29:1, Spring 2011, 71–81, 71.

30. Peter Temple, *Bad Debts* (Sydney: HarperCollins, 1996).

31. *Ibid.,* 4–5.

32. *Ibid.,* 9.

33. *Ibid.,* 185.

34. Peter Corris, *The Dying Trade* (Melbourne: Text, 2012). Originally published McGraw Hill, 1980.

35. Charles Waterstreet, "Brick by Brick," introduction to Peter Corris, *The Dying Trade* (Melbourne: Text, 2012), xii.

36. The ANZAC referred to is the Australia and New Zealand Army Corps that is an integral part of Australian society with its associations of World War I staunch valour despite the knowledge of almost certain defeat and a loyalty to fellow soldiers as much as to a cause.

37. Waterstreet, "Brick by Brick," xii.

38. *Ibid.,* vii–viii.

39. *Ibid.,* xii.

40. Michael Heyward, "About the Text Classics," *Text Publishing,* https://www.textpublishing.com.au/about-the-text-classics.

41. Waterstreet, "Brick by Brick," viii.

42. *Ibid.,* ix.

43. *Ibid.,* xi–xii.

44. *Ibid.,* viii.

45. Stephen Knight, "The Case of the Missing Genre," *Southerly* 48 1988.

46. Knight, *Continent,* 1.

47. Stephen Knight, *Crime Fiction Since 1800: Detection, Death, Diversity* (Basingstoke: Palgrave Macmillan, 2004), 142.

48. Corris, *Dying Trade,* 12.

49. Raymond Chandler, *The Big Sleep* (New York: Alfred A. Knopf, 1939), 152–53.

50. Corris, *Dying Trade,* 20.
51. Waterstreet, "Brick by Brick," ix.
52. *Ibid.,* vii.
53. *Ibid.,* xi.
54. *Ibid.,* x–xi.
55. *Ibid.,* vii.
56. Frank Moorhouse, "Reading Detective Fiction," *Lateshows* (Sydney: Pan, 1990), 64.
57. Stephen Knight, *Form and Ideology in Crime Fiction* (London: Macmillan, 1980), 123.
58. Tvetan Todorov, *The Poetics of Prose,* Trans. Richard Howell (Oxford: Blackwell, 1977), 43.
59. Knight, *Continent,* ix.
60. Moorhouse, "Reading Detective Fiction," *Lateshows,* 61.
61. *Ibid.,* 79.
62. *Ibid.*
63. Smith, "Dark Places," 25.
64. Marele Day, *The Life and Crimes of Harry Lavender* (St. Leonards: Allen & Unwin, 1992).
65. *Ibid.,* 168.
66. *Ibid.,* 1.
67. *Ibid.,* 2.
68. *Ibid.,* 131.

## BIBLIOGRAPHY

Alexander, Cathy. "Garner Cheats Death, Unlike Some of Her Subjects." *Crikey,* November 23, 2012. https://www.crikey.com.au/2012/11/23/helen-garner-cheats-death-unlike-some-of-her-subjects.
Bird, Delys, ed. *Killing Women: Rewriting Detective Fiction.* Sydney: Angus and Robertson, 1993.
Blainey, Geoffrey. *The Tyranny of Distance: How Distance Shaped Australia's History.* Sydney: Macmillan, 1966.
Bryson, John. *Evil Angels: The Trial of Lindy Chamberlain.* New York: Summit, 1985.
Cain, Sian. "Interview. Helen Garner: I Used to Feel Spiteful Because I Never Won Prizes. Now I Can Die Happy." *The Guardian,* December 30, 2017. https://www.theguardian.com/books/2017/dec/30/helen-garner-i-used-to-feel-spiteful-because-i-never-won-prizes-now-i-can-die-happy
Carey, Peter. *True History of the Kelly Gang.* Brisbane: University of Queensland Press, 2000.
Chandler, Raymond. *The Big Sleep.* New York: Alfred A. Knopf, 1939.
Corris, Peter. *The Dying Trade.* Melbourne: Text, 2012.
Day, Marele. *The Life and Crimes of Harry Lavender.* St. Leonards: Allen & Unwin, 1992.
Garner, Helen. *The First Stone: Some Questions about Sex and Power.* Sydney: Pan Macmillan, 1995.
Garner, Helen. *Joe Cinque's Consolation: A True Story of Death, Grief and the Law.* Sydney: Picador, 2004.
Garner, Helen. *This House of Grief: The Story of a Murder Trial.* Melbourne: Text, 2014.
Heyward, Michael. "About the Text Classics." *Text Publishing.* https://www.textpublishing.com.au/about-the-text-classics.
Hooper, Chloe. *A Child's Book of True Crime: A Novel.* New York: Scribner's, 2002.
King, S. "Crime Fiction as World Literature." *Clues: A Journal of Detection* 32:2, 8–19. Doi:10.3172/CLU.32.2.8.
Knight, Stephen. "The Case of the Missing Genre." *Southerly* 48, 1988.
Knight, Stephen. *Continent of Mystery: A Thematic History of Australian Crime Fiction.* Carlton South: Melbourne University Press, 1997.
Knight, Stephen. *Crime Fiction Since 1800: Detection, Death, Diversity.* Basingstoke: Palgrave Macmillan, 2004.

Knight, Stephen. *Form and Ideology in Crime Fiction*. London: Macmillan, 1980.

Knight, Stephen. "Friday Essay: From Convicts to Contemporary Convictions—200 Years of Australian Crime Fiction." https://theconversation.com/friday-essay-from-convicts-to-contemporary-convictions-200-years-of-australian-crime-fiction-98845.

Knight, Stephen. "Peter Temple: Australian Crime Fiction on the World Stage." *Clues* 29:1, Spring 2011, 71–81.

Moorhouse, Frank. "Reading Detective Fiction," *Lateshows*. Sydney: Pan Macmillan, 1990.

Rolls, Alastair, Marie-Laure Vuaille-Barcan, and John West-Sooby. "Translating National Allegories: The Case of Crime Fiction." *The Translator.* 22:2, 2016, 135–43.

Smith, Rosalind. "Dark Places: True Crime Writing in Australia." *JASAL* 8 2008.

Temple, Peter. *Bad Debts*. Sydney: HarperCollins, 1996.

Todorov, Tvetan. *The Poetics of Prose,* Trans. Richard Howell. Oxford: Blackwell, 1977.

Waterstreet, Charles. "Brick by Brick." Introduction to Peter Corris, *The Dying Trade*. Melbourne: Text, 2012.

# Beyond Machismo/
# Beyond Modernity

*Imagining a Postnational Society*
*in Domingo Villar's Inspector Caldas Novels*

Heath A. Diehl

In *Immigration Canada: Evolving Realities and Emerging Challenges in a Postnational World* (2015), Augie Fleras casts nationalism and postmodernism as strange bedfellows, arguing that the former more closely aligns with key attributes of modernity, including "a commitment to a master narrative (uniformity), a coherent state identity (homogeneity), universalism (rules apply to all), centrality (to ensure conformity and control), [and] clarity (rather than ambiguities)."[1] By contrast, nationhood in a postmodern world constitutes, according to Fleras, an embattled, if not entirely outmoded, identity construct. As Fleras writes, "A centralized and fixed mono-uniformity is displaced by a more fluid sense of impermanence, fragmentation, and mutability, thus reflecting a radically skeptical world where everything is relative and contested because nothing is absolute and definitive."[2] In a world, and in a moment, where relativity and skepticism reign, the rigidly-drawn certainty of national boundaries, and the coherence of any identity that such boundaries might anticipate, dissolve and are supplanted by a global geopolitical entity marked by transience, decentralization, and elasticity.

Of course, Fleras is not the only, or for that matter the first, cultural critic to draw a firm line in the proverbial sand between the modern and the postmodern worlds with respect to their conceptions of the nation-state. Indeed, many contemporary cultural critics, including Fleras, trace this line of thought "originally" (as if, in a postmodern moment, any sense of originality can be established or retained) to the early work of Linda Hutcheon, most particularly *The Canadian Postmodern: A Study of Contemporary English-Canadian Fiction* (1988)[3] and *Splitting Images: Contemporary Canadian Ironies* (1991).[4] In the latter text, Hutcheon asserts that "[t]he entire question of Canadian identity has become a kind of playground—or battlefield—for the postmodern as well as the post-colonial defining of 'difference' and value,"[5] suggesting that the "male, Anglo-Saxon, and capitalist defining essences" that might once have lent shape and meaning to a coherent sense of "Canadian identity" are, in the contemporary moment, being undone (read: deconstructed) by the many verbal and visual ironies at work in Canadian cultural artifacts.[6]

Critics like Fleras and Hutcheon write specifically about Canada because, as Richard Gwyn asserts in *Nationalism Without Walls: The Unbearable Lightness of Being Canadian* (1995), that nation constitutes "the world's first postmodern state,"[7] which George Grant, in *Lament for a Nation: The Defeat of Canadian Nationalism* (1965), defines as "the sense that its statehood is not a consequence of typically modern factors such as shared language, ethnicity, and history."[8] However, in the intervening years between the original publication of Grant's work and those of Fleras, Hutcheon, and Gwyn, many nation-states have begun the painful transition into what Fleras terms "[a] postnational society," in which "a plurality of identities and ethnicities [are embraced] within the context of a national community."[9] Fleras goes on to suggest that, within a postnational entity, "belonging to society is not contingent on affiliation to a specific (and usually dominant) ethnocultural group."[10]

Postmodernism has, indeed, impacted our shared sense of political identity on a global scale, most particularly with respect to "the whole question of nationalism, and the related issue of national identity," which, as Richard Kearney notes in "Postnationalism and Postmodernity," "is so central to European politics."[11] In this essay, I am especially interested in the ways in which these debates regarding postmodernity and postnationalism manifest themselves in a series of contemporary mystery novels by Spanish writer Domingo Villar. Consisting at present of two novels—*Water Blue Eyes* (2006)[12] and *Death on a Galician Shore* (2009)[13]—Villar's series follows the investigative pursuits of Inspector Leo Caldas, a native of the autonomous community and historic nationality of Galicia, located in northwest Spain.

Scholars whose works concentrate on the Iberian peninsula suggest that "[p]ostmodernity and postmodernism are as two indispensable socio-cultural phenomena in Spain."[14] In *Postmodernity in Spanish Fiction and Culture* (2010), Yaw Agawu-Kakraba regards Spain "as a nation that ... is still experiencing what can be considered full-blown postmodernity,"[15] arguing that the nation is characterized by "an embedded postmodern politics that critiques identity and the organization of Spanish society itself."[16] Agawu-

Kakraba's use of the word "embedded" is telling, I think, in the way that it at once recognizes the fixedness of postmodernity within contemporary Spanish culture, and acknowledges the sometimes elusive nature of those postmodern politics. This is why, in Villar's work, for instance, the interplay between the traditional and the modern, the rural and the urban, and the like often are experienced as an implicit (even taken-for-granted) part of the diegetic world, rather than explicitly engaged with by the writer or/and the characters. Within the contemporary Spanish nation, Agawu-Kakraba goes on to contend, "the postmodern subject that becomes apparent ... encompasses a plurality of sexual, political, and epistemic relations ... [that are] continuously shifting and constantly rearticulated."[17] As I will discuss later in this essay, the figure that most prominently embodies this postmodern plurality is Villar's sleuth-protagonist, Inspector Leo Caldas.

Villar's Inspector Caldas series dramatizes "the embedded postmodern politics" that characterize the socio-political organization of contemporary Spain through the positing and constant rearticulation of tensions between urbanity and rurality, progress and tradition, and liberalism and conservatism.[18] The dynamic interplay among these tensions, which Villar repeatedly locates in the conflicts and contrasts that exist between his two main characters (i.e., Caldas and sidekick Rafael Estévez), vividly point up the "plurality of identities and ethnicities [that are embraced] within the context of a [contemporary, Spanish] national community."[19]

Beyond mere contrasts between characters, this dynamic manifests itself at the fundamental level of plot and narrative structure. As a genre that is predicated on the positing of a life-or-death antagonism between sleuth and perpetrator, the detective novel of course constitutes an ideal site at which to dramatize and negotiate such tensions. In each of the two initial Inspector Caldas novels, Villar skewers the ideological provinciality of rural Spanish villages, using hot-button issues related to social justice movements for LGBTQ+ and women's rights as a platform for considering what "citizenship" means to Spaniards in the current historical moment and how Spain fits within an increasingly complicated global community.

But Villar does not view the tensions at the heart of his novels (and his native country) in oversimplified, binary terms; rather, even as Villar's novels indict the conservatism that characterizes rural Spain, identifying his perpetrators with anti-progressive ideological formations (like heterosexism, homophobia, misogyny) that must be excised from the narrative/nation, Villar ultimately celebrates his picturesque settings of Vigo and Panxón parish as sites at which progress and tradition can co-exist, at least once the extremist opponents of progress (i.e., the perpetrators) are identified and punished. Ultimately, I argue that Villar's Spain, like the "real" (read: extra-diegetic) nation on which it is based, is a postmodern imagined community (or, in

Fleras' verbiage, a postnational society) built squarely on the foundations of impermanence, mutability, and fragility.

## La Pareja Dispareja, *or the (Spanish)* Odd Couple

Detective fiction has long featured an ill-matched protagonist and side-kick at its narrative center—from Sir Arthur Conan Doyle's Sherlock and Watson, to Agatha Christie's Hercule Poirot and Arthur Hastings, and Mary Daheim's Judith McMonigle Flynn and Cousin Renie. Indeed, in his entry on "Detective Sidekicks," Frederic Joseph Svoboda notes that such figures "have been present in detective fiction since its beginnings, originating with Dupin's unnamed assistant in Edgar Allan Poe's 'The Murders in the Rue Morgue' (1841)."[20] Svoboda goes on to explain that "most sidekicks have served as foils to their brilliant counterparts or as narrators of the detectives' ratiocination."[21] Villar's series identifies itself as part of this tradition very early in its first installment, *Water Blue Eyes*, by introducing the reader to an odd coupling of sleuths—one rational and calm, the other wildly impetuous.

In the opening chapters of this novel, readers meet series protagonist Leo Caldas, a native of Spain's Galicia and a long-time law enforcement officer for the city of Vigo. When readers first encounter Caldas, he is seated in a radio station control booth, listening to call-in complaints from community members as he does on a regular basis for a program of some local fame called *Patrol on the Air*. Time and again Caldas listens patiently to frustrated callers, "knowing he'd be unable to offer anything but comforting words," given that the described infractions fall within the purview not of his department, but of the city police (*Water Blue Eyes*, "Turning"). Rather than express frustration or anger at his impotence, Caldas, at the end of this scene, as "programme number 108 of *Patrol on the Air* [comes] to an end," dispassionately reviews his tally of calls from the day—"City police nine, crazies two, Leo nil"—and, with his signature cool rationality, commits to passing along the complaints to the proper city authorities.

By contrast, Caldas' sidekick, Rafael Estévez, is introduced as a hothead outsider whose transfer to Vigo, according to rumor, "had been a punishment administered in his native Zaragoza," presumably for his "fiery personality" (*Water Blue Eyes*, "Ambiguity"). From the introduction of Estévez into the narrative, Villar emphasizes the man's impatient nature. As the radio program comes to a close, for instance, Caldas checks his phone and learns that he has three missed calls from Estévez—an indication not only of the urgency of the information that Estévez possesses, but also of the "subordinate['s]" (*Water Blue Eyes*, "Turning") hot-blooded temperament. This impression of

Estévez, formed before the reader even "meets" the character, is reinforced in the next chapter when this same subordinate "burst[s] in" to Caldas' office and begins frantically "waving a piece of paper" that contains the address of a murder victim (*Water Blue Eyes*, "Ambiguity"). Later in this same chapter, the reader learns that Estévez was "entrusted" to the "calm influence" of Caldas due to his "impetuous" nature. Characterized as loud, blustery, and ultimately less astute than his "partner in crime," Estévez, like many sidekicks before him, "often participates in the sleuthing process," even though he is almost exclusively "played for comic effect" and his bumbling antics are employed within the narrative to "[suggest] … the depth of the detective's insights."[22] His demeanor stands in marked contrast to Caldas' own—as the narrator explains, "Rafael Estévez … was unable to remain silent, as his DNA did not include his superior's Galician patience" (*Water Blue Eyes*, "Cowering")—and, at first blush, Estévez appears little more than a foil character designed to lend depth and insight into the series protagonist.

Yet to read Villar's mismatched coupling in this manner would be to misunderstand a more complicated dynamic that exists between the two characters, and to overlook completely an important thematic thread that runs through the initial two novels of the series. Specifically, I would suggest that Caldas and Estévez stand as symbolic representations of their native regions— Galicia and Aragon, respectively—and further that these regions, which have enjoyed markedly different histories, together constitute a microcosm of the postnational society that is contemporary Spain. This type of dynamic among character, setting, and national polemics is not uncommon in contemporary European fiction, and, in fact, often figures quite prominently in both detective fiction and, more broadly, the regional novel, of which Villar's detective fiction might be viewed as a subcategory. While this trend is quite pronounced within the genre of contemporary European crime/mystery fiction, some noteworthy examples include: Ann Cleves' Jimmy Perez series, which features the bleak Shetland Islands of Scotland; Petros Markaris' Inspector Haritos series, which provides readers an off-the-beaten-path view of Athens; and Barbara Nadel's Cetin Ikmen series, which invites readers to experience the local color of Istanbul. Some of these novels address this dynamic explicitly, while others approach it in a more implicit manner, but regardless of how directly the authors engage with the contrasts between the north and the south, the urban and the rural, it is undeniable that European crime/mystery fiction places an obvious emphasis on the ways in which location politics shape characters, narratives, and ideologies within the genre.

In his discussion of the "Regional Novel" in Britain, Gary Kelly asserts that "[t]he community of a regional novel … has a particular relationship to the wider nation and empire, often some kind of conflict, resolved or superseded through the plot."[23] Kelly goes on to suggest that "the community may be represented, implicitly or explicitly, as a microcosm of the wider nation and empire."[24] While Kelly is writing specifically about regional novels in the British tradition, his observations resonate quite profoundly with Villar's Spanish detective fiction, perhaps because that genre, broadly cast, often reveals a deep investment in and commitment to the politics of location. As Barbara Pezzotti has advanced in *The Importance of Place in Contemporary Italian Crime Fiction: A Bloody Journey* (2012), "crime fiction ... can deliver the 'sense of a place'" given that "the search for 'whodunit' intertwines with an investigation into the environment of both the victims and the potential culprits."[25]

Villar's novels not only conduct an investigation into the "environment" of contemporary Spain, but also actively celebrate that environment by vividly establishing a sense of place through rich, descriptive passages that do very little to advance the narrative. Villar initially emphasizes the natural beauty of the Galician landscape by revealing it to the reader through the eyes of the outsider, Estévez. As Caldas and his sidekick drive to the scene of Luis Reigosa's gruesome murder, for instance, Estévez delights in the sensual experiences of his adopted region:

> The tide was low, and the strong smell of the sea wafted in through the window. Rafael Estévez liked this smell; it was almost new to him. He looked at the landscape, the intricate relief of fjord-like inlets known as *rías*, that had seduced him from the moment he'd seen it. The sea he'd always been familiar with.... In Galicia, however, swaths of green land gave way here and there to *rías* of varying colours, shielded from the pounding of the Atlantic by streamlined, white-sand islands [*Water Blue Eyes*, "Artist"].

This passage, like many others throughout *Water Blue Eyes,* is rife with vivid sensory details that bring the Galician landscape to life for the reader. As Estévez sees the region with "almost new" eyes, so, too, does the reader enter into Villar's fictional Formosa, an explorer set loose in a landscape that is almost too breath-taking to be believed. For Estévez, who has been familiar with the sea for as long as he can recall, the *rías* of Galicia are somehow more remarkable, more noteworthy than any similar landmark in his native Aragon. He experiences a powerful attraction to this landscape, enticed by its intricate, vivid beauty, and, in tandem, the reader is encouraged to consume with scopophilic relish the many visual delights of the region. In short, this passage demonstrates the ways in which "crime fiction exalts the regional and local specificity"[26] of its settings.[27]

The outsider-as-witness has been a fairly common trope throughout the history of Western literature, but particularly within the category of "regional fiction." In "The Regional Novel: Themes for Interdisciplinary Research," K.D.M. Snell suggests that "[i]n much regional fiction insider-outsider tensions are central to the plot," and Snell goes on to suggest that "[a] recurring phenomenon has been the regional novelist as outside witness, in some cases almost as anthropological visitor, participant-observer and investigator."[28] As a relative newcomer to Galicia, Estévez simultaneously occupies the positions of insider and outsider, particularly in relation to the reader, for whom the sidekick character often serves as a "surrogate" in detective fiction.[29] Unlike Caldas, who is a native to the primary setting of the series, Estévez is not so intimately familiar with this world that he takes for granted local customs and idiosyncrasies that, without explanation, might confound the reader.

At the same time, Estévez is familiar enough with the diegetic world that his ignorance does not serve as a barrier between text and reader. Indeed, Estévez is uniquely positioned to function as an "anthropological visitor" who studies with curiosity the practices of everyday life and the politics of social organization in Villar's fictional Galicia and who, based on his observations, allows readers to draw conclusions regarding the rituals, customs, and behaviors that are observed. Specifically, through Estévez, Villar at least initially invites the reader to explore and delight in the visual pleasures of his world—and the invitation is that much more compelling precisely because readers, like Estévez, are strangers in a foreign land that exists as a "puzzle … to be ruthlessly interrogated visually."[30] The delight that readers experience through the outsider-insider Estévez is, I suspect, intensified for non–Spanish readers who are unfamiliar with Galicia given that these readers can more easily identify with (and mimic) Estévez's awe at the landscape and culture.

## Between Tradition and Modernity

While *Water Blue Eyes* invites the reader to engage in the pleasures of looking at the diegetic landscape, the novel does not uncritically romanticize the picturesque, the pastoral, and, by association, tradition; indeed, within the initial few chapters of the novel, in a telling move, Villar juxtaposes the exalted landscape of his native Galicia with the horrific murder of Luis Reigosa, a crime more akin to torture and one that provides great insight into the conversation that the novel advances around postnationality in the contemporary moment. Through this juxtapositioning, Villar points up, as David W. Allen suggests in *The Fear of Looking or Scopophilic-Exhibitionistic Conflicts* (1974), that pleasure in looking (i.e., scopophilia) always and already presupposes an equally compelling fear of looking, and of being looked at (i.e., "scopophobia").[31] To look is to consume and (attempt to) understand wholly, which, in the case of the nation, translates to the external imposition of Modern conceptions of nationhood that are predicated on the ideals of mono-uniformity, homogeneity, and control. (This is perhaps why the looking in this novel, at least where the landscape of Galicia is concerned, is performed by the outsider, Estévez.) The link between looking, codification, and consumption derives from the colonial enterprise, which, both historically and ideologically, is intimately intertwined with the modern nation-state. What provokes pleasure in the looker is the ability to see the self in the Other, an effect most often achieved through forced assimilation or/and acculturation. What provokes fear in the looker is the prospect of unknowability, both of self and of nation—not only that those entities cannot be wholly codified in language or/and thought, but also that there are elements lurking within both the self and the nation that cannot be anticipated and that likely will challenge, if not completely re-draw, the once assumed indelible boundaries of the nation.

The interplay between the pleasure and the fear of looking is foreshadowed by the scene that immediately precedes the initial investigation of Reigosa's flat and corpse:

> Toralla was a small island. There were only a few mansions, beaches and tracts of wilderness on barely twenty hectares opposite the most exclusive residential area of the bay. But something unusual stood out in the small paradise, a twenty-floor high-rise that, at the height of urban brutalism, had been built with no regard for the harmony that the island had preserved until then. Caldas had always thought that if it had been constructed five centuries before, it would have been enough to scare Francis Drake away [*Water Blue Eyes,* "Artist"].

At once apparent in this passage is the stark contrast that is drawn between the natural beauty of the Galician landscape—here embodied by the quaint "paradise" of Toralla—and the modern high-rise in which Reigosa resided. Like the contrasts that are repeatedly underlined between Villar's protagonist and sidekick pairing, the island and the structure share an "unusual," even unnatural, coexistence, the two having been cobbled together without "regard for … harmony"—aesthetic, ideological, or otherwise. To be sure, I am not attempting here to conflate the kinds of contrasts witnessed in Villar's characters and the kinds of contrasts witnessed in his setting; however, I do want to draw the reader's attention to the presence of these parallel contrasts because collectively they point to the struggles over national identity that, in this essay, I suggest are central to 21st-century Spanish experience.

Equally significant is the allusion to Brutalism as the aesthetic reference point for the high-rise. In *Brutalism: Post-War British Architecture* (2018), Alexander Clement describes Brutalism as "an uncompromisingly modern form of architecture which appeared and developed mainly in Europe between approximately 1945 and 1975."[32] In *Brutalism,* Clement notes, "[t]he use of modern materials predominates: concrete, steel and glass, although other more traditional ones were used in this period too, such as marble, stone and brick, but in a distinctively modern way."[33] Clement goes on to explain that the Brutalist style is "characterized by large, sometimes monumental, forms brought together in a unified whole with heavy, often asymmetrical proportions. When concrete was used it was usually un adorned and rough-cast, adding to its unfortunate reputation for evoking a bleak dystopian future."[34] I would suggest that Villar characterizes Reigosa's high rise as part of the Brutalist tradition—a tradition that mirrors not only the contrasts between Caldas and Estévez, but also the violent nature of the crime perpetrated against Reigosa—as a very explicit means of highlighting the tensions between tradition and modernity that drive the narrative and circumscribe meaning in *Water Blue Eyes*. In this tradition, the high-rise stands as an assault on the landscape, an aesthetic transgression, just as Reigosa's murder stands as a blight on the postnational Spanish society. By this I mean that Reigosa's murder at once stands as a powerful reminder of the mono-uniformity of the Modern era that, in a post-national Spain, must be forcefully reinstated through the excision of the sexual Other. In this way, his murder both clumsily reinstates and simultaneously indicts the systems of heterosexism, heteronormativity, and binary gender that are synonymous with the Modern nation.

Similar to how the heavy, rough-cast high-rise sits uneasily against the idyllic backdrop of Toralla, Reigosa's murder exists uncomfortably within the ideological framework of contemporary Galicia and within the narrative structure of *Water Blue Eyes*. To understand the uneasy relationship between narrativity, ideology, and plot, it is first necessary to discuss briefly the nature of the crime that exists at the narrative center of *Water Blue Eyes*. Reigosa's murder is a brutal and violent affair that seems principally designed to dehumanize the victim, a motivation that takes on added significance given that the victim self-identifies as a gay man within a fairly orthodox heteronormative culture. Upon initially entering the bedroom where Reigosa was murdered, the narrator observes that the victim's "naked body was contorted into an unnatural position" (*Water Blue Eyes*, "Find"), a description that doubly underscores the abnormality of the crime with the words "contorted," which denotes the twisting or bending of an object out of its normal shape, and "unnatural."

Later in this same chapter, the "unnatural" aspect of the crime is emphasized again when the method by which Reigosa was murdered is revealed:

> The body displayed a huge area of bruised skin. The damage started at his stomach and extended down to his legs…. The skin was so shrivelled up that Caldas had the impression that he had a tanned hide before him rather than human skin. He'd never seen anything like it. Judging from Doctor Barrio's astonished expression, he hadn't either [*Water Blue Eyes*, "Find"].

While both Caldas and Barrio have enjoyed lengthy careers in law enforcement, and presumably during that time both have witnessed any number of violent crimes (including murder), the men's reactions suggest that this particular crime is markedly beyond the pale. For Caldas, he has no mental benchmark (other than the "tanned hide" of a skinned animal) with which to compare and make sense of the body before him, an observation that suggests both the heightened degree of damage inflicted upon the victim and the ways in which that physical damage dehumanizes the person against whom it was directed. Caldas can only stare in astonishment at the corpse and ponder the "horrendous blackness" that mars "the lifeless body"— ambiguous rhetoric that speaks to the unspeakability of the crime (*Water Blue Eyes,* "Poison"). The astonishment that is exhibited by Caldas and Barrio is echoed by Estévez, who, upon seeing the body, "cup[s] his testicles and mov[es] away from the body," exclaiming, "Holy fuck, what's *that* he's got there?" (*Water Blue Eyes,* "Find").

The object of Estévez's horror, it turns out, is Reigosa's penis, which, the reader learns, "looked like the empty shell of a barnacle: dark and wrinkled." The narrator goes on to observe, "And one could just make out, as black as all the rest, the saxophonist's testicles. They were the size of raisins, and had the same texture" (*Water Blue Eyes,* "Find"). While Barrio initially cannot determine the exact cause of Reigosa's death, hypothesizing at the scene of the crime that the perpetrator "poured some kind of abrasive substance on him" (*Water Blue Eyes,* "Find"), later in the novel, the forensic specialist determines that Reigosa was injected with formaldehyde, which precipitated a "kind of toxaemia," or blood poisoning, that ultimately killed Reigosa (*Water Blue Eyes,* "Poison"). To Caldas, Barrio describes the crime as an "execution ... worthy of Caligula" (*Water Blue Eyes,* "Poison") and confirms Caldas' suspicion that "[t]he pain must have been excruciating" (*Water Blue Eyes,* "Find"). The gruesomeness of this crime is underscored by the allusion to Caligula, the "Roman emperor from A.D. 37 to 41," whom, according to one biographer, "started out as a tyrannical ruler and degenerated into a monster,"[35] precisely because he subjected the citizens of Rome to systematic torture and dehumanization.

## The Expectation and Desire for (Re)Solution

To suggest that Reigosa's murder sits uneasily within the narrative of *Water Blue Eyes* should not be terribly surprising, given that detective fiction inherently posits crime—often, but not always, a murder—as the central narrative enigma to be probed, unraveled, and ultimately expunged. In *S/Z: An Essay* (1974), Roland Barthes clarifies the textual dynamics at work within detective fiction, noting two key premises on which such narratives are founded. In the first place, Barthes explains, such narratives "[imply] a truth to be deciphered."[36] Barthes goes on to argue that such narratives operate according to "hermeneutic terms [that] structure the enigma according to the expectation and desire for its solution."[37] For Barthes, as well as any number of other literary/cultural critics who have written about the genre, detective fiction turns on the withholding of the identity and motive of an unsub—short for unknown or unidentified subject—for the bulk of the narrative. At the same time, the revelation of the unsub's identity and motive is a foregone conclusion, as it provides the sense of closure that both George N. Dove[38] and Larry Landrum[39] regard as a precondition of the form. Thus, while the genre of detective fiction constitutes a form deeply invested in its own coherence and narrative/ideological unity, the crime at its center forestalls the achievement of that coherence and unity by remaining unresolved for most of the narrative, thereby sitting uneasily within the narrative structure.

In *Water Blue Eyes*, narrative coherence is achieved in the final chapters of the novel when Villar reveals that Reigosa was murdered by Mercedes Zuriaga, the wife of Reigosa's wealthy, long-time lover, Dimas, who admits to having felt "threatened" by the relationship and who had "promise[d] herself she would not be cast aside after so many years of sacrifices" (*Water Blue Eyes*, "Motive"). This climactic moment clears up the two key questions that have driven both Caldas and Villar's readers through the narrative and provides the story a sense of internal unity—a characteristic that is indicative of the kinds of Master Narratives that dominated both fiction and geopolitical conceptions of the Nation in the Modern period. That Caldas is, by the close of the novel, not only aware of the perpetrator's identity, but also in possession of evidence (including a verbal confession) that she committed the crime, suggests that Mercedes will be punished for the murder despite the fact that the reader is not permitted to witness a jury conviction, a prison sentence, or even a remorseful lament. Such punishments—whether explicit or implied—usually suggest that the diegetic world is ruled by an overarching sense of order, virtue, and justice; it also intimates that the extra-diegetic world, as mirrored in the realist fiction, is organized according to similar values.

It is, of course, possible for the revelation of the unsub to facilitate narrative closure without simultaneously enacting ideological order and justice. Indeed, many works of detective fiction—especially more recent ones penned by writers from historically underrepresented groups—present a resolution to the crime while, at the same time, problematizing the ideological unity of the text.[40] Such is the case with Villar's Inspector Caldas novels. In *Water Blue Eyes*, for instance, even when Reigosa's murder is solved, the narrative does not achieve the kind of complete "intelligibility of the story"[41] that critics like Barthes, Dove, Landrum, and Catherine Belsey in *Critical Practice* (1980) attribute to the detective novel. This is so in large part because the crime is so shocking and deplorable that it cannot be explained—let alone justified—through even the most deranged of motivations. Stated differently, in light of the heinousness of some crimes, "the law seems pale in its remedies, leaving [characters and readers] restless and unfulfilled in [their] craving for satisfaction."[42]

Additionally, the inability (or unwillingness) of the narrative to achieve ideological order points to the ways in which Villar's antagonists function within the larger conversation regarding postnationality in which his series engages. Specifically, by identifying the antagonist, here Mercedes Zuriaga, with anti-progressive ideological formations (like heterosexism and homophobia) that prohibit the achievement of ideological order, Villar acknowledges the fragile nature of postnational societies; however, by ultimately excising Mercedes—and the anti-progressive ideological formations for which she stands—from the narrative of *Water Blue Eyes,* Villar intimates that within postnational Spain, progress and tradition can co-exist, even if the relationship between those two forces is unstable and ever-changing. Of course, the ideological valence of *Water Blue Eyes* is not entirely progressive and, at least with respect to its representation of Mercedes Zuriaga, the novel does not advance a particularly nuanced or original idea. In fact, the novel at once appears to hark back to the Golden Age, in which the rooting out of the individual (evil) perpetrator often brought about narrative resolution through the reinstatement of a lawful social order.

To understand the ideological dynamics of the text, it is necessary first to discuss briefly the gender politics of machismo, since, I argue, Reigosa's murder constitutes a recapitulation—however brief and ineffectual—of that ideological formation. In general terms, machismo refers to a form of toxic masculinity that structures self-identities and power relationships among men, women, and children in Iberian and Iberian-descended cultures. Within this ideological framework, LGBTQ+ individuals stand as non-entities not only because their identities cannot be codified or explained through the "logic" of machismo, but also because their identities threaten the very foundations of the ideology by pointing up its gaps and omissions. Perhaps this is why Mercedes Zuriaga tortures and dehumanizes Reigosa in such a manner—the murder a literal retaliation for the kinds of ideological "damage" that LGBTQ+ identities are believed to inflict upon machismo. Unfortunately, Villar's novel does not acknowledge, much less confront, the irony or conflict embedded in the fact that the perpetrator in *Water Blue Eyes* is a woman who has suffered under, but has also become imbricated in, the system of machismo. This task becomes the reader's.

One of psychologist Albert Bandura's "eight forms of 'moral disengagement,'" dehumanization constitutes the systemic stripping away of an individual's or a group's human qualities, to the point that that individual, or those group members, are seen as "less civilized or[/and] less sentient."[43] When "human-looking creatures" are seen as "not really people," then, as David Livingstone Smith explains, "we don't have to treat them as people. They can be used instrumentally, with complete disregard for their human worth—they can be killed, tortured, raped, experimented upon."[44] The murder of Reigosa, which strips him of his basic humanity and renders him bestial, or, little more than a "tanned hide," constitutes a direct attack on his sexual orientation (especially since the primary target of the attack is his genitalia, the center of his sexual expression). In this way, the murder also enacts a defense of machismo, against which Reigosa's sexual orientation, and, more broadly, any LGBTQ+ identity, is posited as antithetical. It is, of course, highly problematic, but perhaps not terribly surprising, that Villar's critique of machismo—both here and in *Death on a Galician Shore*—comes at the expense of a female character. Whether perpetrator (Mercedes Zuriaga) or victim (Rebeca Neira), Villar's female characters seem always and only to be sacrificial lambs whose transgressions (of law, of gender norms, of "sexual propriety") enact both a defense and a critique of machismo.

Mercedes' explanation for why she murders Reigosa also points directly to machismo as a motivating force. Machismo sometimes is misunderstood as simply a system of power whereby women are rendered subservient to men. However, women in Iberian and Iberian-descended cultures often experience machismo not simply as a reification of traditional masculinity, but also and simultaneously as an expression of traditional femininity *as power*. In *Machos Maricones & Gays: Cuba and Homosexuality* (1996), Ian Lumsden regards machismo as characterized by "the pursuit and conquest of women," which he suggests "demonstrate[s] men's sexual virility."[45] At the same time, Lumsden argues, "women themselves expected men to assert their machismo," and he goes on to explain, "[s]ince they were rendered powerless in so many other respects, many women enjoyed, indeed exploited, their power to attract men."[46]

As I note above, Mercedes admits to feeling threatened by the clandestine relationship that her husband shares with Reigosa, and even devotes a significant amount of time to pondering "how she might be able to make [the relationship] end if she needed to" (*Water Blue Eyes*, "Motive"). But Mercedes only decides to act when she discovers that her husband is being blackmailed about the relationship and "might be forced to make a choice and abandon her for Reigosa" (*Water Blue Eyes*, "Motive"). The threat of abandonment and the social stigma that that gesture would portend is so tangible and fear-inducing for a beautiful and vain woman like Mercedes that she is willing to resort to a heinous act of murder in order to prevent that unlikely possibility. The reader might assume—rightly so, I think—that this threat is even more deeply-felt for two reasons: (1) Mercedes is, by all accounts, out of Dimas' league—indeed, when Caldas meets her, he is "surprised that Dimas Zuriaga was married to such a woman" (*Water Blue Eyes*, "Excuse")—and therefore to be abandoned by a man like Dimas might be felt as doubly humiliating; and (2) Dimas' lover is a man. For a woman like Mercedes, Dimas' gay relationship signals her waning power over her husband and, as such, poses a direct challenge to her own sense of self. The murder, then, is an affirmation of her own identity both within the marriage and within the nation through the recapitulation of the predominant social organizing principle on the Iberian Peninsula: machismo.

## Filling a Vast Geographic Space with the Diversity of the World

If Mercedes stands as a figurehead for the ideological formation of machismo, then the fact that her violation of the law is exposed and she presumably is punished for those infractions points to the waning hold that machismo has on Iberian and Iberian-descended cultures. In *Beyond Machismo: Intersectional Latino Masculinities* (2016), Aída Hurtado and Mrinal Sinha open their argument by suggesting that "[o]ne of the most persistent social narratives in our society is the notion of machismo, with its inherent sexism, as a defining feature of all Latino cultures."[47] Hurtado and Sinha go on to explain some of the implications of viewing Machismo as this kind of monolithic Master Narrative, including that Iberian-descended communities "are generally perceived as homogenous in nature, with little internal diversity regardless of differing geographical location, national origin, or educational levels."[48] In other words, Master Narratives fail to provide "complex, realistic, and rich"[49] understandings of individuals and the nations of which they are part, instead substituting "simplistic, one-dimensional, and truncated portraits that deny … a realistic and multifaceted picture" of their subjects.[50] Such "sanitized" and "oversimplified" representations "[deprive readers] of a conceptual lens that would help them better comprehend the world around them."[51] Admittedly, there is something rather reductive and stereotypical in Villar's treatment of the Woman's entrapment within the ideological framework of machismo. While certain kinds of "differences" are salvaged within Villar's imagined postmodern community, others—at least within the initial two installments of the series—continue to be understood (or, rather, misunderstood) in traditional ways.

*Water Blue Eyes* challenges this common Master Narrative of Machismo, first by having a female figurehead for an ideological formation that historically and currently is uncritically equated with male superiority and misogyny. Near the end of the novel, during Mercedes' confession, Caldas remarks, "Pity about the dog," referring to the key piece of evidence that tipped him off to her identity as the murderer. Mercedes immediately corrects him, saying, "No, inspector, pity about men" (*Water Blue Eyes,* "Motive"). This statement, which is targeted at her weak-willed, and weak-stomached accomplice, Isidro Freire, who failed to keep the dog hidden during Caldas' visit to the Zuriaga home, echoes an earlier statement in which Mercedes characterizes Freire as "[a]nother coward, just like Dimas. They're all cowards" (*Water Blue Eyes,* "Gap"). Machismo, according to Lumsden, constitutes a system in which males and females exist in a complimentary, if hierarchal, relationship. Yet in *Water Blue Eyes,* the male characters—most particularly Reigosa, Dimas, and Freire—repeatedly fail to fulfill the expectations of that ideological formation with respect to gender expression and gendered behavior. Furthermore, the one male character whose identity most closely aligns with traditional Machismo (i.e., Estévez) is played for comic effect. All of these factors work to challenge the authority and the centrality of Machismo as an organizing principle within the novel and within the nation.

A second way in which Villar's fiction challenges this common Master Narrative of Machismo is by rendering it subordinate to a form of law and order that is more attentive to inclusion and diversity. As forensic physician Miguel Lorente explains in a *Huffington Post* article from 2016, "Machismo utilizes violence directly against everything and anything that challenges imposed identity standards.... Machismo is directed, above all, at those who question masculinity and the values associated with it."[52] In the past, in both Iberian and Iberian-descended cultures, Machismo has often influenced the ways in which justice is defined and served, with those who challenge the ideological formation always and already viewed as enemies of the nation, even if they are the victims of violent crime. Indeed, sometimes the nation itself perpetrates the violence against those individuals as a means of maintaining the authority of Machismo.

In the existing two novels of his Inspector Caldas series, Villar refuses to cast individuals from historically embattled groups as enemies of the nation; instead, he repeatedly goes to great lengths to illustrate the violence that Machismo historically has inflicted on the marginal and to avenge that violence with swift and severe legal sanctions. In *Water Blue Eyes,* for instance, Caldas initially might be viewed as fairly traditional with respect to sex-gender norms. This is especially true in relation to his choice of profession (i.e., a lone wolf police detective) and his failed relationship with Alba. However, Caldas also is a character with refined culinary tastes, as well as a studied palette with respect to fine wine, and he ultimately is the character who solves the murders of two gay men, Reigosa and Orestes Grial, the DJ behind the blackmail scheme, and brings the murderer to justice.

Similarly, in the second Inspector Caldas novel, *Death on a Galician Shore*, Caldas is called on to investigate the mysterious drowning of a young (male) sailor, and, in the process of doing so, discovers and insists on solving a decade-old cold case murder of a young, unwed mother. Interesting in this novel is that Caldas' investigation eventually uncovers evidence that the young woman, Rebeca Neira, was gang raped before being murdered by a couple of sailors. The crimes were covered up by the sailors and several of their friends—all men whose identities align very closely with the "codified roles" of traditional Machismo—mostly out of fear of retaliation by the Alpha Male among the group, who was also the one primarily responsible for Neira's rape and murder.

While historically a woman like Neira would be regarded as an object to be used and discarded without consequence at the hands of Machismo, Villar insists that she is a human being with a story that demands to be told and a right to integrity and justice. In the same way, men like Reigosa and Grial historically have been sacrificed—often quite violently—on the altar of Machismo, regarded not only as gender outlaws, but also and simultaneously as outlaws of the nation.[53] Villar, though, will not allow these men to be demonized and ostracized, but instead demands that they be acknowledged, even, or perhaps especially, in death, as citizens of the nation. What Villar presents in the figure of Leo Caldas is a more modern and global form of the masculinity that stands in marked contrast to the core values and central tenets of Machismo. No longer regarded as a Master Narrative with all of the privilege and entitlement that that designation enjoys, machismo becomes, in the Inspector Caldas novels, an outmoded form of social organization that threatens the health and longevity of the nation and its populace. This is, of course, not to suggest that machismo is completely eradicated within the series; after all, Villar is writing within the realist, not the fantasy, tradition. Men like Estévez remain homophobic brutes. Women like Mercedes Zuriaga continue to perpetuate their own subjugation within the system of hypermasculine social organization by lashing out at those gender and sexual Others who threaten the minimal privilege that she enjoys. And characters like Luis Reigosa and Rebeca Neira are still sacrificed in the interests of a waning, but still powerful ideological formation. The one glimmer of hope that Villar offers his readers is his sleuth-protagonist, a man not untouched by machismo, but one who nonetheless manages to straddle the chasm between tradition and modernity quite skillfully.

In the final analysis, Villar's novels remind readers that they live in a world where progress—particularly in the form of social justice movements that act in the name of LGBTQ+ and women's rights—is still often perceived as threats against the body of the Modern Nation and the traditions (like Machismo) that the Nation is perceived to embody. In the interests of the

Modern Nation and its claims to unity and coherence, Villar makes clear, proponents of those traditions can and do attempt to eliminate any and all threats. But Villar also very wisely asserts that while these acts of brutality might momentarily silence or/and eliminate the threats, ultimately, we exist in a world and in a moment where the nation itself is constantly being refined and re-defined to accommodate the rich diversity of citizens that comprise it. In other words, *Water Blue Eyes* and *Death on a Galician Shore* mark contemporary Spain as a postnational society in which the citizens, both real and imagined, are engaged in an intellectual project "to understand [their] ongoing experiment in filling a vast yet unified geographic space with the diversity of the world."[54]

NOTES

1. Augie Fleras, *Immigration Canada: Evolving Realities and Emerging Challenges in a Postnational World* (Vancouver: University of British Columbia Press, 2015), 380.
2. *Ibid.*
3. Linda Hutcheon, *The Canadian Postmodern: A Study of Contemporary English-Canadian Fiction* (Oxford: Oxford University Press, 1989).
4. Linda Hutcheon, *Splitting Images: Contemporary Canadian Ironies* (Toronto: Oxford University Press, 1991).
5. *Ibid.,* 84.
6. *Ibid.*
7. Richard Gwyn, *Nationalism Without Walls: The Unbearable Lightness of Being Canadian* (Toronto: McClelland and Steward, 1997), 243.
8. George Grant, *Lament for a Nation: The Defeat of Canadian Nationalism* (Montreal: McGill-Queen's University Press, 2005), lx.
9. Fleras, 380.
10. *Ibid.*
11. Richard Kearney, "Postnationalism and Postmodernity," *Symposium* 8.2(2004): 227.
12. Domingo Villar, *Water Blue Eyes,* trans. Martin Schifino (Mount Pleasant, SC: Arcadia Books, 2016), Kindle edition.
13. Domingo Villar, *Death on a Galician Shore,* trans. Sonia Soto (London: Hachette Digital, 2011), Kindle edition.
14. Yaw Agawu-Kakraba, *Postmodernity in Spanish Fiction and Culture* (Cardiff: University of Wales Press, 2010), Kindle edition. "Introduction."
15. *Ibid.*
16. *Ibid.,* "Chapter 1."
17. *Ibid.*
18. In this essay, I focus almost exclusively on *Water Blue Eyes,* due mostly to space considerations, although the observations that I make are, I would argue, equally attributable to *Death on a Galician Shore.* I chose to concentrate on the former because, as the first Inspector Caldas novel, *Water Blue Eyes* sets the stage (narratively, ideologically, etc.) for the series that follows and therefore serves as the ideal benchmark.
19. Fleras, 380.
20. Frederic Joseph Svoboda, "Detective Sidekicks," *The Guide to United States Popular Culture,* eds. Ray Broadus Browne and Pat Browne (Madison: University of Wisconsin Press, 2001), 230.
21. *Ibid.*
22. Svoboda, 230.
23. Gary Kelly, "Regional Novel: Generic Traits and the Development of the Regional Novel in Britain," *Encyclopedia of the Novel,* vol. 2, ed. Paul Schellinger (London: Routledge, 1998), 1082.

24. *Ibid.*

25. Barbara Pezzotti, *The Importance of Place in Contemporary Italian Crime Fiction: A Bloody Journey* (Madison: Fairleigh Dickinson University Press, 2012), 1.

26. Pezzotti, 1.

27. The exaltation of regional and local specificity can be witnessed across a number of subgenres of crime/mystery fiction, but especially those that devote equal emphasis to character and plot, such as the cozy and the hardboiled P.I. novels. This is so because the crime/mystery genre takes as a given that the sleuth-protagonist is a product of his/her/their environment and therefore must be located within that environment in order to be understood.

28. K.D.M. Snell, "The Regional Novel: Themes for Interdisciplinary Research," *The Regional Novel in Britain and Ireland, 1800–1990,* ed. Snell (New York: Cambridge University Press, 1998), 43.

29. Svoboda, 230.

30. Simon Ryan, *The Cartographic Eye: How Explorers Saw Australia* (Cambridge: Cambridge University Press, 1996), 197.

31. David W. Allen, *The Fear of Looking or Scopophilic-Exhibitionistic Conflicts* (Charlottesville: University of Virginia Press, 1974), 6.

32. Alexander Clement, *Brutalism: Post-War British Architecture*, 2nd ed. (Ramsbury, Marlborough: Crowood Press, 2018), 7.

33. *Ibid.*

34. *Ibid.*

35. Aloys Winterling, *Caligula: A Biography* (Berkeley: University of California Press, 2011), 1.

36. Roland Barthes, *S/Z: An Essay,* trans. Richard Miller (New York: Hill and Wang, 1974), 75.

37. *Ibid.*

38. George N. Dove, *The Reader and the Detective Story* (Bowling Green, OH: Bowling Green State University Popular Press, 1997), 65.

39. Larry Landrum, *American Mystery and Detective Novels: A Reference Guide* (Westport, CT: Greenwood Press, 1999), 82.

40. American hardboiled detective fiction writer Sue Grafton offers a compelling example of this trend; I have discussed the ways in which Grafton presents a resolution to the crime while, at the same time, problematizing the ideological unity of the text in two previous publications, including: Heath A. Diehl, "'W' is for Woman: Deconstructing the Private Dick in Sue Grafton's Alphabet Series," *Murdering Miss Marple: Essays on Gender and Sexuality in the New Golden Age of Women's Crime Fiction,* ed. Julie H. Kim (Jefferson, NC: McFarland, 2012), 120–41; and Heath A. Diehl, "'There are times when an old rule should be abandoned, or a current rule should not be applied': Narration, Innovation and Hardboiled Fiction in Sue Grafton's 'T' Is for Trespass," *TEXT* 37(2016): 1–13, accessed at http://www.textjournal.com.au/speciss/issue37/Diehl.pdf (2 January 2019).

41. Catherine Belsey, *Critical Practice* (London: Routledge, 1980), 79.

42. Sue Grafton, *"K" Is for Killer* (New York: Henry Holt, 1994), 285.

43. Sherry Hamby, "What Is Dehumanization, Anyway?" *Psychology Today,* June 21, 2018, accessed at https://www.psychologytoday.com/us/blog/the-web-violence/201806/what-is-dehumanization-anyway (2 January 2019).

44. David Livingstone Smith, *Less Than Human: Why We Demean, Enslave, and Exterminate Others* (New York: St. Martin's, 2011), 159.

45. Ian Lumsden, *Machos Maricones & Gays: Cuba and Homosexuality* (Philadelphia: Temple University Press, 1996), 37.

46. *Ibid.*, 38.

47. Aída Hurtado and Mrinal Sinha, *Beyond Machismo: Intersectional Latino Masculinities* (Austin: University of Texas Press, 2016), xi.

48. *Ibid.*

49. Derrick P. Alridge, "The Limits of Master Narratives in History Textbooks: An Analysis of Representations of Martin Luther King, Jr.," *Teachers College Record* 108.8(2006): 662.

50. *Ibid.,* 663.
51. *Ibid.,* 680.
52. Miguel Lorente, "Eradicating Machismo and Bringing Equality Is the Only Way to Install Peace and Coexistence," *Huffington Post,* December 31, 2015, accessed at https://www.huffingtonpost.com/miguel-lorente/machismo-and-violence-mis_b_8899576.html (2 January 2019).
53. This attitude should not be terribly surprising within a culture that has embraced machismo as a national ideal since its very origins. Indeed, the ideology of machismo is deeply imbricated in the colonial enterprise, which is itself emblematic of Spanish history and culture across time. As Donald J. Mosher and Silvan S. Tomkins explain, "The ideological script of machismo descends from the ideology of the warrior and the stratifications, following warfare—victor and vanquished, master and slave" (60). See Donald J. Mosher and Silvan S. Tomkins, "Scripting the Macho Man: Hypermasculine Socialization and Enculturation," *The Journal of Sex Research* 25.1(1988), 60–84.
54. Charles Foran, "The Canada Experiment: Is This the World's First 'Postnational' Country?," *The Guardian, January* 4, 2017, accessed at https://www.theguardian.com/world/2017/jan/04/the-canada-experiment-is-this-the-worlds-first-postnational-country (2 January 2019).

## Bibliography

Agawu-Kakraba, Yaw. *Postmodernity in Spanish Fiction and Culture.* Cardiff: University of Wales Press, 2010. Kindle.
Allen, David W. *The Fear of Looking or Scopophilic-Exhibitionistic Conflicts.* Charlottesville: University of Virginia Press, 1974.
Alridge, Derrick P. "The Limits of Master Narratives in History Textbooks: An Analysis of Representations of Martin Luther King, Jr." *Teachers College Record* 108.8 (2006): 662–86.
Barthes, Roland. *S/Z: An Essay.* Trans. Richard Miller. New York: Hill and Wang, 1974.
Belsey, Catherine. *Critical Practice.* London: Routledge, 1980.
Clement, Alexander. *Brutalism: Post-War British Architecture.* 2nd ed. Ramsbury, Marlborough: Crowood Press, 2018.
Dove, George N. *The Reader and the Detective Story.* Bowling Green, OH: Bowling Green State University Popular Press, 1997.
Fleras, Augie. *Immigration Canada: Evolving Realities and Emerging Challenges in a Postnational World.* Vancouver: University of British Columbia Press, 2015.
Foran, Charles. "The Canada Experiment: Is This the World's First 'Postnational' Country?" *The Guardian,* January 4, 2017, accessed at https://www.theguardian.com/world/2017/jan/04/the-canada-experiment-is-this-the-worlds-first-postnational-country.
Grafton, Sue. *"K" Is for Killer.* New York: Henry Holt, 1994.
Grant, George. *Lament for a Nation: The Defeat of Canadian Nationalism.* Montreal: McGill-Queen's University Press, 2005.
Gwyn, Richard. *Nationalism Without Walls: The Unbearable Lightness of Being Canadian.* Toronto: McClelland & Stewart, 1997.
Hamby, Sherry. "What Is Dehumanization, Anyway?" *Psychology Today,* June 21, 2018, accessed at https://www.psychologytoday.com/us/blog/the-web-violence/201806/what-is-dehumanization-anyway.
Hurtado, Aída, and Mrinal Sinha. *Beyond Machismo: Intersectional Latino Masculinities.* Austin: University of Texas Press, 2016.
Hutcheon, Linda. *The Canadian Postmodern: A Study of Contemporary English-Canadian Fiction.* Don Mills, Ontario: Oxford University Press, 2012.
Hutcheon, Linda. *Splitting Images: Contemporary Canadian Ironies.* Toronto: Oxford University Press, 1991.
Kearney, Richard. "Postnationalism and Postmodernity." *Symposium* 8.2 (2004): 227–248.
Kelly, Gary. "Regional Novel: Generic Traits and the Development of the Regional Novel in Britain." *Encyclopedia of the Novel,* Vol. 2. Ed. Paul Schellinger. London: Routledge, 1998. 1081–84.

Landrum, Larry. *American Mystery and Detective Novels: A Reference Guide.* Westport, CT: Greenwood Press, 1999.

Livingstone Smith, David. *Less Than Human: Why We Demean, Enslave, and Exterminate Others.* New York: St. Martin's, 2011.

Lorente, Miguel. "Eradicating Machismo and Bringing Equality Is the Only Way to Install Peace and Coexistence." *Huffington Post,* December 31, 2015, accessed at https://www.huffingtonpost.com/miguel-lorente/machismo-and-violence-mis_b_8899576.html.

Lumsden, Ian. *Machos Maricones & Gays: Cuba and Homosexuality.* Philadelphia: Temple University Press, 1996.

Mosher, Donald J., and Silvan S. Tomkins. "Scripting the Macho Man: Hypermasculine Socialization and Enculturation." *The Journal of Sex Research* 25.1 (1988): 60–84.

Pezzotti, Barbara. *The Importance of Place in Contemporary Italian Crime Fiction: A Bloody Journey.* Madison: Fairleigh Dickinson University Press, 2012.

Ryan, Simon. *The Cartographic Eye: How Explorers Saw Australia.* Cambridge: Cambridge University Press, 1996.

Snell, K.D.M. "The Regional Novel: Themes for Interdisciplinary Research." *The Regional Novel in Britain and Ireland, 1800–1990.* Ed. Snell. New York: Cambridge University Press, 1998. 1–53.

Svoboda, Frederic Joseph. "Detective Sidekicks." *The Guide to United States Popular Culture.* Eds. Ray Broadus Browne and Pat Browne. Madison: University of Wisconsin Press, 2001. 230–31.

Villar, Domingo. *Death on a Galician Shore.* Trans. Sonia Soto. London: Hachette Digital, 2011.

Villar, Domingo. *Water Blue Eyes.* Trans. Martin Schifino. Mount Pleasant, SC: Arcadia Books, 2016.

Winterling, Aloys. *Caligula: A Biography.* Berkeley: University of California Press, 2011.

# Black Money, Gray Skies

## Financial Crimes in Modern Icelandic Thrillers

### JEAN GREGOREK

"What happened? This used to be a sleepy little place."
—Hinrika in *Trapped*

"The intricate acrobatics of high finance that occur somewhere in the stratosphere have all manner of parallel expression in dances on the ground."
—Randy Martin, Introduction,
*An Empire of Indifference: American War
and the Financial Logic of Risk Management*[1]

Icelandic writers in crime genres have noted that the small scale and
extreme weather conditions of Iceland make their crime fiction a version of
the classic Golden Age or country house mystery, with its isolated locations
and limited suspects.[2] However, Icelandic crime, as an emergent genre barely
20 years old, is essentially contemporary—an offshoot of the popular trend
of "Nordic Noir," with a very different genealogy than the more politically
and socially conservative English model. Nordic or Scandinavian crime fiction is renowned for its gritty social realism, its liberal-reformist politics, its
criticism of the widening cracks in Scandinavian welfare states, and its focus
on the changes being wrought by globalization.[3] Scandinavian detectives are
remarkable for their ordinariness; they are unheroic everymen (or women)
observing the increasing levels of social decay and criminality in their once-
tranquil, largely homogeneous societies. Iceland has surfaced as a strong con-
tributor to the Nordic Noir genre, producing well-crafted, critically acclaimed
crime novels and television that continue to be extremely successful in international markets. A number of Icelandic texts turn to a very precise event:
the 2008 financial crisis that devastated the Icelandic economy, resulting in

77

the subsequent fall of the government and a period of national soul-searching that continues into the present moment. If the impact of financial catastrophe on this tiny northern nation was greater measured by loss per capita than anywhere else, the national response was also unique, as Iceland is to this day the only country to imprison the bankers determined to be most responsible.

In the wake of the rapid economic boom and subsequent collapse, or *kreppa*, the question of what happened to traditional Icelandic values has unsurprisingly been brought to the fore. Recent thrillers by native Icelanders—Arnaldur Indriðason, Yrsa Sigurðardóttir, Lilja Sigurðardóttir, and Ragnar Jónasson—and by British writers with Icelandic connections like Quentin Bates and Michael Ridpath, as well as internationally-distributed television series *Trapped, Cover Story,* and *The Lava Field,* use the well-trodden formula of the police procedural in order to examine the state of the nation post-crisis. In many of these texts Icelandic culture and traditions are portrayed as submerged and in need of recovery. A colony of Denmark for seven centuries, Iceland became a sovereign republic in 1944, only to be swept into the orbit of the United States during the Cold War. Throughout its long colonial and neocolonial history, the country has struggled to maintain its own language and cultural identity, and to assert itself as a modern European state. Thus it is unsurprising that the manifold disruptions of the crisis have called forth a new emphasis on Icelandic heritage and a tendency to look back to versions of Iceland's past: its Viking origins; the 19th-century movement for independence from Denmark; the period before Iceland became a member of NATO and home to a major American military base.

The outpouring of quality commercial crime fiction, film, and television is itself one of the results of this post-*kreppa* cultural resurgence. As critics have noted, the topical content of Scandinavian crime fiction has made this genre an accessible vehicle for depicting the social impact of neoliberal globalization. Icelandic thrillers follow this general trend; however, a number of Icelandic texts are striking in their attention to the architecture of globalized finance capital. As early as 1990, David Harvey observed that the "structure of the global financial system is now so complicated that it surpasses most people's understanding."[4] While this is undoubtedly true, it is notable how many Icelandic procedurals engage in the attempt. Perceiving the culture of finance as a source of corruption—often a foreign, mostly American, import—it becomes the object of police investigations. The investigation then incorporates factual information about the workings of fraudulent schemes for inflating share prices, laundering funds, and evading taxes. Most significantly, the violent crimes in these crime fictions are always associated with the turn to neoliberal financialization. Detectives "follow the money" and uncover multiple connections between acts of murder, arson, and rape, and the behind-the-scenes operations of unregulated finance that motivate these more sensational crimes. The world of banking and finance is portrayed as criminogenic and shown to merge with organized crime and unethical practices that harm the body politic. This leads to a number of unflattering fictional portraits of bankers, accountants, and executives.

The present essay focuses, not on the numerous portraits of greedy, testosterone-fueled bankers *per se*, but on the various ways that these Icelandic texts foreground the impact of finance capital, money made *from* money, accumulation based not on traditional modes of production but, in Harvey's words, "instead on the capturing or diverting of value from one part of the system to another." The frequency with which finance and its accompanying free-market rationality serve as the ultimate generator of crime is a distinctive feature of much Icelandic detection, and the harshest judgments in these texts are usually reserved, not for actual murderers, but for unscrupulous bankers and financiers who undermine national institutions in their own self-interest. The critique of neoliberal privatization and finance capital places Icelandic crime fiction in the wider post–2008 body of literature known as "financial fiction" or "Crunch Lit," and helps explain the growing transnational appeal of contemporary Icelandic visual and print media.

## When the Music Stopped

Iceland has become a much-studied textbook case of financial overreach leading to disaster. While economists still debate the effectiveness of various governmental responses, all concur that in the years leading up to 2008 Iceland went through a period of "collective madness."[5] In the 1990s, under the influence of American economic experts and their neoliberal ideology, the government of Iceland embarked upon a program of economic modernization designed to turn Iceland into a nation of shareholders. A program of deregulation, corporate tax reduction, and the privatization of public assets, including the banking sector, set the stage for the most rapid expansion of a financial industry in history. By 2007 Iceland was the fourth richest country in the world measured by GDP per capita.[6] According to Michael Lewis, Iceland's stock market "multiplied in size nine times from 2003–2007," and the average Icelandic family grew three times as wealthy in 2006 as it had been in 2003.[7] Easy access to foreign credit gave the newly deregulated banks plenty of money to play with, and soon Icelandic investors were buying up companies in England and Scandinavia. Speculators also invested heavily in the "carry trade," the practice of shifting funds (so-called "hot money") to various sites around the globe in search of ever-higher rates of return through the crossing of time zones, national borders, and currencies. The influx of new money funded a lavish lifestyle for Iceland's bankers, and, as Roger Boyes observes, "since the privatization of the banks, 136 Icelandic companies had been registered in the tax haven of Tortola in the Caribbean."[8]

But this small country's experiment with Wall-Street style international finance came to a screeching halt in October of 2008. When the September Lehman Brothers' bankruptcy led to a global credit crunch the three major Icelandic commercial banks could not service their debts; the banks had grown so much larger than the national economy that the Central Bank of Iceland could not guarantee payment and the banks collapsed. Almost overnight, the Icelandic króna lost nearly half its value; the Icelandic stock market plunged; pension funds shrank; household purchasing power plummeted; unemployment tripled; construction projects were abandoned on the spot. As the economic depression deepened, many of the wealthiest bankers fled the country. It soon became clear that deregulation and lack of government oversight had allowed the New Vikings, as they were called, mostly young, male, and trained in the United States, to create a wildly irresponsible banking sector that built its "wealth" on a house of cards.[9]

In January 2009 famously placid Icelanders erupted in what became known as the "Pots and Pans Rebellion," a series of demonstrations that led to the fall of the government of Prime Minister Geir Haarde (later charged with negligence in office) and its replacement by a new center-left government under its first female Prime Minister Jóhanna Sigurðardóttir.[10] Responding to public pressure, the first post-crisis Parliament set up a Special Investigative Commission and a Special Prosecutor to look into the causes of the meltdown and to pursue the most egregious cases of fraudulent activity. The Commission's first report uncovered an interrelated set of government and business failures. The report cites a "cultish," male-dominated banking culture; "incestuous" relations between the political elite and the financial sector; a cowed media; and a series of influential papers commissioned by the Iceland Chamber of Commerce emphasizing the need for laissez-faire economic policies and the self-regulation of financial institutions. (An example: "It would be much more sensible to let players on the market set their own rules and implement them rather than rely on public regulation which is burdensome and costly.")[11] As of fall 2018, the Special Prosecutor's work has resulted in the convictions and one-to-six year jail sentences of about 25 bankers and financiers, mainly for such crimes as insider trading, market manipulation, and "gross breach of fiduciary duty."[12] This has been a slow process, and some cases are still being appealed. Boyes explains the essential problem in sorting out the legal mess as "the mystification of capital—that is, the extraordinary web of cross-ownership, with holdings changing hands at such a dizzy pace that it was almost impossible to pin down who had responsibility for what."[13]

Iceland is a young country, gaining its independence from Denmark in

1918, and becoming a republic only in 1944. Sudden wealth and international financial clout appeared—for a short time, at least—to mark a new beginning for a poor and obscure island in the North Atlantic. As Vilhjálmur Arnason comments, Icelanders had incentives to be convinced that finance was the road to prosperity: "As consumers, they gained from this state of affairs, and as citizens of a small nation they took pride in it."[14] The country is now decisively on the economic rebound, due in part to an aggressive campaign to attract tourism, which is shifting the economic base yet again.

## "Crunch Lit": Narrating the Financial Crisis

Katy Shaw's recent study, *Crunch Lit*, asserts that the 2008 global credit crunch and ensuing recession inspired a new wave of financially themed fiction. Shaw, along with most contemporary analysts of Crunch Lit or Financial Fiction, focuses on "literary" texts rather than genre fiction in her assessment of this emerging category.[15] But much Icelandic crime fiction would seem to fall squarely into Shaw's definition of Crunch Lit: contemporary realist narratives that "grapple with the fallout from the financial crisis and dissect[s] the wreckage left in its wake."[16] The fictional texts Shaw considers—Don DeLillo's *Cosmopolis*, John Lanchester's *Capital*, Adam Haslitt's *Union Atlantic*, Sebastian Faulks's *A Week in December*—generally highlight the excessive lifestyles and moral deafness of British and American financiers, and then go on to dramatize the impact of the credit crunch on these flawed but not completely unsympathetic protagonists. Crunch Lit generally seeks to depict a sociology of banking culture in fictional form, presenting "stories of male bankers and their specific sets of circumstances [as] representative of a much broader body of professional people subject to the pressures of financialization."[17] Often these are morality tales, many of which provide the appropriate come-uppance and/or ethical awakening for the banker characters. These credit-crisis novels also serve a didactic function, offering the reader some basic knowledge of a highly specialized arena. For Shaw, these realist fictions confront "the dominant narrative that the events of the credit crunch were too complicated for ordinary people to understand," and challenge "the unrepresentability and confusing status of finance as a contemporary subject."[18]

Shaw's useful study correctly assesses the intentions of the texts she examines, and points to the conscious efforts of novelists to elucidate the ethical dilemmas produced by the financial meltdown. Yet a number of Marxist-influenced critics, following in the tradition of Fredric Jameson's influential essays on postmodernism, point to the problems that the immateriality of finance capital poses for conventional literary realism. Jameson theorizes that this post–Fordist historical phase "in which an entire centre or region abandons production altogether in order to seek maximization in those non-productive spaces ... speculation, the money market, and finance capital in general," leads to a new dominant logic, and to "radically new forms of abstraction" that move beyond the modes of realism and modernism.[19] Literary critics have asserted that capital's new deterritorialization, and the velocity of its circulation, "strains the assumptions of our narrative models," and conclude that "in today's fictions, individuals are likely to confront systems and structures not only beyond their own capacity to evaluate but ... beyond the novel's capacity as well."[20] As Alison Shonkwiler notes, "the elimination of visible production in the age of financialization enables the elimination of visible *relations* of production," concealing ultimate sources of value, and making it difficult to identify a specific agent or agency.[21] In the era of digital hyperspeeds, legal tax shelters, and financial products deliberately designed to obscure the level of risk, the very possibility of "following the money" is so improbable as to constitute a utopian dream. Or, as LiPuma and Lee pose the rhetorical question: "How does one know about, or demonstrate against, an unlisted, virtual, offshore corporation that operates in an unregulated electronic space using a secret proprietary trading strategy to buy and sell arcane financial instruments?"[22]

Moments of economic crisis open up new possibilities for representation as well as new incentives to make the attempt. Although an exact mapping of the infinite transactions taking place "somewhere in the stratosphere" remains an unattainable goal, Crunch Lit at least attempts to demystify common financial terms and practices, and often to produce a moral accounting that rarely takes place in real life. Examples of Crunch Lit that fall into the category of commercial genre fiction go even further in "papering over" the inadequacies of realist representation, constructing reassuring myths of the ultimate legibility of finance and providing a culprit or culprits responsible for the catastrophic consequences of the crash. But the actual process of tracing the flow of money, along with the final location of value, can only be represented by absence, or in the most attenuated or abbreviated form. Forensic accounting, even if it were adequate to this task, is not a discourse that adapts well to popular narrative. So in financially-themed film and television we typically see a few shots of computer screens or a whiteboard; in print versions, the inclusion of a few lines in which the detective learns the name of a shell company or hears the confession of a con artist.[23] While clearly working within the boundaries of the Scandinavian procedural, Icelandic texts tweak its formula somewhat to allow content pertinent to a critique of finance capital. Some common textual strategies include (1) identifying the Icelandic criminals as a *group* of elites, a collective agent rather than a single Machiavellian fraudster or a lone psychopath; (2) linking financial misdeeds with both violent crime run amok and the erosion of the welfare state—showing the hidden workings of finance to lead to moral and social disintegration; and (3) opposing finance to recognizable forms of productive labor, i.e., farming, fishing, and manual work.

The return to honest labor usually means work done historically by men, and therefore the anti-capitalist critique in these texts is decisively gendered. Many post-crash crime dramas are dramas of masculinity, dramas in which true "Icelandic-ness" is embodied in an earlier Viking or peasant ideal, forged through hardship and characterized by male muscle, stamina, and self-sufficiency.[24] Banking and speculative finance are portrayed as parasitic, unproductive, and ultimately un–Icelandic, compared to "real work" and "real trade." The new class of financiers gained popular support in part through casting themselves as hypermasculine "Business Vikings," boldly circling the globe in search of fortune, tapping into nationalistic sentiments of Icelanders as "a special breed of people."[25] Critical Icelandic fictions reconfigure this image of Icelanders as a "special breed" by challenging the cosmopolitan "New Viking" and replacing him with older versions of masculinity that retain contact with land and sea. That this is an idealized and nostalgic—not to mention gender exclusive—rendition of an often painful and impoverished rural past does not make it any less useful to these authors as a shorthand for Icelandic authenticity. Female detective protagonists do feature in some Icelandic examples[26]; however, the three bestsellers discussed below examine contemporary Icelandic national identity through contested ideas of appropriate maleness.

In Arnaldur Indriðason's *Black Skies* and Michael Ridpath's *66 Degrees North* the police detectives are American-Icelandic hybrids, representatives of a nation too oriented toward the United States or poised between the two identities. Both detectives respond to this bifurcation by attempting to recover their Icelandic roots: learning more about their family histories and learning to appreciate the Icelandic cultural traditions that have been largely displaced by American cultural imperialism. In the final example, the 2015 television drama *Trapped,* the possibility of a redeemed and reformed post-crisis nation is raised, not so much by cultural revival as by the Icelandic landscape, a symbolic as well as literal terrain that resists the flows of global capital, and through the quintessentially Icelandic character—and physique—of the detective himself.

## Black Skies: *Iceland on the Brink*

Arnaldur Indriðason's 2009 novel *Black Skies* (*Svörtuloft*) opens with a gruesome account of the torture and murder of an old man. However, the plot soon reveals that this initial seemingly incomprehensible act of cruelty turns out to be retribution from a traumatized victim of child sexual abuse. The real crime on which the plot hinges, the mystery that detective Sigundur Oli eventually solves, is a money laundering scheme involving four Icelandic bankers and a Swedish speculator from a Luxembourg bank. The funds being laundered through Icelandic banks are generated from the child pornography industry, although the millions being made so effortlessly dulls the consciences of all the participants. The money laundering is shown to lead to murder in the present and alerts the detective to the past and ongoing abuse of children for internationally distributed pornographic films. The setting of *Black Skies* is during the heyday of the economic boom, a Reykjavík awash with money, just before the financial meltdown. Most of the characters in the novel are associated with the new economy—investment bankers, accountants, engineers directing the many new building projects. The narrative then exposes the very unsavory source of some of the mobile capital fueling this new economy. And the novel levels a number of criticisms at Iceland's politicians, holding them responsible for destructive cuts in social services and in health care, as well as for their collaboration with the runaway financial sector.

The title of the novel, *Svörtuloft,* comes from the distinctive lava cliffs on the Snaefellsnes Peninsula in the west of Iceland. These cliffs are known for their extreme danger to ships, as over the centuries many have crashed against these rocks, the name of which translates as "Black Ceiling" or "Black Fort," "the pitch-black precipice being the last thing fishermen would see looming over them as their ship went down."[27] Due to its imposing brutalist architecture and dark stone exterior, this is also the nickname of the Central Bank of Iceland. The dramatic architecture of the Central Bank looms large in the cityscape of Reykjavík, "fortress-like … clad with heavy, pitch black gabbro from the East Fjords" (182), a constant reminder of the clout of the new financial industry and the corrupt merger of finance and national politics. Thus the Icelandic title of the novel condenses the image of this unique but inhospitable Icelandic terrain with the building that most embodies the Icelandic attempt to indigenize global finance. Written immediately after the banking collapse but set just before it, the novel's title clearly points to the further shipwrecks that await.

The novel's narration is divided between two points of view: that of the mentally disturbed murderer, Andres, the abused child now grown, and that of the Reykjavík policeman, Sigundur Oli. The incorporation of the killer-slash-victim's perspective is a fairly regular feature of Nordic Noir and has the effect of increasing sympathy for this figure over the course of the novel. Sigundur Oli is a recurring character in Indriðason's popular Erlendur series, 14 novels that focus on the middle-aged detective Erlendur Sveinsson, who hails from the rural hinterlands and maintains a skeptical perspective on an

Iceland becoming ever more unrecognizable and "Americanized." Erlendur is only an absent presence in this novel of the economic boom, which instead features Erlendur's sidekick Sigundur Oli. Sigundur Oli is more culturally American than he is Icelandic—he attended a police academy in the Unites States, and he prefers American sports, television, music, and vacations. Right-wing in his politics, a follower of Milton Friedman, Sigundur Oli both envies and admires his newly wealthy compatriots, and supports his country's more assertive position in the world; as the narrator explains, he follows "the success of Icelandic businessmen at home and abroad. He was impressed by their drive and enterprise, especially when it came to buying up household name companies in Britain and Denmark" (68). Through most of the text, Sigundur Oli represents a libertarian, highly individualistic conception of the self against the social; we learn that he "rarely felt any sympathy for the luckless individuals he came across in the line of duty ... his usual attitude was that these people were responsible for their own plight" (189). But the novel charts Sigundur Oli's growing frustration with the arrogance of the New Vikings as he realizes that their interests do not, after all, serve the nation as a whole. He comes to realize his own responsibilities for relationship failures in his past and rediscovers an attachment to his parents—particularly his father—and possibly, to his fellow Icelanders. Thus, his character stands for a nation deluded for a time but beginning to wake up from the absurd dream of wealth without end.

Divergent class-based value systems are registered through the characters of Sigundur Oli's parents. His father is a master plumber and socialist while his more politically conservative white-collar mother works as a manager in an accountancy firm that has been taken over by an international corporation. The aspirational, snobbish mother is criticized for undervaluing her former husband, who, although he does not always stand up for himself, represents the admirably stoic type of Icelandic male who works with his hands and faces the hardships of life without complaint. Sigundur Oli must throw off his mother's prejudices and learn to appreciate his father's blue-collar values. Over the course of the novel father and son grow somewhat closer, and Sigundur begins to see his father as an honorable alternative to the more successful but self-serving "money men" he used to admire. This reconnection of father and son provides an alternative to the perverse relation between Andres and the stepfather who exploits him. Sigundur Oli also starts to take more notice of the poor and broken people he meets in his daily policing; he now finds himself touched by the "luckless individuals" like Andres that he once disdained.

Sigundur Oli and the novel attach little blame to Andres, committer of the murder of his stepfather—Andres has long been unhinged by his childhood abuse—rather, narrative suspense and ultimate blame center on the small group of Icelandic bankers who murder one of their own in order to protect their laundered money. As is typical of Icelandic thrillers, the group of bankers rounded up at the end of the story are not particularly evil. They are merely common opportunists, blinded by greed, and succumbing to a general atmosphere of corruption. And they are not the initiators of this corruption, which is portrayed as coming from abroad. The worst villain, in addition to Andres's abusive stepfather, is the shadowy Swedish investor, an expert in derivatives working out of Luxembourg, who proposes and organizes the money laundering scheme. We barely meet this character in the course of the plot, and only learn about his existence quite late in the novel. But his elusive presence underscores the fact that the Black Fort represents only one node in the vast global network of financial crime.

While child abuse by bad fathers is portrayed as an Icelandic problem of long standing, the circulation of images of sexually assaulted bodies across borders is relatively new, as are the mechanisms through which the profits of this despicable trade are able to generate more profits. The neglect of Iceland's children has dire social repercussions, leading, for example, to Andres's carrying out of his own version of justice. But recently the suffering of abused children has been "disappeared" into the laundered investments helping to drive the boom that supposedly lifts all boats. The police investigation here exposes what the abstractions of finance conceal. Pornography—the visible record of child exploitation—is used as the trace through which the impact of Randy Martin's "intricate acrobatics of high finance" can be located "on the ground," and we see the proceeds of child porn, laundered through Icelandic banks and then sheltered in Caribbean tax havens, erode present-day social coherence as well as the personal integrity of those who have directly profited from these transactions. *Black Skies* thus offers a perfect example of textual linkage between "black money" and interpersonal forms of violence that seeks to connect the dots between the mostly invisible currents of high finance and its material effects.

Like other examples of Crunch Lit, *Black Skies* includes didactic passages that spell out the various problematic activities through which the financial sector is able to expand so quickly. The character of Sigundur Oli's mother, while denigrated for her elitism, represents an older and more responsible banking culture, critical of the New Vikings. She is professionally situated to explain the complicated and risky maneuvers of the newly deregulated banking industry, and in one of several similar passages, she warns Sigundur of the precariousness of the current financial situation in Iceland and predicts the coming meltdown. She also notes the lack of response from the current government: "I don't think Icelandic law has adequate provisions to cover half of what these people are up to. Parliament is a joke—they're thirty years behind what's happening here" (243).

Foregrounding the point of view of the detective Sigundur Oli as he becomes disenchanted with Iceland's present direction enables the novel to contrast the neoliberal entrepreneurial subject, clearly associated with the influence of United States, with a latent Icelandic national consciousness. Immediately after Sigundur Oli solves the case, we learn that he "briefly toyed with the idea of going to bed with a book. He had been given an Icelandic novel for Christmas nearly a year ago which was still in its wrapping, so he took it out of the drawer, tore off the plastic and started reading, only to return it to the drawer shortly afterwards" (324). Whether Sigundur Oli will return to the book—quite likely a copy of Halldór Laxness's classic novel *Independent People*, discussed below—is left up in the air, but the possibility is there; his new-found sense of empathy for his fellow Icelanders implies that even the most alienated are capable of change.

In the meantime, the concluding passage of the novel leaves the reader with a grim picture of the current state of Iceland. It takes place in the Reykjavik cemetery that houses the grave of the Icelandic independence hero Jón Sigurðsson, a motif of Icelandic nationalism which features in several of Arnaldur Indriðason's novels. Literary critic (later Prime Minister) Katrín Jakobsdóttir has called attention to the frequency with which this author uses present-day indifference to Jón Sigurðsson's legacy to signal the waning of Icelandic national identity.[28] The final sentences of *Black Skies* describe the body of the long-neglected victim Andres, found frozen to death near Jón Sigurðsson's grave. A tragic reminder of Iceland's malaise, we see "his deathly white face was turned, eyes half open, to the heavens, as if at the moment he died he had been looking up at the clouds, waiting for them to part for an instant to reveal a patch of clear blue sky" (330).

## Sixty-Six Degrees North: *Iceland on Fire*

Michael Ridpath's 2011 novel, written in English, is one of a series of five detective thrillers set in Iceland. *66 Degrees North*, the second in the series, opens in mid–January 2009, in the midst of the Pots and Pans Rebellion that led to the fall of the government: "Iceland was angry. As angry as it had ever been since the first Vikings stepped ashore in Reykjavík's smoky bay one thousand years before."[29] With the exception of occasional flashbacks, the action of the novel takes place during this difficult year, painting a detailed portrait of post-*kreppa* Iceland, exploring the responses of a range of characters whose livelihoods have been lost in the crash. Here, there is little money to follow, as it has evaporated almost overnight, leaving ordinary people feeling furious—at their political leaders, at the New Vikings, but perhaps mostly at themselves for their own gullibility. The Special Prosecutor has just been appointed—and makes an appearance in the novel—although the novel's characters do not seem hopeful that some form justice will be served; many of the most successful financiers have already absconded to London or New York. A central question taken up by the novel is what justice for bankrupting a whole nation would actually look like.

The first chapter sets up this question and strikes a distinctly cautionary note regarding political activism. Caught up in the fervor of the anti-government demonstration, a group of drunk protestors lure a bank manager out to confront him with the impact of his misdeeds and, in their rage, accidentally end up killing him. They then improvise a plan to cover up the death by making it appear to be suicide. Sticking to their alibis, the demonstrators escape detection, and their success leads some of the original group to secretly join forces and plot to assassinate the bankers and executives they blame for the kreppa. Through its characterization of some of the individual protesters, the novel suggests that their violence is the result of the projection of feelings of shame, humiliation, and inadequacy on to a handy scapegoat. Among others, we meet Harpa, a thirty-something former bank employee, now broke, who bears the guilt of bankrupting her own parents; and Sindri, a stereotypical aging hippie underachiever. Harpa is motivated by a combination of legitimate anger at her former banker boss but also a deep sense of shame at her own participation in his schemes (11). Sindri is looking for an opportunity to raise his profile as a revolutionary Anarchist, although the narrator informs the reader that "the truth was he felt as guilty as the rest of them" (72). The moral of this opening section seems to be that protest is misdirected and unleashes dangerous emotional currents that become impossible to control. The initial manslaughter—or murder—establishes the point that "vigilante justice" is a contradiction in terms.

The aftermath of the Pots and Pans Rebellion is observed through the eyes of detective Magnus Jonson, an Icelandic-American over from the Boston Police Department. Raised on a farm in rural Iceland until the age of 12, Magnus moved to the U.S. after his alcoholic mother's death. Now in his 30s, he has taken a temporary job in Reykjavík, found an Icelandic girlfriend, and is re-acquainting himself with his homeland and its culture, while at the same time reluctantly uncovering layers of long-buried family secrets. Magnus's partial foreignness serves several functions. It motivates numerous discussions over what it means to be Icelandic, broadening this category to include black Icelanders as well as those who have lived outside of the country. And the fact that Magnus has only recently arrived on the scene means that he has no personal experience of the financial crisis, no mixed feelings of culpability and embarrassment, no blind rage to be misdirected. He therefore brings a more clear-headed perspective to the crimes being investigated, and is able to see past the Icelanders' self-perception that they are an exceptionally peaceful people who rarely resort to political violence, which turns out, in the novel at least, to be untrue at this precarious moment in the nation's history.

Ridpath's novel serves as a well-researched guide to Icelandic culture for outsiders, as the text is filled with the specifics of geography, folklore, and references to the Sagas. Detailed accounts of the Icelandic fishing industry and its quota system are provided, and the dire impact of the financial crisis on the lives of fishermen and farmers is given particular attention. The Anarchist Sindri insists that farmers and fishermen are the "real soul of Iceland"; "men who will work hard in tough conditions, who save, who fight to earn a living on the fells and on the waves" (9). While Sindri's motivations and points of view are often ridiculed by the text, his nostalgia for the old ways and the "real soul of Iceland" is not.

A recurring touchstone in Ridpath's novel is Halldór Laxness's 1935 literary classic *Independent People*, and particularly, its protagonist Bjartur, a character much admired by both Magnus and the conspirators taking justice into their own hands. The sheep farmer Bjartur is taken to represent the self-reliant Icelandic peasant determined to hold his own against the harsh forces of nature as well as against exploitative landowners. In Laxness's novel, Bjartur's naiveté leads him to put his trust in corrupt merchant traders and moneylenders, and he falls into the stranglehold of debt, which ultimately results in the loss of his beloved farm. The many parallels between the story of Bjartur and the situation of contemporary Icelanders are not subtle, and Ridpath's characters agree that the pioneer spirit and toughness that Laxness celebrated are in grave danger of being left behind.[30]

Interestingly, Ridpath's novel frames part of its police investigation as a contest over literary interpretation through its references to this and other Icelandic texts, and Magnus is ultimately proved to be the better reader, and therefore, the better Icelander. His familiarity with Laxness's influential tale enables him to unravel an important clue; the conspirators plan to assassinate a banker they refer to only as "Ingólfur Arnarson," a reference to the legendary Viking settler of Iceland and founder of the city of Reykjavík (As Sindri comments, "If the country was still run by people like him, they'd know exactly what to do with the politicians," 6). But, as Magnus recalls, "Ingólfur Arnarson" is also a major character in *Independent People*. Laxness's ironically named Ingólfur is the foppish son of the local landowner who rises in wealth and status as Bjartur's fortunes fall, a savvy modernizer who becomes director of the National Bank of Iceland and then ascends to the position of Prime Minister. Magnus's knowledge of Laxness allows him to decode the conspirators' use of this historic name in time to save the life of the former Prime Minister whose car has been booby-trapped with a bomb. Similar to the overdetermined image of Jón Sigurðsson's grave in *Black Skies*, "Ingólfur

Arnarson" is a figure who signifies *both* Iceland's heroic origins *and* its modern deviation from them, the very beginnings of Icelandic nationalism and its current dissolute state. One possible implication is that the "real soul of Iceland" can be resurrected through strong and uncorrupted modern policemen like Magnus who have not been distracted by the false promises of finance. Unsure throughout the course of the narrative where he belongs, Magnus must decide whether he will return to Boston or remain in Reykjavík. But by the novel's finale Magnus's Icelandic future is beyond doubt—he is an Icelander at heart.

As we have seen, the murders of banking executives are committed by a collective of disaffected Icelanders connected through the spontaneous anti-government protest dramatized in the novel's opening. The group includes Sindri, portrayed as a slovenly and lecherous blowhard; Ísak, a Marxist economics student studying in London, portrayed as a left-wing fanatic; and two fishermen, Einar and Björn, who have been ruined financially in the meltdown. Einar is older, but in his heyday had the reputation of being "one of the toughest captains of the fleet" (36), while Björn is first introduced through a reference to his "powerful arms" and his broad and calloused hand, "a fisherman's hand" (4). Einar and Björn see themselves as patriots, seeking retribution for the unpunished crimes committed against the Icelandic people, and willingly face prison for their actions. The generally respectful representation of these fishermen threatens to complicate the novel's commentary on vigilante justice, and its sympathies at times seem divided. The question is explicitly raised as to whether these killers are righteous, anti-capitalist activists acting on behalf of the nation, or merely common criminals trying to justify their increasing violence.

The text offers a partial resolution to this problem in that blame for the killings of the oligarchs is apportioned in different degrees, with only Ísak, the young Marxist, presented as totally irredeemable, his revolutionary pretensions rationalizing a murderous bloodlust. Thus the melodramatic episode of Ísak's capture, and the nick-of-time rescue of his intended victim Harpa (originally associated with banking, but now repentant and an object of sympathy) provide emotional closure and move the novel back into the territory of a conventional detective novel and away from more political readings. In an unsubtle act of narrative substitution, sheer malice and the need for scapegoats replace anti-capitalist critique. And Magnus, the novel's central consciousness and the model new Icelander, proclaims that the conspirators belong in the category of "criminals, not terrorists" (453), in his summing-up of the case. The question of what counts as justice for mass financial fraud is raised repeatedly throughout this novel, but ultimately elided; the machinery of the detective plot has no room for this more existential problem. This means that in the world of *66 Degrees North* the terrorist threat is neutralized, but the white-collar criminals responsible for the nation's bankruptcy are never forced to account for their actions and are, for the moment, left to go on with their lives. Remarkably, in this novel of financial crime, the originary crimes are, in a sense, forgiven. The majority of the characters agree that the financiers do not deserve death and that violence is not "the Icelandic way."

## Trapped: *"Proudly Icelandic"*[31]

The 2015 television drama *Trapped* (*Ófærð*), created and partly directed by Baltasar Kormákur, relates the story of the small-town detective Andri Olafsson and his police force of two, Hinrika and Ásgeir, as they unravel the mystery of a dismembered torso caught by a local fishing boat. When a winter storm renders the roads and sea lanes impassable, the police must rely on their own resourcefulness to investigate this bizarre find. As in *Black Skies*, over the course of the narrative we learn that what appears to be a brutal and premeditated murder is actually retribution from a traumatized rape victim—in this case a quiet, withdrawn woman named Maria, who kills the man, the local ne'er-do-well Geirmundur, who once raped her and who threatens to do so again. Geirmundur's body is then mutilated and disposed of under the direction of the town's mayor. Geirmundur had been exiled from the town years before, but not before he had been blackmailed by the mayor and his friends, the owners of the town's two largest businesses, into burning down the fish processing factory for the insurance money. This act of arson created the recent tragedy from which the hamlet has not yet recovered—the fire in which 18-year-old Dagný died and her boyfriend Hjörtur left permanently scarred, then framed for an arson he did not commit.

The 2008 fire that opens the series clearly stands in for the wider financial conflagration and its innocent victims, especially those of the younger generation. The speed with which fire can spread out of control makes it an apt, even obvious metaphor for the global banking crisis and the wealth of a nation suddenly going up in smoke. Arson is literally made an extension of the larger financial crisis, as the town fathers justify their insurance fraud as a necessary act of self-preservation when the economy "went up in flames." The insurance payoff was then discreetly funneled into private investment companies that financed the new tourist industries and set in motion a plan to sell land to Chinese developers to build an international port intended to put the village on the map. It turns out that all of the town's current sources of income are contaminated by the blood money extracted from the initial fire. In a nod to China's economic ascendancy and influence, here the Chinese replace the Americans as the prime movers of global finance.

Elemental Icelandic nature is overwhelming in this masterfully photographed, visually stunning drama, filmed mostly on location in the coastal town of Seyðisfjörður, where geography naturally resists and disrupts global flows. Touristic stereotypes of Iceland as nearly untouched wilderness, a "pure, unspoiled, dreamlike island," and therefore a haven of authenticity, are deliberately evoked.[32] We see that *Trapped*'s mountainous terrain has not readily succumbed to the ease of global exchange and communication. Notably, the days when the drama takes place are days the Icelandic weather has drastically slowed down the speed of modern life. In addition to the storm isolating the town from the rest of the world, an avalanche knocks out the electricity and phone service, heightening the tension and obstructing communication even further. The extremes of Iceland therefore create a unique zone where the problematic effects of global interconnectedness can be examined, and the intricacies of these networks can be traced.

When the torso first surfaces—its only markers of identity are that it is white and male—the police assume that it came from the weekly Danish ferry that brings tourists as well as a motley assortment of suspicious characters to the seemingly peaceful coastal village. (Iceland's former status as a colony of Denmark makes the ferry a symbol of both modern globalization and past colonialism.) However, the body turns out to be a local, rather than a foreign threat; the series sets up a variety of perils to be quelled, human and climatic, foreign and native. The police force is similarly mixed: Hinrika and Ásgeir are long-time residents of the town; Andri has been living in Reykjavík, although his wife and her family are locals. The series adopts the common plot of the big-city policeman relocating to the rural backwater. His position as a relative outsider to this community ensures his ability to administer justice impartially—even when it involves, as it eventually does, arresting his own father-in-law for murder.

More corpulent than most, Andri is otherwise a recognizable Nordic Noir detective—an "everyman" type—taciturn, tough but sensitive. *The New York Times* describes him as the Icelandic version of the small-town Western sheriff, "equal parts nobility, incorruptibility, and cranky gloom."[33] Ólafur Darri Ólafsson, the award-winning actor who plays Andri, is familiar to Icelanders from previous Kormákur projects, most notably the survival drama *The Deep* (2012). In this film Ólafur Darri Ólafsson plays Gulli, a real-life fisherman known as the lone survivor of the wreck of a fishing trawler, managing against all odds to survive overnight in the deadly temperatures of the North Atlantic. Portrayed as a medical miracle—his fat apparently insulated him from freezing to death—Kormákur uses Ólafur's Gulli as a reminder of the modest, anti-heroic, peasant sturdiness of Icelanders, of "who we are and where we came from."[34] Loftsdóttir et al observe that in Andri's impassive masculinity he is deliberately presented as the "embodiment of the Icelander," almost "at one with the beautiful and rough landscape."[35] Their reading is supported by the director's assertion that he cast Ólafur Darri Ólafsson, not only for his talents, but because he wanted a lead actor who would actually look like "a mountain—a big burly man."[36]

Physically sturdy but emotionally vulnerable, Andri is having obvious difficulties moving on from a broken marriage, a situation made all the more tense by the fact that his ex-wife has a new boyfriend. His success as a detective hinges in part on his workaholic sublimation of grief, and in part on his dogged policing under the most punishing weather conditions imaginable. Reviews of the show joke about Andri's refusal to zip his coat, and Loftsdóttir notes that despite blizzards and avalanches, "he remains unaffected, as symbolized by his open jacket."[37] The show's final episode has him locked in a freezer by one of the villains—but of course he survives. Andri's Viking physique and inattention to style contrast him to other male characters, in particular the metrosexual hotel manager and the stereotypically smarmy Lithuanian sex trafficker. And unlike Sigundur Oli and Magnus, he is a family man, a devoted father of two daughters with a strong sense of responsibility to others. His character combines the best of the older Icelandic work ethic with a new and more enlightened social consciousness.[38]

The small town in *Trapped* is deliberately presented as a microcosm of contemporary Iceland, and the economic shifts being scrutinized here are the economic shifts currently underway in the nation as a whole. The townspeople live on a modest scale; this is not a wealthy place. Its main industry, fishing, is giving way to tourism, as we see in the expanding harborside hotel. The many scenes in which the enormous Danish ferry towers incongruously over the town establish a visual metaphor of the jarring impact of global transport and tourism on this quiet provincial backwater. The ferry also brings organized crime in the form of the sex trafficking of underage girls— courtesy of the Lithuanian mafia—which has been taking place in partnership with the distinctly sleazy owner of the local hotel. And the ferry enables the return of Geirmundur, the rapist and arsonist, and, on his return, he again attempts to rape Maria, who this time stabs him in self-defense. The police investigation in this drama uncovers criminal collaboration between the village patriarchs—the mayor and the local business owners—and lays the ultimate blame on their seduction by the prospect of foreign capital.

We soon learn that these same town fathers have their hearts set on luring Chinese investors—and enriching themselves by selling them the land— to establish a port that will become a major transport hub as the Arctic ice melts due to climate change and opens up new sea lanes. Arguing that "America is finished. China is the future," the town leaders claim to seek an economic base other than the speculative capital that dissolved so catastrophically in 2008. When one older villager objects to the plan, reminding them, "We've all been here before. We were endlessly promised the earth," the others respond, "This is different. This is about *real* trade." It remains unclear what commodities will be traded, however, and the port project is clearly aligned with the financial machinations of the earlier boom. All of the characters who support it are shown to have been conditioned by the atmosphere of risky speculation and greed that prevailed before the crash, as well as literally funded by the insurance fraud they committed seven years before. The narrative's sympathies lie with the old man's skepticism, as he is portrayed as a typical rural Icelander, skilled at hunting and fishing, disdainful of new ways and of his insufficiently manly son, who works as a port security guard and has fallen under the sway of the town "fathers."

While both women and men fall victim to criminal attacks during the series, the plot forges a number of links between white-collar crimes and gendered violence committed by male characters against women. The trafficking of young African girls helps to finance the expansion of the hotel; Dagný's death is the result of a financially motivated arson; Maria's rape provides the opportunity for her rapist to be blackmailed into committing the arson; the deeply corrupt mayor beats his wife. Much of the violence against women is represented as indigenous rather than as a foreign import. Not all of the male characters who abuse women are Icelandic, but the show subjects two Icelandic perpetrators to extremely sensational and symbolic deaths. The wife-abusing mayor is burned alive by Dagný's father (Andri's father-in law), and the abused wife secretly watches with relief. This murder turns out to be revenge, carried out when the father discovers that the mayor is the architect of the arson that ended his daughter's life. And, of course, the reduction of Geirmudur to decapitated torso evokes the classic image of castration by a vengeful patriarch. The mutilation and disposal of the body, a collaborative effort but ordered by the mayor, serves to protect his own secrets and remove a disobedient "son" as well as to enact a rough justice for Maria's attack.

For reasons that remain somewhat mysterious, the traumatized youth Hjörtur photographs the as-yet-unidentified torso and uploads the images on to the internet, where they continue to circulate, foreshadowing the overlap that will be uncovered between the crimes of financial fraud and misogynist sexual assault. While Hjörtur's actions make little sense in terms of the plot, they do allow for the replay of this gruesome image. On the level of metaphor, the headless, hand-less, anonymous white corpse symbolizes the deracinated Icelander, the opposite of Andri's physical incarnation of the manly Icelandic ideal.

By the concluding episode, all fires have been extinguished. Andri and Hinrika have identified the immediate sources of corruption—they have unraveled the network of subsidiaries that disguised the mutual financial interests of the town fathers, although this process is, typically, represented quite perfunctorily. The torso has been named, the mystery of how and why

Geirmundur died has been solved, the mayor is dead (hideously murdered but in retaliation for his own violence), and the mayor's murderer, the fish factory owner, the hotel owner, and Maria are all under arrest. (I'm hoping Maria gets off for self-defense—it seems a clear case.) Young Hjörtur is no longer feared by the community as a dangerous criminal. He has from the beginning been marked by his love for Dagný and grief at her death, but, in the plot's most hopeful turn, now has a new girlfriend and a new lease on life. The storm passes and the ferry can once again come and go without hindrance.

True to the rules of the detective genre, this tiny police force represents the best of the Icelandic state, and traditional Icelandic fortitude is proved equal to the task of purging the town of threats both foreign and native, at least temporarily. Sadly, Andri's marriage is definitively over and, with the final long shot of a bereft Andri against the landscape, the drama reinforces his existential masculine solitude, but also his affinity with the wildness of this unique place. The town's future is left open, to be explored in future television seasons. But it's worth noting that in the world of *Trapped* there are no suave international bankers or financiers; no characters appear to be enormously rich or powerful. Instead we have small regional players trying, somewhat pathetically, to emulate the real "banksters"—infected by the investor impulse and the temptations of speculative wealth, running their own parallel vigilante "legal" system for their own benefit, ultimately portrayed as out of their league. If the town of Seyðisfjörður is a microcosm of the nation of Iceland, the more culpable villains remain offshore and off-screen, untouchable in the financial centers of New York, London, and Beijing.

## Conclusions

Iceland's dramatic shifts from longstanding rural poverty to global banking powerhouse, and then to Ground Zero of the international financial collapse, has provided its crime writers with a unique perspective on the inadequacy of nation-states in the face of contemporary globalized finance. A number of Icelandic crime fictions draw on the drama of these real events to create fantasy narratives of finance capital as at least momentarily containable. However, it is significant that in all of the above narratives a full accounting, an achievable justice, remains out of reach. There is always the final thread left hanging, the unpunished culprits off-screen or beyond the scope of the novel's geography. In the inadequacy of their final resolutions these Icelandic texts exhibit an awareness of the deterritorialization of capital flows and the ongoing vulnerability of nations—in particular small states—within the circuitry of globalized capital. John Lanchester notes that 10 years after the 2008 crash, little meaningful reform of the financial system has penetrated the major centers of the global economy. There has been "no change or change for the worse" in breaking up the banks that were too big to fail, and "no overall reduction in the level of risk present in the system."[39] We don't know when the global economy will implode again, but we know that it will. Given that knowledge, Iceland—with its spectacular rise and fall and rise—provides a fascinating and instructive real-life example of how a small nation has weathered the inevitable boom and bust cycles of capitalism.

The chronic instability of the networked global economy may well contribute to a widespread craving for reassuring fantasies of knowledge-as-control, in these examples of Crunch Lit, via a measure of financial literacy inserted within an accessible genre fiction. Although the possibility of literally mapping virtualized capital remains a fantasy, this is a highly symptomatic one—the sign of a collective cultural desire to locate the now-elusive sources of value within a particular geopolitical space, to regain control over a network that exists beyond the scope of any single agent. The police procedurals examined above rehearse not only the disciplining of greedy white-collar criminals who brought down a national economy, but also provide mythological versions of the "detectability" and potential containment of transnational capital. They offer narratives in which borders still matter, cultures are still fundamentally distinguishable, and finance capital can be brought to heel, at least for a time—a fictional world readily appreciated by those outside of Iceland, as well as by the natives of this tiny island nation.[40]

## Notes

1. Randy Martin, *An Empire of Indifference: American War and the Financial Logic of Risk Management* (Durham: Duke University Press, 2007), 3.

2. See, for one of several examples, Ragnar Jónasson, "Translating Agatha Christie into Icelandic: One Clue Took Ten Years," *The Guardian*, April 4, 2017.

3. See Jakob Stougaard-Nielsen, *Scandinavian Crime Fiction* (London: Bloomsbury Academic, 2017); Andrew Nestingen, *Crime and Fantasy in Scandinavia: Fiction, Film, and Social Change* (Seattle: University of Washington Press, 2008); Andrew Nestingen and Paula Arvas, eds., *Scandinavian Crime Fiction* (Cardiff: University of Wales Press, 2011); Kristin Bergman, *Swedish Crime Fiction: The Making of Nordic Noir* (Milan: Mimesis International, 2016). Bergman complicates these generalizations somewhat, arguing that works by Swedish female crime novelists do not always fit into them, and pointing to recent texts that expand the boundaries of the Scandi-Noir tradition. On the cultural politics of the popular Swedish Wallander series, see my essay "The Man Who Refused to Smile: Henning Mankell's Wallander Series and Postmodern Cynicism," *Genre: Forms of Discourse and Culture* 50, no. 2 (July 2017): 153–80.

4. Harvey continues, "This 'bewildering world of high finance encloses an equally bewildering variety of cross-cutting activities, in which banks borrow massively short-term from other banks, insurance companies and pension funds assemble such vast pools of investment funds as to function as dominant 'market makers,' while industrial, merchant, and landed capital become so integrated into financial operations and structures that it becomes increasingly difficult to tell where commercial and industrial interests begin and strictly financial interests end." David Harvey, *The Condition of Postmodernity* (Oxford: Blackwell, 1990), 161.

5.  Willlem Buiter, Chief Economist for Citigroup, quoted in Ásgeir Jónsson and Hersir Sigurgeirsson, *The Icelandic Financial Crisis: A Study into the World's Smallest Currency Area and Its Recovery from Banking Collapse* (London: Palgrave Macmillan, 2016), 9.

6.  Sigríður Benediktsdóttir, et al., "The Rise, Fall, and Resurrection of Iceland: A Postmortem Analysis of the 2008 Financial Crisis," *Brookings Papers on Economic Activity*, Brookings Institution Press, Fall 2017, 192.

7.  Michael Lewis, "Wall Street on the Tundra," *Boomerang: Travels in the New Third World* (New York: W.W. Norton, 2011), 2.

8.  Roger Boyes, *Meltdown Iceland: How the Global Financial Crisis Bankrupted an Entire Country* (London: Bloomsbury, 2009), 160.

9.  The American journalist Michael Lewis, in his somewhat sensationalized 2009 observations of Icelandic banking culture, "Wall Street on the Tundra," criticizes its domination by inexperienced but aggressively overconfident males (although in terms of aggression one wonders how different this was from the culture of Wall Street). In his view, this particular banking crisis was in large part due to a penchant for extreme risk common to Icelandic men. A number of studies analyzing the causes of the crisis, including those from within Iceland, have explored gender as a factor. An oversimplified version reads the crisis as a hopeless mess made by men that women now have to "clean up." The *kreppa* did lead to a new emphasis on Icelandic women in politics and in executive positions in the reformed banking industry. However, I agree with Katy Shaw's critique of some post-crisis accounts for their tendency to reframe "a crisis of financialization as a crisis of masculinity" and which therefore risk deflecting attention "away from economic systems and onto gender." Katy Shaw, *Crunch Lit* (London: Bloomsbury Academic, 2015), 90.

10.  She led a coalition of the Social Democratic Alliance and the Left-Green Party; her cabinet was half female. The heads of two of the newly-reconfigured banks were also women. Roger Boyes sees this political shift as a return to an earlier, more egalitarian ethos in Iceland as well as a possible end to the "Age of Testosterone" (201, 202). Jóhanna Sigurðardóttir was prime minister until 2013.

11.  Quoted in Viljhálmur Arnason, "Something Rotten in the State of Iceland: 'The Production of Truth' about the Icelandic Banks," in *Gambling Debt: Iceland's Rise and Fall in the Global Economy*, Paul Durreberger and Gísli Pálsson, eds. (Denver: University of Colorado Press, 2015), 56.

12.  Laura Noonan et al., "Who Went to Jail for Their Role in the Financial Crisis?" *The Financial Times*, September 20, 2018.

13.  Boyes, 116.

14.  Arnason, 58.

15.  Notable exceptions include Andrew Hobarek's insightful reading of Gillian Flynn's *Gone Girl*, "Post-Recession Realism," in *Neoliberalism and Contemporary Literary Culture*, Mitchem Huehls and Rachel Greenwald Smith, eds. (Baltimore: Johns Hopkins University Press, 2017), 237–252, and Jakob Stougaard-Nielsen's account of Stieg Larsson's *The Girl with the Dragon Tattoo* in his *Scandinavian Detective Fiction*. Larsson's wildly popular novel utilizes many of the plot devices I analyze in Icelandic crime fictions.

16.  Katy Shaw, *Crunch Lit* (London: Bloomsbury Academic, 2015), 9.

17.  *Ibid.*, 94.

18.  *Ibid.*, 2, 17.

19.  Fredric Jameson, "Culture and Finance Capital," *The Cultural Turn* (London: Verso, 1998), 153, 154.

20.  Alison Shonkwiler, *The Financial Imaginary: Economic Mystification and the Limits of Realist Fiction* (Minneapolis: University of Minnesota Press, 2017), xii. See also Annie McClanahan, *Dead Pledges: Debt, Crisis, and Twenty-first Century Culture* (Stanford, California: Stanford University Press, 2017) and Shonkwiler and La Berge's edited collection, *Reading Capitalist Realism* (Iowa City: University of Iowa Press, 2014).

21.  Shonkwiler, xiv.

22.  Quoted in Shonkwiler, xv.

23.  The Swedish detective series *Fallet*, a comedy-drama that parodies the tropes and clichés of Nordic Noir, offers a scene in which one of the detectives explains her research

into the corporation known as "McGuffin Batter" to her fellow police. She announces her discovery that "McGuffin" is merely a front "for a sister company controlled by a holding company run by a subsidiary and founded by a large corporation that is owned by a private limited company" (opening of Episode 7). This is as good an example as any of the shorthand used to represent forensic accounting in financial thrillers. The detective then goes on to identify a single individual on the board of all of these shell companies, thus penetrating the fog of finance in one succinct gesture.

24. Kristin Loftsdóttir, Katla Kjartansdóttir and Katrin Anna Lund observe that a number of post-crash Icelandic films follow "the long tradition of placing men as the symbol for Icelanders as a whole" and glorify "the resilience of masculinity as existing in context of harsh Icelandic nature, presenting Icelandic men as heroes in the anti-hero tradition of Nordic Noir." "Trapped in Cliches: Masculinity, Films, and Tourism in Iceland," *Gender, Place, and Culture: A Journal of Feminist Geography* (2017): 8.

25. Kristin Loftsdóttir, "Finding a Place in the World: Political Subjectivities and the Imagination of Iceland After the Economic Crash," *Focaal* 80 (March 22, 2018). Not paginated.

26. See the Thóra Gudmundsdóttir novels of Yrsa Sigurðardóttir and Quentin Bates's Officer Gunnhildur series; Ragnar Jónasson also has a series featuring a female detective.

27. Arnuldur Indriðason, *Black Skies*, trans. Victoria Cribb (New York: Minotaur Books, 2012), 226. Subsequent references in text.

28. Katrin Jakobsdóttir, 53–56. "Meaningless Icelanders: Icelandic Crime Fiction and Nationality," in *Scandinavian Crime Fiction*, Nestingen and Arvas, eds. (Cardiff: University of Wales Press, 2011), 46–61.

29. Michael Ridpath, *66 Degrees North* (London: Corvus Books, 2011), 1. Subsequent references in text.

30. Or supposedly celebrated—this is a common misreading of Halldór Laxness's novel, as Bjartur's cruelty to his wife and children are heavily critiqued in the original text, as are his stubbornness, pride, and ego. However, Laxness's commentary on Bjartur's many faults does not seem to register with the characters in *66 Degrees North*, who use him as a symbol of Iceland's former self-reliance and independent spirit.

31. This is a quote from Sam Wollaston's review of *Trapped*, in which he writes: "*Trapped* certainly shares DNA with its Scandi cousins.... Sparse, stripped-down, simple, real? Check. Concerned as much with the characters and their problems as the plot? Check. A protagonist with some serious issues, who is flawed and worn down by life? Check. A focus not just on crime and solving crime, but on the consequences and victims of crime too? Já ... but this is not merely a copy.... The economic situation adds an uncertain and volatile backdrop. Nordic maybe, but this is also most definitely, and proudly, Icelandic." "Stuck in a Stormy, Moody Fjord with a Killer on the Loose? Yes Please," *The Guardian*, February 15, 2016.

32. Loftsdóttir et al., 2.

33. Mike Hale, "Like Nordic Noir? *Trapped* Is Chilly, and Pulls You In," *The New York Times*, February 17 2017.

34. See Chris Tosan's interview with Baltasar Kormákur, in which he quotes the director: "After the collapse of the Icelandic economy I felt that this is the story to tell, now. It's a metaphor for the collapse we went through.... In 2007 we'd lost our way—sailors became bankers who were buying megastores in London." "Deep Thought: An Interview with Baltasar Kormákur." *The Film Review*, July 9 2013. Not paginated.

35. Loftsdóttir et al., 11.

36. "Interview with *Trapped* Director Baltasar Kormákur." Nordicnoir.TV (website). August 4 2016. Not paginated.

37. Loftsdottir et al., 11.

38. This more sensitive type of male detective is particularly noticeable in contemporary British and Scandinavian television drama. The male protagonists of *Shetland*, *Hinterland*, *Broadchurch* (especially the third season, which focuses on rape), *George Gently* and others are progressive policemen who model an enlightened modern perspective, often educating their backward colleagues and fellow citizens about discrimination against women and gay people. All of these detectives except for George Gently are, not coincidentally, fathers of daughters.

39. John Lanchester, "After the Fall: Ten Years After the Crash," *The London Review of Books*, July 2018.
40. I would like to thank Julie H. Kim, Francesca Sawaya, Nicole Capozziello, and Julia Dzwonkoski for their generous assistance with this essay.

# BIBLIOGRAPHY

Alderman, Liz. "Iceland, Symbol of Financial Crisis, Finally Lifts Capital Controls." *New York Times*, March 14, 2017.

Árnason, Vilhjálmur. "Something Rotten in the State of Iceland: 'The Production of Truth' about the Icelandic Banks," In *Gambling Debt: Iceland's Rise in the Global Economy*, edited by Gísli Pálsson and Paul Durrenberger, 47–59. Boulder: University Press of Colorado, 2015.

Bates, Quentin. *Cold Comfort*. New York: Soho Crime, 2013.

Bates, Quentin. *Frozen Assets*. New York: Soho Crime, 2011.

Benediktsdóttir Sigríður, et al. "The Rise, Fall, and Resurrection of Iceland: A Postmortem Analysis of the 2008 Financial Crisis." *Brookings Papers on Economic Activity*. Brookings Institution Press (Fall 2017): 191–308.

Bjarnason, Egill. "Iceland Seeks Closure After Financial Crash." *Christian Science Monitor*, October 15, 2018.

Boyes, Roger. *Meltdown: How the Global Financial Crisis Bankrupted an Entire Country*. London: Bloomsbury, 2009.

Calhoun, Craig. Introduction to *Business as Usual: The Roots of the Global Financial Meltdown*, edited by Craig Calhoun and Georgi Derluguian. New York University Press: 2011.

*Cover Story* (2007–2017). Created by Óskar Jónasson and Sigurjón Kjartansson. 3 Seasons. Produced by Sagafilm. Iceland. *Fallet*. (2017). Created by Rikard Ivshammar and Erik Hultkvist. 1 Season. Produced by SVT 1. Sweden.

Gregorek, Jean. "The Man Who Refused to Smile: Henning Mankell's Wallander Series and Postmodern Cynicism." *Genre: Forms of Discourse and Culture* 50, no. 2 (July 2017): 153–80.

Hale, Mike. "Like Nordic Noir? *Trapped* Is Chilly, and Pulls You In." *The New York Times*, February 17, 2017.

Harvey, David. *The Condition of Postmodernity*. Oxford: Blackwell, 1990.

Huehls, Mitchum, and Rachel Greenwald Smith, editors. *Neoliberalism and Contemporary Literary Culture*. Baltimore: Johns Hopkins University Press, 2017.

Indriðason, Arnuldur. *Black Skies*. Translated by Victoria Cribb. 2009. New York: Minotaur Books, 2012.

Indriðason, Arnuldur. *The Shadow District*. Translated by Victoria Cribb. New York: Minotaur Books, 2017.

Jakobsdóttir, Katrín. "Meaningless Icelanders: Icelandic Crime Fiction and Nationality." In *Scandinavian Crime Fiction*, edited by Andrew Nestingen and Paula Arvas, 46–61. Cardiff: University of Wales Press: 2011.

Jameson, Fredric. "Culture and Finance Capital." In *The Cultural Turn: Selected Writings on the Postmodern*, 136–161. London: Verso, 1998.

Jónasson, Ragnar. *Blackout*. Translated by Quentin Bates. 2011. New York: Minotaur Books, 2016.

Jónasson, Ragnar. *Snowblind*. Translated by Quentin Bates. 2010. New York: Minatour Books, 2015.

Jónasson, Ragnar. "Translating Agatha Christie into Icelandic: One Clue Took Ten Years." *The Guardian*, April 4, 2017.

Jónsson, Ásgeir and Hersir Sigurgeirsson, *The Icelandic Financial Crisis: A Study into the World's Smallest Currency Area and Its Recovery from Banking Collapse*. London: Palgrave Macmillan, 2016.

Kormákur, Baltasar, *The Deep*. Film. Blueeyes Productions. Iceland. 2012.

Lanchester, John. "After the Fall." *London Review of Books* 40, no. 13 (July 2018): 1–8.

*The Lava Field.* Directed by Reynir Lyngdal. 1 Season. Pegasus Productions. Iceland. 2014.

Laxness, Halldór. *Independent People.* Translated by J.A. Thompson. 1935. New York: Vintage Books, 1997.

Lewis, Michael. *Boomerang: Travels in the New Third World.* New York: W.W. Norton, 2011.

Loftsdóttir, Kristín. "Finding a Place in the World: Political Subjectivities and the Imagination of Iceland After the Economic Crash." *Focaal* 80 (March 22, 2018).

Loftsdóttir, Kristin, Katla Kjartansdóttir, and Katrin Anna Lund. "Trapped in Cliches: Masculinity, Films, and Tourism in Iceland." *Gender, Place, and Culture: A Journal of Feminist Geography* 2017: 1–18.

Martin, Randy. *An Empire of Indifference: American War and the Financial Logic of Risk Management.* Durham: Duke University Press, 2007.

Martin, Randy. *Financialization of Daily Life.* Philadelphia: Temple University Press, 2002.

McClanahan, Annie. *Dead Pledges: Debt, Crisis, and Twenty-First Century Culture.* Stanford: Stanford University Press, 2017.

Nestingen, Andrew. *Crime and Fantasy in Scandinavia: Fiction, Film, and Social Change.* Seattle: University of Washington Press, 2008.

Nestingen, Andrew, and Paula Arvas, editors. *Scandinavian Crime Fiction.* Cardiff: University of Wales Press, 2011.

Noonan, Laura, et al. "Who Went to Jail for Their Role in the Financial Crisis?" *The Financial Times,* September 20, 2018.

Nordicnoir.TV. "Interview with Trapped Director Baltasar Kormakur." August 4, 2016. No page numbers.

Ridpath, Michael. *66 Degrees North.* London: Corvus Books, 2011.

Shaw, Katy. *Crunch Lit.* London: Bloomsbury Academic, 2015.

Shonkweiler, Alison. *The Financial Imaginary: Economic Mystification and the Limits of Realist Fiction.* Minneapolis: University of Minnesota Press, 2017.

Shonkwiler and La Berge, editors. *Reading Capitalist Realism.* Iowa City: University of Iowa Press, 2014.

Sigurðardóttir, Lilja. *Cage.* Translated by Quentin Bates. London: Orenda Books, 2019.

Sigurðardóttir, Lilja. *Snare.* Translated by Quentin Bates. 2015. London: Orenda Books, 2017.

Sigurðardóttir, Lilja. *Trap.* Translated by Quentin Bates. 2018. London: Orenda Books, 2019.

Sigurðardóttir, Yrsa. *Someone to Watch Over Me.* Translated by Philip Roughton. New York: Minotaur Books, 2013.

Stougaard-Nielsen, Jakob. *Scandinavian Detective Fiction.* London: Bloomsbury Academic, 2017.

Tosan, Chris. "Deep Thought—An Interview with Baltasar Kormákur." *The Film Review,* July 9, 2013.

*Trapped* (2015). Created by Baltasar Kormákur and Sigurjón Kjartansson. 1 Season. Produced by RVK Studios. Iceland. Broadcast on BBC 4 2016.

Woolaston, Sam. "Stuck in a Stormy, Moody Fjord with a Killer on the Loose? Yes Please." *The Guardian,* February 15, 2016.

# Imagined Geographies and Colonial Marginals in *Miss Smilla's Feeling for Snow*

Somdatta Bhattacharya

> "It is freezing, an extraordinary –18°C, and it's snowing, and in the language which is no longer mine, the snow is *qanik*— big, almost weightless crystals falling in stacks and covering the ground with a layer of pulverized white frost."
> —*Miss Smilla's Feeling for Snow*[1]

This is how Peter Høeg begins his hugely successful tale of loss, innocence, greed, crime, detection and adventure, and this first paragraph includes all that is at the center of the narrative—snow, desolation, loss of a homeland and mother tongue. On the surface, *Miss Smilla's Feeling for Snow* is a detective story. It begins as a classic example of detective fiction: it seems to include all three major elements that describe and define such a narrative—"a detective of some kind, an unsolved mystery ... and an investigation by which the mystery is eventually solved."[2] However, as the narrative develops, in an often bafflingly complex and layered text full of flashbacks, allusions and intertextual references, the certainties that shape the genre are questioned, and the reader is left with clues and possibilities, and the "solution" remains painfully elusive.

Smilla Qaaviqaaq Jaspersen lives in Copenhagen, in the "White Cells" of the city that is often described as sterile. Born of a Greenlandic Inuit mother and a prosperous Danish doctor, Smilla lives the life of a reluctant Dane in the city. She is thrown into an obsessive search for answers when her neighbor Isaiah, a child, is killed. The state claims that it was an accident while Smilla, who can read signs left behind in the snow that covers the

101

rooftop from where Isaiah plunged to death, believes that it cannot be. What follows is a journey of relentless pursuit where Smilla reads signs, pursues leads, ignores threats and faces powerful forces, to solve the riddle. With the help of Peter Føjl, another neighbor who was close to Isaiah, Smilla discovers that the child's death is connected to a conspiracy centered on Gela Alta, in a Greenlandic glacial island. She learns that a couple of past expeditions to the island have found something valuable and that Isaiah's father had died in one such expedition. The antagonists now plan to return to the island, and Smilla is determined to sneak onto the ship to uncover the truth. She gains entry onto the ship in the guise of a stewardess and finds out that the ship's crew is under the command of a mysterious Tørk Hviid. In the end, it is revealed that the secret in the island is a meteorite which has infested the surrounding areas with a lethal worm. Isaiah's father was in fact a victim of the parasite, and the boy was forced off the roof because he had accompanied his father and had the worm dormant in his body. The novel ends where Smilla, using her intuitive sense of ice and snow, chases Tørk onto thin ice.

The novel, in its postmodern pastiche of the genre of detective fiction, undercuts the genre's basic premise wherein "the point of an analytic detective story is the deductive solution of a mystery."[3] The novel ends in an admission that there are no solutions or conclusions:

> Tell us, they'll come and say to me. So we may understand and close the case. They are wrong. It's only what you do not understand that you can come to a conclusion about. There will be no conclusion [410].

As Hans Henrik Møller has argued, "Although Smilla knows all the Inuit snow … she never quite succeeds in finding the murderer, in combining all the threads into a single pattern thereby providing a sense of closure."[4] I argue that it is in this denial of closure (and move away from the logocentric patterns of the detective story) that the narrative reveals itself as an intersectional space of competing narratives. The story here is not (only) a murder mystery; it uses a murder plot to reconstruct several larger "events." Møller has pointed to this interpretation: "It moves from … the possibility of determining the cause of one single death to the impossibility of comprehending the consequences of a meteor threatening the entire world, from fiction to metafiction."[5] In this essay I try to explore another trajectory—to read the novel as a narrative of postcolonial trauma and a nativist resistance to colonial hegemony and greed.

Edward Said built his monumental work on Orientalism on a central principle: "geography is socially constituted."[6] In Said's discourse, colonialism produces "imaginative knowledge" that produces the colonized space as barbaric, uncultured and, in essence, "Orient." This act of "designating in one's mind a familiar space which is 'ours' and an unfamiliar space beyond 'ours,' which is 'theirs,' is a way of making geographical distinctions that can be entirely arbitrary." This act of producing an imaginative space through the production of imaginative knowledge is often unilateral: "imaginative geography of the 'our land / barbarian land' variety does not require that the barbarians acknowledge the distinction. It is enough for 'us' to set up these boundaries in our own minds; 'they' become 'they' accordingly, and both their territory and their mentality is designated as different from 'ours.'"[7] The idea of discursive production of space and the colonial designation of the Other space as an imaginative geography are both interesting tools to unlock the narrative of *Smilla*. It is interesting to read the narrative as an intersectional space where two imaginative geographies collide—one that is constructed by Smilla as an exile longing to return to her roots in Greenland, and the "barbaric" territory constructed by Danish political, economic and colonial interests in Greenland. This contestation, I argue, unravels around a number of intersecting postcolonial themes that the novel presents. The novel is not (only) about solving a murder mystery in the glaciers of Greenland; it is rather about a number of puzzles that a colonial, and later a capitalist, hegemony and subordination throw up.

At the center of the narrative is Smilla's repeated affirmation of her identity as a Greenlander. Her mother, an Inuit hunter, had met Dr. Moritz Jaspersen, the Danish doctor who had come to Greenland to research trigeminal neuralgia, in North Greenland. The marriage ended when Smilla was three years old. Later, after her mother's death, the custody of the children was given to the father, and both Smilla and her brother were taken to Denmark. This exile from her Greenlandic roots remained a painful experience for Smilla as she struggled to escape the metropolitan world of Denmark for Greenland. The official file on Smilla provides a glimpse into this struggle, and her rebellion against assimilation into the Danish society:

> Your mother reported missing on 12 June 1963, while hunting. Presumed dead. Your brother commits suicide in September '81…. Custody transferred to the father after the mother's death…. To Denmark September 1963. Reported missing, searched for, and found by the police six times between '63 and '71, twice in Greenland [88].

The report goes on to list a number of transgressions she continued to commit as she was denied a return to Greenland. Finally, we find her, at the beginning of the narrative, in an apartment housing, "White Cells," in Copenhagen.

Smilla's personal history is enmeshed in the colonial history of Greenland. Greenland's Inuit populations have lived under Danish hegemony for centuries. The modern colonization of Greenland dates back to the 1720s.[8] It was a crown colony controlled by Copenhagen, and the Danes kept the land in isolation from the 18th century, fearing foreign immigration. The Danish state controlled and monopolized Greenlandic trade. As Christian

Egander Skov has argued, "Danish colonial policies were to a large degree informed by what could be seen as a paternalistic wish to protect the native Inuit from abuse and the dangers of modern life."[9] This was stressed in the characterization of the Danish colonialist as a benevolent hegemon. By 1953, Greenland was designated as an integral part of Denmark. As Robert Petersen has pointed out, a sense of entitlement governed the Danish hegemony of Greenland. "The difference was that the 'colonies' outside Greenland were occupied with the purpose of economic and strategic exploitation, while Greenland was regarded as an inherited dependency."[10] The relationship seems, at least on surface, peaceful and mutually agreed upon. However, "this was, among other things, due to the fact that the Greenlandic community had no organization above the household level, and thus lacked anyone who might be interested in defending his power."[11] The outcome of this lack of political organization is a startling array of restrictions and rules and regulations that the Danish state imposes on the Greenlander. Smilla now needs a visa to visit her homeland, as the colonial administration assumes the power to define and redefine her identity. At one point, her visa application is denied "summarising several private matters" (88). The paternalist state often bares its fangs in the narrative, and all pretenses of being a benevolent benefactor of colonial subjects are shed in moments when the state suspects Smilla of rebellion: "we can throw you in the clink at any time," Smilla is threatened at one point in the narrative, "imprisonment … in a little soundproof room with no windows is, I have been told, particularly uncomfortable for somebody who grew up in Greenland" (90–91). Smilla constantly brings out this tension below the surface at both the landscapes of her exile: Copenhagen and Thule.

Smilla's hybrid identity is at the center of the narrative of the novel. She is acutely aware of it and has developed the attitude of an outsider in Danish society. At the core of Smilla's life in Copenhagen and her sojourns in the city is a continuous affirmation of her identity as a nomadic Inuit, and a refusal to conform to the homogenous Nordic identity:

> I have arranged my apartment like a hotel room—without getting rid of the impression that the person living here is in transit. Whenever I feel the need to explain it to myself, I think about the fact that my mother's family, and she herself, were to some extent nomads [9].

I read this also as a refusal to forget a history of colonial displacement. This colonial history of Greenland recurs throughout the narrative:

> Not one day of my adult life has passed that I haven't been amazed at how poorly Danes and Greenlanders understand each other. It's worse for Greenlanders, of course. It's not healthy for the tightrope walker to be misunderstood by the person who's holding the rope. And in this century the Inuit's life has been a tightrope dance

on a cord fastened at one end to the world's least hospitable land with the world's most severe and fluctuating climate, and fastened at the other end to the Danish colonial administration [79].

This affirmation of a Greenlandic identity and refusal to forget that what binds her to the Danish society is a history of colonialism is also a refusal to be interpellated into a homogenous Nordic identity. The colonial metropolis and its state apparatus, with their barely disguised suspicion of the Inuit, underline the Otherness that underscores Smilla's responses to Denmark. Throughout the narrative, the state, which holds one end of the "cord" on which the Greenlanders are doing a "tightrope walk," seems to use Smilla's identity as a Greenlander to frustrate her attempts to uncover the truth. When all else fails, they question her identity. Her investigating Isaiah's death is a threat to the colonial authority: "In a little country like ours, you are a sensitive issue, Miss Jaspersen. You have seen and heard a lot" (90). The Danish colonial state can watch over Smilla and keep her in its sights in the "white cells" and the stifling cityscape. But she becomes a threatening unknown when she enters Greenland. Smilla's repeated efforts to run away from her father's metropolis and Danish schools to her mother's Greenland should be read as a constant rebellion to escape interpellation into the colonial state.

One of the levels at which this interpellation takes place is at the level of language. The colonial subjects are constantly told that the "golden ascent would take place in Danish" (105). Loss of language through colonial violence is seen as a cultural onslaught on the Inuit's life. Imposition of the Danish language on the uprooted Greenlander's life is key to her/his acculturation into the colonial metropolis. The state, to begin with, presents it to the colonial subject as a ticket to cultural and economic prosperity. Smilla remembers how she was initiated into this process:

> When we moved from the village school to Qaanaaq, we had teachers who didn't know one word of Greenlandic, nor did they have any plans to learn it. They told us, for those who excelled, there would be an admission ticket to Denmark and a degree and a way out of the Arctic misery [105].

All lucrative jobs are attached to the Danish language. Greenland's virtual annexation as "Denmark's northernmost county" is accompanied by this cultural annexation that wipes out the Greenlandic language. The realization that the migration, both spatial and linguistic, to the Danish colonial metropolis has resulted in the loss of one's own language and culture, sinks in slowly but surely:

> Then you arrive in Denmark and six months pass and it feels as if you will never forget your mother tongue. It's the language you think in, the way you remember your past. Then you meet a Greenlander on the street. You exchange a few words. And suddenly you have to search for a completely ordinary word. Another six months

pass. A girlfriend takes you along to the Greenlanders' House in Lov Lane. That's where you discover that your own Greenlandic can be picked apart with a fingernail [105].

Colonial education plays a determining part in this process of acculturation. As Barbara Arneil points out, colonial ideology has always believed in acculturation through education: "Classical liberal theory is … deeply wedded to the idea of progress through education rooted in the need to relinquish customary 'ways and modes.' If there is resistance to such 'improvement' at home, stronger forces may be needed, including separation from the home environment in workhouses or segregated schools." Arneil mentions how this "liberal ideology" of colonialism recommends boarding schools for children from the subject race.[12] It is with claustrophobia and revulsion that Smilla remembers her boarding schools. Smilla recounts how education in Denmark not only made her lose her language but it changed the way she was seen and perceived by her Greenlandic peers, at Rugmarken's School, "near the welfare barracks for migrants" (45). This education forces Greenlandic children to acculturate into the Danish mainstream by undermining their own cultural values. Charles Hobart's study of the influence of the school on the acculturation of Greenlandic children points out a crucial aspect of this colonial education:

> Control of the school system differs sharply in autonomous and in colonial or wardship societies. In the former, members of the society allocate a portion of its resources for the training of the next generation, conformably with the core values and the master trends of the society. There is rarely debate over where or how or what kind of education is to be offered; societal consensus usually exists on these questions. In colonial or wardship societies, however, the decisions as to where and how and what kind of education is to be offered or imposed are usually made by representatives of the dominant society rather than by representatives of those affected.[13]

The rupture between preschool/community life and school life leaves the Greenlandic child often confused and linguistically challenged. Smilla mentions how Isaiah would switch over to Danish, to express a polite form of address alien to his Greenlandic cultural practices (45). On the other hand, this linguistic hegemony endangers the rich linguistic diversity that Isaiah had inherited from his Greenlandic roots: "there isn't one language in Greenland. There are three" (106).

We see Smilla's struggle against this linguistic/cultural hegemony when she says about the Greenlandic language, "I have tried to learn it again" (105). The narrative itself constantly harks back to this refusal to give up one's mother tongue and it brings up Greenlandic terms and words in opposition to the Danish/European linguistic hegemony. A case in point is Smilla's use of the North Greenlandic word *sinik* as measure of distances:

Sinik is not a distance, not a number of days or hours. It is both a spatial and temporal phenomenon, a concept of space-time, it describes the union of space and motion and time that is taken for granted by the Inuit but cannot be captured by any European everyday language [278].

Through language Smilla brings out submerged histories, linguistic experiences erased by colonial violence. Smilla harks back to this in her memories of her mother, the hunter in the Arctic. Life with her mother was one of being at one with nature and it was often at odds with the world of her father, the famed doctor from Denmark. The colonial philosophy of life which her father brings into the Arctic is alien to the ways of life that Smilla's mother and her clan have practiced for generations. For instance, "compassion is not a virtue in the Arctic. Rather it is a kind of insensitivity" (30). Appropriation by her father and the Danish colonial culture meant a deep alienation from this life of nature: "some part of it was no longer accessible to me in the obvious way that it had been before" (31). Remembering the language, fighting back against this cultural amnesia, harking back to the words of her mother— "Smilla ... I have carried you in *amaat*" (30)—can be read as attempts to recapture the pre-acculturation life of native purity. Smilla's taking up Isaiah's cause is, in one sense, part of this struggle to assert the underdog's refusal to kowtow, to challenge the colonial assertion of authority over native culture. It is only metaphorically fitting that the culmination of this struggle, and Smilla's triumph, comes on the glacial landscape of the Arctic, the landscape that the colonial authority has failed to master.

Robert Young has shown that dispossession, landlessness and exile are typical of colonial violence: "These are all postcolonial struggles, typically dealing with the aftermath of one of the most banal and fundamentally important features of colonial power: the appropriation of land."[14] One of the outcomes of this is the flocking of these dispossessed to the slums of metropolitan cities, centers of colonial power. In *Smilla*, the "White Cells" stands for the dispossession that the Greenlanders have had to go through: The "White Cells" where Smilla, and Isaiah and his mother Juliane, live are "a number of prefabricated boxes of white concrete" (5). For a Greenlander, this is a forced movement from the vastness of Greenland: "vast open landscape. The horizons. You head towards them and they keep receding. That is Greenland" (102). This movement from open landscapes to the closed, sordid interiors of constricted urban houses is both confusing and traumatic, which we note in both Isaiah and Juliane. Isaiah's silence and Juliane's alcoholism are fueled by this. As Smilla notes, "The Greenlandic hell is the locked room" (90). The claustrophobia of living in a crowded metropolis is acknowledged metaphorically often in the narrative: for instance, "no one who has lived side by side with animals which have plenty of room can ever visit a zoo" (41). In another instance, a visit to the Copenhagen county morgue to see Isaiah's dead body reminds Smilla of a Danish boarding school: "I regularly work at suppressing the memory of them" (14). These memories also bring back memories of vast open spaces of Thule that she had lost. It is in this context that Smilla's comments about Newton's bucket experiment is interesting. Smilla is enamored by Newton's idea of Absolute Space, "that which stands still, that which we can cling to" (38). Greenland and its vast icy landscapes that she had roamed with her mother is undoubtedly Smilla's Absolute Space. Smilla clings to her memories of the sweeping landscape of Greenland and it acts as an affirmation of her identity: "I have lost my cultural identity for good, I usually tell myself. And after I've said this enough times, I wake up one morning, like today, with a solid sense of identity. Smilla Jaspersen—Greenlander *de luxe*" (120). Smilla's search for truth is punctuated by such moments where she is assertive about her Greenlandic identity.

The narrative presents the marginal life of the colonial Other—the Greenlander—through the story of Juliane. In the colonizer's city, her life is reduced to a series of official documents. As Smilla notes, "For many Greenlanders, the most difficult thing about Denmark is the paperwork.... There is a certain elegant and delicate irony in the fact that even a practically illiterate life like Juliane's has sloughed off this mountain of paper" (21). Added to that is the fact that Juliane has learnt to submissively subject herself to state surveillance: "she has been on social security and under the electron microscope of the authorities for so long that she has stopped imagining that anything can be kept private" (20). I argue, adapting Yael Berda, that this "security meta-framing" regulates the Greenlander in the colonial metropolis and regulates the process of making the Greenlander into a "citizen":

> Histories of surveillance of movement in North America and Europe have shown that these practices are fundamentally tied to the making of citizenship .... However, in postcolonies, these technologies were perpetuated to control displacement and exclusion of those classified as refugees, intruders, illegal aliens, and migrant workers. The legacies of colonial systems that managed civil populations, contributed to the current global mobility regime organized around a trinity of security threats: immigration, crime, and terror.[15]

In this sense, the "white cells" are both a refuge and an internment camp. Juliane is provided for by the state, in return for her subjecting herself to a constant surveillance that produces her as a citizen and the colonial Other simultaneously. While the "papers" bestow on her legitimacy as a citizen, they also produce, classify, and affirm her identity as a migrant Other. It is interesting to make note of the lists of papers that Smilla discovers in Juliane's home, for they sketch a history of her negotiations with the colonial state: "little appointment slips from the alcoholism clinic ... her birth certificate, fifty coupons from the bakery ... (when they add up to 500 kroner you get a free pastry). An appointment card from the Rudolph Bergh VD clinic, old tax deduction cards" (21). This list clearly marks Juliane's position in the imperial metropolis as one of dependence, and one of constant surveillance as she is forever portrayed as prone to alcoholism and a possible transmitter of VD. As Arneil has pointed out, colonialism's concern with the idle and irrational foreigner and citizen can be "traced back to chapter five of the Second Treatise of John Locke's *Two Treatises* when he famously argues that God gave the world to the 'industrious and rational.'"[16] The colonial state that reveals itself in Juliane's documents of her negotiations with it fits the description of the kind of colonial government recommended by J.S. Mill for the colonized Other:

> What they require is not a government of force, but one of guidance. Being, however, in too low a state to yield to the guidance of any but those to whom they look up as the possessors of force, the sort of government fittest for them is one which possesses force, but seldom uses it: *a parental despotism or aristocracy.*[17]

This unequal negotiation with the imperial city and the migrant Other has turned Juliane into a retreatist, apathetic to both her life and her relationship with her son. She mourns her son, without really comprehending what has happened to him. She has in fact lost both her husband and her son to colonial greed. We see her clinging on to these bits of papers—"the nappies were the only thing I threw out" (21)—while slowly wasting away in the unfamiliar surroundings of Copenhagen. As the narrative notes, she is communicative only when drunk.

The fact that Smilla herself was under constant surveillance comes through later in the narrative. Everything she has ever done is recorded and filed away, for further reference, for predicting patterns of behavior. The investigative detective Ravn opens his dark green file and gives her a glimpse of her past. It is revealed to Smilla they have been recording her life, and that this knowledge will be used in defining/deciding her citizenship. As she has been told, "We have sniffed around a bit. The information is absolutely correct. On this basis, I think we have to assume that we are dealing with a very independent young woman who has unusual resources which she has administered with ambition and talent" (88). The file has recorded every move that she has made, from her birth to her arrival in Denmark to her various attempts to run away from school and the clutches of the city. The marginal life of the colonial Other is surveiled, recorded and administered and legislated upon by the colonial authority. The knowledge on the subject thus produced is used to understand and classify the other (independent, ambitious and talented, and thus a threat). Smilla's rebellion against this structure of surveillance is manifest in her distaste for the small black telephones in the *Kronos*:

> I don't like being watched. I hate punch cards and clocking on and off. I am allergic to cross-referenced lists. I loathe passport controls and birth certificates, obligatory

school attendance, mandatory disclosure of information, alimony, legal liability, oaths of confidentiality—the whole rotten monstrosity of government controls and demands that fall on your head when you come to Denmark. All the things that I normally I sweep out of my mind but which may still confront me at any moment, perhaps manifested in a little black telephone [274].

In sharp contrast is the life of Smilla's nomadic hunter mother, who, living in Thule and the vast expanses of Greenland, remains perpetually outside the grasp of the colonial authority. After they meet and fall in love in Greenland, Smilla's father unsuccessfully tries to get the mother to move with him to the "base." She refuses: "As for anyone born in North Greenland, the suggestion of being cooped up was intolerable for my mother" (31). Instead, he is made to move with her to the barracks and live with her. Here the tables are turned. Here the colonizing Dane is trapped in the world of the colonized: "present without being able to take any real part, dangerous as a polar bear, imprisoned in a land which he hated by a love which he did not understand and which held him captive, over which he seemed to have not even the slightest influence" (31). The marriage ends when he leaves in a livid, profane rage, in a final rejection of the wild Thule life that flourishes outside the purview of the colonial authority. Smilla's mother is now replaced in his life by Benja, a docile and rather ornamental young wife. She is a sharp contrast to the fierce independence that Smilla's mother represents.

It would be tenable to argue that Smilla's journey into the unknown, to find the truth about Isaiah's murder, is in essence a journey from the crippling surveillance of Copenhagen to the vast, uncharted and free expanses of Greenland. The novel is divided into six parts—the first three parts take place in the city, the next two take place on the sea, while the final section unravels on the icy glaciers of Greenland. It is interesting to read the city and sea sections of the novel as almost Kafkaesque. Here I go with the definition of "Kafkaesque" as formulated by Frederick Karl:

Kafka has lent his name to an entire range of meanings that help interpret the appalling history of later twentieth century.... For Kafkaesque at its most meaningful and exalted denotes a world that has its own set of rules, its own guidelines, its own form of behaviour that cannot be amenable to the human will. Kafkaesque, in fact, seems to denote a will of its own, and it is, apparently, destructive of human endeavours. Clearly, it runs counter to human directions or goals or aims, and it serves as a form of bedevilment.[18]

The city is ruled by a gigantic bureaucratic mesh that filters everything. It is an enormously well-ordered machinery that constantly frustrates Smilla's efforts to seek answers. Smilla's search for answers, and meanings, constantly come up against a stalling, threatening colonial authority. It is almost reminiscent of the opening lines of *The Trial* ("Someone must have been telling lies about Joseph K."): Someone must be telling lies about Isaiah and what befell him. It is this bureaucracy that has irretrievably buried the Greenlander, the colonial Other, in heaps of paperwork. Smilla struggles to glean the lives of Isaiah and his mother from the mesh of paperwork that has defined and interpellated their lives into the colonial machinery: "The state bureaucracy's front line of paper: application forms, documents, and official correspondence with proper public authorities" (21). Looming over all these is the elusive specter of the Cryolite Corporation, and an interesting episode is Smilla's foray into the archives of the Corporation, which reads like a colonial subject's despairing search for meaning in the colonial archive.

Isaiah's father has died two years earlier in one of the expeditions into Greenland conducted by the Cryolite Corporation, Juliane gets a widow's pension from the Corporation, and Smilla is determined to find the truth about the expedition and is hoping to find answers in the archives. As she sneaks into the building, Smilla wonders, "Is this a Portrait of Denmark's relationship with its former colony? Disillusionment, resignation, and retreat? While retaining the last administrative grip: control over foreign policy, mineral rights, and military interests?" (72). The archive itself and its cavernous shelves are portrayed as mercilessly ordered, "a piece of history. About the politically and economically most profitable investments in Greenland." Many postcolonial critics have pondered over the politics of the colonial archival intent. As Bhekizizwe Peterson notes, in the context of South Africa, "colonial and apartheid authorities consistently denied the existence of any legacy among Africans worth preserving, an attitude borne out in their insistence that Africans had no history. Alternatively, where robust forms of local knowledge could not be ignored or denied, colonial authorities sought to reshape and appropriate such 'archives' into the service of colonialism."[19] In front of Smilla's prying eyes, the archive refuses to give away any secrets at first. As if echoing Peterson, she finds the archive itself, "quite simply the crystallisation of the wish to put the past in order. So that busy, energetic young people can come waltzing in, select a specific case ... and waltz out again with precisely that segment of the past" (74–75). It seems the archive is designed to obfuscate, to mislead, to whitewash a crime: "The whole thing looks clean and above board. It's tragic, and yet no more than an accident. Nothing to explain why a little boy, two years later, falls off a rooftop in Copenhagen" (75).

Smilla's journey to find the truth about Isaiah's murder is a movement from this slippery elusiveness of the colonial bureaucracy and cavernous archives to the vast expanses of Greenland where she is able to put her feet firmly down on the hardened ice. The last section of the novel, "The Ice," begins, unlike the earlier sections, with an assured Smilla, without any trace of the diffidence or self-doubts that haunt the character in the previous sections: "The *Kronos* is on its way into the ice. I can see it in the distance, veiled by ten millimetres of safety glass fogged up by the salt crystallized on the outside. That does not make any difference. I feel it as if I were standing on it" (363). Smilla is back in the familiar territory. It is her native knowledge— of snow, ice, melting glaciers and the frozen sea—that is her weapon against the colonial obfuscator. This is where the colonial imaginative geography finds its match in the native's experiential landscape. Peterson has talked about the material realities of the colonial subject's life that often escape the colonial archive, "stored in the stubborn memories of people, in suitcases and plastic bags under beds, in wardrobes and in ceilings."[20] He calls it an "experiential archive." I read an experiential archive in Smilla's instinctive understanding of the Greenlandic space: "Yet they still want to conquer the ice. They want to sail through it and build oil drilling platforms on it.... It's a waste of time calculating impossibilities. You can try to live with the ice. You can't fight it or change it or live instead of it" (365). It is no coincidence that Smilla's final victory over the killers of Isaiah comes on the barren landscape of snow and ice, and it is Smilla's knowledge of ice that wins in a battle against the colonial greed for power. It is her certainty about the minutiae of the landscape's character that determines the fate of the aggressor:

> Tonight the temperature will drop even more, and there will be a snowstorm. He will only live a couple of hours. At some point he will stop, and the cold will transform him; like a stalactite, a frozen shell will close around a barely fluid life until even his pulse stops and he becomes one with the landscape. You can't win against the ice [410].

This is a stunning reversal for the colonial imaginative geography of the subject territory—trapped in its own discourse, defeated by the subject's experiential landscape and refusal to forget or forgive.

While this marks both Smilla's triumph over Isaiah's killers and her statement on those who try to exploit the arctic landscape for commercial greed, it is not an isolated victory for the native in the narrative. The narrative does throw up various episodes where the native instinct and the "experiential archive" of the native life continuously challenge and subvert the colonial authority. For instance, Smilla remembers how her mother used to give away stuffed falcons she had hunted to European visitors and ethnographers with an apparent display of generosity, and later would get nylon ropes, scissors, clothes and such in return. "She got whatever she asked for. By wrapping her guest in a web of fierce, mutually obliging kindness" (67). Here is an interesting reversal of roles: the colonized here is no more an innocent, irrational simpleton. Her courtesy to the colonizer was "full of pallid premeditation":

> That is why Thule will never become a museum. The ethnographers have cast a dream of innocence over North Greenland. A Dream that the Inuit will continue to be the bowlegged, drum-dancing, legend-telling, widely smiling exhibition images

that the first explorers thought they were meeting south of Qaanaaq at the turn of the century. My mother gave them a dead bird. And made them buy half the store for her. She paddled a kayak that was made in the same way they were made in the seventeenth century, before the art of kayak building disappeared from North Greenland. But she used a sealed plastic container for her hunting float [68].

Smilla shares this legacy of native ingenuity that *used* the colonial encounters in several ways to their own advantage.

In the case of Smilla's mother, the native has, unbeknownst to the colonial authority, absorbed and transformed the colonial apparatus. Smilla reads the same potential in Isaiah's life in Denmark: "He would have been able to absorb Denmark and transform it and become both" (68). His death at the hands of colonial greed can be read as a failure to realize that potential. Smilla's quest and final revenge, then, involve fulfilling a promise. I argue that the final icy judgment in the quote above ("You can't win against the ice") is a retrieval of native knowledge, assertion of an understanding of space that negates all attempts to reshape it or represent it in a colonial discourse.

We may conclude our discussion by going back to the idea with which we set off our discussion, of the text as an intersectional space where competing narratives of hegemony collide. In this context, it would be interesting to read *Smilla* as anti-colonial writing. It uses, and then inverts, the stereotypes celebrated in colonial writings on colonies. It appropriates the master narrative of the subject as ignorant, barbaric and unwelcome, and then turns it around to empower the subject to retaliate. The subject now traps her/his master in a landscape he neither can understands nor survive.

NOTES

1. Peter Høeg, *Miss Smilla's Feeling for Snow* (London: Vintage, 2012), 1.
2. Charles J. Rzepka, *Detective Fiction* (Cambridge: Polity, 2005), 10.
3. John T. Irwin, *The Mystery to a Solution: Poe, Borges, and the Analytic Detective Story* (Baltimore: Johns Hopkins University Press, 1996), 1.
4. Hans Henrik Møller, "Peter Høeg or the Sense of Writing," *Scandinavian Studies* 69 (Winter 1997): 40.
5. *Ibid.*
6. Ashley Dawson, "Edward Said's Imaginative Geographies and the Struggle for Climate Justice," *College Literature* 40 (2013): 35.
7. Edward W. Said, "Orientalism," *The Georgia Review* 31 (Spring 1977): 167.
8. Robert Petersen, "Colonialism as Seen from a Former Colonized Area," *Arctic Anthropology* 32 (1995): 118–26.
9. Christian Egander Skov, "Radical Conservatism and Danish Imperialism: The Empire Built 'Anew from Scratch,'" *Contributions to the History of Concepts* 8 (Summer 2013): 75.
10. "Colonialism as Seen from a Former Colonized Area," 119.
11. *Ibid.*
12. Barbara Arneil, "Liberal Colonialism, Domestic Colonies and Citizenship," *History of Political Thought* 33.3 (2012): 500.
13. Charles W. Hobart, "The Influence of the School on Acculturation with Special Reference to Greenland," *The Journal of Educational Thought* 2.2 (1968): 98.

14. Robert J.C. Young, *Postcolonialism: A Very Short Introduction* (Oxford: Oxford University Press, 2003), 50.
15. Yael Berda."Managing Dangerous Populations: Colonial Legacies of Security and Surveillance," *Sociological Forum* 28 (September 2013), 627.
16. Arneil, "Liberal Colonialism, Domestic Colonies and Citizenship," 496.
17. *Ibid.*, 503.
18. David John Farmer, *The Language of Public Administration: Bureaucracy, Modernity, and Postmodernity* (Alabama: University of Alabama Press, 1995), 251.
19. Bhekizizwe Peterson, "The Archives and the Political Imaginary," Refiguring the Archive (Springer, 2002), 29.
20. "The Archives and the Political Imaginary," 32.

BIBLIOGRAPHY
Arneil, Barbara. "Liberal Colonialism, Domestic Colonies and Citizenship." *History of Political Thought* 33.3 (2012): 491–523.
Berda, Yael. "Managing Dangerous Populations: Colonial Legacies of Security and Surveillance." *Sociological Forum* 28 (September 2013): 627–630.
Dawson, Ashley. "Edward Said's Imaginative Geographies and the Struggle for Climate Justice." *College Literature* 40 (2013): 33–51.
Farmer, David John. *The Language of Public Administration: Bureaucracy, Modernity, and Postmodernity.* Alabama: University of Alabama Press, 1995.
Hobart, Charles W. "The Influence of the School on Acculturation with Special Reference to Greenland." *The Journal of Educational Thought* 2.2 (1968): 97–116.
Høeg, Peter. *Miss Smilla's Feeling for Snow.* London: Vintage, 2012.
Irwin, John T. *The Mystery to a Solution: Poe, Borges, and the Analytic Detective Story.* Baltimore: Johns Hopkins University Press, 1996.
Møller, Hans Henrik. "Peter Høeg or the Sense of Writing." *Scandinavian Studies* 69 (Winter 1997): 29–51.
Petersen, Robert. "Colonialism as Seen from a Former Colonized Area." *Arctic Anthropology* 32 (1995): 118–126.
Peterson, Bhekizizwe. "The Archives and the Political Imaginary." In *Refiguring the Archive,* edited by Carolyn Hamilton et al., 20–37. New York: Springer, 2002.
Rzepka, Charles J. *Detective Fiction.* Cambridge: Polity, 2005.
Said, Edward W. "Orientalism." *The Georgia Review* 31 (Spring 1977): 162–206.
Skov, Christian Egander. "Radical Conservatism and Danish Imperialism: The Empire Built 'Anew from Scratch.'" *Contributions to the History of Concepts* 8 (Summer 2013): 67–88.
Young, Robert J.C. *Postcolonialism: A Very Short Introduction.* Oxford: Oxford University Press, 2003.

# "A new beginning for good people"

## National Identity and the New South Africa in Deon Meyer's Crime Fiction

### Colette Guldimann

In postapartheid South Africa crime thrillers have emerged as the new form of the political novel or politically engaged fiction. This is the controversial claim by well-known South African literary scholar, Leon de Kock.[1] His pronouncement was a crucial intervention into the academic debate about the sudden and rapid proliferation of crime fiction within South Africa after the transition to democracy in 1994. While crime fiction (and non-fiction) has emerged as the definitive genre of contemporary South African writing, it was far less common during apartheid.[2] The reasons for this have been widely discussed but are perhaps best articulated by South Africa's most celebrated and widely read crime writer, Deon Meyer. When questioned in an interview on National Public Radio in the United States in 2006 about the timing of his novels and whether a global audience can now identify with a white policeman as a hero, Meyer states:

> Absolutely. I think it would have been totally impossible to write a book about policemen, or former policemen, in the old South Africa under the apartheid regime. What Nelson Mandela and F.W. De Klerk did for me personally was they freed up police detective heroes and private eyes so that one can write about them. I don't [think] it is possible to have a protagonist in a police state as a hero.[3]

Meyer's observation about the impossibility of a police hero within a repressive state is borne out by the circumstances in other African countries. Despite its very different political circumstances, Morocco provides another example of this since crime fiction exploded onto the literary scene only after the end of the repressive political regime of King Hassan II, known as the Years of Lead. Between 1963 and 1997, Morocco produced only one police procedural. The Years of Lead were characterized by "violent police suppression" and human rights violations[4] and the police novel disappeared from Morocco and indeed the Arab world more broadly, because "it was impossible to depict a cop as a sympathetic character" and Arabic crime fiction developed a tradition of "privileging the rogue hero or outlaw during the period of police repression and brutality."[5] The mid–1990s in Morocco gave rise to long awaited political transformation and it was this period of heady optimism that gave rise to various new forms of cultural production including, most significantly, the birth of the Arabic police novel.[6]

Yet the possibility of genre fiction resulting in any kind of politically engaged writing was an initial blind spot in South African critics' responses to the emergence of this form of fiction. In a particularly influential 2010 essay, Michael Titlestad and Ashlee Polatinsky examined the *oeuvre* of South African writer, Mike Nicol, who made the transition from (what they read as) serious fiction to the popular crime genre and declared that this represented a withdrawal from historically engaged fiction in favor of a genre which reduces complex questions about historical truth to generic devices.[7] Using Roland Barthes' distinction between the "readerly" and "writerly" text, they claimed that while serious literary fiction "compels the reader into active engagement," making the reader an agent of historical meaning, crime fiction is "readerly" and "all that is required is passive consumption" as these texts "are always in the service of the status quo."[8] They conclude by suggesting that crime fiction represents "a dilution" of South African literature that is "more global" than individuated.[9] This essay will show that the two are not mutually exclusive and that the global crime fiction genre can be used to present narratives that work at multiple levels, simultaneously local and global.

A debate raged within South African literary publications with various critics defending crime fiction against Titlestad and Polatinsky's claims and arguing for it as a form that is not only able to, but is actually, perhaps, best suited to political and social commentary and critique. These critics, including Ranka Primorac (2011), Christopher Warnes (2012), Samantha Naidu and Elizabeth Le Roux (2014), Colette Guldimann (2014) and Leon de Kock (2016), were informed by global trends in crime fiction and the critical debates that emerged around postcolonial and transnational fiction in other parts of the world. As a result of this intervention, crime fiction has now been accepted as a "legitimate" form of postapartheid cultural expression and is slowly being incorporated into the academic canon, with several established South African journals devoting special issues to the subject.

While many critics now recognize South African crime fiction as a form that is intervening in social and political issues, there has been no examination of national identity and its reconfiguration after the political transition to democracy in 1994. This essay will map the shifting nature of national identity, in relation to the borders of the nation-state, on the one hand, and the globalization of crime on the other, by identifying three stages in the writing of Deon Meyer. Meyer, hailed as the King of South African crime fiction in the media, is undoubtedly the pioneer of postapartheid crime fiction. He has won an impressive array of international crime writing awards and his books have been translated into over 20 languages. In addition to his international stature there are several other reasons that make Meyer an interesting subject for this study. Meyer is a white Afrikaner who grew up with a politically conservative father who believed in apartheid.[10] He also writes in his mother-tongue, Afrikaans, despite his perfect command of the English language, as a way of contributing to the survival of this "small African language."[11] His crime writing career followed in the wake of South Africa's transition to democracy, a crucial factor in its emergence as stated earlier. Meyer published his first crime novel in Afrikaans, *Feniks*, in 1996, just two years after the country's first democratic elections, followed by *Orion* in 1998 and *Proteus* in 2000 (all in Afrikaans). The first English translation, of *Feniks*, appeared in 1999 as *Dead Before Dying*, followed by *Dead at Daybreak* (*Orion*) in 2000. This was published concurrently with Meyer's third Afrikaans title, *Proteus*. It is thus important to be aware that there was a brief period in Meyer's early career when he was addressing only Afrikaans speaking readers in South Africa. Currently English translations typically follow two years after the Afrikaans publication (in addition to translations into another 26 languages). Thus, while Meyer's initial novels engaged the South African context, he soon began to situate South Africa within global themes as translations created an international readership.

Meyer initially insisted that he wrote for sheer entertainment and shied away from political commentary about his novels, but as his international reputation developed, he became more candid about the relationship between his writing and the politics of the country. In an interview in 2011, which was available on Meyer's website at the time, he refers to postapartheid South Africa as a "work in progress," and expresses his sense of responsibility, as someone who comes from "the cultural group responsible for apartheid," to "make this place work."[12] In one of the earliest academic articles about Meyer, Ranka Primorac claimed that Meyer's thrillers present the "self-assigned" cultural work of appropriating "symbols from the past" and repositioning them.[13] Despite his initial insistence that he writes for sheer entertainment, I argue that Meyer is using crime fiction as a means of both representing the country and intervening in this "work in progress."

A crucial tool in thinking about Meyer's *oeuvre* is Leon de Kock's 2016 book, *Losing the Plot: Crime, Reality and Fiction in Postapartheid Writing*. De Kock is the first critic to provide a sustained reading of the emergence of crime writing (fiction and non-fiction) in relation to the social and political upheaval of the transition from apartheid to the newly democratic South Africa and to map crime writing as a response to this monumental event. In analyzing the "relatively sudden, and major, shift" in SA writing from "liberal-humanist and late-modern forms of fiction to genre-based" crime fiction, de Kock suggests that we should read this shift, not as capitulation to the seductions of the popular market but "as symptomatic of a bigger movement, of a seismic social shift."[14] *Losing the Plot* thus "proposes a way of looking at the field of South African [crime] writing in the 1990s, 2000s and the current decade that pivots around a continuingly problematised notion of transition."[15] The term "transition" as de Kock defines it, was "that putatively transformative shift from one 'state' to another in which an entire nation found a form of secular redemption from purgatorial political conditions" of the past.[16] De Kock describes how an initial wave of optimism, "evident in the early phase of upbeat transitional ferment," was followed by a "gradual and deepening sense of 'plot loss' among South African writers and intellectuals of all stripes."[17] The transition or "switch" to a "new dispensation" serves as a "founding marker" in the "collective consciousness" of the new South Africa.[18] De Kock argues that the concept of transition and its "uptake, problematisation and forensic-diagnostic investigation" serves as a pivot in postapartheid literary culture.[19]

The majority of academic work on Meyer's novels is engaged with his representation of white policemen or PIs and their own personal "transition" from the old apartheid police force to the new democratic South African Police Service and this is read as a metaphor for the greater national process of discarding the past and working towards reconciliation.[20] Yet while this is true of Meyer's earlier novels, there has been less critical attention to his later work and no sustained overview of shifting ideas about the nation-state within his *oeuvre* as a whole. I propose that Meyer stands as a prime example of De Kock's claim that postapartheid writing constitutes both an "investigation" into, and a "search" for, the "'true' locus of civil virtue in decidedly disconcerting social conditions."[21] There is no doubt that the personal transition Meyer's white male protagonists undergo provides models of new forms of white, and Afrikaner, masculinity in postapartheid South Africa, and that these narratives target a South African readership using the global framework of the hardboiled detective.[22] Yet the investigation into, and search for, the true locus of civil virtue take on increasingly complex forms in Meyer's later fiction. I will identify the shifts in this investigation in three of Meyer's novels, starting with the period when he was just emerging as an international writer due to publication of English translations, through to one of his most recent novels: *Heart of the Hunter* (2003), *Cobra* (2014), and *Fever* (2017). While critics have focused largely on Meyer's white detectives, I will demonstrate here how two of Meyer's black characters enact their own search for the true locus of civil virtue and, in doing so, become representative of what it means to a South African true to the country's democratic values on which the transition was founded. *Heart of the Hunter* presents a reconfiguration of South African identity following the transition to democracy. Published more than 10 years later, *Cobra* presents a clear case of plot loss through the main protagonist, Benny Griessel, yet this is countered by a renewed focus on civil virtue in a global context, while *Fever* presents the dystopian outcome of that search for civil virtue.

The three novels I have selected represent different stages in post-transition South Africa and I will show how Meyer, while using global crime fiction forms, is responding to conditions within South Africa. Meyer's work is very much in line with international crime novels of the late 20th century when, according to Eva Erdmann, "as the boom in crime fiction took off, the pursuit of the criminal was displaced by the search for cultural identity."[23] The distinguishing feature of this type of crime fiction was the "fact that the main focus is not on the crime itself, but on the setting, the place where the detective and the victim live," what she calls the *"locus criminalis."*[24] The criminological search for evidence is transposed to "epistemologies of cultural anthropology, ethnographic and national characteristics, and the structure of the genre is governed by the spectrum of cultural identities."[25] Erdmann might well be describing Deon Meyer's *Heart of the Hunter.*

# Heart of the Hunter *(2003)*

*Heart of the Hunter* was published in English in 2003, nine years after South Africa's transition to democracy, while the Afrikaans original was published in 2000. While several critics have identified that Meyer sets up a connection between the main protagonist, Thobela Mpayipheli, and the newly democratic South African nation in the novel, I argue that Meyer utilizes the crime genre in order to reconfigure South African identity within the context of the political transition. This early novel, Meyer's third, demonstrates the necessity of South Africa's coming to terms with its violent apartheid past and constitutes a new South African identity through the figure of Thobela, who was the first black protagonist in Meyer's *oeuvre*. For Naidu and Le Roux, Thobela represents "an ideal of democracy."[26] For Leon de Kock, Thobela "embodies the intricate complexity of postapartheid dispensation."[27] While all these critics allude to national identity, none develop the argument fully. I have argued that Meyer uses the "ambiguities and grey interzone" of the thriller sub-genre to displace the clear-cut black and white distinctions of the detective novel and replaces these with "multiple interpretations that encourage thinking beyond binary categories."[28] This is necessary in order to represent a character, who, like South Africa, is in a state of "transformation." The original Afrikaans title, *Proteus*, gives a clearer indication of the Protean shape-shifting metaphor Meyer is invoking.

The narrative of the novel takes the form of a road chase from Cape Town to Lusaka in which the protagonist, Thobela Mpayipheli, is pursued by the Presidential Intelligence Unit (PIU) and the media coverage of this chase. Through creating this focus of public attention Meyer succeeds in focusing on a critical question: "is Tiny Mpayipheli a bad guy or good guy, a hero or a villain? Is he virtuous or villainous within the redefined terms of the new dispensation."[29] At the start of the narrative, Thobela Mpayipheli is a 40-year-old family man, working as a gofer for a BMW motorcycle dealership and living with his common law wife and her son in the Cape Town township of Gugulethu. While set in postapartheid South Africa, the apartheid past quickly intrudes into the present. Thobela's past comrade in the anti-apartheid struggle, Johnny Kleintjies, has been kidnapped in Lusaka, Zambia, and Thobela feels honor-bound to deliver the ransom: a computer disc. Kleintjies was responsible for integrating the various intelligence units prior to democracy and the disc contains sensitive information about South Africa's past. The recently created Presidential Intelligence Unit is, however, also after the disc and they attempt to apprehend Thobela at the airport. Thobela evades capture and begins his road trip across South Africa on a motorbike, resulting in the aforementioned road chase. Through the media coverage and its attempt to uncover the true identity of Thobela, readers are presented with conflicting representations. Media reports shift back and forth between "good" and "bad" as Thobela's past is presented from various perspectives. Following information released by the PIU, and the fact that he is being pursued by the forces of law and order, journalist Alison Healy denounces Thobela as the "Big, bad Xhosa biker" in the press.[30] This negative image gives rise to a variety of responses and characterizations of Thobela that continue throughout the text. Responding to Healey's journalism, a member of the public, Immanuel, a shoeshine man, tells Healy that what she has written about Thobela are "not right," that he is in fact a "good man" and a "war veteran" (150–51). Readers learn that Thobela is a former soldier from *Umkhonto we Sizwe* (MK), the armed wing of the African National Congress formed to fight apartheid by violent means. As the road chase and media fanfare continue, so does the contradictory information about Thobela. Adding to this array of representations are narrative flashbacks to Thobela's past where readers learn he was no ordinary MK soldier but rather one hired out to the KGB as an assassin. In a series of double-crossings reminiscent of John le Carré,

Thobela's mission is never completed. It is revealed that the PIU has two moles in its highest ranks—the director and deputy-director—one an informant for the CIA, the other for *Al-Qaeda*. Kleintjies is found dead and the data on Kleintjies' disc is destroyed. While the overt mystery driving the narrative is the identity of a PIU spy, code-named *"Inkululeko,"* the real mystery of the text is bound up with uncovering the true identity of Thobela, as his physical journey becomes a metaphorical one, into the heart of the hunter.

Thus, while Meyer makes use of the "present tense" of the thriller action, as opposed to the backward looking whodunit, there is a parallel movement in his text where interpretations of the present are continually impacted upon by the narratives from the past. To date Meyer has only two novels which depart from the traditional crime formula of having an investigator, whether a police officer or PI, as the central character: *Heart of the Hunter* and *Fever*. They are also the only two novels where the crime is not obvious and the reader has to work out what it is, prompting a questioning of the very nature of crime. The thriller form, I have argued, is crucial to what Meyer achieves in *Heart of the Hunter*, and, in this regard, the work of Julian Symons, who has identified eight ways in which the crime thriller deviates from the traditional detective narrative, is useful.[31] These divergences lie in plot, detective, method, clues, characters, setting, puzzle value, and social attitude.[32] While the detective story takes the crime as the starting point and works backwards, the narrative of the crime thriller moves forwards and delves inwards, into the character's psychology, and asks, "What stresses would make A want to kill B?"[33] This relates closely to setting. While plot and clue requirements dominate the detective narrative, in the thriller, setting is an integral part of the crime itself, the *locus criminalis*. Meyer uses these two aspects of the crime thriller to interrogate and reconfigure South African identity in relation to both the past and the present.

If the protagonist can be defined as "good" and the forces at work as "wicked," then, according to Martin Priestman, we have the characteristics of the anti-conspiracy thriller.[34] There is no doubt in the reader's mind, by the end of the novel, that the PIU represents the bad guys as there are two informants within its ranks. Significantly, we are told that the unit is constituted because the vice-president wants a new intelligence service "without a past," an obvious reference to the transition and a fresh start, which turns out to be a complete failure as past allegiances still dictate how its members behave (51). The question about just how "good" Thobela is emerges through Healy's journalism "pitted against statements by the state," signaling a "fierce public-sphere contestation" about how to "read" Thobela and his actions: is he, as the government media suggest, a "Frankenstein of the struggle" or a "Robin Hood"?[35] This "media fanfare," de Kock suggests, represents a "test case" of who is more truthful and more "good," who can be trusted to further the "fragile, infant democracy."[36] In a discussion about how the government might manipulate the media, Janina Mentz, of the Presidential Intelligence Unit, tells the minister of intelligence that "the line between the hero and the villain is very narrow ... it depends on how the facts are interpreted" (190). It is precisely this ambiguity that Meyer launches in order to get his readers to question what it means to be a "good" citizen in a newly democratic, post-transition South Africa.

The process is not only a social one, played out within the media, but an introspective one that Thobela himself must undergo, as part of the psychology of the crime thriller. Crucial to this is Thobela's relationship with his Xhosa ancestors. While de Kock reads this as a "romantic" representation, I suggest that this can be read politically as it provides a context within which his past actions can be assessed.[37] Meyer inserts Thobela into a line of historical Xhosa figures—Phalo and Rharhabe, Nquika and Maqoma—who, I argue, are carefully selected to span a period pre-dating colonial conflict and extending into the period of the frontier wars between the Xhosa and the advancing British colony in the Eastern Cape.[38] The first of these, Phalo, was paramount chief of the Xhosa people from 1736 until his death in 1775. He is significant, historically, since he was the last king of an independent and united Xhosa nation. Thobela's bloodline thus reaches back to a period of pre-colonial domination in Southern Africa. The other historical figures, Rharhabe, Nquika and Maqoma, were all warriors engaged in the battle against colonial domination in the frontier wars that broke out between the Xhosa and British Cape colony three years after Phalo's death.[39] Thobela's connection with his warrior ancestors is reinforced from various perspectives. Orlando Arendse, the drug lord, says "[t]hree hundred years ago he would have been the one in front, charging the enemy" (218). Most significantly, however, the text attributes Thobela's motivation to join the armed struggle to his ancestors: "he longed to be one of Nxele's warriors who stood shoulder to shoulder, who broke the spear with a crack over his knee" (370). Thobela's motivation thus echoes one of South Africa's great figures in the struggle for liberation, Nelson Mandela. In his oft-quoted "I am prepared to die" statement from the dock at the Rivonia Trial in 1964, Mandela articulates how his political motivation came from listening to his elders' stories of the wars fought by his ancestors in defense of the country:

> In my youth in the Transkei I listened to the elders of my tribe telling stories of the old days ... those of wars fought by our ancestors in defence of the fatherland. The names of Dingane and Bambata, Hintsa and Makana, Squngthi and Dalasile, Moshoeshoe and Sekhukhuni, were praised as the glory of the entire African nation. I hoped then that life might offer me the opportunity to serve my people and make my own humble contribution to their freedom struggle. This is what has motivated me in all that I have done.[40]

Thobela's years as a fighter in MK are thus positioned within a longer historical context of the fight against colonialism, and his status as a "good man" and a "war veteran" as Immanuel, the shoeshine man, tells Alison Healy is confirmed (150–51). The "crime" here is thus attributed to colonialism and its heir, apartheid.

When Healy learns that Thobela has been an assassin and not an ordinary MK soldier, she reverts to the language of common crime: "How many people did he murder?" (272). The retort by Zatopek van Heerden, former policeman and Thobela's friend, sums up the novel's suggestion that concepts of good and bad are relative. Thobela, he says, "murdered no one. He fought a war" (272). It is the thriller's emphasis on setting that is used to contextualize Thobela's actions within South Africa's history. Yet Meyer is reconfiguring identity for a new post-transition South Africa, and it is Thobela's ancestral voices that guide him on his journey as he has to re-evaluate his past actions. When he learns that his common law wife, Miriam, has "gone missing" Thobela's past as an assassin comes back to haunt him. He wonders whether the "same words" were used "for the people he had killed": "One day his victims would return ... repayment for his cowardice, for the misuse of his heritage, for breaking the code of the warrior.... [His ancestors] drooped their heads in shame" (369). Thobela's interiorized reconsideration of his violent actions might be read as a reconfiguration of South African identity from a past in which violence was justified, within the context of the anti-apartheid struggle, to a democratic present where it must be renounced. Warnes, for example, has argued that Meyer's police thrillers provide a fictional "justification for a functioning criminal justice system and a society based on rule of law" and thus a move away from individual violence or retribution towards a resolution through the system.[41]

While I agree that there is an element of truth in the above, this argument would only hold true if Thobela continued to renounce violence and the novel ended with a redemptive message. Meyer is, however, attempting something more complicated in line with the project of configuring identity as South African. The end of the novel remains true to Protean shape-shifting: Thobela resorts, once again, to violence, including his former weapon of choice as an assassin: the assegai. This is carefully situated within the narrative as a necessary response to a new threat. In a final bloody confrontation, Thobela and van Heerden face two killers who are not identified, but careful reading suggests that they are from the CIA and are after the data on the disc and ultimately killed in the battle. This return to violence is one that is constituted in terms of the new South African nation, the "fragile democracy" that must be protected. Thobela and van Heerden, black and white, represent a new national team, united in protecting the South African nation by preventing information from falling into the hands of those who will abuse it.

Rather than eschewing violence, as some have suggested, Meyer shifts it away from the oppositional politics of the anti-apartheid struggle in order to reconstitute a new *national* identity. The disc, and the data it contains, is destroyed in a symbolic gesture, suggesting that is no "truth" about South Africa's past.

In a conversation between Thobela and Tiger Mazibuko, a member of the PIU, on the final pages of the novel, Thobela gives Tiger the following advice: "Ask yourself: how long ... before things change? A new administration, or a new system or a new era. They are using you, Mazibuko" (417). With this the text ultimately questions the "transition" as a "switch" that has been successfully implemented as a definitive break with the past and thus undermines the "teleological thrust implicit in the notion of a transition to democracy."[42]

## Cobra *(2014)*

*Heart of the Hunter* is clearly engaged in a search for the true locus of civil virtue and its focus, like Meyer's other early novels, is on the context of the South African transition. That investigation continues in a novel published 11 years later, where the search, although still South African, is framed within a global context. *Cobra* (2014) reflects the global trend in representing the deterritorialization and transnationalization of crime, themes Meyer first introduced in his 2011 novel *Trackers*.[43] *Cobra* utilizes *Heart of the Hunter's* structure of a kidnapping in exchange for sensitive data, but the boundaries have shifted in order to represent a revised version of what it means to be a true South African. This time the data comes from outside the borders of South Africa and the threat is from both within and without the country.

*Cobra* is part of Meyer's "Benny Griessel" series, police procedurals featuring white policeman, Griessel, as the main protagonist. Griessel, who appears in seven novels to date, is the epitome of the hardboiled cop: a recovering alcoholic, whose private life is in typical disarray. He is also one of Meyer's white characters who have managed to make the "transition" from apartheid to the new South African Police Service. Griessel's drinking and emotional issues are directly linked to his role as a cop "under apartheid":

> It didn't matter how hard he used to believe he was only fighting the good fight against crime, that he was on the side of the good guys, there was always the niggling little voice in the back of his head. You couldn't avoid the hatred in the others' eyes...[44]

Griessel's guilt demonstrates that the role of the police under apartheid was a largely political function, as opposed to a community service. Under apartheid only one in every 10 members of the police force was actually engaged in traditional investigation of crimes while the other nine were involved in policing the plethora of apartheid legislation.[45] Meyer's white detectives all struggle with this legacy.

The source of crime in this novel is transnational. David Adair, a British citizen and professor at Cambridge University, flees to South Africa, making use of Body Armour, a bodyguard and security service. The bodyguards, former policemen, are murdered, and Adair is kidnapped. As the investigation unfolds, readers learn that Adair has developed an algorithm, adopted by the United States and the European Union, in order to identify terrorists through international banking activities. We later learn that Adair privately loaded a new version of his algorithm and had gathered information about corrupt activities by members of the British government. Adair was planning to use this data to force governments into greater banking transparency, and it is this information that the kidnappers are after. Griessel and his team are attempting to track down both Adair and the data when, in a twist of the plot, they are removed from the case by the South African State Security Agency (the SSA). The police team discover that the SSA has been spying on their investigation because, it is suggested, the South African government wants this data in order to blackmail the British government. At this point Griessel experiences a sense of impotence and despair that is common to hardboiled detectives:

> He had become irrelevant in a vocation that demanded deeper thought and insight and intelligence. In a country and a world that was changing far faster than he could adapt to it. What was *wrong* with him? [Chapter 32].

This disorientation is similar to experiences articulated by Kurt Wallender, Henning Mankell's hardboiled police detective in *The White Lioness*:

> Where do I go from here? He said to himself. I don't want to get involved in a kind of violence that will be incomprehensible to me as long as I live. Maybe the next generation of policemen in this country will have a different kind of experience and have a different view of their work. But it's too late for me.[46]

While both novels investigate contract killings, what differentiates Griessel and Wallender, however, is the South African context of transition: Wallender sees the incomprehensible violence as something new, something he is not equipped to deal with, a rupture from a less violent past. For Griessel, on the other hand, it is the return of the past, and "it felt like it was back to the bad old days [of apartheid] again"; and just as in those old days "he was increasingly reluctant to tell people he was a policeman" (Chapter 32). Here Griessel embodies the sense of "plot loss" described by de Kock, where the "forward march" of transition has been derailed, leaving "indeterminacy" in its place.[47]

Yet while Griessel is the main protagonist, *Cobra* presents an alternative to this sense of "plot loss" through another character: Captain Mbali Kaleni, "the only woman in the Violent Crimes Team" (Chapter 23). Kaleni is frequently described by her ethnic origin, as Zulu, and, through her presence in three novels, has become renowned as a police officer who could "recite every article in the Criminal Procedures Act" and "always acted strictly according to these regulations" (Chapter 23). At the point when Griessel's team receive the order to stop the investigation into recovering the data (and locating Adair) it is Kaleni, with ambitions of becoming the National Police Commissioner, who stands up to Police authority. Accused of insubordination and questioned about "what the hell has got into [her]," she replies with an impassioned speech:

> My father used to tell me stories of how he did not dare use his phone, because the security police were always listening. He was part of the struggle, Colonel. Back when the secret services conducted all the important criminal cases, when they told the police what to do. When everybody was spying on each other. And everything was hushed up by the media.... Today it is happening again. Now parliament is passing this Security Bill. Why? Because they want to hide things. Now this. State security eavesdropping on us, and taking over a criminal case. Just like in apartheid times. We are destroying our democracy, and I will not stand by and let it happen.... I owe it to my parents' struggle and I owe it to my country. You and the brigadier too. You owe it to the comrades who gave their lives for the cause [Chapter 30].

Here Kaleni aligns being a true police officer not with obedience to authority but with fidelity to the founding principles of the anti-apartheid struggle, which gave birth to democracy in South Africa; a democracy that is now being undermined by the actions of the post-transition government. In contrast with Griessel's confusion about his position in the new country, Kaleni has recourse to a set of foundational principles embodied in her direct family history. This is similar to the way Thobela measures his actions against a set of historical antecedents but with rather different outcomes. While *Heart of the Hunter* is concerned with blurring the boundaries between good and evil, particularly in relation to South Africa's past, *Cobra* redraws a distinct divide, necessary for the country's present and future. Here Kaleni, the good cop, must stand against evil within the government and, with this, Kaleni is positioned as the touchstone of a loyal police officer, and true South African citizen, standing up to national corruption. In her outspoken resistance against the forces of law and order in favor of the spirit of what it means to be a true South African, Kaleni is reminiscent of the historical figure of Steve Biko who, under apartheid, formulated Black Consciousness which redefined a true Black South African as someone who resisted apartheid and its laws.

Inspired by Kaleni's speech the team continue the investigation, unofficially, and eventually, at the end of the novel, the incriminating data ends up in Kaleni's safekeeping. She does not hand it over to any of the possible authorities, including the police, for fear that it will end up in the hands of those who can abuse it. One character in the novel states that with "great power comes great responsibility" and that the South African government cannot be trusted with the great power that would result from having the data (Chapter 31). When asked what she intends to do with the disc, Kaleni replies:

> "I'll keep it as a safeguard."
> "Against what?"
> "Against people who want to harm our democracy, and spirit of my father's struggle."
> Nyathi just nodded. He couldn't think of a better guardian for it [Chapter 60].

The novel does not take this any further but ends with the character representing the "'true' locus of civil virtue" in South Africa standing against the corruption of the present.

Discussing the internationalization of crime fiction Andrew Pepper and David Schmid warn against celebratory accounts and exoticization of the genre and argue that if crime fiction is the "new world literature par excellence" it must use the genre's capacities to "reflect, in critical and imaginative ways, on the processes of globalization in general, or on the growing transnationalization of crime and policing networks in the contemporary era."[48] Since Adair was planning to use the data to force the U.S. and EU into adopting greater banking transparency, Kaleni is thus aligned with a greater transnational project, using the idea of national identity against corrupt government actions that take place as a result of globalization. At this point Meyer's *oeuvre* thus still presents an alternative to the "plot loss" experienced by character like Griessel.

## Fever *(2017)*

Published in Afrikaans (*Koors*) in 2016 and in English in 2017, *Fever* is Meyer's greatest departure from conventional forms of crime fiction. *Fever* presents a post-apocalyptic dystopian future in which 95 percent of the world's human population has been eradicated by a virus manufactured for this purpose, though this is only revealed at the end of the novel. Although there is a murder, the crime is not apparent and, by the end, the reader is left wondering what the actual crime is. The narrator and protagonist is Nico Storm, who, along with his father, Willem Storm, survived the fever as a teenager. He is reflecting from the future, when he is 47 years old—while the novel's central narrative ends when he is nineteen—looking back into the period following the fever's devastation. The novel is located within a recognizable current-day South Africa, and specific and accurate geographical details are included. In fact, the opening pages contain a map of present-day South Africa and its national borders. What is noticeable, in this regard, is that no character is identified by racial group or characteristics. The discerning reader, especially in South Africa, can easily decode characters' races from names and details about their past, yet this is an interesting departure from Meyer's previous novels where racial categories are identified, often to present differences that are ultimately overcome. In a South Africa where the majority of existing signs of civilization have been destroyed, Nico's father, Willem, founds a new society. While obviously engaging with global narratives of environmental disaster, I propose that *Fever* is also a continuation of Meyer's investigation into national identity and the search for that true locus of civil virtue in *another* new South Africa. De Kock has pointed out how much of the new postapartheid writing consists of narratives and counternarratives that set up a "dialectic around the very notion of a fresh start," which is the fashion in which the transition to the new postapartheid South Africa was positioned.[49]

Following de Kock's claim I argue that *Fever* should be read as Meyer's exploration of South Africa's "fresh start," which would explain why race is absent from characters' descriptions since a major shift of the transition was discarding the racial nomenclature of apartheid. In a similar vein, Willem is cautious about avoiding linguistic connotations of the pre-apocalyptic order. While in terms of the novel's setting within the future, the past would be the present-day "new" South Africa, Willem's discussion sounds reminiscent of the language of the "transition." He struggles to find the appropriate language to describe the new society he wants to found; he claims that he does not "know what to call it yet" since "'[s]ettlement' and 'colony' are such loaded words in this country. Former country…"[50] This sounds strikingly like a description of the postapartheid transition. Resembling the project in Meyer's other novels, of separating the "good" from the "bad," Willem's goal is to find "good people of every sort" (Chapter 13). His project is built on his understanding of Western civilization dating back to the ancient Greeks:

> Hennie read aloud: "A New Beginning for Good People," with a heavy Afrikaans accent.
> "Yes, it's in English," Pa said. "We want to reach everyone."
> "We are starting a sanctuary, a community that will have justice, wisdom, moderation and courage…"
> "It's from Plato," said Pa. "From *The Republic*" [Chapter 15].

Willem's only concept of civilization, society and time is based on ancient Greek thought. He perceives the failure of the previous South Africa within a teleological narrative of progress, and this is what he attempts to reinstate with his new community: "he started to elaborate passionately on the Greeks and their civilization, culminating with a sigh of deep regret: 'We were capable of so much, and so much, we lost'" (Chapter 11).

My argument for reading this new society as an allegory for South Africa is strengthened by Meyer's choice of location for "a new beginning": Vanderkloof (Chapter 7). Vanderkloof is the Afrikaans name of an existing town in the *Northern Cape* province of *South Africa* located on the *Orange River* and South Africa's second largest dam, *Vanderkloof Dam*. One of two hydro power stations in South Africa is powered by generators from the dam. These strategic elements are cited by Willem as the rationale behind Vanderkloof as the best place in South Africa for a new beginning. This is once again located within discourses of Western civilization: Vanderkloof is uniquely suited to "Maslow's hierarchy of security": a "natural fort, thanks to the hills with their cliffs, and the dam" (Chapter 9). It is interesting to notice that Willem thinks about the borders of his new community in terms of the traditional nation-state: a means to deflect an "enemy," defined as a threat from beyond the borders. As there is "only one easily navigable road in" there is "only one flank to defend, unless the enemy arrived with a fleet of ships, which is most unlikely on the Orange River" (Chapter 9).

While Vanderkloof—later renamed Amanzi from the Xhosa and Zulu word for water—is chosen for its strategic location, we are also given interesting information about its political past. Willem relates that while visiting the town in the pre-apocalyptic South Africa, he learned that "most of Vanderkloof's inhabitants shared the Orania ideology of whites only, or Afrikaner only, or whatever it was they hoped to achieve" (Chapter 32). Orania is a whites-only, Afrikaans-speaking town, also located along the *Orange River* in the *Northern Cape* Province. The town was founded by Carel Boshoff, Sr., as a registered company shortly before white-minority rule ended in South Africa. Boshoff Sr. was an Afrikaner intellectual and son-in-law of one of the architects of apartheid, Hendrik Verwoerd, and the town is currently run by his son, Carel Boshoff, Jr.[51] Residents claim that the aim of the town is to create a stronghold for *Afrikaans* and the *Afrikaner* identity by keeping their language and culture alive. Critics accuse the town authorities of rejecting the transition to the new South Africa and trying to recreate apartheid South Africa. It might be more productive to think of Orania not so much as going backwards but as resisting the teleological narrative of transition. Residents cite a cultural argument of wishing to preserve their linguistic and cultural heritage—not unlike the so-called theoretical underpinnings of the apartheid ideology of "separate development"—and their desire to protect themselves from the high levels of crime outside Orania, that is, within South Africa. The cultural argument is rendered rather disingenuous since speaking Afrikaans, as many black South Africans do, is not the main criteria for joining Orania: it requires being defined an ethnic, and thus white, Afrikaner. Black South Africans are not permitted to live in Orania.[52] Ironically, Orania residents claim the right to self-determination provided by the *Constitution of the new postapartheid South Africa*.[53]

The only difference between Vanderkloof and Orania, readers learn, was that the Vanderkloof inhabitants wanted to avoid the "racist stigma" of Orania, so "this town," which provides the site of Willem's new beginning, was a "sort of clandestine Orania, where the more cowardly separatists lived" (Chapter 32). Thus, although Orania attempts to defy the transition into postapartheid South Africa, the town of Vanderkloof, while making no such public statement, covertly adhered to the pre-transition ideology of apartheid. It is on the site of this ambiguous history that Willem chooses to found his new community, chosen for its strategic geographical features, as though the physical features of a landscape can erase the past. This history of Vanderkloof, I argue, stands for the attempt to build the new South Africa on the foundations of the apartheid past.

Willem's new community thrives initially, and it is, significantly, when the "first democratic election of leaders" takes place that Willem decides that the Afrikaans name Vanderkloof is "in no way suitable" (Chapter 23). It is renamed Amanzi, the Zulu and Xhosa word for water. The name is suggested by "Granny Nandi Mahlangu" and adopted with a round of instantaneous applause (Chapter 23). Here is another echo of South Africa's past and the transition since Meyer's text uses the discourse that is commonly adopted to differentiate the "first democratic election" in 1994 from the previous elections with an exclusively white electorate. The question then, is what happens to this new community and what does it suggest about Meyer's shifting investigation of the new South Africa? Amanzi's reputation attracts people and groups from the former South Africa and from beyond its now defunct borders. Technology is reconstructed as people with various expertise arrive and contribute towards the development of Amanzi.

Willem's understanding of nationality as a fiction is introduced through yet another Western source: the work of historian, Yuval Noah Harari, from his widely read book *Sapiens: A Brief History of Humankind* (2014):

> Pa said we are the only organism whose behaviour can change dramatically because we create fiction. Fiction that is so great and powerful that it bound people in larger and larger groups, to accomplish greater and greater things. Yuval Noah Harari described these as imagined realities, social constructs and myths. These stories of ours, these social constructs, were ideas like nationalism among people of different tongues or cultures, or religions, or political ideologies [Chapter 70].

Harari's idea that *homo sapiens'* domination of earth is due to their ability to cooperate is clearly referenced in *Fever*: "this human ability to create a social construct, an imagined reality of myth, and believe in it, led directly to our ability to cooperate in our thousands and later in millions" (Chapter 70). The question then becomes: can Amanzi find a national fiction that unifies this new community comprised of different tongues, cultures, religions and political ideologies, a group resembling the South African nation in 1994 which was constructed as united, despite the fractures and divisions of apartheid and colonialism?

The model presented, and widely celebrated at the time, was Nobel Peace Laureate and former Anglican Archbishop Desmond Tutu's metaphor of the "Rainbow Nation" or the "Rainbow People of God." The image and promise of the rainbow nation gained currency in popular discourse and rapidly developed into the "popular mythology" of a multicultural South Africa.[54] It was widely propagated by Nelson Mandela in his capacity as first President of the new South Africa. Describing how myth can change human behavior Willem cites Harari's version of the French Revolution in *Sapiens* as a perfect example of how a unifying myth can change human behavior "overnight": "in 1789 a large number of French rejected the myth of the divine right of kings to rule, and adopted the myth of the sovereignty of the people" (Chapter 70). While Willem cites this, from Harari, as a successful transition due to collective myth, South Africa's transition, overnight, was less so.[55] While the image and discourse of the Rainbow Nation took hold in an initial wave of optimism that characterized the "transitional ferment," this was followed by a gradual and deepening sense of "'plot loss' among South African writers and intellectuals of all stripes."[56]

The "new beginning" in Amanzi ultimately fails to find a unifying myth, and the group fractures along old fault lines. There is a lengthy standoff between Willem and the military leader of Amanzi, Domingo, both atheists, whose ideas are rooted in ancient Greek thought, on the one side, and Pastor Nkosi Sebego, who wants to establish a religious state founded on Christianity with "God as our President," on the other (Chapter 86). Just prior to the split, Willem makes an impassioned plea to the community to embrace his ideas about equality and freedom. This, once again, uses the language of South Africa's transition and the political ideal of equality. Willem claims that the fever which wreaked devastation everywhere had one positive outcome in South Africa: "It made us all truly equal" (Chapter 81). Willem's description of the country before the fever as one of "perpetual separation" reads like a catalogue of the apartheid past:

> We were separated by tribe and clan, by colour and race, by legislation and religion, by language and culture, by our divergent economic realities and by our ideologies. The more we argued and fought about our differences, the more we focussed on them, the more they divided us [Chapter 86].

Rather than repeating the divisions of the past, Willem asks Amanzi to focus on the things that unite the community. He gives his own addition, cast in global terms, to Plato's view of democracy in order to accommodate South African differences:

democracy not only afforded a kind of equality to the equal as well as the unequal, but also a freedom to the believers and the unbelievers, to the Christians and the Muslims, Hindus and Buddhists, ancestor worshippers and agnostics [Chapter 81].

Willem enjoins the community of Amanzi to "embrace," "enjoy," and "use" this freedom and to "work together to make it bigger" (Chapter 81) and thus attempts to incorporate South African differences into an extended version of the Greek model of democracy. Willem's rhetoric fails, and Pastor Sebego leaves with half the residents of Amanzi on a "Great Trek" to found his own community, named the "New Jerusalem" (Chapter 96). The reference to the Great Trek—a movement of Dutch-speaking colonists up into the interior of South Africa in 1835 in search of land where they could establish their own homeland, independent of British rule—solidifies the allegory of how Amanzi perpetuates South Africa's history of division and fracture. While the split is represented in religious terms and race is not mentioned, it is apparent to the South African reader, or anyone who does their research, that Nkosi Sebego is Tswana, an ethnic African, while Willem is white and his side-kick Domingo is "Coloured." The community of Amanzi, built on the ruins of Vanderkloof, is split, once again, on the basis of race.

Where then is the crime in *Fever*? The first chapter opens with Nico, the narrator, stating: "I want to tell you about my father's murder." Yet, as it turns out, Willem is killed accidently by a group sent by his wife to make contact with him and rescue him. Willem's wife, Nico's mother, is one of a group of people who engineered the Fever virus. Reading *Fever* through an ecocritical lens would bring up the debate about whether the crime should be located within anthropocentrism or ecocentrism. Nico's opening statement, however, is hardly the language of crime fiction; it is not the "story" about a murder and thus suggests none of the "plot" that is all important to the solving of a murder in crime fiction. The subsequent lines of the first chapter, bear out my reading of the novel as political allegory. Nico informs the reader: "This is the story of my life. And the story of your life and your world too, as you will see" (Chapter 1). While the global reader might read this as a narrative about environmental catastrophe, there is little doubt that the South African reader, or those familiar with South African history, would interpret "your world" as a reference to current day South Africa. It is important to recall here that Meyer writes in Afrikaans and is thus addressing a constituency of Afrikaans readers. While this does not preclude a global audience from identifying with Meyer's work—and his international sales figures prove that this is very much the case—his *oeuvre* demonstrates that he is closely engaged with the South African politics of the transition.

The real crime then, I would argue, is the failure of the people, and government, of Amanzi to hold true to the ideals of the new community and to fall back instead into difference and division. De Kock describes the looming disillusionment and disorientation experienced in the post-transition years by those "still rooted in a social imaginary that continues to hold dear the founding tenets of the 'new' democracy," and this, he claims, sets the scene for postapartheid literary culture and why it is characterized by crime fiction.[57] The discrepancy between the ideals on which the new democracy was founded and the outcome in the later post-transition years, created the conditions for "wide-ranging investigation into the causes of the perceived inversion, or perversion, of South Africa's 'reimagined destiny.'"[58] This derailing of the tenets of the new democracy has come to be "regarded as criminal," and the crime fiction genre thus comes conveniently to hand since it "typically sets out to pinpoint a culprit," and thus, implicitly, the "sources of social and political perversity."[59]

Pinpointing the "sources of social and political perversity" is clearly the case in *Heart of the Hunter* and *Cobra* where the culprits are located within the forces of law and order: the PIU, the government (in South Africa and elsewhere), the SSA. The discrepancy between the founding ideals and the post-transition outcome is a crucial pivot of the plot in both novels. While Adair's kidnapping is the ostensible crime in *Cobra*, which sets the narrative in motion, the real crime which drives the plot forward is the intervention of the South African SSA and the derailing of the tenets of the new democracy. By linking this to government corruption in the United Kingdom, Meyer creates a transnational network of crime. The criminal derailing of South Africa does, initially, result in the sense of "plot loss" that de Kock has formulated. Yet this is simultaneously recuperated by Meyer's characters who continue to uphold the founding tenets of the transition and who thus represent that "'true' locus of civil virtue" within the fragile new democracy.

*Fever* does not offer the readily identifiable redemptive characters present in the earlier texts. The end of the novel is ambiguous: it suggests that Nico returns to Amanzi and continues to (re)build it, yet its founding figures have departed. Willem and Domingo are dead, and Sebego has left to found his own town. While the culprits responsible for Willem's murder are from the organization who have manufactured the virus, this is clearly not the problem that is investigated in *Fever*: Willem is murdered late within the narrative, and, by that time, the community of Amanzi has already failed to find a unifying myth and has split along the lines described. While Willem is a spokesperson for the tenets of Western democracy, founded on ancient Greek ideals, his vision fails to unify the people of Amanzi. He is also presented as fallible since he lies to the people in his capacity as leader of the community. I have argued that as an allegorical exploration of the transition to the new South Africa, *Fever* investigates the discrepancy between the ideals on which the "new" democracy was founded and the outcome in post-transition years. While there is no clearly identifiable culprit, the search for the "'true' locus of civil virtue" also yields no positive result. At one level then, *Fever* is the ultimate expression of losing the plot within South African crime fiction's investigation of political transition.

One can thus witness Meyer's shift from *Heart of the Hunter* where a new national identity is reconstructed for the democratic post-transition South Africa to *Cobra*, set much later in the post-transition period, where losing the plot emerges but can still be recuperated. *Fever*, the most ambiguous of Meyer's novels, presents a re-enactment of the new start promised by South Africa's transition and Amanzi's losing of the plot. Yet, as stated previously, Nico is narrating from the future and the narrative end of *Fever* may signal a new beginning. There is a gap of 24 years between the end of the story and Nico's narration and readers have no idea what has transpired in that time. The founding fathers of Amanzi—Willem, Domingo, and Sebego—espoused values based on discourses drawn from the Western repository of knowledge that came to South Africa through colonialism and ultimately proved to be divisive. Set in the future, the post-apocalyptic South Africa, where the repository of Western knowledge has been destroyed (except for those who remember it), the novel also represents a rupturing of the Western teleological narrative of transition. This end might also represent a return to, or of, South Africa's pre-colonial past:

> Pa [Willem] stood still. He looked at the hills, the clouds, all the shades and textures. "Hell, Nico, it's beautiful."
>
> …
>
> "I think it must have been like this, before the Europeans came. You know, Africa" [Chapter 19].

## NOTES

1. Leon de Kock, *Losing the Plot. Crime, Reality and Fiction in Postapartheid Writing* (Johannesburg: Wits University Press, 2016), 34.

2. While it is true that crime fiction was not a commonly used genre in South Africa, during apartheid and before, various researchers are recovering pockets of crime fiction that were published prior to 1994. See, for example, Colette Guldimann's (2019) article about pioneering black hardboiled fiction published in *Drum* magazine in South Africa during the 1950s.

3. Deon Meyer, "Deon Meyer: Probing South Africa in Crime Fiction," interviewed by L. Wertheimer on National Public Radio (NPR), 27 May 2006. http://www.npr.org/templates/story/story.php?storyId=5435833. Accessed February 15, 2019.

4. Jonathan Smolin, "Anxious Openings: Globalization in the Moroccan Arabic Police Procedural," *Middle Eastern Literatures* 17, no. 3 (2014): 285.

5. Jonathan Smolin, "Political Malaise and New Arabic Noir," *South Central Review* 27, no.1 (2010): 82. It is interesting to note that this was also true of writing by black South Africans under apartheid.

6. *Ibid.*

7. Michael Titlestad and Ashlee Polatinsky, "Turning to Crime: Mike Nicol's *The Ibis Tapestry* and *Payback*," *Journal of Commonwealth Literature* 45, no. 2 (2010): 259.

8. *Ibid.*, 269.

9. *Ibid.*, 270.

10. Agustin Reyes-Torres, "Investigating the New South Africa: An Interview with Deon Meyer on *Dead Before Dying*," *Anglistica* 15, no.1 (2011): 84.

11. Deon Meyer, "Deon Meyer: Probing South Africa in Crime Fiction," interviewed by L. Wertheimer on National Public Radio (NPR), 27 May 2006. http://www.npr.org/templates/story/story.php?storyId=5435833. Accessed February 15, 2019.

12. Deon Meyer, interview with Jonathan Clayton (2011). Available at http://www.deonmeyer.com/interviews/times.html. Accessed October 10, 2011.

13. Ranka Primorac, "Dialogues Across Boundaries in Two Southern African Thrillers," *The Journal of Commonwealth Literature* 46, no. 1 (April 2011): 168.

14. Leon de Kock, *Losing the Plot: Crime, Reality and Fiction in Postapartheid Writing* (Johannesburg: Wits University Press, 2016), 36.

15. *Ibid.*, 2.

16. *Ibid.*

17. *Ibid.*, 3.

18. *Ibid.*, 2.

19. *Ibid.*, 9–10.

20. See Agustin Reyes Torres, "Deon Meyer's *Dead Before Dying*: Voices and Representation of the New South Africa," *ES Revista de Filologia Inglesa* 33 (2012): 271–284.

21. De Kock, *Losing the Plot*, 6.

22. See Christopher Warnes, "Writing Crime in the New South Africa: Negotiating *Threat* in the Novels of Deon Meyer and Margie Orford," *Journal of Southern African Studies* 38, no. 4 (2012): 987.

23. Eva Erdmann, "Nationality International: Detective Fiction in the Late Twentieth Century," in *Investigating Identities Questions of Identity in Contemporary International Crime Fiction*, edited by Marieke Krajenbrink and Kate M. Quinn, 11–26 (Amsterdam: Rodopi, 2009), 19.

24. *Ibid.*, 12.

25. *Ibid.*, 20.

26. Samantha Naidu and Elizabeth le Roux, "South African Crime Fiction: Sleuthing the State Post-1994," *African Identities* 12, nos. 3–4 (2014): 288.

27. De Kock, *Losing the Plot*, 46.

28. Colette Guldimann, "The Protean New South Africa in Deon Meyer's *Heart of the Hunter*," *scrutiny2: Special Issue on South African Crime Fiction* 19, no. 1 (2014): 83.

29. De Kock, *Losing the Plot*, 49.

30. Meyer, Deon. *Heart of the Hunter*, translated by K.L. Seegers (London: Hodder and Stoughton, 2003), 113.

31. Colette Guldimann, "The Protean New South Africa in Deon Meyer's *Heart of the Hunter*," *scrutiny2: Special Issue on South African Crime Fiction* 19, no. 1 (2014): 80–92.

32. Julian Symons, *Bloody Murder: From the Detective Story to the Crime Novel* (Harmondsworth: Penguin, 1985).

33. Guldimann, "The Protean New South Africa," 85.

34. Martin Priestman, *Crime Fiction: From Poe to the Present* (Plymouth: Northcote House, 1998), 43.

35. De Kock, *Losing the Plot*, 51.

36. *Ibid.*

37. *Ibid.*, 50.

38. Meyer's acknowledgements in *Heart of the Hunter* provide multiple sources for his historical research into this area.

39. For a more detailed discussion see Colette Guldimann, "The Protean New South Africa in Deon Meyer's Heart of the Hunter," *scrutiny2: Special Issue on South African Crime Fiction* 19, no. 1 (2014): 80–92.

40. Nelson Mandela, "I Am Prepared to Die," *Nelson Mandela Centre of Memory* (1964). Available at http://db.nlesonmandela.org/speeches/pub_view.asp?pg=item&itemID=NMS010&txtstr=prepared%20to%20die. Accessed September 20, 2011.

41. Warnes, "Writing Crime," 991. 5

42. De Kock, *Losing the Plot. Crime*, 11.

43. Deon Meyer, *Trackers*, translated by K.L. Seegers (London: Hodder and Stoughton, 2011), Ch. 15.
44. Deon Meyer, *Cobra*, translated by K.L. Seegers (London: Hodder and Stoughton, 2014), Ch. 32.
45. Mark Shaw, *Crime and Policing in Post-Apartheid South Africa* (London: C. Hurst, 2002), 1.
46. Henning Mankell, *The White Lioness*, translated by Laurie Thompson (London: Vintage, 1988), 118.
47. De Kock, Leon. *Losing the Plot,* 3.
48. Andrew Pepper and David Schmid, editors, *Globalization and the State in Contemporary Crime Fiction* (London: Palgrave Macmillan, 2016), 2.
49. De Kock, *Losing the Plot,* 11.
50. Deon Meyer, *Fever*, translated by K.L. Seegers (London: Hodder and Stoughton, 2017), Ch. 9.
51. Pumza Fihlani, "Inside South Africa's whites-only town of Orania," *BBC News*, October 6, 2014.
52. *Ibid.*
53. *Ibid.*
54. De Kock, *Losing the Plot,* 3.
55. While the accuracy of Harari's history was been widely questioned, engaging in this debate is not my concern here. I am interested in how Harari's narratives are being utilized by Meyer in order to represent ideas about South Africa's transition to a new start.
56. De Kock, *Losing the Plot,* 3.
57. *Ibid.,* 4.
58. *Ibid.*
59. *Ibid.*

## BIBLIOGRAPHY

De Kock, Leon. *Losing the Plot. Crime, Reality and Fiction in Postapartheid Writing.* Johannesburg: Wits University Press, 2016.
Erdmann, Eva. "Nationality International: Detective Fiction in the Late Twentieth Century." In *Investigating Identities Questions of Identity in Contemporary International Crime Fiction*, edited by Marieke Krajenbrink and Kate M. Quinn, 11–26. Amsterdam: Rodopi, 2009.
Fihlani, Pumza. "Inside South Africa's whites-only town of Orania." *BBC News*, October 6, 2014. https://www.bbc.com/news/world-africa-29475977
Guldimann, Colette. "Against the law: Arthur Maimane's pioneering hard-boiled black detective fiction in *Drum Magazine*." *Safundi: The Journal of South African and American Studies* 20, no. 3 (2019): 259–276. https://doi.org/10.1080/17533171.2019.1573456
_____. "The Protean new South Africa in Deon Meyer's Heart of the Hunter." *scrutiny2: Special Issue on South African Crime Fiction* 19, no. 1 (2014): 80–92. https://doi.org/10.1080/18125441.2014.906235
Harari, Yuval Noah. *Sapiens. A Brief History of Humankind.* London: Vintage, 2014.
Mandela, Nelson. "I Am Prepared to Die." *Nelson Mandela Centre of Memory* (1964). Available at http://db.nlesonmandela.org/speeches/pub_view.asp?pg=item&itemID=NMS010&txtstr=prepared%20to%20die. Accessed September 20, 2011.
Mankell, Henning. *The White Lioness.* Translated by Laurie Thompson. London: Vintage, 1988.
Meyer, Deon. *Cobra.* Translated by K.L. Seegers. London: Hodder and Stoughton, 2014. Kindle.
_____. "Deon Meyer: Probing South Africa in Crime Fiction." Interviewed by L. Wertheimer on national public radio (npr), 27 May 2006. http://www.npr.org/templates/story/story.php?storyId=5435833. Accessed February 15, 2019
_____. *Fever.* Translated by K.L. Seegers. London: Hodder and Stoughton, 2017. Kindle.
_____. *Heart of the Hunter.* Translated by K.L. Seegers. London: Hodder and Stoughton, 2003.

_____. "Interviewed by Jonathan Clayton." (2011). Available at http://www.deonmeyer.com/interviews/times.html. Accessed on October 10, 2011.

_____. *Trackers*. Translated by K.L. Seegers. London: Hodder and Stoughton, 2011. Kindle.

Naidu, Samantha, and Elizabeth le Roux. "South African Crime Fiction: Sleuthing the State Post–1994" *African Identities* 12, nos. 3–4 (2014): 283–294. https://doi.org/10.1080/1472 5843.2015.1009621

Pepper, Andrew, and David Schmid, editors. *Globalization and the State in Contemporary Crime Fiction*. London: Palgrave Macmillan, 2016.

Priestman, Martin. *Crime Fiction: From Poe to the Present*. Plymouth: Northcote House, 1998.

Primorac, Ranka. "Dialogues Across Boundaries in Two Southern African Thrillers." *The Journal of Commonwealth Literature* 46, no. 1 (April 2011):157–172. https://doi: 10.1177/0021989410396043

_____. "Introduction: in/visibility and African Thrillers." *Journal of Postcolonial Writing* 49, no. 1 (February 2013): 71–73.

Reyes Torres, Agustin. "Deon Meyer's *Dead Before Dying*: Voices and Representation of the New South Africa." *ES Revista de Filologia Inglesa* 33 (2012): 271–284.

_____. "Investigating the New South Africa: An Interview with Deon Meyer on Dead Before Dying." *Anglistica* 15, no. 1 (2011): 79–89.

Shaw, Mark. *Crime and Policing in Post-Apartheid South Africa*. London: C. Hurst & Co., 2002.

Smolin, Jonathan. "Anxious Openings: Globalization in the Moroccan Arabic Police Procedural." *Middle Eastern Literatures* 17, no. 3 (2014): 283–298.

_____. "Political Malaise and New Arabic Noir." *South Central Review* 27, no. 1 (2010): 82–90.

Symons, Julian. *Bloody Murder: From the Detective Story to the Crime Novel*. Harmondsworth: Penguin, 1985.

Titlestad, Michael, and Ashlee Polatinsky. "Turning to crime: Mike Nicol's *The. Ibis Tapestry* and *Payback*." *Journal of Commonwealth Literature* 45, no. 2 (2010): 259–273. https://doi.org/10.1177%2F0021989410366895

Warnes, Christopher. "Writing Crime in the New South Africa: *Negotiating Threat* in the Novels of Deon Meyer and Margie Orford." *Journal of Southern African Studies* 38, no. 4 (2012): 981–991. https://doi.org/10.1080/03057070.2012.742364

# Sacred Games

## The Interplay of Nationalism and Existentialism in a Multicultural Nation

SOMALI SAREN

The distance between nations is rapidly shrinking as the numbers of people and organizations crossing borders are increasing day by day. A "nation" can no longer simply be defined as "a large body of people united by common descent, history, culture, or language, inhabiting a particular state or territory."[1] Nations in the world now, more than ever, are becoming rapidly globalized and consequently multicultural. Multiculturalism is primarily studied in the context of developed nations that are seeing a recent surge in immigration, and as a form of resistance to the phenomenon the idea of nationalism is turning into a stronger political force. But in a multicultural nation like India, the idea of national identity has been problematic since its very inception. In India multiculturalism is inherent; here, various religious and cultural ideas dispute over domination of the national discourse. How a subject residing in such a state understands national identity is a complex study that will be undertaken here while examining Indian writer Vikram Chandra's crime novel *Sacred Games*.[2] At a time when the debates around national identity are taking new turns every day, embedding such a serious discourse in a popular genre without being too scholarly is a feat that needs to be studied and appreciated.

In India, as Ashutosh Varshney[3] points out, the idea of nationalism involves a contest between separate ideas: two separatist nationalisms, secular nationalism and Hindu nationalism. The demand of two Indian communities for a sovereign nation, Sikhs' demand for Khalistan and Kashmiri's demand for an independent nation, is known as the separatist nationalism. India, however, has also been facing many separatist factions in Northeast India for the demand of separate states or for full autonomy. Officially newly Independent India was born as a secular nation and continues to be so, as guided by the Constitution. Hindu nationalism was born as a byproduct of 1947's partition which deemed Pakistan as a Muslim nation and India as a nation with Hindu majority. Assimilation remains the criteria of Hindu nationalists for the inclusion of the minorities. These contesting factors are the main players in the discourse of Indian national identity, and Chandra has successfully managed to focus on them throughout his text.

Contemporary authors, by introducing detectives from minority groups—be it in terms of race, gender, class or sexual orientation—have repeatedly proven that the structure of crime narrative is favorable for the discourse of identity politics. Vikram Chandra's police detective Sartaj Singh too belongs to a minority religious group in India, namely Sikh. Despite being a multicultural country, the apparent peaceful existence of secular India is constantly being threatened by a strong undercurrent of communal tension. In such circumstance how the detective and the other characters surrounding him attempt to shape their intertwined national and existential identities will be examined through the crime novel *Sacred Games*.

Though the characters represented in the novel belong to the same nation, they inhabit and experience extremely dissimilar spaces. Thereby it exposes the nation's unattainability of a stable inclusive national identity based on social and cultural equality. Ironically it is the same contested nationalisms, I argue, that confer on the detective Sartaj Singh and the gangster Ganesh Gaitonde a similar kind of inner and outer journey. This has been highlighted by the parallel narrative and common elements in their stories. Disparity between the expectation and the reality of dynamic modern urban India destabilizes the characters' self-identity and impel them to examine their "inauthentic existence." Therefore, the detective and the criminal will be analyzed in light of Heidegger's[4] concepts concerning existentialism to argue that their existential crisis is reflective of the existing complexities in social or national identity formation. "Thrown" into a chaotic world dominated by hierarchical and religious identity, these two characters, by connecting through their existential identity simultaneously suggest a common national consciousness forming beyond the loftiness of social, cultural or political discourse.

## The Setting: A Multicultural and Postcolonial India

Contemporary crime fictions have been much dedicated to the specificity of its setting, so much so that "the crime itself appears to be at best merely a successful stunt. It almost seems as if the inventories of criminal motives and case histories have been exhausted, so that crime fiction's primary distinguishing characteristic has become the locus criminalis."[5] Be it the country, the city or the whole world, the textual space implicated in crime fiction always has been, as Auden calls it, "the Great Wrong Place" of crime and criminality. The financial and commercial capital of India, Bombay, depicted in Vikram Chandra's *Sacred Games,* is appropriate for such a description.

Varshney points out some factors that keep a nation united, such as, ethnicity (e.g., Japan), religion (e.g., Pakistan), territory (e.g., Switzerland) and ideology (e.g., the United States).[6] In case of India the construction of national identity is in constant conflict between the three defining factors of territory, culture and religion. "Unity in diversity" is a catchphrase that has been infused into Indian consciousness from a very young age. As a secular nation of numerous religions (including Hindu, Muslim, Christianity and many other minority religions), castes and class, it apparently peacefully accommodates diverse cultural and social practices. In terms of territory and religion India is considered to be mainly a Hindu nation for its "sacred geography" and dominant Hindu population. However, the inclusions of certain provisions, like articles 29 and 30[7] in Indian constitution, ensured conservation of the distinctive cultures of the minorities. The actual living experience though suggests two existing mindsets opposing in nature: there are the secularists who reinforce the view of peaceful existence of different religions; and, on the other hand, there are the communalists who reach out to history to highlight differences and continuous conflicts existing since past. Owing mainly to the British strategy of creating communal tension to "divide and rule," especially between the Hindu and the Muslim, the nation sustains an irreparable rift.

Ironically under the British rule not only communalism but also nationalism was born. The force of communalism—for instance, "communities" structured and held together by Hindu or Muslim religious or ethnic identities—was subdued under the immediate need for nationalism to overthrow the colonialists. However, independence came with the condition of partition. Two countries were formed out of British India: Pakistan and India. While Pakistan's national identity was based on Islam, India chose to be a secular nation, as conceptualized by Jawaharlal Nehru, an Indian independence activist and the first prime minister of Independent India. Nehru believed that by creating a national identity based on the past would be problematic. Therefore, instead, he tried to build it based on modernization and economic development. But post-independence, the communal forces were revived and led by the RSS (Rashtriya Swayamsevak Sangh) and its chief Vinayak Damodar Savarkar with greater force to realize the dream of a Hindu nation. For the Hindu nationalist the elements of loyalty and emotion are too abstract to hold a nation together. The communalists' persistent call for homogeneousness is endangering to minority population as it equates communalism with nationalism.

Modern cities are "palimpsests, comprised of remnants from earlier landscapes, always susceptible to erasure or brought into different relations with emerging structures—social relations redefined spatially as habitat."[8] Bombay is no different. In his treatment of the past, by touching on the pivotal moments for India since its Independence, Chandra establishes the long history of crime and unrest that has germinated enough hatred to provoke the present transgression. Post-independence India has to struggle and overcome conflicts in order to create an idea of the nation. Immediately after independence Nehru's vision was to build an India that is "committed to protecting cultural and religious difference rather than imposing a uniform Indianess."[9] But the fissure resulted from partition continues to torment post-independent India till today. Maria Varsam coined the term "concrete dystopia" to define "those events that form the *material* basis for the content of dystopian fiction which have inspired the writer to warn of the potential of history to repeat itself."[10] In the present context the *material* basis are the 1947's Partition of India along with post-independence communal violence such as 1992's Babri Masjid demolition in Ayodhya (in the state of Uttar Pradesh), followed by 1993's Bombay bomb blast which itself was a result of chain of events leading from the demolition of the mosque in Ayodhya. These nationwide historical events form the basis for Chandra's dystopic vision of Bombay, therefore turning Bombay into a microcosm of modern India.

In India modernity was brought in through the neoliberal economic policy reform of the 1980s and 1990s. Bombay was "the first Indian town to experience economic, technological, and social changes associated with the growth of capitalism in India."[11] In the 1990s independent India—the country which had inherited weak economy along with extraordinary cultural (in linguistic, religious and ethnic forms) divisiveness, social authoritarianism and injustice rather than a healthy interacting melting pot of different races and communities—witnessed rapid changes through economic liberalization. Government's withdrawal of the strict state control and restriction on functioning of market saved the country from the ongoing economic crisis and resulted in economic development, but concomitantly also "generated spectacular new forms of inequality between social groups, regions, and sectors."[12] Now with the earlier existent social hierarchy there emerged the geographical strata. Numerous studies have declared Bombay to be the least homogeneous city in India. The urban space consists of two starkly different kinds of population occupying contrasting physical spaces: Dharavi, one of the largest slums of the world, is just few miles away from the richest parts of the city. Keeping up with the reality, the scene of action in *Sacred Games* goes back and forth between rich and poor areas of the city. The growing inequality is accompanied by the pitfall of the united nation. In the midst of social inequality and agitation, the financial capital of India, Bombay, begets large numbers of gangs and their battles for domination, and it can be argued that the reason behind the growing formation of illegal gangs is a symptom of neoliberal discrepancy.

Chandra's novel contains four chapters called "Insets" which do not actually move the central story along. For genre fiction it might appear to be a bit digressive, but they could serve as what Barbara Piatti and others call a "projected space,"[13] which "follow[s] a specific function and add[s] extra layers of meaning to the geography of a narrated world."[14] The first "inset" consisting of Sartaj's mother's narrative, connects the rationale behind the main crime story to its very beginning. Her story of losing her sister during the 1947's partition riots, as they were fleeing from newly born Pakistan to reach India, acts as a premonition for what a secular India might face in future. It is the beginning of Hindu-Muslim divide which still haunts India and turns out to be a major source of the mystery of the present crime narrative. Here Vikram Chandra responsibly carries the burden of "Partition's post-amnesia," a process which Ananya Jahanara Kabir describes in her work: "The Indian novel in English is handcuffed to the history of Partition in two ways. It is shaped by the politics that resulted in Partition and that created a specific post–Partition subject, exemplified by the Indian Muslim as a minority figure; and it is shaped by the ways partition has been remembered, forgotten and re-remembered by successive generation of writers."[15] The second inset featuring an ex–secret intelligence officer, K.D. Yadav who is suffering from gradual memory loss, is important not for its contribution to the mystery but for its introduction to the newly independent secular nationalism of Independent India. Lying on the hospital bed he reminiscences about his meeting with Nehru, his operation in the jungles of northeast India in the aftermath of 1962's Indo-China war, his encounter with the Naxalites.[16] Above all this section highlights the Indian national identity that is highly dependent on the discourse of "us" vs. "them"; here the geographical border defines nationalism. When K.D., an O.B.C (backward caste), questioned the lack of diversity in the intelligence organization that consists mostly of Brahmin (the "highest" caste in Hindu) members, he was always told, "Think, K.D … of who we are fighting. Yes. The *dushman* [enemy]. They were there, and here we are. Them and us" (326). The third and fourth insets are fragments of individual stories depicting the discontent of post-independent India and the long-lasting aftermath of the Partition.

At first *Sacred Games* appears in compliance with the structure of classical detective fiction by laying out a dead body (of gangster Ganesh Gaitonde) and the assignment of a detective (Inspector Sartaj Singh) to solve the mystery of the death. But as the narrative unfolds the genre seems to get modified and overturned owing to, as Chandra himself points out, "numerous layers of history and events [that] play a part in the protagonists' lives, and they themselves never know the larger picture. Ostensibly, Gaitonde and Sartaj seem to belong to the classical detective tradition—like Moriarty and Holmes—but in fact, they hardly ever meet. Instead they, like all of us, tend to be caught up in events that are far bigger—in a huge web of agendas and politics and ideologies."[17] The author himself has admitted that there was a conscious effort on his part to subvert the genre. Subversion is the most preferred device of the postcolonial writer to challenge the status quo. But Chandra's experimentation does not stop there. By setting up the story of a police detective and a gangster in the postcolonial multicultural world he reinvigorates the identities of such stereotypical characters and uses them as a medium to analyze the complexities of contemporary Indian national identity.

The setting of the story, then, acts as an agent in the formation of the narrative and the characters. As Robert Tally observes, "Space and spatial relations are not merely a backdrop or setting for events, an empty container to be filled with actions or movements.... Rather, space was both a product … and productive; it produces us, in fact."[18] Indeed the author throughout the text produces two opposing spaces—legitimacy and illegitimacy—but the parallel narratives of the two representatives, Detective Sartaj Singh and gangster Ganesh Gaitonde, from both spaces, demonstrated the stark differences and yet a connection. They both reflect how "the deepest problems of modern life flow from the attempt of the individual to maintain the independence and individuality of his/her existence against the sovereign powers of society, against the weight of the historical heritage and the external culture and technique of life."[19] Therefore while representing the conflicts of a modern postcolonial city through a crime text, the city itself emerges as a key character in every aspect of the narrative. Reading against this background, the text then becomes a spatial struggle of the detective and the criminal figures and all the other characters hailing from the two spaces, and thus representing Bombay as a battleground. Their identities transpired to be spatial constructions, and crime becomes a means to acquire more space.

## Sartaj Singh: The Detective and Passive Secular Nationalist

By opening the market for privatization and global capital flow, India finally altogether gave away Gandhi's vision of national identity built around vast rural India and embraced Nehru's vision of an India sailing high on large industries and technology. The Indian national identity, then, became more and more in tandem with the Western urban development models. The identity of the nation and its nationals became concentrated in the cities. As Diener and Hagen observe, cities contain the power to shape the national identity, citizenship and belonging:

> The political geographies of urban space and place derive from power; the city simultaneously produces, concentrates, distributes, and consumes power. That power, in its varied tangible and intangible forms, shapes the spatiality of the urban landscape, structures social relations, and conveys meanings, among them senses of collective belonging.
>
> Urban landscapes, in both their material, symbolic and mental forms, are therefore constitutive and symbolic of the shifting contours of social relations and national identity.[20]

Accordingly, whoever holds the power in India's city centers could create or remake the narrative of nationalism.

The multiculturalism that defines India is a threat for the neo-nationalists. In India, the neo-nationalists exist primarily in the form of two organizations: the previously mentioned RSS and Shiv Sena (the extremist political party based on the state of Maharashtra). Taking a cue from the reality, Chandra creates a fictional underground group called Kali Sena, whose primary mission is to build a "Hindu rashtra," a nation for Hindus; and a political party called *Rakshaks*. *Rakshaks* has been mentioned in Sartaj's previous adventure too—the short story titled "Kama"[21] (desire). In "Kama" Kshitij, a young member of *Rakshak*, murders his father Mr. Chetanbhai. His father and mother were engaged in unconventional amorous activities and Kshitij's extreme conservative Hindu conscience could not accept it. *Sacred Games* begins with the recent shift of power in the State government. The government of so-called secular Congress has been replaced by the same *Rakshaks*. This explicitly refers to the Shiv Sena's first formation of Maharshtrian Government in 1995. Besides their hatred for Muslims, they are also known for their contempt for the "outsiders" or immigrants from other parts of the country (like Tamils, Biharis, etc.) who came to the city and "stole jobs and land" (220). The city atmosphere is now changing. After coming into power, the ministers of this "muscular right-wing organization" "had toned down their ranting nationalism, but they would not give up on their battle against cultural degeneration and western corruption. 'They promised to reform the city'" (17).

Amidst this new Bombay, Inspector Sartaj Singh is going on with his regular work when, out of the blue, he is informed of the hideout of the most infamous gangster Ganesh Gaitonde. He soon reaches the location and finds the gangster locked inside a big cube-like building with hardened walls. Gaitonde, the G-company boss, starts making conversation with Sartaj from the inside while Sartaj unsuccessfully attempts to break the door. Disregarding

Sartaj's continual demands for surrender, Gaitonde starts narrating his life story to Sartaj. Finally, Sartaj breaks in, but inside he finds the dead body of Gaitonde and a woman who is later identified as Jojo. Though the novel starts with Gaitonde's death his voice continues to narrate the rest of his story. The third-person narrative of Sartaj and the ghost narrative of Gaitonde overlap each other while progressing towards the revelation of the mystery of his death.

It is no mystery that Gaitonde was killed by a bullet; he shot himself after shooting an unknown woman. Yet this mystery is far more complicated than "the thin, pointed narrative of your ordinary murder case, where there was a corpse, an unknown killer or killers, and you were looking for a motive." "Here there were two dead, one had obviously killed the other, and what did it matter what their relationship was? How would you know? Why would you care?" (140) are the questions needing answers which could not be solved with conventional methods. Appropriately so, Sartaj's detection method was not conventional either; it often defies the western scientific and logical process by giving way to mere chance and coincidence. It is instinct that plays the biggest part, and Sartaj has learned to trust it, so much so that sometimes, "you had the truth in your mouth but no evidence in your hands. And sometimes you acted on this knowledge, you planted evidence, wrote an FIR leaving out certain facts and putting others in. Justice had sometimes to be manipulated into being properly blind" (557). Capturing criminals did not involve a thrilling car chase either or sprinting through crowded streets. Sartaj would have liked all of it, but here hunting criminals meant "intimidating a woman and an old man in their own home. This was tried and tested policing technique, to disrupt family and business until the informant sang, the criminal caved, the innocent confessed" (212). Because, in postcolonial India, the nature of a crime is unlike its western counterpart; there is not just a single mystery but multiple crimes of different degrees and classes that Sartaj has been assigned to solve. "Policing was often a scattered business that required setting aside one job to attend to another" (78). The metropolis is vulnerable to not just terrorism and gang wars but also to small time burglaries and murders for personal revenge. Investigations of these broad ranges of crimes reveal the growing distance of the capitalist city from the anticipated nation-state of Nehru. A death in a slum is insignificant, and "nobody minds" (78) if the case remains unresolved—a murder in poverty is of little interest as "dead bodies there were just dead, devoid of any enlivening possibilities of professional praise, or press, or money" (19). Sartaj still wants to bring justice in every corner. As a detective Sartaj's job is to fill in "a void, a blank of the unexplained, more properly, the unnarrated ('How did this happen? What happened on the night of the murder?')"[22] aspects of these crimes. He, however, is consumed by the void when it comes to the mystery occurring outside of the bourgeoisie society, a mystery from the periphery. Being an upholder of bourgeoisie ideology Sartaj successfully solves another mystery and finds out who has been blackmailing Kamala Pandey, an Air Hostess. But why did Gaitonde kill himself? Who is the mystery man in the slums of Bengali Bura who was involved in multiple crimes? These are the questions insoluble for him that render the supposedly linear narrative of crime revelation non-linear, fragmented, and necessitating accommodation of the voices of the marginalized, those who are living on the periphery, to fill in those unresolved blanks. For instance, while Gaitonde's narrative comprises half of the work, one of the novel's four insets reveals the story of the mystery man Aadil, another example of the failure of "India Shining."

As a Sikh policeman in Bombay Sartaj embodies the cultural tension present in the megapolis. Sartaj's Sikh identity makes him an outsider despite being born and brought up in the city. Mary—the sister of the murder victim Jojo and Sartaj's future love interest—has concerns about the possibility of being seen with Sartaj: "she wouldn't want her neighbours wondering either, about visits from policemen, or strange Sikhs" (270). His difficulty in conceding to his community stereotype further complicates his stance. He is a member of a community that suffered during the partition violence in conflicts with the Muslims. But, his junior Kamble observes, for a *sardar* he is "too soft on them [Muslims]" (541). But Sartaj prefers his societal identity as a policeman over the communal and asserts that he is rather "too soft for a policeman" (541). Sartaj represents the idea of a secular India. His secret desire of putting up a picture of Guru Govind Singh (a Sikh spiritual Guru) on the police station wall that is already decorated with other religious figures is exclusively "a somewhat twisted assertion of secularism" (5).

It is not only his cultural identity that pushes him into the alienated state but also his professional life. Sartaj as a part of the repressive state apparatus instills fear and disgust: "[c]itizens, and especially women, were always subdued with policemen, careful, scared, formal" (166). As a state apparatus the police have the power to intimidate people. Legitimization of such reprehensible acts contributes in "recolonizing" people. They are often seen as "monsters, set aside from everyone else" (106). Claire Chambers in her study of Chandra's short story "Kama" fittingly quotes David Arnold's argument that postcolonial policing is a continuation of colonial past:

> Although created to serve colonial needs, the police passed largely unchanged into Indian hands and have remained of central importance to the political fortunes of Independent India. A colonial institution, designed to uphold colonial rule, and control over which was jealously guarded, the police became mainstay of post-colonial state-power.[23]

Rather than being an upholder of morality the law-keeper becomes the protector of the influential section of the society. It is the same Chandleresque world of crime and degeneration: "It's not a very fragrant world, but it's the world you live in."[24] The civilians, specifically the bourgeoisie, do not want to acknowledge this world for all its filth and dirty work, such as Sartaj's rich ex-wife Megha. In the short story "Kama" she confessed that she hated the world Sartaj lives in. And Sartaj had wanted to say, "it's your world also, ... I live in the parts you don't want to see."[25] He is not an anti-establishment figure but rather a representative of it whose position ironically imposes estrangement from the society.

The clash between the ideology of the state and the individual's moral obligations and responsibility towards his/her community often complicate the conscience of the postcolonial detective. His/her awareness of the corrupt and flawed system leads to inner conflict, and hence the veering of the genre's rational strand towards the philosophy of emotions, towards existentialism. But as a state apparatus Sartaj unquestionably accepts existing order. Violence, intimidation, corruption, bribery, and political partiality have been depicted as natural parts of police activities, as long as they serve the purpose of the powerful, and Sartaj seldom feels the need to challenge it. Thus, Parulkar's—the deputy commissioner of police and Sartaj's mentor—accumulation of illegal wealth stacked in a foreign bank and his posh apartment under the name of his niece are presented through Sartaj's eyes in an uncritical manner. He thereby stays clear of stirring "the unspoken 'fear' of the bourgeoisie," that is questioning, "about the origin of their wealth; those energetic attempts of maintaining the façade of the civilizing process would come to nothing if awkward questions were asked about the ways in which money was accumulated."[26]

Nevertheless, it is still the role of the detective to act as the anchor of this decentered world. Sartaj understands that "what they wanted was only that someone in a uniform, a robe, somebody with three lions on their shoulder should say, yes, I see how it came about, first this happened, and then that, and so you did this and then this" (158). But Sartaj is not the hero-figure a detective has often been portrayed as. His dedication to the job does not emanate from any sense of moral or social obligation but rather from his helpless surrender to the quotidian "inauthentic" existence. As Claire Chambers argues, to Sartaj "work functions more as a distraction from existential despair than for the benefit of his community."[27] His alienation is then, as we have observed, not self-inflicted, unlike the impressive detective figures like Holmes, Phillip Marlowe, Sam Spade et al. Rather he is in the league of Ian Rankin's detective John Rebus who needs the work to make sense of the world. In *Even Dogs in the Wild* the idea is voiced explicitly by Rebus when Brian Holroyd was seeking revenge by murdering people who abused his father in his childhood. Rebus acknowledges the poetic justice of the whole case as he thought, "What did it matter if Brian Holroyd was out there, picking off his abusers and their abettors?" And next moment his thoughts changed to "Yet somehow it did—it did matter. Always had, always would. Not because of any of the victims or perpetrators, but for Rebus himself. Because if none of it mattered, then neither did he."[28] Sartaj too had to delve deep into his detective persona to make himself feel more relevant in this world. He is functioning through the same sense of inevitability that dominates his understanding of the world. He believes that everything happens because that is how they are supposed to: "I catch them because that's what I do, and they run because that's what they do, and the world keeps turning" (105). He is doing what he is expected to do for "being-there," what Heidegger termed as *Dasein*,[29] or "a way of life shared by the members of some community."[30] As *Dasein* he is surrendering to *das Man* or "the they" or "Others." *Das Man* is defined by Heidegger as being-with-others in everyday life without any question; it equates not to other people but the ontological phenomenon of a specific culture. When *Dasein* as a being is afraid to encounter the limitedness of life, in a mode of denial, the being joins the crowd to avoid the existential anxiety. As we can observe throughout the text, in his loneliness Sartaj often realizes the finiteness of life. For example, in the first chapter, Sartaj stood near the window looking at the parking space below. Suddenly it occurred to him "how easy it would be to keep leaning over, tipping until the weight carried him … the crack of the skull, a quick crack and the silence" (24). The thought frightened him. To wash it off he leaves the house to be among the crowd in a club. Being a policeman Sartaj finds it easier to do what is historically and culturally expected of him. This is indicative of his "inauthentic" existence, an existential element that brings him closer to the other characters, specifically Ganesh Gaitonde.

## Ganesh Gaitonde: The Gangster and Accidental Hindu Nationalist

The criminal, who has been vilified and presented as an aberrant that needs to be punished to re-establish a just society, now has become a product of an unjust society and a contender for hero figure. Instead of the detective it is the criminal who narrates the "unnarrated" crime story, which is otherwise reconstructed by the detective based on his deductions. In the process of filling the void Gaitonde gives us insights into the other by-products of the flourishing city, tucked away from the mainstream society, the underworld of crime.

Conceptually Indian society is founded on equality, but in reality, the hierarchical nature is evident in every sphere of life, and to have a place at the top of that stratified society, to have the most coveted possession, power, is what everyone aims for. Though India practices mixed economy where private and public sectors go side by side, in cities like Bombay it is more capitalistic in nature. Henri Lefebvre's observation regarding urban space is relevant here:

> Social place is allocated according to class, and social planning reproduces the class structure and reflects the balance of power among actors. This is either on the basis of too much space for the rich and too little for the poor, or because of uneven development in quality of places, or indeed both.[31]

Neoliberalism promised and delivered market prosperity. The growing wealth of the city became synonymous with opportunities, thereby attracting poor people from rural areas who arrived in the city to benefit from the booming economy only to end up living in the mushrooming slums right next to the prosperous neighborhoods. Industrialization and growth of the city also attract people from the neighboring states and countries, "*ganwars* who come from Bihar or Andhra or *maderchod* Bangladesh … [who come] in thousands, to work as servants and on the roads and on the construction sites" (20). This movement creates a vast conglomeration of people, resulting in battles for space as "in this city, the rich had some room, and the middle class had less, and the poor had none" (79). The "bitter secret" of survival in the metropolis is "*paisa phek, tamasha dekh* … if you have money to throw, you could watch the spectacle" (11); the stark disparity became a prominent attribute which in turn gave rise to criminal gangs. The have-nots found ways to claim their space and wealth—from those who have—through the means of extortion, smuggling, drug trafficking, and other illegal activities. Crime then becomes a means to acquire more space, which in turn represents an instance of the failure of the Nehruvian state.

Then, to have power in a crowded city like Bombay is frequently symbolized by the ownership and control of space, the ability to set boundaries. Gaitonde realizes this early in his career of crime. Gaitonde's journey towards his strong presence began with him acquiring control over a piece of land in the city. He narrates:

> I knew it in my bones, if you don't own land you are nothing.… I had already seen the land, and had walked up and down it, and knew it was the right place.… So we gave money to the municipality, to one clerk and to two officers, and the land was mine to build on [107].

He built the *basti* (slum) of Gopalmath, his very own domain. He made it from scratch, clearing the wasteland of weeds and bushes, by fighting other gangs who questioned his authority. The *kholis* (one-room houses) in the slum filled up fast with people from all castes and creeds: "Dalits and OBCs, Marathas and Tamils, Brahmins and Muslims" (111), and from this crowd Gaitonde created his gang G-company. Gopalmath gave Gaitonde a sense of spatial power, a sense of belonging to the city: "I had needed to fight it not only for territory, but for legitimacy. I was now Ganesh Gaitonde of Gopalmath, and nobody could dispute my right to stay in the city" (111).

Another way to gain control over people is by imposing order. Suketu Mehta, in his book *Maximum City: Bombay Lost and Found,* observes that "the gangs flourish because they form a parallel justice system in a country with the world's largest backlog of court cases.... A dispute over a flat, which takes twenty years in court, is taken care of in a week or a month by the underworld."[32] That is why, Gaitonde, though a criminal, is hailed as the messiah by people. He establishes his own law and means of justice, a trait of gangster fiction epitomized by Mario Puzo's *The Godfather* (1969). People come to Gaitonde for solutions to avoid "the endless and useless law courts" and he "listened to all sides of the case and gave a decision, a fair and fast ruling that would be enforced by [his] boys, with force if necessary." He was proud of having power "to give men and women whatever they wanted, to reach inside their guts and pull out whatever dirty little dreams they had hidden in there for a lifetime, and make it real" (475).

Bombay has witnessed gruesome gangster terrorism in reality too, one of the most infamous being the murder of the affluent owner of a Bombay music company who was shot dead by the Dawood Ibrahim gang for not paying heed to their monetary demands. In the novel Gaitonde's "daily skim" is said to be "greater than annual corporate incomes" (30). In the American context it is the desire to fulfill one's "American dream" that resulted in the growing members of underworld gangsters. When studied in the Indian context it becomes a counter narrative to "India Shining." Due to its most favored location by the seaports Bombay has rapidly risen to become the financial center of India. This sea port not only invites easy access to business but also illegal activities. Gaitonde narrates his first experience as a criminal novice, his journey across the sea with his mentor Salim Kaka to execute a deal with foreign gold smugglers; and the same gold that Gaitonde appropriates by killing Salim Kaka is used as his own capital to slowly climb the ladder of the underworld power structure.

Gaitonde maintains spatial control through cellular technology. In her study of the remarkable Bombay *film noir* from 2002, *Company,* Lalitha Gopalan takes note of the significance of the telephone's ubiquity in the film. She defines its function as that of a "double-edged sword." On the one hand "its expansiveness maps a territory for the underworld that is no longer beholden to conduct its activities in the dark alleyways of the modern city."[33] But on the other the hand, the telephone becomes "a device that can be subjected to eavesdropping and surveillance,"[34] as both the gang members and the police manipulate the technology to gain information on their opponents. Chandra's novel, at the very beginning, established a connection between the two worlds through a phone call from the underworld to Sartaj that states: "Do you want Ganesh Gaitonde?" (28). But it was Gaitonde himself who phoned Sartaj about his whereabouts. Therefore, he himself sets the stage for his denouement and the tone of the power relation between the detective and the criminal. In the power play between the two characters Gaitonde always has had the upper hand. In his ghost narrative the gangster recounts his first encounter with Sartaj. He was in the disguise of an employee of an import-export company. Sartaj tried to look through him using his "police-man's trick of sudden questions" and "calculated glance" (597) but failed to recognize him. In contrast, Gaitonde marked him as the policeman in "a crisp khakhi uniform and a tall pagdi" (596) who was friendly and amusing but also very attentive. It is in this brief encounter Gaitonde measured the detective, and in his last moment when he wanted to tell his story to the world he decided to call Sartaj because, he explains: "I remembered the generosity, unusual for anyone, incredible in a policeman, and I remembered you. You have a policeman's cruelty in your eyes, Sartaj, in your swagger, but under that studied indifference there is a sentimental man" (858). Ultimately, Gaitonde's helplessness and despair and eventual defeat under uncontrollable circumstances make him and Sartaj alike.

Space has always been instrumental to enforce a particular version of nationalism. This has been the case when the Hindu nationalists destroyed the mosque in Ayodhya, a mosque believed to have been built (in 1528) after destroying a temple dedicated to Rama (a Hindu deity). This particular incident was followed by a series of inter-communal riots. In Bombay Shiv Sena actively organized riots causing a large number of deaths. In protest of the demolition and killing of Muslims, don Dawood Ibrahim choreographed 13 bomb blasts in the city. In the novel Dawood Ibrahim has been fictionalized as Suleiman Isa. Suleiman, as we are informed, tied up with Pakistani government to plant a bomb in the city he himself was born in to take revenge for the Muslims who had been murdered.

Gaitonde always believed only in the religion of money, and his company had members from all castes and creeds. But as riots broke, his own men turned against Muslims, and the Muslim inhabitants emptied and left their *kholis*. And then there was pressure from his men who asked him the inevitable question: "Bhai is with us, or with the Muslims" (391). Gaitonde hesitated to take a side as he wonders: "Who was I, who had always regarded the would-be attackers of the mosque and its defenders as equal fools?" (391). His neutral standing demotivated his followers who started taking part in the riots, leaving him alone. This makes Gaitonde realize what greater power trumps his limited spatial control of Gopalmath, and the collective spatial identity he had created starts falling apart under the greater social narrative.

When Bipin Bhosle, the Rakshaks MLA offered Gaitonde money to dislocate the Muslim population in a nearby slum, the gangster found a way out: he burnt the slum. Finally, the man who believed in nothing found a sense of acceptance in the collective identity of Hindu. Gaitonde muses, "There were Hindus, and there were Muslims. Everything sits in pairs, in opposites, so brutal and so lovely" (395). And he decides, "Suleiman Isa was the Muslim don, so I was the Hindu bhai. It was necessary" (408). His eternal professional enmity with Suleiman gets colored in communal and national colors as Suleiman was not only a Muslim but also a betrayer of the country who spied for Pakistan and took help from them to attack the city. It has also been suggested that the existing gang-war between Ganesh Gaitonde, a Hindu gangster, and his rival Suleiman Isa, the Muslim gangster is a rehearsed version of the Partition violence.

The transformation of Gaitonde took a new shape when Swami Sridhar Sukla, an extremist Hindu Guru and founder of an underground group named Kalki Sena, took him as his disciple and started pursuing him to join his Hindutva cause, and simultaneously K.D., the officer in highly secret government service, hired him as a spy to help him fight foreign threats for the country. Gaitonde incidentally became a crusader for both: the idea of a Hindu nation and the present secular nation. By embodying these two contradictory aspects without a deeper understanding of the consequences Gaitonde steps into the whirlwind of contradictions. By completely surrendering his soul to Guru-ji, Gaitonde felt he had been reborn: "Something had died in me, and now there was a newness in its place. Guru-ji had made me again" (743). So eventually he too, like Sartaj, without questioning, fully embraced the identity that his environment was bestowing upon him. In different stages of his life his existence had been deeply interwoven with the lives of various people: firstly, Kanta Bai and Paritosh Shah, his accomplices; Subhadra, his wife; Guru-ji and Jojo, his closest companion. Every time one of them passes away or abandons him, the existential anxiety of *Dasein* surfaces. For example, after Gaitonde serves his role in Guru-ji's plan and the latter alienates Gaitonde, the gangster ponders: "I knew he wouldn't come back.... I was alone. Once again ... and again there was a rupture inside me, an endless, raw-edged chasm, and I was falling into it. I was alone" (839). Akin to Sartaj, Gaitonde's being is dependent on the *das Man*, rendering his *Dasein* an "inauthentic" existence.

## Contested Nationalism, Existentialism and Identity

In the wide spectrum of what national identity means to citizens, we can consider three kinds of people in the novel. On one side there are Sartaj and K.D., those who strive to uphold Nehru's dream of secular India. On the other end of the spectrum are the Guru-ji and his underground group whose view of nationalism equates to a Hindu nation. And then there are the characters like Gaitonde and Parulkar who oscillate between these two, either in utter confusion or for opportunism. The city itself then becomes a space of ideological struggle.

As Henri Lefebvre writes, "What we call ideology only achieves consistency by intervening in social space and in its production, and by thus taking on body therein."[35] To give his ideology a living body Guru-ji turns into the main perpetrator in this mystery. Ironically, as opposite to a stereotypical criminal figure, his motive is to disrupt the present disorderliness to reinstate a sense of order he thought necessary. He wanted to create a homogenous nation for Hindus: "a perfect nation, run according to ancient Hindu principles" (509). His vision of utopia is embodied in the *ashrams* (religious retreat) he had built all over India. Gaitonde could see the "logic and progression" in it:

> Chaos seeped in past his steel fences, his blue gates, his protective mantras. All over the country, the ashrams were laid out according to the same exact plan.... The whole landscape focused always on the marble pyramid, which resembled our old Indian temples.... Far from this central point, at the very outskirts, there were the menial buildings, the laundries, ... the public toilets.... Arranged in the middle there were the schools ... and the dormitories for married couples.... These made a precise circle around the white pyramid itself, beyond which there was only liberation....
>
> There was an order here that was the order of Guru-ji's intellect. Reading these landscape was like listening to a sermon.... I could now see very clearly his vision, his idea for what the country should be, then the whole world [812–13].

Guru-ji's utopia is the same capitalist ideal masked in an ordered structure. To spread this structure beyond the fences of the ashrams the self-styled godman through all his spiritual speeches and practices rationalizes the urgency of an apocalypse:

> All these United Nations, these dreamy-eyed do-gooders.... They think they have stopped war, but all they ensure is a state of constant, smouldering war. Look at India and Pakistan bleeding each other for more than fifty years. Instead of a final, glorious battle, we have a long, filthy mess.... Every golden age must be preceded by an apocalypse [838].

His plan is to resume previous kinds of communal riots throughout the country but in larger scale; he wanted to start a battle against "Muslims, communists, Christians, Sikhs. Anyone else who doesn't like this perfect nation. Militant Dalits also" (509). To start the war, he needed to plant a nuclear bomb in the city and blame it on a fictional Islamic terrorist organization named Hizabuddeen. Gaitonde helped Guru-ji to smuggle a huge number of arms to the country. But unbeknownst to him one of the shipments carried in a nuclear weapon too. When Gaitonde confronts Guru-ji, the latter refuses to be persuaded by Gaitonde's vain attempt to save the world. This strange turn of events leads to Gaitonde—a gangster who has unhesitatingly killed people—developing an intense desire to save the life of billions. Where does this desire stem from? I would argue it is the nationalism embedded in one's everyday existence.

How are people from various class, caste and creed supposed to build a national consciousness that doesn't discriminate? From observation of life in the city, I suggest that everyday life builds national identity and holds the multicultural existence together. It is everyday life that installs

> predictability and bodies, things and spaces become subject to ordering processes. And the small everyday orderings can be subsumed under larger national orderings, merging the local with the national. Moreover, the persistence of such common patterns over time underpins a common sense that this is *how things are* and this is *how we do things*. There is thus an interweaving of conscious and unreflexive thought which typifies everyday practice and communication[36] [19].

The city is overcrowded, polluted, discriminating to its people. Nevertheless this existence—with "the enormous bustle of millions on the move, the hurtling local trains with thick clusters of bodies hanging precariously from the doors, the sonorous tramp and hum of the crowd inside the tall hall of Churchgate Station"—is what makes them feel alive and bring them together.

Here national consciousness is not based on myth or history, or by association with an "imagined community"; instead, it is very concrete, spatial in nature. It is the sense of home in the bustling city of Bombay that gives the character a common national identity. They are so entangled in their space through quotidian practices that even an upcoming doom could not separate them from the city which itself contains their identities. Gaitonde, instead of going back to his sojourn in Thailand, decides to stay back in India to search for Guru-ji and stop him, ignoring the danger of being killed by his enemy or encountered by the police. Gaitonde muses: "Where would home be when home was gone? Could you have a home away from home when there was no home? No I couldn't go anywhere, I couldn't leave.... I would stay right here, close to the field of battle, in it, I would stop Guru-ji.... I would save my home" (841). The attachment other characters feel towards the city is similar. Throughout, Sartaj has displayed a certain degree of possessiveness over his own space. He is devoted towards his duty because "he didn't like people getting killed on his beat" (78) and even in last moments he would rather carry on with his duty. Sartaj's partner Kamble feels the city needs to be reborn and he would not hesitate to die with it. Same sentiments are reflected in other characters like Gaitonde's friend Jojo and Sartaj's love interest Mary.[37] Sartaj sums it up for everyone:

Perhaps Kulkarni was wrong about the people of Bombay, perhaps they would stay in their city even if they knew that a great fire was coming. They would wait for the bomb in these tangled lanes, grown out of the earth without forethought or plan. People came here from gaon [village] and vilayat [abroad], and they found a place to sit, they lay down on a dirty patch of land, which shifted and settled to take them in, and then they lived. And so they would stay [785].

The knowledge of fast approaching death ushers *Dasein* towards "anticipatory resoluteness"; that is, finally *Dasein* stops viewing death as a long distant event and becomes aware of its finitude and its power to define the self, thus, *Dasein* becomes "authentic." Martin J. Walsh explains how Heidegger uses this term as a movement away from "facticity" of everydayness:

Human being, *Dasein* grasps the possibilities of its situation as a challenge to its own power of becoming what it is freely capable of becoming. It reaches out beyond itself and aims at what it is not yet. It strives to understand and appropriate its world and it strives to create and become its authentic self.[38]

Despite Gaitonde's spatial power and Sartaj's "recolonizing" power, the characters ultimately remain powerless. They cannot alter or control the bigger narrative in the power center. But as "authentic being" they can define the self with or without the "they." The realization of having a limited amount of time on this earth allows *Dasein* to decide which factical possibilities are important and meaningful to it. Both Gaitonde and Sataj, in the face of imminent death, are in full awareness of being "thrown" into the world, and "choose" to continue with the "they-self" and it is this "choice" that brings the two opposing characters at a meeting point.

Existential anxiety is always accompanying the being even in its inauthenticity. Interpreting Heidegger, Anna Rowan observes that there are two stages of being "authentic": *becoming* authentic and *continue being* authentic.[39] But this authenticity is slippery, and a being can slip back anytime into everyday inauthentic existence. *Continue being authentic* is when *dasein* consciously puts effort to retain its authenticity. Gaitonde in a fit of anger shoots Jojo whom he considered his closest ally. In her death he accepts his limitedness and the pointlessness of it all; the killing, money-making all seemed to him futile. He realized his surrender to *das Man* had cost this situation: "I was defeated.... What I did or didn't, do was irrelevant. Or worse, it was entirely relevant. Whatever I chose to do would contribute to his plan, would end in fire. The world wanted to die, and I had helped it along. He had set up the sacrifice, and every action of mine was fuel. I couldn't stop it." His inability to control the direction of his own action left his future existence to inauthenticity. Thus, he decides to end his life in order to avoid being slipped back to inauthenticity. He rather "chose" to die in his "authentic being," as he surmises, "but I can ... stop myself. This is the only and last thing I can choose. In this, I can defeat even you, Guru-ji. I can stop myself" (857). The mystery of why Ganesh Gaitonde killed himself in the bunker is solved in the voice of the dead man himself: "I do it because I know who I am" (859).

Sartaj from the beginning had intertwined his existence with Mr. Parulkar, his mentor. Parulkar was great with political games; his loyalty changed with every change in the government. Sartaj admired him for it and depended on him for support in both personal and professional front. Early in the book he couldn't even imagine being his own self without him. Parulkar makes him feel secure in his position. The thought of Parulkar's possible dismissal from the force "flung him into anger" and left him in a sudden uncertainty of what if "Parulkar was gone, what of Sartaj? What would become of him?" (10). But in the face of impending doom he finally refuses to define his existence as entwined with others and chooses to be the primary author of his life. He understood that "every connection came freighted with loss, every attachment with the possibility of betrayal. There was no avoiding this conundrum, no escape from it, and no profit from complaining about it" (943). So, when Parulkar's enemy asks Sartaj to expose his boss's corruption, he did betray him to save this world. But even when the bomb has been disposed of and the world has been saved, he dwelled on the finitude of it all: "Sartaj didn't feel any safer. Inside him, even now, there was that burning fuse, the ticking fear.... Sartaj couldn't keep the question at bay: *You want to save this? For what? Why?*" (877).

The only Sikh inspector in the city, Sartaj was known for his suave appearance and was once featured in a magazine as "The City's Best-Looking Bachelor." But lately he had lost his glory. Even if in an understated manner, Sartaj has always striven to be recognized as the hero who saved the day. It reflected in his stubbornness to do the right thing, to catch the murderer. Or when he found the infamous Gaitonde in the bunker and asserted, "Gaitonde was mine," hoping no commissioner would arrive to snatch his prize. But finally when he did become the hero, when he did locate the nuclear weapon he wasn't ready to be defined by the "they" anymore, and he *continues being* authentic; he continues to exist in his everyday space but now "he was not afraid of happiness or heartbreak that lay ahead. He was newly alive, as if he had been freed of something" (945).

It is more of a passage to a greater understanding of the present milieu which gives an existential edge to the text. The conflict between the good and the bad is overshadowed by "the entrance of existential and tragic seriousness into realism."[40] Therefore, the plot is less concerned with the trope of "detective versus criminal," and more focused on how the figures cope with the postcolonial existence and seek an "authentic" existence. In the dystopic set up of the city where the idea of control is a mere illusion, the pursuit of the perpetrator by the detective, in the end, has been established as a *leela* or game. And "[to] win is to lose everything, and the game always wins" (44). Who is right? Who is wrong? These are questions that will remain unanswered. Because, "on the field, all actions were only provisionally moral, and the game was eternal. So was Ganesh Gaitonde a bad man? Was Nehru a bad man?" (308–09).

## Conclusion

Closure is an important part of detective fiction. In the last part of the narrative everything comes back to normalcy, so that everyday life can be resumed without doubts and fears of the unknown. Contemporary writers of the genre have played around with this element quite liberally to produce a crime novel that is desirable in this new era of diversity. At one level Chandra's story seems to attest to a conventional closure. Sartaj locates the bomb and crisis is averted. However, eliminating the underlying tensions owing to the multicultural setting seems to be an impossible task.

The divisiveness based on differing cultures, religion and class dominating the society makes it impossible to constitute a uniform national identity. Instead, the characters take shelter in their private experience of the nation-state to build mutual connection. Since nations are "not only constructions, but also *continually in the making*,"[41] national identity too continually reinvigorates itself to infuse nationalism among its citizens. In current India the Nehruvian secular nationality is being gradually silenced by the right-wing's Hindutva nationalism. In 2019 India's re-election of a political party that feeds on the ideology of Hindu domination and minority assimilation is a confirmation of that in reality.

Sartaj too realizes this fact and therefore a sense of impermanence looms behind it all. In order to make sense of the world, in the end Sartaj dismisses the necessity of a closure and asserts that "[t]o be alive [is] enough."

NOTES

1. *Lexico, s.v.* "nation," accessed May 20, 2019, https://www.lexico.com/en/definition/nation.

2. Vikram Chandra, *Sacred Games* (2006; Reprint, Gurgaon: Penguin Books, 2014).

3. Ashutosh Varshney, "Contested Meanings: India's National Identity, Hindu Nationalism, and the Politics of Anxiety," in *Daedalus*, vol. 122 (1993), 227–61.

4. Martin Heidegger, *Being and Time*, trans. John Macquarrie and Edward Robinson (Oxford: Basil Blackwell, 1965).

5. Eva Erdmann, "Nationality International: Detective Fiction in the Late Twentieth Century," in *Investigating Identities: Questions of Identity in Contemporary International Crime Fiction*, eds. Marieke Krajenbrink and Kate M. Quinn (New York: Rodopi, 2009), 12.

6. Varshney, "Contested Meanings," 233.

7. Article 29 in Indian Constitution enables any section of Indian citizen belonging

to minority community to conserve their distinct language, script or culture. Article 30 gives minorities the right to establish their own linguistic and religious institutions.

8. James Hay, "Piecing Together What Remains of the Cinematic City," in *The Cinematic City*, ed. David B. Clarke (London: Routledge, 1997), 226.

9. Sunil Khilnani, *The Idea of India* (London: Penguin Books, 2003), 167.

10. Maria Varsam, "Concrete dystopias: Slavery and Its Others," in D*ark Horizons: Science Fiction and the Dystopian Imagination*, eds. R. Baccolini and T. Moylan (New York: Routledge, 2003), 209.

11. Sujata Patel, "Bombay/Bombay: Globalization, Inequalities, and Politics," in *World Cities Beyond The West: Globalization, Development, and Inequality*, ed. Josef Gugler (New York: Cambridge University Press, 2004), 328.

12. Akhil Gupta and K. Sivaramakrishnan, "Introduction: The State in India After Liberalization," in *The State in India After Liberalization*, eds. Akhil Gupta and K. Sivaramakrishnan (Oxon: Routledge, 2011), 3.

13. In their study of literary geography Barbara Piatti and others have suggested five components of fictional spaces: setting, projected space, zone of action, marker and routes. The projected space is described as places of the characters' dream, nostalgia or longing.

14. Barbara Piatti, Anne-Kathrin Reuschel, and Lorenz Hurni, "Dreams, Longings, Memories—Visualising the Dimension of Projected Spaces in Fiction," *Proceedings of the 26th International Cartographic Conference* (Dresden: International Cartographic Association, 2013), 1–18, accessed May 14, 2019, http://www.literaturatlas.eu/files/2014/01/Piatti_ICC2013_final.pdf.

15. Ananya Jahanara Kabir, "'Handcuffed to History': Partition and the Indian Novel in English," in *A History of the Indian Novel in English*, ed. Ulka Anjaria (New York: Cambridge University Press, 2015), 120.

16. Naxalites are followers of Mao's doctrines. Marked by state and central governments as terrorists, they waged their fight in 1967 against the landlords, businessmen and politicians who they believed had been unjust to the poor, specifically the Dalit and Tribal population.

17. Vikram Chandra, "A Conversation with Vikram Chandra," Interview by Jai Arjun Singh, Jabberwock. Blogger, 25 Aug. 2006. Web. 16 Aug. 2016.

18. Robert T. Tally, Jr., "This Space That Gnaws and Claws at Us," in *Epistemocritique: Litterature et saviors* 9 (2011).

19. George Simmel, "The Metropolis and Mental Life," in *Metropolis: Centre and Symbol of Our Times*, ed. P. Kasinitz (Basingstoke: Macmillan, 1995), 30.

20. Alexander C. Diener and Joshua Hagen, "The City as Palimpsest: Narrating National Identity Through Urban Space and Place," in *The City as Power: Urban Space, Place, and National Identity*, eds. Alexander C. Diener and Joshua Hagen (Lanham, MD: Rowman & Littlefield, 2019), 3.

21. Vikram Chandra, "Kama," in *Love and Longing in Bombay* (1997; Reprint, Gurgaon: Penguin Books, 2010).

22. Slavoj Zizek, *Looking Awry: A Introduction to Jacques Lacan Through Popular Culture* (Cambridge: MIT Press, 1991), 58.

23. Claire Chambers, "Postcolonial *Noir*: Vikram Chandra's 'Kama,'" in *Detective Fiction in a Postcolonial and Transnational World*, eds. Nels Pearson and Marc Singer (Farnham: Ashgate, 2009), 37.

24. Raymond Chandler, *The Simple Art of Murder* (New York: Pocket Books, 1944), 17.

25. "Kama," 151.

26. Mary Evans, *The Imagination of the Evil* (London: Continuum, 2009), 25.

27. "Postcolonial *Noir*," 38.

28. Ian Rankin, *Even Dogs in the Wild* (London: Orion, 2016), 285.

29. Heidegger, *Being and Time*.

30. John Haugeland, "Reading Brandom Reading Heidegger," *European Journal of Philosophy* 13 (2005), 423.

31. Henri Lefebvre, *The Production of Space*, trans. Donald Nicholson-Smith (Oxford: Blackwell, 1991), 44.

32. Suketu Mehta, *Maximum City: Bombay Lost and Found* (New York: Alfred Knopf, 2004), 309.

33. Lalitha Gopalan, "Bombay Noir," *Journal of the Moving Image* 13 (2015), 73.
34. *Ibid.*, 73.
35. Lefebvre, *Production*, 44.
36. Tim Edensor, *National Identity, Popular Culture and Everyday Life* (Oxford: Berg, 2002), 19.
37. Jojo and Mary are also sisters, another similar aspect in the parallel trajectories of Sartaj and Gaitonde.
38. Martin J. Walsh, *A History of Philosophy* (London: Geoffrey Chapman, 1985), 537.
39. Anna M. Rowan, "Dasein, authenticity, and choice in Heidegger's *Being and Time*," *Logo I Ethos* 1 (2016), 99.
40. Erich Auerbach, *Mimesis: The Representation of Reality in Western Literature* (Princeton: Princeton University Press. 2003), 481.
41. Ghassan Hage, "The spatial imaginary of national practices: dwelling—domesticating/being—exterminating," *Environment and Planning D: Society and Space* 14 (1996), 463–85.

## Bibliography

Auerbach, Erich. *Mimesis: The Representation of Reality in Western Literature.* Princeton, New Jersey: Princeton University Press. 2003.
Chambers, Claire. "Postcolonial *Noir*: Vikram Chandra's 'Kama.'" In *Detective Fiction in a Postcolonial and Transnational World*, edited by Nels Pearson and Marc Singer, 31–46. Farnham: Ashgate, 2009.
Chandler, Raymond. *The Simple Art of Murder.* New York: Pocket Books, 1944.
Chandra, Vikram. 1997. "Kama." In *Love and Longing in Bombay.* Gurgaon: Penguin Books, 2010.
_____. 2006. *Sacred Games.* Gurgaon: Penguin Books, 2014.
_____. 25 Aug 2006. "A Conversation with Vikram Chandra." Interview by Jai Arjun Singh. Jabberwock. Blogger, Web. 16 Aug. 2016.
Diener, Alexander C., and Joshua Hagen. "The City as Palimpsest: Narrating National Identity Through Urban Space and Place." In *The City as Power: Urban Space, Place, and National Identity*, edited by Alexander C. Diener and Joshua Hagen, 1–22. Lanham, MD: Rowman and Littlefield, 2019.
Edensor, Tim. *National Identity, Popular Culture and Everyday Life.* Oxford: Berg, 2002.
Erdmann, Eva. "Nationality International: Detective Fiction in the Late Twentieth Century." In *Investigating Identities: Questions of Identity in Contemporary International Crime Fiction*, edited by Marieke Krajenbrink and Kate M. Quinn, 11–26. New York: Rodopi, 2009.
Evans, Mary. *The Imagination of the Evil.* London and New York: Continuum, 2009.
Gopalan, Lalitha. "Bombay Noir." *Journal of the Moving Image* 13 (2015): 64–90. http://jmionline.org/article/bombay_noir.
Gupta, Akhil, and K. Sivaramakrishnan. "Introduction: The State in India After Liberalization." In *The State in India After Liberalization*, edited by Akhil Gupta and K. Sivaramakrishnan, 1–28. Oxon: Routledge, 2011.
Hage, Ghassan. "The Spatial Imaginary of National Practices: Dwelling—Domesticating/Being—Exterminating." *Environment and Planning D: Society and Space* 14, no. 4 (August 1996): 463–85. doi:10.1068/d140463.
Haugeland, John. "Reading Brandom Reading Heidegger." *European Journal of Philosophy* 13 (2005): 421–428. doi:10.1111/j.1468–0378.2005.00237.x.
Hay, James. "Piecing Together What Remains of the Cinematic City." In *The Cinematic City*, edited by David B. Clarke, 211–231. London: Routledge, 1997.
Heidegger, Martin. *Being and Time.* Translated by John Macquarrie and Edward Robinson. Oxford: Basil Blackwell, 1965.
Kabir, Ananya Jahanara. "'Handcuffed to History': Partition and the Indian Novel in English." In *A History of the Indian Novel in English*, edited by Ulka Anjaria, 119–132. New York: Cambridge University Press, 2015.

Khilnani, Sunil. *The Idea of India*. London: Penguin Books, 2003.

Lefebvre, Henri. *The Production of Space*. Translated by Donald Nicholson-Smith. Oxford: Blackwell, 1991.

Mehta, Suketu. *Maximum City: Bombay Lost and Found*. New York: Alfred Knopf, 2004.

Patel, Sujata. "Bombay/Bombay: Globalization, Inequalities, and Politics." In *World Cities Beyond the West: Globalization, Development, and Inequality*, edited by Josef Gugler, 328–347. New York: Cambridge UP, 2004.

Piatti, Barbara, Anne-Kathrin Reuschel, and Lorenz Hurni. "Dreams, Longings, Memories— Visualising the Dimension of Projected Spaces in Fiction." In *Proceedings of the 26th International Cartographic Conference*, 1–18. Dresden: International Cartographic Association, 2013. Accessed May 14, 2019. http://www.literaturatlas.eu/files/2014/01/Piatti_ICC2013_final.pdf.

Rankin, Ian. *Even Dogs in the Wild*. London: Orion, 2016.

Rowan, Anna. "Dasein, authenticity, and choice in Heidegger's *Being and Time*." *Logos i Ethos* 41, no.1 (2016): 87–105. http://dx.doi.org/10.15633/lie.1795.

Simmel, George. "The Metropolis and Mental Life." In *Metropolis: Centre and Symbol of Our Times*, edited by Philip Kasinitz, 30–45. Basingstoke: Macmillan, 1995.

Tally, Robert T., Jr. "This Space That Gnaws and Claws at Us." *Epistemocritique: Litterature et saviors* 9 (Autumn 2011). https://epistemocritique.org/this-space-that-gnaws-and-claws-at-us/.

Varsam, Maria. "Concrete dystopias: Slavery and Its Others." In *Dark Horizons: Science Fiction and the Dystopian Imagination*, edited by Raffaella Baccolini and Tom Moylan, 203–224. New York: Routledge, 2003.

Varshney, Ashutosh. "Contested Meanings: India's National Identity, Hindu Nationalism, and the Politics of Anxiety." *Daedalus* 122, no. 3 (1993): 227–61. http://www.jstor.org/stable/20027190.

Walsh, Martin J. *A History of Philosophy*. London: Geoffrey Chapman, 1985.

Zizek, Slavoj. *Looking Awry: An Introduction to Jacques Lacan Through Popular Culture*. Cambridge: MIT Press, 1991.

# "Congress has never heard a voice like mine"

## Law, Legal Fictions and National Legal Culture in Native American Detective Writing

### ALEXANDRA HAUKE

## U.S. Congress, the Marshall Trilogy and Legal Fictions

On January 3, 2019, former New Mexico Democratic Party chairwoman Deb Haaland (Laguna Pueblo tribe) was sworn into the 116th U.S. Congress as one of the first two Native American women members[1] and is now the representative for New Mexico's 1st congressional district. Haaland ran her campaign for election in November 2018 under the tagline #BEFIERCE, addressing and speaking out for women's rights—especially women of color—by pushing for political reforms in education, abortion access, and sexual harassment laws as well as for climate injustice by supporting the Standing Rock water protectors in their protests against the Dakota Access Pipeline. For Haaland's proponents, her win means that New Mexico has made history in its state politics: it signifies "a victory for working people, a victory for women, and a victory for everyone who has been sidelined by the billionaire class"; and it confirms that "every New Mexican and American has the chance to thrive regardless of our skin color, neighborhood, religion, gender, who we love, or the size of our bank account."[2]

With 19 percent of its members from minority groups, the 115th U.S. Congress was already more ethnically diverse than any before it; however, only two members—Tom Cole (Chickasaw) and Markwayne Mullin (Cherokee)—were registered Native Americans among the 100 senators and 435 representatives.[3] The small number of indigenous individuals that make up the country's population (less than 2 percent) is often used to justify this lack of tribal representation in contemporary American politics. However, more tangible reasons for such disregard include the United States' history of exclusion of minority groups—especially natives and women[4]—in all areas of the political sector, and the economic obstacles many tribal peoples cannot overcome when it comes to financing congressional races, which discourage them from running for office in the first place and adds another layer of marginalization to their already difficult positions.

Deb Haaland's rare chance to serve in Congress as of 2019 thus comments not only on the position of such twice- and thrice-marginalized individuals as objects of identity politics, "negative stereotyping," and "social sorting"[5] in the history of American (cultural) politics, but more broadly on the mechanics, possibilities, and effects of law on different social groups. According to the Constitution of the United States, Congress can "make all Laws which shall be necessary and proper for carrying into Execution the foregoing Powers, and all other Powers vested by this Constitution in the Government of the United States, or in any Department or Officer thereof."[6] This makes clear the importance of members from minority groups in legislative roles, as individuals from their communities are statistically subjected to higher rates of victimization, incarceration, and inequalities by primarily white legal institutions[7] and thus rely heavily on representatives working against ethnic disadvantage and white privilege in the government's highest branches. "You want to have influence over people who are making decisions for one of the most vulnerable communities in our country," says Haaland when asked why she decided to run for Congress.[8] Her statement speaks to the centuries-long legal disagreements at the heart of federal-tribal relations in the U.S., rooted in the Supreme Court's historical "lack of coherent doctrine"[9] and its "rudderless exercise in judicial subjectivism,"[10] resulting in the fact that "federal Indian law is characterized by doleful incidents"[11] because "the Court has injected itself into Indian affairs despite having even more inferior constitutional pedigree than Congress."[12] Tribal politicians like Haaland thus represent a newly gained opportunity for native people to be included in executive processes regarding their own situation, countering the fact that the fate of "the most vulnerable communities" in the U.S. still lies in the hands of the non-native governing majority.

Historically, indigenous tribes were politically "homogenous units" and "primarily judicial in the sense that the council […] looked to custom and precedent in resolving novel and difficult social questions that arose."[13] European contact and the colonizers' seizure of legislative power over all native peoples brought about forceful attempts at providing legal structure to these self-administering tribal nations in the early 19th century, the era of Indian

Removal. The three most significant cases in this federal-tribal legal history, *Johnson v. M'Intosh, Cherokee Nation v. Georgia,* and *Worcester v. Georgia*— communally known as the Marshall Trilogy after their enactor, John Marshall, the fourth Chief Justice of the United States—defined "Indians" as "domestic dependent nations" who "occupy a territory to which we [the U.S. Supreme Court] assert a title independent of their will"; thus, they "occupy a state of pupilage" and their "relation to the United States resembles that of a ward to his guardian."[14] From a 21st-century perspective, these outrageous declarations signify on their own datedness, yet their "legal afterlife"[15] persists in the contemporary ramifications of the colonial era and thus supports the neo-colonial agenda in its efforts to maintain white supremacy in all areas of legal, political, and socio-cultural life. While decrees such as Public Law 93–638 (1975), for example, would finally give federally recognized tribes the right to establish their own constitutions and legal bodies to enact the laws of their national boundaries, tribal peoples' status as victims of nationalization—as what Beth Piatote, in line with an 1856 U.S. attorney general decision, calls "domestic subjects"[16]—has not faltered: a fact that continues to spur on native quests for self-assertion and sovereignty through activism, scholarship, increased political involvement, and literary production.

Deb Haaland's important exclamation "Congress has never heard a voice like mine"[17] signifies on her unprecedented opportunity to become a member of U.S. Congress as a long overdue and necessary step towards increased native (and female) representation in the governmental realm and a significant symbolic move against the constraints of domestic subjectivity in the face of the Marshall Trilogy: in 1823, during *Johnson v. M'Intosh,* Marshall nullified the tribal right of occupancy through his claim that "[d]iscovery is the foundation of title, in European nations, and this overlooks all proprietary rights in the natives" and that, therefore, "all existing titles depend on the fundamental title of the crown of discovery."[18] In the context of this and all following rulings under the Chief Justice, it was clear that there was no opportunity for an "international forum in which [any one] claim could be challenged had the Indians known and objected"[19] and that the Court's legal supremacy would thus become the superlative order of ongoing conquest. For many years, during periods of treaty-making, removal and relocation, assimilation, and termination, native tribes were subjected to similar ordeals; and their inferior legal position continuously put them at a clear disadvantage and robbed them of official platforms to stipulate their terms, claim their needs, and assert their existences and identities. It will come as no surprise, therefore, why Haaland's accession to the never-before-experienced power of occupying a seat in Congress is such an invaluable occurrence in native history: their representative status as native individuals signifies a communal voice that affords domestic subjects the right to be heard and the agency to participate in discussions about the rule of American law, whose "remarkably divergent purposes [of] justifying colonialism in the pursuit of constitutionalism"[20] are still in full effect. Haaland's case highlights that more opportunities for indigenous peoples to tell their own stories are emerging, but that much work is still to be done to allow, for example, a "constitutional amendment incorporating them into the federal-state design" in order to extrapolate much of America's exceptionalism from its legal doctrine[21] and pass sentences on individual case bases instead of standardized convictions rooted in the contradictory congressional-constitutional impulses of Marshallian law.

While such imperatives towards legal representation, visibility, agency, and self-determination are at the forefront of indigenous political activism, Native Americans support these efforts by pushing for more recognition in other sectors as well: first and foremost, literary production. Catherine Rainwater suggests that native writers take to literature for the "considerable, world-altering political power within aesthetic form"[22] and thus advocate anti-colonial discourses to provoke changes in the U.S.'s national identity politics of erasure and exclusion in legal culture. In this essay, I examine the ways in which indigenous literary efforts to (re)write genre fiction such as detective fiction, which has been dominated by the "traditional reliance of fictional detection, particularly in the hard-boiled tradition, on Western, white, male protagonists"[23] until the 1960s and 70s, participate in and enable such decolonizing discourses. Gerald Vizenor's *The Heirs of Columbus* (1991) is one of the earliest examples of indigenous-penned detective novels for the ways it invests in discussions about the legal marginalization of native tribes and the hegemonic practices of genre writing. *Heirs*, like the subgenre on a larger scale, introduces the reader to "worlds in which Native people have the opportunity to enforce, rather than be coerced by, the law"[24] and thus to narrate indigenous pasts, presents, and futures from the point of view of the colonized other. As I will show, the literary and political imperatives of Native American detective writing culminate in revisionist versions of federal-tribal legal history, signifying on the inextricable link between fiction and law and thus on the power of narrative to reshape the American imaginary of "Indians" as both constituting and challenging factors for the myth of national-legal unity. Vizenor's text ultimately explores the potential of this corrective practice by scrutinizing the possibilities for indigenous agency, creativity, and sovereignty.

## Legal History, Law and Literature and Indigenous Detective Writing

There is great consensus among Native American writers and scholars that tribal storytelling is in itself "an act of agency, of asserting control over one's own culture."[25] It "challenges the supposed objectivity of classic historiography,"[26] it is "imaginative self-recreation,"[27] it brings the community together, engages strategies of remembering and surviving, binds the past to the present, and thereby pushes the people unstoppably towards future action. The magnitude of the practices and significances of storytelling in and for native history is far greater than the constraints of this essay allow; it stands to reason, however, that literature, in its many forms, continues to be the primary form of artistic, personal, collective, political, legal, cultural, and activist expression for indigenous peoples because it opens up spaces of possibility to engage in practices of identity-formation amidst the aforementioned contemporary ramifications of the colonial project and to imagine worlds in which those affected by these difficulties are allowed to participate in "the workings of an anticolonial imaginary: visions of alternative futures that may explain, in part, how Indian communities survived the violence"[28] of "the doctrine of discovery and conquest."[29]

Native fictions thus make dealing with the impossible realities of everyday life possible. This is especially significant when it comes to representations and negotiations of law, legal fictions, and national legal culture in literature, as the impossibility of tribal peoples as "dependent sovereigns"[30] and "subjects of empire"[31] dominates the limiting agency of the tribes' domestic subjectivity and can best be processed through the power of verbal critique in narrative. One particularly influential way to examine these fictional attempts to understand real-life practices is to read literary narratives in conversation with legal texts, i.e., to engage in the study of law and literature. With its origins as far as back as classical antiquity and ties to the Western origins of rhetoric, the tradition of conjoint readings of law and literature exhibits both profound "historical depth" and "conceptual as well as quantitative scope"; it is said to have experienced a "revival" in terms of "legal humanism" in American academia in the late 1960s and throughout the 1970s, a time when the field was crowned as a "movement" in its own right.[32] While Klaus Stierstorfer identifies two major reasons for the reemerging interest in law and literature during that time—the rise of the academic job market and the simultaneous rejection of that rise as a reason—the temporal connection between the revival and the emergence of the diverse civil rights movements in the United States further strengthens the emphasized effort of this practice to "rehumanize the law."[33] In the context of tribal history, the founding of the American Indian Movement (AIM) in 1968 speaks to this synergy; in fact, "Red Power activism, more Native American students graduating from university and law school programs, and a federal policy allowing tribes to sue in federal court" led to a high number of tribes raising "indigenous issues in American courts beginning in the 1970s,"[34] the time the Nixon administration put an end to termination policies and the Ford administration introduced efforts towards sovereignty, for example, through the enactment of the Indian Self-Determination and Education Assistance Act in 1975. The surgence of AIM and law and literature as a field also coincide with what is commonly termed "The Native American Renaissance," a period of increased literary production following the 1969 Pulitzer Prize win of N. Scott Momaday's seminal novel *House Made of Dawn* (1968), a text many native writers have named as a significant source of inspiration for their own work and which critics have marked as a breakthrough into a substantial change in the landscape of tribal literature.[35]

These increasing opportunities to fictionalize and thereby expose the inner workings of the federal government from native perspectives gained particular momentum during the last few decades of the 20th century in the form of the novel. Sean Kicummah Teuton observes that, "[w]hether masquerading or assimilating, resisting or recovering, the Native American novel persists, ironically, not only by preserving but in fact by rewriting narrative traditions." In this sense, "from the arrival of the first American Indian novel," namely John Rollin Ridge's *The Life and Adventures of Joaquín Murieta: The Celebrated California Bandit* (1854), "native writers have been forced to meet the demands of a mainstream reading audience that often harbors inaccurate views of Native Americans"[36]—most prominently in popular American genres such as the Western or the crime story. The title of Ridge's novel insinuates elements of both these genres in its form and content: Murieta, whose legacy as a Hispanic folk hero stems from the text's negotiations of the cultural borderlands between Mexico and the United States shortly after the Mexican War (1846–48), tends to a life of revenge through crime after being banished from his land and witnessing his family's wrongful suffering. He "robs the wealthy to support the weak throughout the land"[37] and yet he is often prone to "resembl[ing] romantic portrayals of the noble savage"[38] in his quest to avenge Cherokee land theft. Ridge's story is firmly grounded not only in the aftermath of war and the traditions of the historical novel but also in the results of the Indian Removal Act (1830) and the land redistribution orders of *Cherokee Nation v. Georgia* (1831). Thus situated within the cultural and legal contexts of its time, *Joaquín Murieta* offers the earliest opportunity in the history of the native novel to co-examine law and literature, to identify thereby its central concern—the federal government's crimes against non-whites—and to locate this theme in narratives that would follow in its footsteps. Sabine N. Meyer claims that, due to the unilateral political power of Euro-American institutions in the United States, "Native American texts—both non-fictional and fictional—have inevitably had to engage, thematically as well as aesthetically, with the legal discourses and legal landscapes put in place by the colonizer"; thus, "they can only be understood by placing them within the historical and legal framework of federal Indian law." Most importantly, she goes on, "Native American literature adds its own legal vision to the law, so that we can conceive of the relationship between Native American literature and federal Indian law as a dialogic one,"[39] asserting the fundamental necessity for legal readings of indigenous fiction as articulations of cultural sovereignty and tribal identities in flux. Many scholars have shown that such interdisciplinary readings are effective in a variety of genres across indigenous literatures,[40] essentially because both the crimes of empire and tribal resistance against them have permeated all Native American texts—fictional, nonfictional, oral, and written. Within this frame, the cultural contexts, thematic concerns, and aesthetic features of Ridge's *Joaquín Murieta* point towards a specific legacy of negotiations of legal culture, systemic imperialism, and national identity, namely the efforts of Native American writers in crime and detective writing. Shelley Streeby advocates that Ridge "worked within the conventions of the best-selling crime novel in hopes of making money" and, in *Joaquín Murieta*, "alludes to different types of crime literature, placing his novel within an international field of popular knowledge about crime."[41] Furthermore, "in imagining and exploiting a transnational connection with Indigenous Mexico he perhaps began a trend in Cherokee and other Native novels to come"[42] that traces a direct arc between the historical crimes committed against native peoples and indigenous crime stories as genre as the central emphases of a study of law and literature, respectively.

With the Marshall Trilogy's legal crimes, Ridge's literary efforts, and Deb Haaland's political success in mind, this evolution now leads to the principal concerns of this essay. Native American literature, a set of products emerging from the frameworks of past and present indigenous history and thus from resistant writing against the judicial hegemony of Euro-American rules of law, is at its core concerned with the imperial crime of colonialism, strategies to face this harsh circumstance, and efforts towards self-assertion, justice, and recognition. Situating these ideas within a larger theorization of formal aesthetics and formulaic conventions, it could be argued that all literary works created by native writers in the United States adhere to the larger notion of crime fiction, whose central themes can be traced to the complex workings and diverse iterations of violence and the almost compulsory societal need to understand its reasons, catch its enactors, and prevent its further dissemination. This might explain why those few works in the abundance of scholarship on crime writing that have attempted to outline the role of Native American authors, readers, and subjects[43] either exclusively employ the term "crime fiction" in discussions of the form's agents and concerns or use "crime" and "detective" writing interchangeably without commenting on the blurry terminological boundaries and the larger discordance about generic naming that permeate the form and its many subcategories. While indigenous studies scholar James H. Cox is the first to fill some of the theoretical and epistemological gaps created by the aforementioned studies in his recent article "Native American Detective Fiction and Settler Colonialism" (2017), he also alternates the use of the terms crime and detective fiction to refer to the same body of works and does not address the lacuna in scholarship about Native American detective fiction or engage in in-depth analyses of most of the narratives he mentions. Yet Cox is the first to provide ideas about a by-no-means-exhaustive tribal-penned corpus of novels pertaining to the genre of Native American detective fiction: he engages in its origins in and connections to the golden age of the larger genre of American crime fiction, the significance of its "cultural and political emphases," its "narrow focuses on crime, detection, and punishment" as themes rooted in the "central concerns of Native literary history" more generally, and its leitmotifs, such as the needs of native communities to gain "the authority to determine the future of their children, to protect their tribal nation citizens from sexual assault, and to maintain their land, natural resources, and cultural property"—all in all, to invest in the strategies of "explicitly anti-colonial literature."[44] Reading Cox's outline against my earlier assertion that most of native literature could be classified as crime fiction in a larger sense due to its thematic focus on crimes but not necessarily on detection, I want to address why I see a clear need for the distinction between crime and detective writing in the context of indigenous literatures in the United States, where the former is too general a denominator to carve out the specifics of the latter.

I employ the term "detective"—inflected by the suffix "ive" as denoting a processual practice—in a comprehensive way that allows for an adjectival, methodical, and applied understanding of its mechanics.[45] While detective writing draws from the constituents of crime fiction, such as the violent backdrop of settler colonialism and its legacies, it refuses to put an exclusive focus on a story's outcome and, in turn, this happy ending in the hands of a singular and/or central investigator as proposed by the standardized formulae of detective fiction, thereby detaching the exclusive-associative link between "detective" and "human figure/embodiment of the law." In indigenous literatures, therefore, detective texts stand out from crime stories because they *are* detective in that they narrate in a detective mode and so allow the process of storytelling to take center stage. Such forms of indigenous self-narration emerge as strategies of identity-formation by employing oral traditions, creation stories, and pre-contact legal histories to decenter the linear progression of the straightforward murder-suspect-solution plot structure—a justification tool for the detective as a body of the American state, whose sole purpose is to protect, serve, discover, succeed, and leave the scene. The tribal emphasis on storytelling as an alterNative[46] detective process instead creates anti-hegemonic discourses countering the burden of Columbian "discovery" that weighs heavily on indigenous history. Euro-American detective fiction has enforced the discovery myth in particularly pertinent ways either by appointing white authorities with discovering the truth about perpetrators with "Indian blood," such as in Peter Bowen's *Coyote Wind* (1994), or by imagining indigenous sleuths (often sidekicks of the main white investigator) as stereotypical trackers in the popular dime novels of the 1880s, wherein their close connections to nature ascribe to them practices of discovery non-native detectives are unable to obtain, as in Judson R. Taylor's *Phil Scott, the Indian Detective: A Tale of Startling Mysteries* (1882). In such Western-penned examples, as Dorothea Fischer-Hornung and Monika Mueller observe, authors often structure the "ethnic plot" and the "detective plot" alongside each other, emphasizing the former over the latter and thus engaging with "the distance the detective's particular ethnic group has from 'mainstream' society"[47] in ways that can only enforce the settler-colonial agendas at the core of the discovery narrative. By denying the need for ethnic explanations at the hands of the colonizer and refusing culturally-motivated plot separations, indigenous detective texts shift the focus of the respective tales towards processual uncoverings of historical dispossessions, erasure, and silencing at the hands of the native community—a reversal of the imposition of *being* discovered into active *discovering* through self-narration as well as a conscious employment of people- and sovereignty-oriented language rooted in oral storytelling. "Words are rituals in oral tradition," according to Gerald Vizenor, "from the sound of creation, the wisps of visions on the wind, [...] not cold pages or electronic beats that separate the tellers from the listeners."[48] In this sense, while the indigenous detective novel's backdrop is crime, its emphasis is (self-) detection—i.e., the detec*tive* practice overcomes "the [historical] difficulties of articulating forms of public voice for Native peoples in light of shifting legal paradigms"[49] by enabling organic, non-linear narrative creation.

From this follows that native detective narratives become detec*tive* through a contextual reading of law in conversation with literature, not least because, according to Cox, they expose "the capriciousness of law enforcement in a settler colonial context"[50] on both sides of the native-colonizer divide. Simultaneously, they create scenarios that enable indigenous communities to take (back) control of their legal situations through tribal-centered modes of self-representation—i.e., narration from the native inside—that allow the legally sidelined other to tell their own stories in an anti-colonial manner instead of being subjected to Chief Justice Marshall's 19th-century master narratives about them. Babara Villez suggests that, "[r]ather than tools through which to examine each other, [law and literature] are a pair, two actors in the same project, two facets of one and the same object: a national culture"; they "participate in the construction of a national identity" and thereby "of a citizen's legal culture,"[51] a process that ties the latter inextricably to the former and necessarily forms a connection between the individual's cultural identity—for example, in terms of race, class, or gender—and the respective nation's judicial institutions. I have already touched upon the Marshall Trilogy's archaic character; it is fundamental at this point, however, to refer back to its unwarranted persistence and its condition as a set of what Hope Babcock calls "legal fictions about the conquest of Indians and their nature," lacking "intellectual purpose" in the 21st century and instead "hiding a normative judgment that Indians should not exists [sic] as a separate people"[52]: after two centuries, "the trilogy and its legal implications [still dominate] all facets of Native American life, including Native literary production." They endure as "the foundation of federal Indian law"[53] and thus of native identities as seen by the Supreme Court. Reading Villez's, Babcock's, and Meyer's ideas in conversation, it becomes clear that, in the context of these identities, the national culture that emerges from the rules of the law is that of the Euro-American master and that the concerns of tribal peoples and their identities are always tethered to the federal judiciary's hegemony and its reliance on Marshallian law as a legal fiction. While in the third case, *Worcester v. Georgia*, Marshall tried to soften the radical blows of his first two decisions and contradicted his own statements in the process by fashioning new fictions, he "never directly overruled his earlier views" and thus enabled future courts to "use language from his first two opinions to justify infringing upon tribal sovereignty and ignore his later changes."[54] Babcock argues that all three of Marshall's rulings engaged in the uses and usefulness of the legal fiction doctrine, whereby legal fictions are "statements understood by lawyers and judges to be false, but that lead to a consistent holding in the law [and] are rarely questioned as anything other than a tool the law uses to ensure a fair or consistent conclusion."[55] A look at the history of native disenfranchisement post–Trilogy provides a clear answer to the question whether and how legal fictions become historical fact: through his piercing rhetoric and convincing ability to sell his opinions as facts, Marshall engaged in the establishment of a common us-vs.-them-binary ideology between "Americans" and "Indians" to maintain the general public's satisfaction with the workings of the federal government. Marshall's legal fictions thus work as a "type of storytelling where the fiction is created to make a smooth rule of law"; as a consequence, "the fiction [...] justifies the actions taken by the court"[56] well into the present day.

Considering Sabine N. Meyer's subsequent impulse that "indigenous rights discourses need to be disentangled from the language and structures of colonialism,"[57] it becomes clear why native efforts to write fiction wherein which the authors scrutinize federal and enforce native law have gained more and more urgency in the 21st century. Early law and literature scholarship "used the tools of literary criticism to understand the law, and particularly [the] legal opinions" behind the fictionalized court cases, "as a narrative,"[58] i.e., as legal fictions, according to Babcock. The literature this scholarship examines is itself a fiction about the law and thus concerned with law *in* literature, which now situates the Native American detective genre firmly among the concerns of the study of law and literature, thus combining the twofold impulses of the subgenre mentioned above—detect*ive* narration and discussions of legal (dis)enfranchisement. I argue that native detective novels refuse to acknowledge Columbus's discovery and Marshall's rulings as constitutive of past, present, and future indigenous identities, epistemologies, stories, and practices of meaning-making. Rather, they employ the act of detection—the process of investigation—as an anti-colonial, counter-narrational *modus operandi* overturning the course of discovery imposed on indigenous lives from the imperial outside. In the process, these texts reframe, refocus, and rewrite the discovery narrative in the context of journeys towards self-discovery, sovereignty, and self-assertion from the alterNative inside. By exposing the wrongdoings of the federal government, the limitations of federal Indian law, and the inevitable necessity of future legal reforms, the texts at the center of my analysis become narratives of and about discovery in a variety of ways that go beyond both the simplistic application of "detective" as an investigative authority tied to the law in official or unofficial ways and the straightforward ethnic-vs.-detective-plot-arcs, in which indigenous peoples' identities and actions continue to be overruled. The diegetic worlds of native detective novels are informed not only by the respective legal cases they scrutinize but, first and foremost, by the larger crime behind the entire corpus on the level of native history, representation, and sovereignty—colonialism and hegemonic dominance. The imperial crime of the colonizer on the colonized thus takes center stage and remains as the primary object of resistance after the last page has been turned, even if the diegesis suggests closure on the intratextual level, thus negotiating ways in which the U.S. continues to operate as a neocolonial crime scene.[59] Native American detective writing is thus concerned with producing fictions *contra* legal fictions: as Babcock's reading has convincingly shown, "judges have accepted Marshall's Indian law fictions even when the empirical record supporting them is known to be false. The continuing power of those fictions to inform modern federal Indian jurisprudence is distressing and must be more than simply habit,"[60] a plea echoed by Philip Frickey, who contends that an "appropriate first step would be a judicial acknowledgement of these realities."[61]

My subsequent reading of Gerald Vizenor's *The Heirs of Columbus* (1991) teases out the novel's aesthetic and political emphases as a detect*ive* text—a narrative of (self-) discovery on several levels—and the legal contexts of its intra- and extradiegetic worlds. Vizenor's novel is among the many native detective novels published in the 1990s, a time when the subgenre came to life as an immediate result of the "wealth of academic literature [that] began to emerge on the history and typology of the [detective] genre" in the 1960s and 70s,[62] decades of civil rights activism during which the "feminist counter-tradition,"[63] African American contributions to the form,[64] and the "gay/lesbian police subgenre"[65] gained momentum, as did the institutionalization of multicultural and postcolonial studies in the U.S. between the 1970s and approximately 1990, whose agenda "has been to stress the intersection of various differential discourses such as ethnicity/culture/race, gender, nation, religion, or sexuality" in literature, especially in genre fiction.[66] Gerald Vizenor—alongside, for example, Linda Hogan, Ron Querry, Adrian C. Louis, Louis Owens, Carole laFavor, Sherman Alexie, Mardi Oakley Medawar, Stephen Graham Jones, Sara Sue Hoklotubbe, Tom Holm, Marcie Rendon, D.L. Birchfield, and Louise Erdrich—contributes to the genre of Native American detective fiction fundamental discussions of the impact of legal fictions and the federal government's "powerful sense of settler colonial entitlement"[67] on contemporary native identities and cultural productions; the text shows that, through alterNative perspectives on formula fiction and strategies of self-narration, native communities can break free from the constraints of federal-judicial laws to build worlds in which they are "[r]estrained only by the laws of fiction."[68] As we will see, these liberating efforts echo Vizenor's idea of survivance, put forth in his 1994 study *Manifest Manners: Postindian Warriors of Survivance*,[69] whose implications of native survival, resistance, presence, remembrance, endurance, and perseverance speak to the continuance of native tribes and their stories in the face of centuries of adversity. Survivance functions as "narrative resistance" against the settler-colonial project, as "a sense of native presence [in law and literature] over absence, nihility, and victimry,"[70] whereby native detective novels become extensions of "the new stories of tribal courage" which make up "the core of survivance."[71] Thus, by imagining and practicing the political, legal, and literary sovereignty of indigenous communities, these texts, of which *Heirs* is but one example, lay bare the ways in which dialogic readings of narrative and law assert national-tribal identities as self-governing agents of non-hegemonic narration.

# "Your honor, there is one more incredible discovery to report": Gerald Vizenor's The Heirs of Columbus

Gerald Vizenor's seventh novel has received much critical and scholarly attention from a variety of perspectives. Elizabeth Blair, for example, reads the text as a "whodunwhat" and pays particular homage to its use of "the conventions of the postmodern detective story"[72] while Andrew Uzendoski draws attention to the ways "Vizenor critiques contemporaneous international legal norms in response to global celebrations of the 500th anniversary of Christopher Columbus's first voyage to the Americas."[73] Beyond these contexts, *Heirs* emerges not only as a literary extension of the political movements of the late 20th century outlined above but also as a narrative situated firmly in the legal situations of its time—framed, first and foremost, by the Native American Graves Protection and Repatriation Act (NAGPRA), enacted in 1990.

> The Act first establishes the ownership of cultural items excavated or discovered on federal or tribal land after November 16, 1990. [...] Native American remains and associated funerary objects belong, first, to lineal descendants. If the descendants cannot be identified, then those remains and objects [...] belong, in order of preference, to the tribe on whose land the remains or objects were found, or the tribe having the closest cultural relationship to them[...]. The Act then provides for repatriation of these items upon request of the appropriate descendent or tribe.[74]

Vizenor's work thematizes the theft of indigenous sacred objects—such as medicine pouches, masks, or ceremonial feathers—and human remains, crimes that take center stage in the novel during courtroom hearings, collaborative investigations, and tribal pleas for legal compliance to NAGPRA. The ensuing negotiations of the just ways of following and the corrupt manners of breaking this law draw a direct line to theft—of land, identity, and community—as the original settler crime, established by Marshallian law through the nullification of the tribal right to occupancy and already fictionalized in the first indigenous (crime) novel, Ridge's *Joaquín Murieta*. Through discussions of these kinds of robbery, violence, acceptance, and sovereignty on both sides of the colonizer-colonized divide, *Heirs* emphasizes the necessary acknowledgment of the power of federal-legal fictions on the one hand and tribal storytelling on the other for native identities, communities, and justice.

Vizenor's novel is, at its core, a principal story of survivance that denies the straightforward imposition of settler discovery: Vizenor reimagines Christopher Columbus as a Mayan who "brought civilization to the savages of the Old World," who "escaped from the culture of death and carried our tribal genes back to the New World, back to the great river; he was an adventurer in our blood and he returned to his homeland" (9). This revisionist context, which is narrated by Stone Columbus—heir to both Christopher Columbus and a stone—and founded on the fact that "the great explorer was tribal and he carried our stories in his blood" (4), remains unbelievable to many of the non-native characters in the novel, such as late night radio host Admiral Luckie White. She mocks the Anishinaabe's stories, beliefs, and fluidity of identities through her insistence that "this is serious radio" (9) and that she will not tolerate her listeners' corruption by absurd claims to genetics that defy "the real story" (10) of Columbus's heroism. Luckie is not convinced of Stone's stories without evidence to their truthfulness, thus holding on to the singularity of the discovery narrative and the legal fiction of American conquest and occupancy. Her denial of the possibility for stories to serve as official credos for native ways of living and Stone's contrasting assertion of the same tribal creation story as a marker of sovereignty situates Vizenor's *Heirs* firmly among the concerns of Native American detective writing from the onset, whereby self-narration within and beyond legal contexts allows for a reconsideration of agency in the context of tribal and non-tribal judicial norms and rights.

The novel's subsequent concern with the establishment of the first cross-blood tribal nation at Point Assinika illustrates this struggle: the nation's new location, with its "wild, West Coast, circus-like bingo pavilions," arises in stark contrast to the "urban, East Coast, mannered building"[75] inhabited by the Brotherhood of American Explorers. The principal villains of the novel, the Brotherhood, intend to appropriate for their own purposes the remains of Christopher Columbus, which, as stipulated by NAGPRA, legally belong to the titular heirs, his native descendants. "The number of heirs is a tribal secret" that is never revealed in the text, "but there were nine who told stories that autumn evening at the stone tavern" (14), where, according to Stone's grandmother Truman Columbus, civilization has its origins and where stones told the original creation stories until they were stolen and sold by missionaries and anthropologists. Theft and repatriation are subsequently at the thematic forefronts of *Heirs*' central courtroom scenes, during which the narrative emphasis of indigenous detec*tive* storytelling is established. While the federal government is represented by a single federal judge (Beatrice Lord), a sole member of the Brotherhood (Doris Miché́d), and one private investigator (Captain Treves Brink) during the court hearing "over the rights of tribal stories and the remains of the great explorer" (65), the community of heirs as witnesses, sleuths, and rightful owners of Columbus's bones decenter this unidirectional and one-dimensional understanding of narration, existence, and possession.

Vizenor's use of similar or identical names (such as Christopher/Binn/Stone/Truman Columbus) and the occasional omission of their first names confront the reader with a kind of linguistic puzzle that merges the actual crime plot, defined by the true heritage of Christopher Columbus, with the imperative power of the detec*tive* narrative mechanics to (con)fuse native and non-native (hi)storytelling by cutting across Western linearity and chronology. Within and beyond *Heirs*, "language is our trick of discovery" (169), which is why "Vizenor writes Columbus into the history of the Anishinaabe, carves his name into the family tree," and thereby "essentially disarms history."[76] From this follows that the purpose of the hearing is not to sentence the perpetrator who stole Columbus's remains but "to discover what a crime means in this particular case" (68)—i.e., to narrate (on) the meta-level of legal fictionality where the crimes of colonialism and Marshallian law define indigenous subjectivities and thus rights of belonging. In this context, one of the novel's most meaningful assertions comes from one of the heirs, lawyer-trickster-poacher Felipa Flowers, mother of Stone's daughter Miigis, who declares that "the liberation of our stories is no crime" (60); rather, establishing the heirs' narratives as collective processes of meaning- and identity-making enables the imperative of resilience at the heart of survivance as a resistant strategy against unlawful actions at the hands of the American justice system.

Among these narratives is the testimony of Memphis, the black panther-heir, which bears witness to the sacred focus on the ongoing process of indigenous creation, liberation, and inspiration: "we were created by a trickster mongrel who disguised the outside of creatures with skin and hair, beaks and ears, but we are animals on hold with interior visions [...] and the shaman heals the animals with stories in our blood, not the masks we wear as humans, the mask dies, the stories endure" (70–71). The panther's explanation of the power of narrative and frequent corporeal transformation from human to animal during her interview cut across the federal judge's imaginative abilities and displace the standard detective-novel-interrogation in favor of the tribal traditions of oral storytelling: Memphis cannot bring the state agents any clarity in the case at hand because "the judge and lawyers [...] demanded too much from science, cold reason, and human disguises to see the eyeshine of animals in stories" (72). Instead, she embodies Vizenor's "trickster-sleuth," whose "signature [...] is chaos and chance,"[77] whose interest lies in justice for their community, and whose role as only one of several potential yet never fully realized investigators of the crime not only dips into the non-linear practices of postmodern and post-structuralist narration but also into the fundamental multivocality of tribal storytelling. Memphis "purred to inspire and animate the memories of the judge"; as a consequence, Lord "laughed to consider judicial practices, but she would hold to reason and the best disguises she understood between the nouns and verbs of human existence and the myths of evolution" (72). Such evolution is "highbred delusion," according to the panther (70), which is why *Heirs* refuses to acknowledge indigenous beginnings as tethered to Columbus as the discovering detective, the singular "patriarch or origin."[78] Instead, the novel provides a plethora of heirs across species and genders as the uniters—not the discoverers—of the new cross-blood tribe, whose familial relations extend beyond primary blood lines. The simultaneity of the descendants' roles as witnesses to the theft, potential criminals or accomplices in the eyes of the federal agents, and investigators shedding light on the inner workings of Anishinaabe cultural traditions and worldviews subverts the exclusive responsibilities of the singular Euro-American detective, whose individualism is employed as the primary requisite for legal heroism.

Following Memphis's imaginative account of the powers of tribal stories, Major Chaine Riel Doumet, one of several native investigators in the novel, yet again highlights the significant connection between storytelling and (legal) fictions: he emphasizes that "the modern idea of ownership is not the same as the tribal sense of possession" (76); therefore, "medicine pouches and bones are possessed by shamans, but not owned by museums" (77), the same way native land was already sovereignly treated according to tribal property rights pre European contact; it was not a mythical "property-less Eden"[79] inhabited in unfaltering peace, waiting to be conquered. As he grants the heirs legal and cultural right to repatriation in accordance with both federal and tribal law, Doumet, like Memphis, closes his account by drawing attention to the "problem [...] over the recognition of stories and natural objects as having standing to argue in court." He stresses the necessity of "a sovereign bone court on a barge, a new forum to hear and decide disputes over the reburial of human and animal remains," whereby "the court would protect the rights of tribal bones to be represented in court" (77) in line with "the right of possession to those remains" as outlined in NAGPRA: "Whoever knowingly sells, purchases, uses for profit, or transports for sale or profit" tribal relics without this right "shall be fined [...] or imprisoned [...] or both."[80] Doumet's insistence on the legal significance of bone courts supports the heirs' declaration that "the last rites are never the last words" (78), yet again echoing the NAGPRA clauses outlined earlier in this essay, whereby non-identification or non-traceability of the direct descendants of native belongings leads to the conveyance of property to their respective tribe. The Brotherhood's case is thus nullified from the start, predicated only on false accusations of Felipa's own involvement in the respective theft, which will end with their unsuccessful attempt to use the heirs' stories against them. Ultimately, the "unusual judicial hearing would depend more on imagination than on material representations," an effort in "favor [of] tribal consciousness" (65) that results in Beatrice Lord censuring the Brotherhood for their manipulative tactics against the heirs and the court itself. In this sense, the novel serves not only native justice but also allows the federal judge to prove her lawful integrity by sentencing the colonizer's legal fictions: "The real is the simulation" (86), she speaks to the injustices of tribal oppression before she is invited by the heirs to join them at the stone tavern through a trickster-dream-journey that will traverse her across physical and metaphysical realms, thereby situating the legal representative firmly among the native practices of imagination and narration. The hearing thus shows no reliance on Euro-

American imaginations of detective fiction but rather defies the Western imaginaries of "Indians," legal procedures as well as material profit from indigenous artifacts and thereby "resists romantic nostalgia while recognizing loss"[81] in a truly self-detective and self-assertive manner.

The last tribal witness in *Heirs'* courtroom hearing, Lappet Tulip Browne, another indigenous private investigator, adds an additional layer to the novel's dialogic understanding of law and literature outlined above. When she is encouraged by Judge Lord to "study the law [because] your mind is too bright to waste on investigation," she retorts: "The rules of a legal culture rule out tribal stories and abolish chance in favor of causative binaries. I choose to be a private investigator, to discover the stories my way and avoid male domination" (82). While the judge dismisses the detective profession in favor of the superiority of law, Lappet roots her suspicion and rejection of legal institutions in their domination by male hegemony and their erasure of storytelling as a constitutive practice for native identity- and meaning-making. She emphasizes her individual choice as a specific act of (female) agency that reestablishes the domestic tribal subject as an effective organ of native sovereignty through self-assertion and community-centered activism. Lappet's ironic use of the word "discover" in the context of storytelling ultimately reframes the dominant master narrative about tribal people, anchored in the legal fictions of Marshallian law, into an alterNative model of creation that enforces self-discovery from the indigenous inside. In this sense, investigation—of the "[t]rickster stories [that] liberate the mind in language games" (82), of native being, and of the power to self-govern—has the highest priority in *Heirs* and, by extension, the native detective novel.

What brings my reading of *Heirs* as a detec*tive* text invested in the practices of law and literature full circle at this point of Lappet's ultimate moment of personal and legal self-assertion is its potential as a literary forerunner of the 2009 ratified Constitution of the White Earth Nation, where many of the novel's titular beneficiaries were born. Principally authored by Vizenor himself, the main aim of the Constitution is "to secure an inherent and essential sovereignty, to promote traditions of liberty, justice, and peace, and reserve common resources, and to ensure the inalienable rights of native governments for our posterity."[82] The chapters of the constitutional document cover such important premises as territory and jurisdiction; the rights and duties of the tribe's citizens; governance; boards and community councils; or the powers of its courts, judges, and presidents—concerns that also define the heirs' motivations for justice and legal compensation as well as their plans for indigenous futures of equality and liberty. When Judge Lorde proclaims that "[s]tories, then, are at the core of tribal realities, not original sin, for instance, or service missions," Lappet responds: "Stories and imagination, your honor, but of a certain condition that prescinds discoveries and translations" (80)—

that denies the colonial legacies of legal fictions. Yet, as the investigator continues, the "rules of a legal culture rule out tribal stories" (82) because any challenge to the cultural-political unity and stability of the nation-state in the form of non-normative practices are always already perceived as existential threats to its national identity and narrative—an idea that arguably still persists in American (political) culture in the 21st century. The Brotherhood's attempt to outsmart the heirs by mocking these practices and convincing the Judge of the heirs' absurd, uncivilized traditions by appealing to her rationale as a body of the law echoes the Marshallian idea that a tribal nation is "a weak state" that cannot be trusted to speak the truth, let alone rule American lands because it would "leave the country a wilderness."[83] By contrast, Lappet's account that "the languages we understand are games" because "[t]rickster stories liberate the mind in language games" (82) is rather reminiscent of Jill Doerfler's afterword to the constitutional document of the White Earth Nation, whereby "[t]ribal sovereignty is inherent and is not a privilege that the United States has granted Native nations"[84]—as the legal fiction doctrines would dictate.

Both *Heirs* and the Constitution thus embody sovereignty, democracy, and survivance, concepts, along with constitutionalism, that "are intimately linked to the ideas of national identity, political authority [...], international law and diplomacy, and intergovernmental relations,"[85] and that entitle native tribes to their own decision- and law-making processes. As becomes clear in *Heirs*, Lappet's self-assertive impression on the Judge, the creation of Point Assinika, the rejection of Columbian discovery, the reformulation of tribal history, and the striving for a sovereign, crossblood nation articulate the precontact view of "each Native nation" to operate as "a unique socio-cultural-political body that sought self-fulfillment and maturity on every human level, both internally and externally," without turning settler hegemony on its head par for par in a pursuit of sovereignty as "absolute power."[86] During their testimonies, Felipa, Memphis, and Lappet never ask for more than what is rightfully theirs: their only claims are the bodily remnants of their past, which will allow them to discover and create a new future as a fully sovereign community without federal legal interference. In this sense, the novel does not exchange dominance for dominance or seek revenge on historical hegemony. Rather, it exposes the limitations of federal law, which becomes most evident when Felipa Flowers heads to London to investigate clues pointing towards a potential retrieval of the remains of Pocahontas. She is kidnapped and killed by Doric Michéd's henchmen after she "had rescued a tribal woman from the cruelties of more than three centuries of civilization; she was at peace, unconcerned, and lonesome for the heirs" (115). Scotland Yard homicide inspectors hold Felipa's body for assessment before closing the case without being able to determine the causes of her death; Doric is, in turn, convicted yet released on parole due to circumstantial evidence, a final reminder that, even in the face of a clear violation of NAGPRA's right of possession, the "politics of race [are] never secure" (121) and the "judicial subjectivism" of Euro-American practices of legal justice speak to its "inextricable complicity with the project of colonial conquest and subjugation."[87]

Only when Point Assinika is officially declared a sovereign nation by the heirs, after it "became the wild estate of tribal memories and the genes of survivance in the New World" (119), are Felipa's fate revealed and her remains buried on tribal grounds next to those of Christopher Columbus and Pocahontas. Vizenor does not provide the reader with restorative legal justice for Felipa; yet the repatriation of the remains of the novel's central emblematic tribal figures in line with NAGPRA highlights that "[w]e heal with opposition, we are held together with opposition, not separation, or silence, and the best humor in the world is pinched from opposition" (176)— a claim supported by Judge Lord's pledge to support the sovereignty of Point Assinika (177). *Heirs* ends with a final trial for the new tribal nation when the wiindigoo—the evil, cannibalistic gambler of Anishinaabe creation stories who was embodied by Doric Michéd earlier in the text—is "thawed out by federal operatives, an act of vengeance because two agents were burned by the stolen tavern stone" (177), after he was frozen and kept in a cave by an ice woman at the beginning of the novel. As wiindigoo tests the tribe's oppositional powers by threatening their harmony with violence—an ultimate repetition of the colonial crimes of the past—the heirs resist with the peaceful medicine of storytelling: "Stone is a healer in his stories, and he discovered the course of humor that heals here" (169). Wiindigoo's defeat then opens up a recuperative, repatriated space for Vizenor's epilogue: "Columbus arises in tribal stories that heal with humor the world he wounded; he is loathed, but he is not a separation in tribal consciousness. The Admiral of the Ocean Sea is a trickster overturned in his own stories five centuries later" (185).

Through the successful (re)establishment of the sovereign nation at Point Assinika, *Heirs* ultimately echoes the White Earth Constitution in its claims that "[t]he time has come for tribal nations to rebuild."[88] The novel is detec*tive* in that it uncovers possibilities for such reconstruction processes when the "Eurocentric core" of Indian law fails "the discourse of Native sovereignty"[89]: it finds them in the communal healing practice of storytelling and in the anti-colonial words of the oral, mythic sense of "stories in the blood" (20) that endure in "the signature of survivance" (28) that is native literature, sovereignty, and activism. As such, what the crime in *The Heirs of Columbus* means is that "death is not the end of stories and human rights under law" (78), just as the end of the colonial era does not signify a stop to native disenfranchisement through legal misdemeanors. The Constitution of the White Earth Nation as a fundamental "charter of self-governance"[90] makes dealing with these dispossessions possible in new, legally sovereign ways so that the Anishinaabe can overcome the colonizing reproductions of dominance that define both law and literature. By blurring the edges of the standard detective genre without erasing its contours and allowing tribal identities to assert themselves through tribal-constitutional legal mechanics, Vizenor's novel creates possibilities for indigenous renewal across diverse practices of storytelling and law-making. By bringing the heirs into fruitful conversation with agents of the federal state, the novel is able to mediate spaces where native perspectives on both law and literature have the highest priorities. After all, as Stone Columbus argues, "the heirs are sovereign and the court hears our stories" (78).

Where U.S. federal law closes cases due to circumstantial evidence, the Native American detective novel opens new doors for discussions of tribal-legal agency beyond Marshallian rulings and Columbian discovery. The collective, not the detective, brings about change: ultimately, crime gives way to imagination and to the assertion of sovereign tribal nations, identities, and legal cultures. The practices of generic rewriting at play in Vizenor's narrative reaffirm the legal contexts of NAGPRA and the Constitution of the White Earth Nation in ways that signify on the inextricable link between law and literature in *Heirs* as a Native American detective novel wherein Columbian discovery is decentered in favor of Anishinaabe self-discovery.

"The politics of tribal creation stories never ends" (111), according to Felipa. And this is what it means that U.S. Congress is finally hearing voices like Deb Haaland's: the legal afterlife of the Marshall Trilogy continues to be challenged in 2019 by the heirs of native Columbus.

NOTES

1. The second member is Sharice Davids (Ho-Chunk Nation), who is now the representative for Kansas's 3rd congressional district. As the first openly gay Kansan and only the seventh openly queer member overall elected for Congress, she continuously raises her voice in matters of LGBTQ+ rights and speaks out about the importance of diversity, especially in the political realm. Haaland's and Davids' contributions are thus crucial for contemporary understandings of socio-cultural equality and serve to refocus the fundamental concerns of the American justice system. In this essay, I will exclusively focus on Haaland's position to carve out the significance of her political efforts and their connections to legal theorizations of indigenous cultural products.

2. Deb Haaland, Twitter Post, June 6, 2018, 6:35 am. https://twitter.com/Deb4Congress NM/status/1004220152559239168.

3. GovTrack.us, "Members of Congress," https://www.govtrack.us/congress/members.

4. Cf. Susan Herbst, *Politics at the Margin: Historical Studies of Public Expression Outside the Mainstream* (Cambridge: Cambridge University Press, 1994), 33; David E. Wilkins, *American Indian Politics and the American Political System* (Lanham, MD: Rowman & Littlefield, 2007), especially chapters 2 and 3.

5. Cf. Haaland.

6. *The Constitution of the United States: The Bill of Rights and All Amendments*, Article 1, Section 8, Clause 18, http://constitutionus.com/.

7. Cf. Jeffrey Ian Ross and Larry Gould, eds., *Native Americans and the Criminal Justice System* (New York: Routledge, 2006), especially chapters 8, 9, 10, and 13.

8. Leila Fadel, "Record Number of Native Americans Running for Office In Midterms," National Public Radio, July 4, 2018, https://www.npr.org/2018/07/04/625425037/record-number-of-native-americans-running-for-office-in-midterms?t=1535444817111.

9. Charles E. Wilkinson, *American Indians, Time and the Law* (New Haven: Yale University Press, 1987), 4.

10. David H. Getches, "Conquering the Cultural Frontier: The New Subjectivism of the Supreme Court in Indian Law," *California Law Review* 84, no. 6 (December 1996): 1573.

11. Philip P. Frickey, "Adjudication and Its Discontents: Coherence and Conciliation in Federal Indian Law," *Harvard Law Review* 110 (1997): 1754.

12. Philip P. Frickey, "(Native) American Exceptionalism in Federal Public Law," *Harvard Law Review* 119, no. 2 (December 2005): 436.

13. Vine Deloria, Jr., and Clifford M. Lytle, *American Indians, American Justice* (Austin: University of Texas Press, 1983), xiii.

14. *The Cherokee Nation v. The State of Georgia*, 30 U.S. 1, 5 Pet. 1, 8 L.Ed. 25, https://openjurist.org/30/us/1.

15. Sabine N. Meyer, "From Federal Indian Law to Indigenous Rights: Legal Discourse and the Contemporary Native American Novel on the Indian Removal," *Law & Literature* 29, no. 2 (2017): 270, https://doi.org/10.1080/1535685X.2016.1246902.

16. Beth Piatote, *Domestic Subjects: Gender, Citizenship and Law in Native American Literature* (New Haven: Yale University Press, 2013), 8.

17. Deb Haaland, "Deb Haaland for Congress—Ready," YouTube Video, 0:30, May 8, 2018, https://www.youtube.com/watch?v=GL9aiZtbz-8.

18. *Johnson and Graham's Lessee v. William M'Intosh*. 21 U.S. 543, 5 L. Ed. 681, 8 Wheat. 543. January 25, 2019. https://openjurist.org/21/us/543.

19. Deloria and Lytle, *American Indians*, 4.

20. Frickey, "Exceptionalism," 436.

21. *Ibid.*

22. Catherine Rainwater, *Dreams of Fiery Stars: The Transformation of Native American Fiction* (Philadelphia: University of Pennsylvania Press, 1999), 47.

23. Charles J. Rzepka, *Detective Fiction* (Cambridge: Polity, 2005), 235.

24. James H. Cox, "Native American Detective Fiction and Settler Colonialism," in *A History of American Crime Fiction*, ed. Chris Raczkowski (Cambridge: Cambridge University Press, 2017), 252.

25. Sabine N. Meyer, "From Domestic Dependency to Native Cultural Sovereignty: A Legal Reading of Gerald Vizenor's *Chair of Tears*," in *Native American Survivance, Memory, and Futurity: The Gerald Vizenor Continuum*, eds. Birgit Däwes and Alexandra Hauke (New York: Routledge, 2017), 131.

26. Kimberly M. Blaeser, "The Language of Borders, the Borders of Language in Gerald Vizenor's Poetry," in *The Poetry and Poetics of Gerald Vizenor*, ed. Deborah L. Madsen (Albuquerque: University of New Mexico Press, 2012), 5.

27. Karl Kroeber, "Why It's a Good Thing Gerald Vizenor Is Not an Indian," in *Survivance: Narratives of Native Presence*, ed. Gerald Vizenor (Lincoln: University of Nebraska Press, 2008), 29.

28. Piatote, *Domestic*, 9.

29. Sabine N. Meyer, "In the Shadow of the Marshall Court: Nineteenth-Century Cherokee Conceptualizations of the Law," in *Twenty-First Century Perspectives on Indigenous Studies: Native North American in (Trans)Motion*, eds. Birgit Däwes, Karsten Fitz, and Sabine N. Meyer (New York: Routledge, 2015), 151.

30. Judith Resnik, "Dependent Sovereigns: Indian Tribes, States, and the Federal Courts," *The University of Chicago Law Review* 56 (1989): 671–759.

31. Glen Sean Coulthard, *Red Skin, White Masks: Rejecting the Colonial Politics of Recognition* (Minneapolis: University of Minnesota Press, 2014), 1.

32. Klaus Stierstorfer, "The Revival of Legal Humanism," in *Law and Literature*, ed. Kiernan Dolin (Cambridge: Cambridge University Press, 2017), 9–10.

33. *Ibid.*, 10.

34. Franke Wilmer, "Indigenous Peoples' Responses to Conquest," in *Encyclopedia of Violence, Peace, and Conflict*, eds. Lester R. Kurtz and Jennifer E. Turpin (San Diego: Academic Press, 1999), 185.

35. The term renaissance has been starkly criticized because it suggests a disregard of preceding literary production and enforces the common Western image of "the Indian" as stuck in the past; when seen not so much—or not only—as a nomer for literary creation post Momaday's Pulitzer, however, but even more so for the overwhelming publicity of and interest in that production and also the changes in the political sector, the quintessential meanings of the term do apply.

36. Sean Kicummah Teuton, "The Native American Tradition," in *The Cambridge History of the American Novel*, eds. Leonard Cassuto, Claire Virginia Eby, and Benjamin Reiss (Cambridge: Cambridge University Press, 2011), 1107.

37. *Ibid.*

38. Sean Kicummah Teuton, "The Native Novel," in *The American Novel 1870–1940*, eds. Priscilla Wald and Michael A. Elliott (Oxford: Oxford University Press, 2014), 425.

39. Sabine N. Meyer, "The Marshall Trilogy and Its Legacies," in *The Routledge Companion to Native American Literature*, ed. Deborah L. Madsen (New York: Routledge, 2016), 128.

40. Cf. Meyer, "Legal Discourse"; Piatote, *Domestic*; Weaver, *People*; Duane Champagne and Carole E. Goldberg, *Captured Justice: Native Nations and Public Law* 280 (Durham: Carolina Academia Press, 2012); George D. Pappas, *The Literary and Legal Genealogy of Native American Dispossession: The Marshall Trilogy Cases* (New York: Routledge, 2017); David J. Carlson, *Imagining Sovereignty: Self-Determination in American Indian Law and Literature* (Norman: University of Oklahoma Press, 2016).

41. Shelley Streeby, *American Sensations: Class, Empire, and the Production of Popular Culture* (Berkeley: University of California Press, 2002), 263.

42. Teuton, "Native Novel," 425.

43. See, for example, Gina and Andrew MacDonald's *Shaman or Sherlock? The Native American Detective* (2002); Ray B. Browne's *Murder on the Reservation: American Indian Crime Fiction* (2004).

44. Cox, "Native American," 261–62.

45. This use of the term "detective" is reminiscent of Stephen Rachman's reading of Edgar Allan Poe's Dupin stories, in which the author showed "an interest in the ratiocinative process, not the character of the detective per se, that led [him] to his innovation and away from it as well. He left it to others, notably Sir Arthur Conan Doyle, to explore the possibilities of the character of the detective, of which his deductive methods would be but one facet" ("Poe and the origins of detective fiction," in *The Cambridge Companion to American Crime Fiction*, ed. Catherine Ross Nickerson [Cambridge: Cambridge University Press, 2010], 21).This, in turn, brings to mind Charles Rzepka's distinction between "detective" fiction and stories of "detection" as well as Patricia Merivale's and Susan Elizabeth Sweeney's use of the term "detecting texts," which all challenge literary expectations and ask questions about the roles, purposes, and effects of genre.

46. I borrow this term from Katja Sarkowsky, who, in turn, has adopted it from Drew Hayden Taylor: "'AlterNative' is […] an ironic and humorous concept that does not clearly denote a particular subject position or identity, but that is rather flexibly defined by what it is not: the stereotype of the 'traditional Indian'" (*AlterNative Spaces: Constructions of Space in Native American and First Nations' Literatures* [Heidelberg: Winter, 2007], 21–22, n11). In this sense, alterNative implies a position facing the settler-colonizer from the indigenous inside.

47. Dorothea Fischer-Hornung and Monika Mueller, *Sleuthing Ethnicity: The Detective in Multiethnic Crime Fiction* (Madison: Fairleigh Dickinson University Press, 2003), 12.

48. Gerald Vizenor, *Landfill Meditations: Crossblood Stories* (Hanover: University Press of New England, 1991), 99.

49. Mark Rifkin, "Finding Voice in Changing Times: The Politics of Native Self-Representation during the Periods of Removal and Allotment," in *The Routledge Companion to Native American Literature*, ed. Deborah L. Madsen (New York: Routledge, 2016), 146.

50. Cox, "Native American," 253.

51. Barbara Villez, "Law *and* Literature: A Conjunction Revisited," *Law and Humanities* 5, no. 1 (2011): 210.

52. Hope M. Babcock, "The Stories We Tell, and Have Told, About Tribal Sovereignty: Legal Fictions at their Most Pernicious," *Villanova Law Review* 55 (2010): 803–804.

53. Meyer, "Marshall Trilogy," 127.

54. Babcock, "Stories," 814, 815.

55. Jen Camden and Kathryn E. Fort, "'Channeling Thought': The Legacy of Legal Fictions from 1823," *American Indian Law Review* 33 (2008–2009): 79.

56. *Ibid.*, 85.

57. Meyer, "Marshall Trilogies," 133.

58. Camden and Fort, "Channeling," 79.

59. In *An Indigenous Peoples' History of the United States*, Roxanne Dunbar-Ortiz similarly headlines that "North America is a crime scene," paying homage to Jodi Byrd's exclamation that "the story of the new world is horror, the story of America a crime" (Boston: Beacon Press, 2014), 228.

60. Babcock, "Stories," 830.

61. Frickey, "Exceptionalism," 490.

62. Christine Matzke and Susanne Muehleisen, "Postcolonial Postmortems: Issues and Perspectives," in *Postcolonial Postmortems: Crime Fiction from a Transcultural Perspective,* eds. Matzke and Muehleisen (Amsterdam: Rodopi, 2006), 1–2.

63. Margaret Kinsman, "Feminist crime fiction," in *The Cambridge Companion to American Crime Fiction*, ed. Catherine Ross Nickerson (Cambridge: Cambridge University Press, 2010), 21.

64. Robert E. Crafton, *The African American Experience in Crime Fiction* (Jefferson, NC: McFarland, 2015), 14.

65. Judith A. Markowitz, *The Gay Detective Novel: Lesbian and Gay Main Characters and Themes in Mystery Fiction* (Jefferson, NC: McFarland, 2004), 27.

66. Florian Sedlmeier, "Rereading Literary Form: Paratexts, Transpositions, and Postethnic Literature around 2000," *Journal of Literary Theory* 6, no. 1 (2012): 218.

67. Cox, "Native American," 257.

68. Meyer, "Legal Discourse," 285.

69. This study was later renamed *Manifest Manners: Narratives on Postindian Survivance* (1999).

70. Vizenor, *Survivance*, 1.

71. Vizenor, *Manifest Manners*, 4.

72. Elizabeth Blair, "Whodunwhat? The Crime's the Mystery in Gerald Vizenor's *The Heirs of Columbus*," in *Loosening the Seams: Interpretations of Gerald Vizenor*, ed. A. Robert Lee (Bowling Green: Bowling Green State University Popular Press, 2000), 156.

73. Andrew Uzendoski, "Speculative States: Citizenship Criteria, Human Rights, and Decolonial Legal Norms in Gerald Vizenor's *The Heirs of Columbus*," *Extrapolation* 57, no.1–2 (2016): 21.

74. William C. Canby, Jr., *American Indian Law in a Nutshell* (St. Paul: West, 1981), 385–86.

75. Yvette Koepke and Christopher Nelson, "Genetic Crossing: Imagining Tribal Identity and Nation in Gerald Vizenor's *The Heirs of Columbus*," *SAIL* 23, no. 3 (2011): 6.

76. Kimberly M. Blaeser, *Gerald Vizenor: Writing in the Oral Tradition* (Norman: University of Oklahoma Press, 1996), 96.

77. Blair, "Whodunwhat?," 156.

78. Koepke and Nelson, "Genetic," 8.

79. Andrew P. Morris, "Europe Meets America: Property Rights in the New World," Foundation for Economic Education, January 1, 2007, https://fee.org/articles/europe-meets-america-property-rights-in-the-new-world/.

80. Publ. L. 101–601, 25 U.S.C. 3001 et seq., 104 Stat. 3048 : §1170 (a). January 4, 2019. https://www.govinfo.gov/content/pkg/STATUTE-104/pdf/STATUTE-104-Pg3048.pdf.

81. Koepke and Nelson, "Genetic," 10.

# 184   Crime Fiction and National Identities in the Global Age

182. Gerald Vizenor and Jill Doerfler, *The White Earth Nation: Ratification of a Native Democratic Constitution* (Lincoln: University of Nebraska Press, 2012), 63.
83. *The Cherokee Nation v. The State of Georgia*, 30 U.S. 1, 5 Pet. 1, 8 L.Ed. 25, https://openjurist.org/30/us/1.
84. Jill Doerfler, "A Citizen's Guide to the White Earth Constitution: Highlights and Reflections," in *The White Earth Nation: Ratification of a Native Democratic Constitution*, by Gerald Vizenor and Jill Doerfler (Lincoln: University of Nebraska Press, 2012), 82.
85. David Wilkins, "Sovereignty, Democracy, Constitution: An Introduction," in *The White Earth Nation: Ratification of a Native Democratic Constitution*, by Gerald Vizenor and Jill Doerfler (Lincoln: University of Nebraska Press, 2012), 1.
86. *Ibid.*, 5, 5, 1.
87. Meyer, "Federal Indian Law," 272, 273.
88. Doerfler, "Guide," 82.
89. Sidney L. Harring, "Indian Law, Sovereignty, and State Law: Native People and the Law," in *A Companion to American Indian History*, ed. Philip J. Deloria and Neal Salisbury (Malden: Wiley-Blackwell, 2002), 443.
90. Wilkins, "Sovereignty," 8.

# Bibliography

Babcock, Hope M. "The Stories We Tell, and Have Told, About Tribal Sovereignty: Legal Fictions at Their Most Pernicious." *Villanova Law Review* 55 (2010): 803–31.
Blaeser, Kimberley M. *Gerald Vizenor: Writing in the Oral Tradition*. Norman: University of Oklahoma Press, 1996.
Blaeser, Kimberley M. "The Language of Borders, the Borders of Language in Gerald Vizenor's Poetry." In *The Poetry and Poetics of Gerald Vizenor*, edited by Deborah L. Madsen, 1–22. Albuquerque: University of New Mexico Press, 2012.
Blair, Elizabeth. "Whodunwhat? The Crime's the Mystery in Gerald Vizenor's *The Heirs of Columbus*." In *Loosening the Seams: Interpretations of Gerald Vizenor*, edited by A. Robert Lee (Bowling Green: Bowling Green State University Popular Press, 2000), 155.
Browne, Ray B. *Murder on the Reservation: American Indian Crime Fiction, Aims and Achievements*. Madison: University of Wisconsin Popular Press, 2004.
Camden, Jen, and Kathryn E. Fort. "'Channeling Thought': The Legacy of Legal Fictions from 1823." *American Indian Law Review* 33 (2008–2009): 77–109.
Canby, William C., Jr. *American Indian Law in a Nutshell*. St. Paul: West, 1981.
Carlson, David J. *Imagining Sovereignty: Self-Determination in American Indian Law and Literature*. Norman: University of Oklahoma Press, 2016.
Champagne, Duane, and Carole E. Goldberg. *Captured Justice: Native Nations and Public Law* 280. Durham: Carolina Academia Press, 2012.
*The Cherokee Nation v. The State of Georgia*. 30 U.S. 1, 5 Pet. 1, 8 L. Ed. 25. January 15, 2019. https://openjurist.org/30/us/1.
*The Constitution of the United States: The Bill of Rights and All Amendments*. Article 1, Section 8, Clause 18. January 17, 2019. http://constitutionus.com/.
Coulthard, Glen Sean. *Red Skin, White Masks: Rejecting the Colonial Politics of Recognition*. Minneapolis: University of Minnesota Press, 2014.
Cox, James H. "Native American Detective Fiction and Settler Colonialism." In *A History of American Crime Fiction*, edited by Chris Raczkowski, 250–62. Cambridge: Cambridge University Press, 2017.
Crafton, Robert E. *The African American Experience in Crime Fiction*. Jefferson, NC: McFarland, 2015.
Deb Haaland. "Deb Haaland for Congress—Ready." YouTube Video, 0:30, May 8, 2018. https://www.youtube.com/watch?v=GL9aiZtbz-8.
Deloria, Vine, Jr., and Clifford M. Lytle. *American Indians, American Justice*. Austin: University of Texas Press, 1983.
Doerfler, Jill. "A Citizen's Guide to the White Earth Constitution: Highlights and Reflections."

In *The White Earth Nation: Ratification of a Native Democratic Constitution*, by Gerald Vizenor and Jill Doerfler, 81–94. Lincoln: University of Nebraska Press, 2012.

Fadel, Leila. "Record Number of Native Americans Running for Office in Midterms." National Public Radio. July 4, 2018. https://www.npr.org/2018/07/04/625425037/record-number-of-native-americans-running-for-office-in-midterms?t=1535444817111.

Fischer-Hornung, Dorothea, and Monika Mueller, eds. *Sleuthing Ethnicity: The Detective in Multiethnic Crime Fiction*. Madison: Fairleigh Dickinson University Press, 2003.

Frickey, Philip P. "Adjudication and Its Discontents: Coherence and Conciliation in Federal Indian Law." *Harvard Law Review* 110 (1997): 1754–84.

Frickey, Philip P. "(Native) American Exceptionalism in Federal Public Law." *Harvard Law Review* 119, no. 2 (December 2005): 431–90.

Getches, David H. "Conquering the Cultural Frontier: The New Subjectivism of the Supreme Court in Indian Law." *California Law Review* 84, no. 6 (December 1996): 1573–655.

Haaland, Deb. "Tonight, New Mexico made history. #nmpol #nm01 #ruready #befierce." Twitter. June 6, 2018. https://twitter.com/Deb4CongressNM/status/1004220152559239168.

Harring, Sidney L. "Indian Law, Sovereignty, and State Law: Native People and the Law." In *A Companion to American Indian History*, edited by Philip J. Deloria and Neal Salisbury, 441–59. Malden: Wiley-Blackwell, 2002.

Herbst, Susan. *Politics at the Margin: Historical Studies of Public Expression Outside the Mainstream*. Cambridge: Cambridge University Press, 1994.

*Johnson and Graham's Lessee v. William M'Intosh*. 21 U.S. 543, 5 L. Ed. 681, 8 Wheat. 543. January 25, 2019. https://openjurist.org/21/us/543.

Kinsman, Margaret. "Feminist crime fiction." In *The Cambridge Companion to American Crime Fiction*, edited by Catherine Ross Nickerson, 148–62. Cambridge: Cambridge University Press, 2010.

Koepke, Yvette, and Christopher Nelson. "Genetic Crossing: Imagining Tribal Identity and Nation in Gerald Vizenor's *The Heirs of Columbus*." *SAIL* 23, no. 3 (2011): 1–33.

Kroeber, Karl. "Why It's a Good Thing Gerald Vizenor Is Not an Indian." In *Survivance: Narratives of Native Presence*, edited by Gerald Vizenor, 25–38. Lincoln: University of Nebraska Press, 2008.

Markowitz, Judith A. *The Gay Detective Novel: Lesbian and Gay Main Characters and Themes in Mystery Fiction*. Jefferson, NC: McFarland, 2004.

Matzke, Christine, and Susanne Muehleisen, eds. *Postcolonial Postmortems: Crime Fiction from a Transcultural Perspective*. Amsterdam: Rodopi, 2006.

Matzke, Christine, and Susanne Muehleisen. "Postcolonial Postmortems: Issues and Perspectives." In *Postcolonial Postmortems: Crime Fiction from a Transcultural Perspective*, edited by Matzke and Muehleisen, 1–16. Amsterdam: Rodopi, 2006.

"Members of Congress." Govtrack.us. January 18, 2019. https://www.govtrack.us/congress/members.

Merivale, Patricia, and Susan Elizabeth Sweeney. *Detecting Texts: The Metaphysical Detective Story from Poe to Postmodernism*. Philadelphia: University of Pennsylvania Press, 1999.

Meyer, Sabine N. "From Domestic Dependency to Native Cultural Sovereignty: A Legal Reading of Gerald Vizenor's *Chair of Tears*." In *Native American Survivance, Memory, and Futurity: The Gerald Vizenor Continuum*, edited by Birgit Däwes and Alexandra Hauke, 119–34. New York: Routledge, 2017.

Meyer, Sabine N. "From Federal Indian Law to Indigenous Rights: Legal Discourse and the Contemporary Native American Novel on the Indian Removal." *Law & Literature* 29, no. 2 (2017): 269–90. https://doi.org/10.1080/1535685X.2016.1246902.

Meyer, Sabine N. "In the Shadow of the Marshall Court: Nineteenth-Century Cherokee Conceptualizations of the Law." In *Twenty-First Century Perspectives on Indigenous Studies: Native North American in (Trans)Motion*, edited by Birgit Däwes, Karsten Fitz, and Sabine N. Meyer, 148–71. New York: Routledge, 2015.

Meyer, Sabine N. "The Marshall Trilogy and Its Legacies." In *The Routledge Companion to Native American Literature*, ed. Deborah L. Madsen, 123–34. New York: Routledge, 2016.

Morris, Andrew P. "Europe Meets America: Property Rights in the New World." Foundation for Economic Education. January 1, 2007. https://fee.org/articles/europe-meets-amer ica-property-rights-in-the-new-world/.

*The Native American Graves Protection and Repatriation Act.* Publ. L. 101–601, 25 U.S.C. 3001 et seq., 104 Stat. 3048 : §1170 (a). January 4, 2019. https://www.govinfo.gov/content/pkg/ STATUTE-104/pdf/STATUTE-104-Pg3048.pdf.

Pappas, George D. *The Literary and Legal Genealogy of Native American Dispossession: The Marshall Trilogy Cases.* New York: Routledge, 2017.

Piatote, Beth. *Domestic Subjects: Gender, Citizenship and Law in Native American Literature.* New Haven: Yale University Press, 2013.

Rachman, Stephen. "Poe and the origins of detective fiction." In *The Cambridge Companion to American Crime Fiction,* edited by Catherine Ross Nickerson, 17–28. Cambridge: Cambridge University Press, 2010.

Rainwater, Catherine. *Dreams of Fiery Stars: The Transformation of Native American Fiction.* Philadelphia: University of Pennsylvania Press, 1999.

Resnik, Judith. "Dependent Sovereigns: Indian Tribes, States, and the Federal Courts." *The University of Chicago Law Review* 56 (1989): 671–759.

Rifkin, Mark. "Finding Voice in Changing Times: The Politics of Native Self-Representation during the Periods of Removal and Allotment." In *The Routledge Companion to Native American Literature,* edited by Deborah L. Madsen, 146–56. New York: Routledge, 2016.

Ross, Jeffrey Ian, and Larry Gould, eds. *Native Americans and the Criminal Justice System.* New York: Routledge, 2006.

Rzepka, Charles J. *Detective Fiction.* Cambridge: Polity, 2005.

Sarkowsky, Katja. *AlterNative Spaces: Constructions of Space in Native American and First Nations' Literatures.* Heidelberg: Winter, 2007.

Sedlmeier, Florian. "Rereading Literary Form: Paratexts, Transpositions, and Postethnic Literature around 2000." *Journal of Literary Theory* 6, no. 1 (2012): 213–33.

Sopelsa, Brooke, and Brian Latimer. "Rep.-elect Sharice Davids, a gay Native American, is ready to 'shape the future' of America." NBC News. December 18, 2018. https://www. nbcnews.com/feature/nbc-out/rep-elect-sharice-davids-gay-native-american-ready-shape-future-n948891.

Stierstorfer, Klaus. "The Revival of Legal Humanism." In *Law and Literature,* edited by Kiernan Dolin, 9–25. Cambridge: Cambridge University Press, 2017.

Streeby, Shelley. *American Sensations: Class, Empire, and the Production of Popular Culture.* Berkeley: University of California Press, 2002.

Teuton, Sean Kicummah. "The Native American Tradition." In *The Cambridge History of the American Novel,* edited by Leonard Cassuto, Claire Virginia Eby, and Benjamin Reiss, 1107–21. Cambridge: Cambridge University Press, 2011.

Teuton, Sean Kicummah. "The Native Novel." In *The American Novel 1870–1940,* edited by Priscilla Wald and Michael A. Elliott, 423–35. Oxford: Oxford University Press, 2014.

Uzendoski, Andrew. "Speculative States: Citizenship Criteria, Human Rights, and Decolonial Legal Norms in Gerald Vizenor's *The Heirs of Columbus.*" *Extrapolation* 57, no.1–2 (2016): 21–49.

Villez, Barbara. "Law *and* Literature: A Conjunction Revisited." *Law and Humanities* 5, no. 1 (2011): 209–19.

Vizenor, Gerald. *Landfill Meditations: Crossblood Stories.* Hanover: University Press of New England, 1991.

Vizenor, Gerald. *Manifest Manners: Postindian Warriors of Survivance.* Middletown: Wesleyan University Press, 1994.

Vizenor, Gerald, and Jill Doerfler. *The White Earth Nation: Ratification of a Native Democratic Constitution.* Lincoln: University of Nebraska Press, 2012.

Weaver, Jace. *That the People Might Live: Native American Literatures and Native American Community.* New York and Oxford: Oxford University Press, 1997.

Wilkins, David. "Sovereignty, Democracy, Constitution: An Introduction." In *The White Earth Nation: Ratification of a Native Democratic Constitution,* by Gerald Vizenor and Jill Doerfler, 1–8. Lincoln: University of Nebraska Press, 2012.

Wilkins, David E. *American Indian Politics and the American Political System.* Lanham, MD: Rowman & Littlefield, 2007.
Wilkinson, Charles E. *American Indians, Time and the Law.* New Haven: Yale University Press, 1987.
Wilmer, Franke. "Indigenous Peoples' Responses to Conquest." In *Encyclopedia of Violence, Peace, and Conflict,* edited by Lester R. Kurtz and Jennifer E. Turpin, 179–95. San Diego: Academic Press, 1999.

# Memory, Witnessing and Race at the End of the World

*Rick Moody's "The Albertine Notes"*
*as Metaphysical Detective Fiction*

ANDREW HOCK SOON NG

Focusing on Rick Moody's dystopian short story, "The Albertine Notes," this essay reads the narrative against the framework of the metaphysical detective fiction to reflect on two distinct concerns that are nevertheless related to conventions of the genre: the first involves an epistemological inquiry into the nature of memory and forgetting, and whether effecting the latter serves salvific ends or renders the subject's being (*Dasein*) inauthentic. To make my case, I turn to the writings of Maurice Blanchot, whose perspective on the relationship between forgetting, death and witnessing is particularly pertinent to my discussion of the main character's negotiation between precisely these categories that locates him in a liminal, impossible situation as a witness—a situation where different temporality collides and thus disrupts his subjectivity from stable grounding. In my view, that the story prominently involves a memory-altering drug, Albertine, and its influence on the central character, Kevin Lee, figuratively reinforces this epistemological point: Kevin's inability to clearly establish his temporal reality because of Albertine's effect is, in this regard, a metaphor implicating his compromised function as witness and, by extension, the veracity of his testimony, which is the narrative since the story is told from his point of view. My analysis's other concern has to do with the possible contentions shed by the narrative with regards to American crime fiction featuring ethnic investigators by especially white authors. Here again does Moody's text effect narrative ambiguity by complicating its representation of race matters, refracted through its Asian American protagonist, in such a way that it could be interpreted as both redemptive and indirectly discriminatory, the latter of which would then rehearse the problem inherent in the genre whereby "the Asian eye [is] thus [made to] read its culture through the code developed by the dominant culture. The oppositional nature of ethnic and cultural life was minimized as a fixed, stereotypical picture of an isolated minority group was pitted against a fixed 'white-American power structure.'"[1]

The abovementioned lines of enquiry, which will be pursued in sections two and three respectively in my discussion are, to a significant extent, determined by my reading of Moody's text as a fiction of detection inclined towards the metaphysical subgenre. That is, as a metaphysical detective story, "The Albertine Notes" can thus be interpreted as reflecting the kinds of concerns often associated with the subgenre that are, moreover, expressed by its formal conventions. In the case of the story under investigation, its non-linearity and the unreliable narrator textually intimates the ambiguity relating to its epistemological inquiry into memory and witnessing, while its intertextual propensity compels a comparison with other American crime fiction featuring ethnic detectives to serve as a kind of commentary on the problems with the genre's depiction of race matters. It is important to note, however, that "The Albertine Notes" is technically not a work of detective fiction, but more science fiction in the speculative vein involving the trope of detection. Thus, the section following this introduction is necessarily aimed at, first, situating the text within the broad subgenre of the metaphysical detective fiction in order to warrant the inclusion of Moody's text in this collection, and second, providing a context for the issues subsequently explored in the remainder of this essay.

## "The Albertine Notes" as Metaphysical Detective Fiction

To provide a context for navigating my argument hereafter, I will provide at this juncture a brief summary of "The Albertine Notes." Accordingly, "The Albertine Notes," as noted above, is set in a dystopic American future when an atomic bomb has already destroyed much of Manhattan, rendering "fifty square blocks of your city ... suddenly [looking] like a NASA photo of Mars."[2] Once a global center of culture and commerce, it has been reduced to a "center of nothing, except maybe the center of society ladies with radiation burns crowding the trauma units at the remaining hospital. Manhattan was just landfill now. And there are no surprises in a landfill" (405–06). The plot revolves around the protagonist and narrator, Kevin Lee, an Asian-American survivor who is trying to eke out a living in the aftermath as an investigative journalist for a magazine operating out of "a makeshift lobby, in a building on Staten Island, the least affected precinct of the beleaguered New York City" (395). His assignment: to write a piece on the drug, Albertine, and its domination of the ruined city's traumatized population. Kevin's attempt to uncover as much as he can about this narcotic that induces mainly pleasurable memories—a necessity in the aftermath—soon leads him to the realization about the drug's ability to also transport memory back and forth in time in a way that the user can directly influence history *via memory*. The drug, in other words, allows its user to not only "*remember the future*" (398), which suggests tripping forward in time to acquire mental images that will become part of present memory, but also change the past by, for example, killing someone "*in a memory*" in order to eliminate his existence in the present (414).

I will not go into the intricacy of the narrative's plot since this is unnecessary for my present concern and would risk simplifying its otherwise highly complex (even complicated) account, with its time-travelling premise that renders its chronology ambiguous and any conspicuous narrative linearity difficult to establish. Nevertheless, an important development is how Kevin is invariably introduced to the drug as he hopes to better understand its origin (i.e., how "Albertine appeared in a certain socio-economic sector not long after the blast" [396]) and effect, and potentially unravel who its secretive kingpin, Eduardo Cortez, really is. As advised by one of his informers, Cassandra, a female Asian junkie, to know Albertine, "you have to be *inside*. Take the drug, then you'll be inside" (402). In the course of his investigation, Kevin will discover how the drug not only enthralls its users with good memories (403) (if also bad ones, as it turns out [399]), but also allows, say, user A, and under certain controlled environment, to become a memory in user B's memory, thereby effectively allowing A to then track, spy on, monitor and indirectly influence B's action in her memory. In fact, as noted above, user A can even kill B "*in a memory*" (415) by erasing the image of B in an act of remembering to remove her from existence in the present. With the story moving not only in and out of memory, but also between temporalities—causing them to become indistinguishable from each other—it is inevitable that Kevin's point-of-view will grow increasingly unreliable as well.

Midway through the narrative, Kevin's investigation gradually consolidates into an attempt to identify who "Addict Number One" is (414). This is to ostensibly save him and prevent the city's destruction, which is supposedly due to Cortez's desire to establish his Albertine empire—i.e., by eliminating Addict Number One, and hence the origin of Albertine, in historical memory so that Cortez can always already subject the survivors of Manhattan to addiction. As the narrative reaches its denouement, Kevin will learn he had been a pawn all along in an experiment to try and change the course of history through Albertine's memory work. That he is an investigative journalist and the many individuals he encountered during his assignment, as the narrative intimates, may be nothing more than memories carefully managed for him by social scientists in a makeshift laboratory who are trying to undo the past to save the city. I use the term "may be" because by this point in the story, Kevin himself—and by extension, the reader—is no longer assured of his reality as he shifts in and out of Albertine's effect, and is flooded with all kinds of distorted remembrances and contradictory emotions, so much so that he wonders:

> What's [his] memory? Memory's the groove. It's the all-stars laying down their grove, and it's you dancing, chasing the desperations of the heart, chasing something that's so gone, so ephemeral you know it only by its traces.... [Its] the lie, the story you never get right, the better place. Memory is the bitch, shame factory, the curse and the consolation [461].

Kevin will also learn that the terrorist responsible for city's destruction was "not a highly trained sleeper cell of foreign nationals" (458) but Cortez himself, whose objective was to subjugate the city in order to turn himself into the authoritative "condition of the economy" in post-apocalypse New York. But perhaps most important and surprising of all is the fact that Kevin will discover he *is* Addict Number One, or more accurately "Addict Zero" (461), all along, whose death others are trying to prevent. Chronology-wise, it is no longer perceivable if the past has caught up with the present, or if New York's devastation was prevented, since Kevin's self-realization of his true identity and role in the story fundamentally does not clarify which event—Manhattan destroyed or otherwise—has actually occurred. Either way, however, Kevin obviously no longer poses a threat to Cortez, who would have always already succeeded or failed, the latter because "that'll mean that Eddie doesn't need to go back in time to try to find [Kevin] ... that Eddie has given up trying to control the past, in order to control the present," while the former because the future where "Eddie comes up with the idea of detonating the blast" will be "eliminate[d] ... in which case Manhattan will still be standing the entire present" (459).

From the outline above, it is clear that while "The Albertine Notes" is not a detective fiction in the traditional sense, it certainly qualifies as a fiction of detection, especially one underscoring a metaphysical dimension. A more accurate designation for Moody's story would be science fiction metaphysical detective fiction,[3] but for my discussion, I will focus only on its metaphysical detective inclination.[4] A couple of telling clues attest to its broad belonging to this subgenre. First, although it is unlikely "The Albertine Notes" directly references renowned examples of the subgenre, it is nevertheless interesting to note that it expresses certain qualities similar to them. One instance is its setting in New York, which of course brings to mind Paul Auster's ludic *The New York Trilogy* (1987), arguably the most recognizable text of the subgenre[5]; then there is also the motif of the investigator who eventually discovers he is the target of investigation himself, or has been somehow involved in the crime all along—a motif fundamentally undermining the ontological stability necessary to detective fiction whereby the investigator assumes the position of the all-knowing gaze. While the former is reminiscent of Peter Ackroyd's *Hawksmoor*, published two years earlier, the latter unmistakably echoes Douglas Adam's *Dirk Gently's*. Third, that the investigation in "The Albertine Notes" reaches a non-closure—does Kevin's revelation save Manhattan or not?—is also a common feature of the subgenre, whose premise is often less about solving a conundrum (usually criminal, but not necessarily),[6] and more about grappling with complex philosophical issues involving, among others, the notion of being and consciousness, and the relationship between time and space. According to critics, Patricia Merivale and Susan E. Sweeney, who coined the subgenre's term, a metaphysical detective fiction is

> a text that parodies or subverts traditional detective-story conventions—such as narrative closure and the detective's role as surrogate reader—with the intention, or at least the effect, of asking questions about mysteries of being and knowing, which transcend the mere machinations of the mystery plot. Metaphysical detective stories often emphasize this transcendence, moreover, by becoming self-reflexive (that is, by representing allegorically the text's own processes of composition).[7]

It would seem that the metaphysical detective fiction, while evidencing the process of detection or investigation, is not about crime and its resolution at all, although crime is commonly evoked as a trope in order to engender such a process. It is a subgenre that emphasizes insoluble mysteries due to their epistemological ambiguity, which in turn disrupts ontological certainty, thus "inevitably cast[ing] doubt on the reader's ... attempt to make sense of the text" by subverting the (usually male) authoritative gaze to deny readerly identification with the investigator (who, as such, would be the "surrogate reader").[8]

In the final analysis, the metaphysical detective fiction leaves the reader questioning the nature of knowing and of "What, if anything, can we know? What, if anything, is real?"[9] And while it deploys, as mentioned, familiar trappings of the traditional detective fiction such as a criminal event transposing into an intricate puzzle that invites investigation via a series of clues, its concern is less with arriving at, and more with transcending, the known or knowable. This is achieved frequently through the postmodern metafictional strategy of self-reflexivity, whereby the work of fiction "examines its own nature as a signifying practice and by implication, points to its own provisionality as a meaning-making system."[10] In other words, it is fiction aware of, and making known, its artifice, or its representational function, and hence, the limits of its signifying capacity, or what Charles Russell calls "its own unfolding as a construct of meaning." Alternatively, self-reflexivity can also be described as a technique in which an "artwork sees itself as already defined by existent discourse that it can lay bare before the artist and viewer."[11] Or to restate Russell's proposition differently, it is artwork that underscores its intertextual dependence on, in order to variously ironize and transgress, previous/ other discourse—a perspective not dissimilar from Merivale and Sweeney's concerning the metaphysical detective text's attempt at parodying or subverting traditional detective-story conventions.

Even without considering for now how "The Albertine Notes" reflects the two abovementioned self-reflexive positions, based on its premise of a detection culminating in an ambiguous non-closure that concurrently involves the imbrication between time and memory (and to a lesser extent, space as well), it seems unmistakable the narrative could broadly reflect metaphysical detective fiction. The experience of temporal disjunction and devoiding of reality as a result of using Albertine, thus disrupting the cause-and-effect continuum, could be interpreted, in this regard, as the narrative's means for transcending the "machinations of the mystery plot" in order to implicate complex notions about being and knowing. The text appears to strongly suggest this with its consistent proffering of various theories regarding Albertine's origin and rise (including one implicating C.G. Jung's concept of the "collective unconscious" [420–21]), culminating in the outlandish view "that Albertine has infinite origins. That she appeared in the environment all at once, at different locations, synchronously, according to some kind of philosophical or metaphysical randomness generator" (447). This is, however, merely one of several theoretical positions espoused by a story whose interest is apparently more in narrative experimentation (non-linearity, representing multiple realities, plot instability implying a warped state of consciousness) so as to indirectly engage with philosophical questions about time and memory. The origin of Albertine, in the end, is left indeterminate, but this is because it is no longer the story's central concern, which has shifted to Kevin's memory work and his role in the city's salvation. But as noted, even this development remains tentative. In fact, there are only two certainties at the end of the novel, i.e., the city, as it currently stands, lies in ruin, and Kevin has been programmed to soon forget absolutely everything related to the blast and its repercussion so that he can be "reborn," as it were, to a new memory—and hence self-unaffected by the trauma of Manhattan's obliteration.

An appreciation of how "The Albertine Notes" underscores its metaphysical concerns will be the objective of the following section. As my discussion will demonstrate, the way in which epistemological professions are metafictionally explored is by rupturing the narrative's linearity through an unreliable narrator. However, rather than motivations such as incomplete knowledge or understanding, self-denial, and dissimulation to disguise the truth from others (and even self, as in the case of Kazuo Ishiguro's *Remains of the Day*), Kevin's unreliability has more to do with his drug addiction and subsequent subjection to an experiment whose consequence is the distortion of his memory and temporality. It is also possible that his unreliability may be due to trauma resulting from witnessing the destruction of New York, although this is less evident in the narrative, and hence will only be tangentially considered in my analysis. Notwithstanding its inclination towards a tale of detection that emphasizes metaphysical concerns, "The Albertine Notes" nevertheless remains rooted in the tradition of the crime fiction in that it conspicuously involves a terrible crime whose result is the death of an entire city and life as its inhabitants know it, after which an investigator is tasked with learning about its consequence (Albertine's incremental rise), culminating in the discovery of the identities of both the crime's perpetrator and cause, which are Cortez and Kevin himself respectively. Yet another way in which Moody's text could be said to effect metafictionality is by reading it in an intertextual relationship not only with other metafictional detective texts, but the American crime fiction genre as well in order to highlight issues about the latter's conventions. In the third part of this essay, I will show how interpreting "The Albertine Notes" as a metaphysical detective fiction potentially clarifies certain ideological problems regarding race that continue to persist in American crime narratives featuring Asian American investigators.

## Death, Forgetting and the Impossible Witness

There is invariably a number of epistemological questions that "The Albertine Notes" likely poses, but for my purpose, I will focus primarily on its exploration of the link between memory and time particularly in terms of how its disruption or sustenance affects subjectivity. As such, rather than a depiction of how history affects memory, Moody's text seems more concerned, on the one hand, with how memory can reshape history in a way that is true to the past, but also exorcised of its debilitating content so that the subject can be figuratively "reborn" to a new self, freed from painful remembrances. However, the narrative at the same time seems to be positing the possibility that such a process, following Maurice Blanchot, frees the subject from death only to plunge his being into inauthenticity—a circumstance that Kevin arguably resists in his desire to remember even after being given the chance to forget the "awful things" (459) he had witnessed on the fateful day of the blast. To clarify these points, I will first pursue an argument involving the imbrication between space and memory, specifically how the former defines and shapes the latter. Indeed, that Kevin frequently refers to familiar Manhattan landmarks that have become obliterated suggests a degree of mourning, which in turn reveals the extent his memory, and by extension, self, is defined by space, whose loss can significantly disrupt the subject's sense of historical continuity. Drawing on Blanchot's meditation on, variously, time, forgetting, being and otherness, I will next demonstrate how Kevin negotiates forgetting and remembering that inevitably plots him in an impossible position of responsibility as a witness.

"The Albertine Notes" could be said to "reveal one of the fundamental problems in mapping the past into real and imagined landscapes: that is, the reliance on space as a container of time."[12] In the narrative, this problem is in fact accentuated due to the evaporation of space that leaves no trace of its presence for which time can be contained. And what it is about time that is contained is fundamentally memory, whereby landmarks and architectures, for example, serve beyond their utility as dwellings to, moreover, assume the role of memorialization sites. Features of space such as, in the case of a city, buildings and other (re)constructed localities, in other words, not only bear material, but psychological, function as well, and thus often indirectly affect its inhabitants' subjectivity. Its loss, particularly as a result of a traumatic event, can prove destabilizing, even fragmenting, for a subject whose self-identity and belonging are intricately connected to it. When this occurs, it invariably begs the question how subjective coherence can still be maintained through memory-work relating to space when the referent (the said space) is no longer there to ground it.

Evident throughout the narrative is Kevin's tacit grief over the destruction of his beloved New York, which he deems "the greatest city in the world" (405) that indirectly intimates how closely his subjective wellbeing is connected to his dwelling. Kevin is potentially mourning over not just the death of his city but also his original subjectivity due to its profound determination by the environment he once inhabited. In this regard, Kevin's condition seems to reflect the correlative relationship between memory and space that historian Joëlle Bahloul explicates. Although his argument concerning domestic space is more narrowly inclined towards the house, I see it as equally applicable to larger places of dwelling, such as the city. Accordingly,

[the] remembered past is lodged in the monotonous repetition of the necessary acts of concrete experience. The memory that "invents" it, and rewrites it, is the product of this relentless repetitiveness…. The domestic … world makes up the woof of remembrance, or memory. The house is "inhabited" by memory. Remembrance is moulded into the material and physical structures of the domestic space.[13]

For Bahloul, what defines memory are past actions and encounters occurring in the "domestic … world" represented in material space, i.e., the house. Or to rephrase Bahloul's observation slightly differently, what informs memory is, among others, the subject's experience of lived space, or place that in turn, also determines his sense of self-identity. That Kevin's subjective position is deeply intertwined with his landscape is evident not only in his appraisal of New York as the world's superlative cosmopolis, but also his prideful claim of it as "my city" (405), whose obliterated landmarks he longingly catalogues throughout the narrative—New York's renowned skyline, the Statue of Liberty, City Hall, the New York Stock Exchange, Chinatown, and so forth—to conspicuously signal his grief. Manhattan, to borrow Bahloul's phrase, thus serves as "the woof of remembrances" structuring Kevin's subjectivity, and its destruction would invariably be registered by him as a kind of self-devoiding.

Admittedly, while revisioning memory-time through drugs could likely prevent Kevin's figurative death by the disaster, what this preservation entails is less clear in terms of its significance for Kevin after the event of his forgetting. As the Deconstructionist, Jesse Simmons, tells him at the end of the experiment and after he has learned his true identity and role in the circumstance:

> "You may have forgotten that Manhattan was ever a city by the time you get home tonight. You might have forgotten all of this, all this rotten stuff, this loneliness, even this speech I'm giving you now. In fact, we have tried to pinpoint forgetting, Kevin, we have targeted it, in such a way as to wipe clean you own memories of the blast. Because you actually had a pretty rotten time that day. You saw some awful things" [459].

Forgetting, in an ironic sense, becomes a means to reverse Kevin's symbolic death corresponding with the dissolution of a city that so intricately determined his subjectivity. In having his memories wiped clean of the devastation, Kevin is "returned" to an originary moment in which the blast never occurred and his subjectivity never defined by Manhattan because the latter never existed in his memory in the first place. Kevin's subjectivity could start over in a way akin to figurative rebirth—a prospect that would certainly appear attractive to him since his personal life even before the catastrophe had been mainly a series of missed opportunities and failures (a point I will revisit in the next section) culminating in drug addiction, the last of which has been forgotten until the experiment returned it to his consciousness. In erasing Kevin's memory of the blast, the scientists are possibly expressing the "feel[ing] there cannot be any experience of the disaster, even if we were to understand disaster to be the ultimate experience. This is one of its features: it impoverishes all experience, withdraws from experience all authenticity."[14] It is, hence, to both save Kevin from (figurative) death and reinvigorate his

*Dasein* with authenticity—since for Blanchot, death belongs to the inauthentic because it is outside the grasp of being's power, or will—that his forgetting is being experimentally induced. But is forgetting an escape from death, as Moody's text seems to suggest, or merely a "detour," to use Maurice Blanchot's term, from it? For Blanchot, forgetting is "movement that steals away [to] allow ourselves to turn toward what escapes (death), as though the only authentic approach to this inauthentic event belonged to forgetting. Forgetting, death: the unconditional detour. The present time of forgetting delimits the unlimited space where death reverts to the lack of presence."[15] Karmen McKendrick contends in her exegesis of this passage, forgetting is an act of "moving through time" by detouring "towards death" in order "to open [being] to the outside beyond experience."[16] This "beyond experience," McKendrick explicates, is the realm of silence, "an unknown … the outside/within of language. Yet our sense of this unknown is not pure future—that which we shall find—nor is it presence, as if we could see it before us. Silence calls to memory, to our sense of having forgotten. It calls, more precisely, to what we could never remember, never re-collect, because it began without origin, in fragmentation, as the very site of disruption."[17] Forgetting, therefore, is not a movement away from death, but one paralleling it; it is a condition that returns the subject, if not to "the lack of presence," to one where presence is unknown because it lies somewhere between outside and within language, as something always within, but also outside, of the subject's grasp. Forgetting may relocate the subject away from authentic death, only to position his being (*Dasein*) in "fragmentation" and "disruption"—a being without articulation, bounded by silence.

Blanchot posits that complete forgetting, which is what is hoped for in Kevin's case, can only be attained if the act of forgetting itself is also forgotten. As Blanchot observes, "To enter into this movement of redoubling"—a movement that broadly characterizes Kevin's "next forgetting" (459)—is not tantamount "to forget[ting] twice; it is [instead] to forget in forgetting the depth of forgetting, to forget more profoundly by turning away from this depth that lacks any possibility of being gotten to the bottom of."[18] Forgetting completely, in other words, does not somehow sustain memory, the therefore being (subjectivity), but only relegates it to somewhere outside, even while existing within, language—memory that is encapsulated in language, but can no longer be spoken because it is now silent, unknown. Tellingly, that Moody's text is likely conversant of forgetting's paradox, i.e., it sustains, by rendering *Dasein*'s death inauthentic, is evident when Kevin, even in his drug-induced state, realizes that his attempt at writing the Albertine's story, which would in turn (although without his realization) reveal his own, has arrived at nothing, or once again, silence. Pursuing what seems to him a futile, confusing investigation, he comes to the conclusion that he has "produced shit" (442), and eventually admits in the end that his "journalist exposé [has completely broken] down" (461), thus exposing nothing (silence) about either Albertine or himself to him. Indeed, without being told who he is by the social scientists, it is likely that Kevin will continue to struggle with subjective inauthenticity due to a profound gap in his memory induced by forgetting. For this reason, I interpret Kevin's *aporia* as reinforcing Blanchot's perspective on forgetting as not so much an escape from death but an encounter with an experience that fundamentally positions the subject in silence and nothingness because it is an experience beyond the language's capacity to articulate. Based on this reading, it is therefore apparent, and to restate my point, that the symbolic salvation engineered for Kevin to help him survive the destruction of Manhattan is actually reductive of his being, which is rendered inauthentic—a subjectivity premised on nothingness. Interestingly, that the narrative does not take the reader beyond the point of Kevin's second forgetting may evince the impossibility of such a continuity because, on the one hand, disremembering would have occurred, but also alternatively, Kevin would have been relegated by his forgetting to an "outside" of language, and hence can no longer find articulation for being. Death, to paraphrase Martin Crowley's reading of Blanchot, is not the "object" of Kevin's "ability" in the sense that death is not an enabling condition, "but rather its abolition."[19]

Tellingly, despite the social scientists' good intentions for Kevin to help him soon forget the past, there is possible resistance on his part that the narrative subtly hints in at least two ways. The first is again found in Simmons's revelation; notwithstanding what he tells Kevin regarding wiping clean his recollection of Manhattan and, by extension, the "pretty rotten" fateful event of its obliteration, she would also go on to explain, "However, if in the future, during the next forgetting, you want to remember this or other events from your life we have a suggestion for the future, Kevin, *just play back your audio recordings*" (459). That Simmons uses the term "want," I opine, demonstrates her acknowledgment of an ingrained desire in Kevin to memorialize the past that no induced forgetting can ultimately dissolve. This perhaps stems from her recognition of how deeply connected Kevin's subjectivity is to the habitation they have lost—a recognition developed from observing his consistent reminiscences of the shapes, sights, sounds and feel of Manhattan when under Albertine's influence. In "wanting" to retain remembrance, Kevin arguably evinces a degree of refusal to completely abandon the memory of his original being in order to embrace a subjectivity that is inauthentic. The second clue to Kevin's will to remember is intimated at the close of story when Kevin takes a boat ride into the ruins of Manhattan. Despite the onset of forgetting, Kevin seems to resist it by focusing his concentration on the image that characterizes the city of New York most meaningfully to him—that of the immigrant:

I'm going backward, through the neighborhood of immigrants, so now I step on the easternmost part of the island, same place the Italians stepped, same place the Irish stepped, same place the Puerto Ricans stepped, and I'm going in there now, because as long as it's rubble I don't care how hot it is, I'm going in … and I can hear the voices, even though it's been a while now, all those voices layered over one another, in their hundred and fifty languages, can't hear anything distinct about what they are saying, except that they're saying, *hey, time for us to be heard* [463].

I will return to this passage again for discussion later, but suffice for now to note that in Kevin's fusion of his final memory of the city with the subjective position with which he invariably identifies racially, historically and culturally, it is arguable that he is deliberately effecting refusal of what was not his choice in the matter (i.e., forgetting) in the first place rather than allowing himself to be engulfed by it, however much it would "save" him. Here again is apparently an example of the entrenched affinity between space and subjectivity whereby the memory of one necessarily evokes and preserves the other. In this case, it is possible that in bringing the two images together in his fading thoughts, Kevin is shoring up resistance against the disremembering engineered for him by Simmons and her team. Additionally, that the social scientists also recognize his tacit rebuff against forgetting is evident in the fact they engineered a targeted forgetting for him that could be deactivated by the audio recordings Kevin made during his "investigation" of Albertine.

What compels Kevin's rejection of forgetting, as I see it, is possibly an unconscious assumption of responsibility corresponding with a witness's. Kevin, it could be said, desires remembrance in order to memorialize both his lost city and original *Dasein*. In wanting to remember, Kevin is already projecting himself into the future as a subject who will uphold, rather than, deny historical memory; a subject who grounds presence and authenticity rather than nothingness and inauthenticity; who speaks rather than embraces silence. After all, as overwhelming and unspeakable an event the destruction of Manhattan may be, it is, in the words of Giorgio Agamben, "only if language bears witness to something to which it is impossible to bear witness, can a speaking being experience something like a necessity to speak."[20] What constitutes that impossible "something" is akin to a holocaust (whether nuclear devastation or genocide, which is Agamben's focus) because to speak it only confronts language with *aporia*. Yet, it is because it is impossible to speak that it demands speaking. In denying forgetting, Kevin is effectively adopting the position of the impossible witness in the future, one who is compelled to speak even though what can be said escapes language. It is for this reason that despite the existence of Kevin's audio recordings, even Simmons and her team seem to implicitly agree that only Kevin himself can bear witness to the history up until the blast, thereby reinforcing Blanchot's contention that

> to testify is always on the one hand to do it at present—the witness must be present
> at the stand himself, without technical imposition.... One cannot send a cassette to
> testify in one's place. One must oneself be present, raise one's hand, speak in the first
> person and in the present, and one must do this in order to testify to a present, to an
> indivisible moment, that is, at a certain point to a moment assembled at the tip of an
> instantaneousness which must resist division.[21]

A cassette, in Blanchot's estimation, may record the past, but it cannot link the past to the present that underscores testifying. It cannot, in other words, be a witness because it only speaks *of* the past, and not *to* the future; it reverberates in the past but will remain silent in the future. For memorialization to take effect, however impossible, testifying must be accomplished by a first-person speaking subject who serves as a conduit between past and future. He is the "indivisible moment," the "instantaneousness which must resist division" between past and future so that the two temporalities always already collapse into the present.

Kevin's impossible position as witness—the desire to remember a cataclysmic event that consciousness cannot contain, to deploy language when confronted with silence—may describe his future circumstance, but there are clues in "The Albertine Notes" that potentially already implicate it. There is, on the one hand, Kevin's journalistic breakdown noted earlier that suggests a struggle to articulate what is essentially unspeakable. The realization the story he is attempting to write is also "shit" underscores his concomitant location within and outside language. On the other, there is the strategy of disrupting narrative linearity that, in turn, renders Kevin's credibility as narrator suspect, not so much in terms of whether what is happening is real, but more if an event is actually happening, or happening in memory, and whether it is a past or future event (since, as mentioned, Albertine can also cause its user to paradoxically remember the future). The text segues, without clear temporal distinction, into various scenarios including conversations with several people for his story: an interrogation by Cortez's henchmen (442); warning with a high school crush *in the past* about the *present* catastrophe (444); a telephone exchange with his father only to be told he had already been told just days earlier not to call again, although Kevin has no recollection of the latter (434); the slaughter of the social scientists by Cortez's men, which probably did not happen (455) and so forth. All of which suggests that they may not be actually happening, but are memories within memories, or memories collapsed into each other to the point that Kevin is experiencing multiple presents. Resulting from this fluid interchange of settings and events is an increasing difficulty in establishing the narrative's chronological sequence, so much so that in the end, it is not even clear if Kevin has yet to cross over to, or has already arrived beyond, his next forgetting. Finally, there is the degree of metafictional self-consciousness that "The Albertine Notes" tellingly exhibits regarding its transgression of linear time when on one occasion, Kevin is told by an expert he is interviewing how "it is impossible to exist in linear time at all" (446). Since Kevin is the reader's proxy, this scenario is arguably tantamount to the text drawing the reader's attention to its deliberate act of subverting familiar temporal sequence, and by extension, Kevin's reliability as a narrator, and hence, witness. That Kevin is moreover told by the same individual how New York likely never "actually exist[ed]" but is merely "an illusion purveyed by a malevolent scientist" and a "collective hallucination … to rationalize" the present state of ruination only adds to the confusion regarding the narrative's linearity and the credibility of what Kevin is witnessing since this would suggest it is Kevin's experience *after* his second forgetting we have been privy to all along.

## The Ambivalence of Race Matters

According to Dylan Trigg, to witness is to "speak of what is heard in the present and what remains to be said in the past to [therefore] confer an afterlife upon the temporality of trauma, one that outlives the immediacy of the event."[22] Testifying, as such, involves updating the past for the present so as to confer on the traumatic event of former a continuity that lingers beyond the originary moment. It is, in Trigg's term, a "haunted dynamic," which he further explains is the "intimate, if disturbed"[23] connection adopted by the relationship between event and place resulting from a disaster. Such a dynamic can lead to a recognition of "the persistence of an event that continues in spite of the absence of its original containment."[24] As an embodiment of the past, the witness can continue to preserve a containment, or place, that otherwise is tragically lost—a circumstance that potentially describes Kevin's position in "The Albertine Notes." Importantly, and as the passage quoted earlier concerning Kevin's final thoughts before the onset of his impending forgetting, the past that he ostensibly seeks to preserve for the future fuses the memory of Manhattan with the image of the immigrant, thereby effectively reimagining the "original containment" from a racial perspective. That is, the past that will "haunt" and hence inform the future will be one racially marked, not by whiteness alone, but its racial other as well. In this sense, Kevin could be interpreted as representing an impending future whose space, while ruined, also potentially augurs redemption in that racial ideology is no longer marked by difference but singularity declaring "*time for us to be heard*" (463). This perhaps explains the ideological import of an Asian American character in a story in which race matters, while not exactly muted, are also never fully explored either. As I see it, only an ethnic hero can achieve this narrative end because his otherness also compels the self to recognize its own "irreplaceable singularity," what "makes [it] unique," but also its own "loss," or absence, without the other.[25] Or, to explain my point in a different way, that whiteness as a racial category is the "unmarked marker" would only flatten the distinctiveness of otherness because it itself is indistinctive, thereby reinforcing dichotomy without reconciliation.[26] In this sense, Moody's text could be compared to Dale Furutani's detective novels (featuring the Japanese-American investigator Ken Tanaka), which according to Theo D'haen, "conduct[s] a complex debate with the … [racial] ideology of the [genre] and finally refashion it in a form, and with a set of characters and concerns, commensurate with our present age. Specifically, they foreground the ideal of a truly multicultural America."[27]

But race is fundamentally a curious feature in Moody's story because it does not contribute to the narrative in any significant way, thus begging the question of not only its abrupt emphasis at the close of the narrative, but also why Kevin's ethnicity is consistently made into an issue. Several times in the narrative, Kevin would recount his family's disappointment in him, and his inability to assume the image of the model minority stereotype often attributed to successful immigrants, such as his father, who "was an IT venture capitalist and my mother was a microbiologist" (397). He would, for example, compare his family's tenacity—the ability to "hang on," like his grandfather who "left behind his country [and] never gave a thought" (430) with his inability to stick it through his university studies, resulting in him dropping out from Fordham (397). Alternatively, he would express self-reproach for failing to live up to the reputation of "incredibly smart" Asian kid who "was supposed to have calculus right at my fingertips, and … know C++ and Visual Basic and Java and every fucking computer language," but instead found himself hyperventilating whenever confronted with exams (440). That Kevin's family has invariably given up on him is evinced in a telephone exchange with his father whereby he is told of the reminder not to call again just days earlier, although he has no recollection of the incident (434). In all this, it is possible to read Kevin's predicament as resulting from having committed cultural betrayal, whose discourse frequently "[regulates] fidelity and communal belonging" amongst Asian Americans.[28]

Accordingly, the story's deployment of an ethnic hero not only appears to spearhead racial difference as a marker of singularity and uniqueness, but also challenges the stereotype of the high-achieving, hardworking minority as the only favorable subjectivity. However, on closer examination and more importantly, when read against the framework of the American crime genre, it is less clear if the text's representation of racial matters is unambiguously affirmative at all. This returns me to the point made earlier concerning reading "The Albertine Notes" as an intertextual reference highlighting certain problems relating to racial ideology that are inherent in detective fiction featuring ethnic investigators—a point I want to briefly explore in the remainder of this section. Admittedly, Moody's text departs from the usual trend in American crime fiction in which, as Maureen Reddy describes, "race matters are denied, displaced or otherwise so thoroughly disguised that many readers overlook them."[29] However, its concern over racial matters is, at the same time, either rather tangential and does not amount to any serious engagement with them, or worse, tacitly reproduces the sort of racial politics often found in the genre whereby "a person of color [is moved] to the center of [the] narrative without necessarily altering the white structure."[30] Reddy, moreover, views this contention as particularly evident in crime writing featuring ethnic central characters (the investigators) by white writers—a circumstance that Moody's text palpably reflects. As she argues, "there are serious issues involved in white authors' creation of characters of color; these issues include not only the problems of appropriation and commodification … but other difficulties as well, some of which touch on authenticity in terms of believability and verisimilitude."[31]

To warrant my claim that "The Albertine Notes" exhibits the racial problems inherent in American crime fiction by white authors featuring principal characters who are non-white, I will briefly consider some examples from the text. First, while Kevin's frequent expression of disappointment with himself that announces his filial and cultural betrayal may suggest an attempt at "believability and verisimilitude"—that is, not all Asians conform to the image of the model minority—it serves to underline his subjectivity with a lack as well, not to mention how little bearing it has on the story as a whole. This, ironically, ends up reinforcing the stereotype of the model minority as the benchmark to which the ethnic other should aspire. Additionally, that the story's villain, Eduardo Cortez, belongs to an ethnic minority commonly associated with drug trafficking not only rehearses racial typecasting but also, when juxtaposed with Kevin, ascribes the two individuals with dissimilar and oppositional values as migrant others, and thus indirectly typecasts the Asian protagonist (as model minority) as well. Implied hence is the idea that if the immigrant is to be the privileged subjectivity of the future America, it should be the one familiarly recognized as exemplary (Asian), not criminal and violent (Latin American), by the present dominant racial group (which the writer represents). It is therefore inevitable that the text's inclination towards racial matters would be rendered uncertain when it demonstrates both an avoidance and reinforcement of racial stereotyping.

Second, even Kevin's function as (anti)hero is strategically corresponded with limitations that bear racial significance. For instance, his desire for a Caucasian woman, Serena, is disallowed development because this would upset the propriety intersecting race and sexuality that delicately underscores American detective fiction. Accordingly, while a white male hero/Asian female interest would ostensibly be encouraged, the other way around would not. Consequently, Kevin can merely be Serena's friend and confidante, but not her lover, whose role is unsurprisingly reserved for a white male character originally suspected to be Addict Zero until Kevin discovers he is that person, thus also redeeming the former by shifting lack to, and aligning criminality solely with, ethnic others, i.e., Kevin and Cortez respectively. And as if to underscore the unmistakable whiteness of Serena's love interest, he is tellingly given the name Paley. Related to this point is the third whereby Kevin is not only rejected by a white woman as a potential love interest, but also figuratively infantilized in the story, as evident near the end when it is revealed that his microbiologist mother is ultimately responsible for Kevin's present predicament, beginning with her introduction of an experimental drug (a combination of "Lithium, some SSRIs and a memory enhancer" [460])—later to be known as Albertine—to him with the excuse of helping him study for school examinations, when all the while she is preparing him for the task of future witness and keeper of America's memory. In this regard, it is possible to interpret Kevin's addiction as a metaphor for oedipal dependence that not only symbolically infantilizes, but also emasculates, him to reinforce his "lack" as male subject and at the same time nullify his sexual (yellow) peril against the white male.

Finally, it is notable that the Caucasian male in Moody's narrative is given minimal presence and role, usually in the guise of scholars Kevin interacts with, or comes across, during his research, and of course, Paley. On the one hand, this is in tandem with the narrative's ideological attempt to establish synonymity between immigrant subjectivity and Americanness, thus necessitating subtle attenuation of the authoritative, dominant white male that is textually achieved through his limited, cameo appearances. Moreover, the fact that Paley is a potential victim the hero is attempting to protect, and that the scholars are largely ineffectual (Conrad Dixon dies from addiction, while Ernest Wentworh will be revealed to be way off the mark in his theorization of Albertine) seems to further support this interpretation when considering its implication of the symbolically castrated white man. On the other hand, however, the demotion of the Caucasian male to secondary characters in the text could equally be read as a narrative strategy intended to safeguard, rather than jeopardize, the "superiority" of white masculinity over other raced masculinities. Take Serena's boyfriend again as a representative case in point. Unlike Kevin and Cortez, whose masculine lack or "inferiority" is marked by emasculation or corruption, Paley's masculinity is informed by innocence, education and lofty ambitions ("[he] went to NYU ... and he wanted to make movies" [416]). Kevin's endeavor to rescue him, as such, not only expresses the protagonist's affection for Serena, acknowledgment of Paley's blamelessness and/or feeling of guilt, but when read against a gendered framework, the text's ideological motivation to prevent the supremacy of white masculinity from endangerment as well. In this sense, if the other white male characters are unimportant and expendable, it is because their ineffectuality intimates a possible threat to the superiority of white masculinity. Admittedly, my claim these characters are white is fundamentally tenuous since it is based solely on their names (unlike non-white characters like Kevin and Cortez, whose racial background is detailed), which would then however bring us back to Koshy's point about whiteness as an "unmarked marker" and reinforce my argument regarding the text's subtle maintenance of white masculinity's supremacy as status quo.

Based on the preceding observations, it is arguable that although Moody appears conscientious about avoiding racial indiscretions often committed in American fiction of detection on one level, he nevertheless makes them on another, thus demonstrating the difficulty encountered by white writers when depicting major characters who belong to ethnic minorities. Somehow, the unmistakable sympathy and understanding expressed by Moody for his protagonist does not allow his text to transcend the fraught racialized ideology inherent in the genre but render it ambiguous instead whereby the narrative strategies he deploys to circumvent it could be read as rehearsing it at the same time.

## Conclusion

The ambivalent treatment of race matters patently adds another layer of uncertainty to "The Albertine Notes" that interpretatively commensurate with the metaphysical detective fiction's inclination towards narrative ambiguity and non-closure. In this regard, although dissimilar considerations underscore my discussion—i.e.an epistemological inquiry into the nature of memory and its relationship with forgetting and witness on the one hand, and the way in which the text illuminates issues inherent in a specific genre on the other—they are nevertheless connected to my reading that frames Moody's text against the conventions and concerns of the metaphysical detective story. Admittedly, the ascription of the narrative to this category of fiction is ultimately an interpretive claim on my part, but I believe such a motivation can be fruitful especially in terms of the interpretive complexities it is able to yield as a result.

NOTES

1. Norman K. Denzin, "Chan Is Missing: The Asian Eye Examines Cultural Studies," *Symbolic Interaction* 17, no. 1 (1994): 69–70. Inset quote from Elia Shohat, "Ethnicity-in-Relations: Toward a Multicultural Reading of American Cinema," in *Unspeakable Images: Ethnicity*

*and The American Cinema*, ed. Lester D. Friedman (Urbana: University of Illinois Press, 1991), 217.

2. Rick Moody, "The Albertine Notes," in *McSweeney's Mammoth Treasure of Thrilling Tales*, ed. Michael Chabon (Harmondsworth: Penguin, 2004), 397. All subsequent references are from this edition.

3. Science fiction oriented metaphysical detective fiction is rare but not altogether unusual, as evidenced by the highly surreal works of Japanese writer, Kobo Abē (e.g., *The Face of Another* [1966] and *The Box Man* [1973]). Western examples include Richard Morgan's *Altered Carbon* (2002), which bears cursory similarity with Moody's story and features a Japanese-American protagonist helping a man in a dystopic future to uncover the killer of his original self in the past, and Douglas Adam's *Dirk Gently's Holistic Detective Agency* (1987).

4. A development in postmodern writing, this subgenre of crime fiction is also known by various other terms such as "deconstructive mysteries" (Patrick Brantlinger, "Missing Corpses: The Deconstructive Mysteries of James Purdy and Franz Kafka," *Novel* 20, no. 1 [1987]: 24–40), "post-nouveau roman detective [fiction]" (Michel Sirvent,"Reader-Investigators in Post-*Nouveau Roman*: Lahougue, Peeters, Perec," in *Detecting Texts: The Metaphysical Detective Fiction from Poe to Postmodernism*, eds. Patricia Merivale and Susan Sweeney [Philadelphia: Univ. of Pennsylvania Press, 1998], 157–78) and the "ontological detective story" (Elena Gomel, "Mystery, Apocalypse, and Utopia: The Case of the Ontological Detective Story," *Science Fiction Studies* 22, no. 3 [1995]: 343–56). Although the third comes closest to describing Moody's narrative, as we shall see, I will use the term "metaphysical detective fiction" throughout since this is the most label most commonly associated with this kind of texts in scholarship.

5. This publication date refers to the version that includes all three parts of the trilogy.

6. Examples of metaphysical detective fiction that do not feature a criminal investigation include the third book of Auster's trilogy, *The Locked Room*, and Thomas Pynchon's *The Crying of Lot 49* (1965).

7. Patricia Merivale and Susan Sweeney. "The Game's Afoot: On the Trail of the Metaphysical Detective Story," in *Detecting Texts: The Metaphysical Detective Fiction from Poe to Postmodernism*, eds. Patricia Merivale and Susan Sweeney (Philadelphia: University of Pennsylvania Press, 1998), 2.

8. *Ibid.*

9. *Ibid.*, 4.

10. Paul Maltby, *Dissident Postmodernists: Barthelme, Coover, Pynchon* (Philadelphia: University of Pennsylvania Press, 1991), 22.

11. Charles Russell, "The Context of the Concept," in *A Postmodern Reader*, ed. Joseph Natoli and Linda Hutcheon (Albany: State University of New York Press, 1993), 293–294.

12. Mike Craig and Penny S. Travlou, "The City and Topologies of Memory," *Society and Space* 19 (2001): 167.

13. Joëlle Bahloul, *The Architecture of Memory: A Jewish-Muslim Household in Colonial Algeria, 1937–1962*, trans. Catherine du Peloux Ménagé (Cambridge: Cambridge University Press, 1996), 29.

14. Maurice Blanchot, *The Writing of the Disaster*, trans. Ann Smock (Lincoln: University of Nebraska Press, 1986), 51.

15. Maurice Blanchot, *The Infinite Conversation*, trans. Susan Hanson (Minneapolis: University of Minnesota Press, 2008). 196.

16. Karmen McKendrick, *Immemorial Silence* (Albany: State University of New York Press, 2001), 29.

17. *Ibid.*, 27.

18. Maurice Blanchot, *The Infinite Conversation*, 195.

19. Martin Crowley, "Possible Suicide: Blanchot and the Ownership of Death," *Paragraph* 23 no. 2 (2000):193. Without delving into details since it is beyond the scope of my discussion, it is nevertheless interesting to note that Kevin's induced forgetting of Manhattan's existence (and the blast's occurrence) can be correlated with Cathy Caruth's definition of trauma in the sense they both are experiences whose claim is unconsciously refused by the

subject in order to ensure survival. In Caruth's postulation, "trauma is not locatable in the simple violent or original event in an individual's past, but rather in the way that its very unassimilated nature—the way it was precisely not known in the first instance—returns to haunt the survivor later on" (Cathy Caruth, *Unclaimed Experience: Trauma, Narrative, and History* [Baltimore: Johns Hopkins University Press, 1996], 4, emphasis in the original). Note how Kevin's forgetting is meant to recalibrate the past in such a way that it never happened. In this way, the past will remain unknown and unknowable to Kevin, and would not thus be assimilated by his consciousness to become a memory

20. Giorgio Agamben, *Remnants of Auschwitz: The Witness and the Archive*, trans. Daniel Heller-Roazen (New York: Zone Books, 2005), 65.

21. Maurice Blanchot, *The Instant of My Death*, trans. Elizabeth Rottenberg (Stanford: Stanford University Press, 2000), 32–33.

22. Dylan Trigg, "The Place of Trauma: Memory, Hauntings. and the Temporality of Ruins," *Memory Studies* 2 no. 1 (2009): 93.

23. *Ibid.*, 91, 95.

24. *Ibid.*, 91.

25. Maurice Blanchot, *The Writing of the Disaster*, 13.

26. Susan Koshy, "Morphing Race into Ethnicity: Asian Americans and Critical Transformations of Whiteness," *Boundary 2* 28, no.1 (2001): 154.

27. Theo D'Haen, "Samurai Sleuths and Detective Daughters: The American Way," in *Sleuthing Ethnicity: The Detective Multiethnic Crime Fiction*, eds. Dorothea Fischer-Hornung and Monika Mueller (Madison: Farleigh Dickinson University Press, 2003), 39. See also the discussion on the Tanaka novels in Berten and D'Haen's study (Hans Berten and Theo D'Haen, *Contemporary American Detective Fiction* [Basingstoke: Palgrave Macmillan, 2001]). That racial matters, according to the two scholars, are possibly revisioned in these novels to cast multiracialism in a more positive light is likely to do with the fact that Furutani is an ethnic writer himself. Furutani, however, appears to be an exception in this regard when seen against other ethnic authors of American crime fiction, based not only on Berten and D'Haen's, but also Maureen T. Reddy's assessment of their works. For Reddy, see Maureen T. Reddy, "Race and American Crime Fiction," in *The Cambridge Companion to American Crime Fiction*, ed. Catherine Ross Nickerson (Cambridge: Cambridge University Press, 2010), 135–47, and Maureen T. Reddy, *Traces, Codes and Clues: Reading Race in Crime Fiction* (New Brunswick: Rutgers University Press, 2003).

28. Leslie Bow, *Betrayal and Other Acts of Subversion* (Princeton: Princeton University Press, 2001), 11.

29. Maureen T. Reddy, "Race and American Crime Fiction," 135.

30. Maureen T. Reddy, *Traces, Codes and Clues*, 153.

31. *Ibid.*, 156.

## BIBLIOGRAPHY

Agamben, Giorgio. *Remnants of Auschwitz: The Witness and the Archive*, trans. Daniel Heller-Roazen. New York: Zone Books, 2005.

Bahloul, Joëlle. *The Architecture of Memory: A Jewish-Muslim Household in Colonial Algeria, 1937–1962*, trans. Catherine du Peloux Ménagé. Cambridge: Cambridge University Press, 1996.

Berten, Hans, and Theo D'Haen. *Contemporary American Detective Fiction*. Basingstoke: Palgrave Macmillan, 2001.

Blanchot, Maurice. *The Infinite Conversation*, trans. Susan Hanson. Minneapolis/London: University of Minnesota Press, 2008.

Blanchot, Maurice. *The Instant of My Death*, trans. Elizabeth Rottenberg. Stanford: Stanford University Press, 2000.

Blanchot, Maurice. *The Writing of the Disaster*, trans. Ann Smock. Lincoln/London: University of Nebraska Press, 1986.

Bow, Leslie. *Betrayal and Other Acts of Subversion*. Princeton: Princeton University Press, 2001.

Brantlinger, Patrick. "Missing Corpses: The Deconstructive Mysteries of James Purdy and Franz Kafka," *Novel* 20. 1 (1987): 24–40.

Caruth, Cathy. *Unclaimed Experience: Trauma, Narrative, and History*. Baltimore: Johns Hopkins University Press, 1996.

Craig, Mike, and Penny S. Travlou. "The City and Topologies of Memory," *Society and Space* 19 (2001): 161–77.

Crowley, Martin. "Possible Suicide: Blanchot and the Ownership of Death," *Paragraph* 23, no. 2 (2000): 191–206.

Denzin, Norman K. "Chan is Missing: The Asian Eye Examines Cultural Studies," *Symbolic Interaction* 17, no. 1 (1994): 63–89.

D'Haen, Theo. "Samurai Sleuths and Detective Daughters: The American Way," in *Sleuthing Ethnicity: The Detective in Multiethnic Crime Fiction*, eds. Dorothea Fischer-Hornung and Monika Mueller, 36–52. Madison: Farleigh Dickinson University Press, 2003.

Gomel, Elana. "Mystery, Apocalypse, and Utopia: The Case of the Ontological Detective Story," *Science Fiction Studies* 22, no. 3 (1995): 343–56.

Gruesser, John Cullen. *Race, Gender and Empire in American Detective Fiction*. Jefferson, NC: McFarland, 2013.

Koshy, Susan. "Morphing Race into Ethnicity: Asian Americans and Critical Transformations of Whiteness," *Boundary 2* 28, no.1 (2001): 153–94.

Maltby, Paul. *Dissident Postmodernists: Barthelme, Coover, Pynchon*. Philadelphia: University of Pennsylvania Press, 1991.

McKendrick, Karmen. *Immemorial Silence*. Albany: State University of New York Pres, 2001.

Merivale, Patricia, and Susan Sweeney. "The Game's Afoot: On the Trail of the Metaphysical Detective Story," in *Detecting Texts: The Metaphysical Detective Fiction from Poe to Postmodernism*, eds. Patricia Merivale and Susan Sweeney, 1–24. Philadelphia: University of Pennsylvania Press, 1998.

Mills, Alice, and Claude Julien, eds. *"Polar Noir": Reading African-American Detective Fiction*. Tours: Presses Universitaires François-Rabelais, 2005.

Moody, Rick. "The Albertine Notes," in *McSweeney's Mammoth Treasure of Thrilling Tales*, ed. Michael Chabon. 385–463. Harmondsworth: Penguin, 2004.

Reddy, Maureen T. "Race and American Crime Fiction," in *The Cambridge Companion to American Crime Fiction*, ed. Catherine Ross Nickerson, 135–47. Cambridge: Cambridge University Press, 2010.

Reddy, Maureen T. *Traces, Codes and Clues: Reading Race in Crime Fiction*. New Brunswick: Rutgers University Press, 2003.

Russell, Charles. "The Context of the Concept," in *A Postmodern Reader*, ed. Joseph Natoli and Linda Hutcheon, 287–98. Albany: State University of New York Press, 1993.

Shohat, Elia. "Ethnicity-in-Relations: Toward a Multicultural Reading of American Cinema," in *Unspeakable Images: Ethnicity and the American Cinema*, ed. Lester D. Friedman, 215–50. Urbana: University of Illinois Press, 1991.

Sirvent, Michel. "Reader-Investigators in Post-*Nouveau Roman*: Lahougue, Peeters, Perec," in *Detecting Texts: The Metaphysical Detective Fiction from Poe to Postmodernism*, eds. Patricia Merivale and Susan Sweeney, 157–78. Philadelphia: University of Pennsylvania Press, 1998.

Trigg, Dylan. "The Place of Trauma: Memory, Hauntings, and the Temporality of Ruins," *Memory Studies* 2, no. 1 (2009): 87–101.

# From Istanbul to the East End
# in the Work of Barbara Nadel

PETER CLANDFIELD

In *Death by Design* (2010), the twelfth volume in Barbara Nadel's ongoing Istanbul-based police procedural series, the protagonist Inspector Çetin İkmen goes undercover to London during an investigation of traffic in counterfeits, drugs, and people. Beforehand, İkmen reviews what he knows about the foreign city, in a passage that points to key concerns of Nadel's fiction and of this essay:

> His mind flew back [...] to his only visit to the British capital back in the 1970s. It had been a grimy, dark place then, not unlike the İstanbul of the same period. Back then the London bobbies he had gone over to observe had usually finished their shifts drinking and smoking in pubs. Then, just like Turkey, Britain had been plagued by industrial unrest and political agitation. Now London, at least, was the shining heart of the global financial world and bobbies[,] so he heard, were more likely to go to the gym than to the pub. But İkmen was no fool and he knew that this new, bright London had been bought at a very high price. He'd read about the miners' strike in the 1980s, about how Margaret Thatcher had dismantled the country's heavy industries. Now the British lived by their banks, their advertising agencies and businesses with odd names like hedge funds and futures—things he didn't understand.[1]

While İkmen here contemplates limits to his and perhaps many people's grasp of contemporary London, the novel uses his perspective both to defamiliarize the city and yet, gradually, to bring out its parallels with his home city. Individual volumes of the series do recall (if often critically) orientalist tropes regularly featured in traditional British detective fiction, but the cumulative, cross-volume emphasis is on Istanbul as a modern metropolis with contemporary challenges similar to those of London. Both cities have seen rapid population growth along with proliferating development and redevelopment schemes whose results are not always aligned with ordinary public needs such as sustainable employment, reliable mobility, and affordable housing. As Nadel's work suggests repeatedly, clashes between global economics and local concerns can fuel forms of populism that are overtly intolerant or—more insidiously—that promote consumerist individualism as the sovereign good.

Nadel's books regularly challenge neat oppositions between globalized elitism and localized populism, pointing, particularly, to alliances between international finance and property industries and leading populist politicians. *Death by Design* indicts the hypocrisies and posturings of former London mayor and current UK prime minister Boris Johnson without actually having to name him. The seventeenth volume in the Istanbul series, *Land of the Blind* (2015), deals comparably with Recep Tayyip Erdoğan, the Turkish leader who has pursued neoliberal economic policies while promoting religiosity and manipulating popular opinion against the supposed influence of international secular elites. While it plots sinister links between amoral capitalism and manufactured consumer populism, Nadel's work also explores alternatives grounded in ordinary, localized kinds of diversity. *Death by Design* imagines utopian as well as disastrous possibilities for London, and the UK capital's contemporary complexities and parallels with Istanbul are also addressed in the second procedural series Nadel began in 2012, now running concurrently with the Turkish one. *Land of the Blind* revolves around the 2013 protests provoked by the Turkish government's plans to redevelop the city's Gezi Park—a genuine, if inconclusive, popular revolt against state-imposed gentrification. If Nadel's volumes identify contrived and manipulated kinds of populism as more fundamental menaces to their cities than individual criminal acts, they also invest hope in constructive procedures for protecting and renovating localized democracy.

## Settings and Procedures

In English-language crime narratives, Istanbul has featured as an atmospheric departure point, as in Agatha Christie's *Murder on the Orient Express* and its film adaptations (most effectively the 1974 Sidney Lumet version) or as a corrupt, brutal environment that protagonists struggle to escape, as in Alan Parker's 1978 film *Midnight Express*. In contrast to such depictions, Nadel's books take time and make space for nuanced views of the city, its place in Turkey, and its connections with the rest of the world. In a 2009 interview with novelist and blogger Richard Kunzmann, Nadel details her engagement with the territory of her series:

Turkey is a rapidly evolving country with a long and very involved history and so every book that I write about it is the result of a lot of research [....] I read all the latest literature and journalism from both inside and outside Turkey; and I am in close contact with friends and colleagues based in the country[.... T]here is also a "Turkey of the mind," a place I carry with me all the time [... as] the result of many years of contact with the place, its people and its myths.[2]

In a 2013 interview with another novelist/blogger, J. Sydney Jones, Nadel summarizes her reception: "I've had generally good local reaction with great support from Turkish newspapers and periodicals[....] That said it has to be remembered that Turkish literary criticism is much more polite and less punitive than that in my native UK."[3] Despite these comments, perhaps the sharpest criticism of the Istanbul series appears in a 2010 essay by Turkish academic critic Hande Tekdemir, who sees the version of Istanbul that Nadel presents in the first four İkmen volumes as "a modern caricature" of the historical city that is "suggestive for interrogating the way representations of Istanbul reflect the search for identity in the post-imperial centers of Britain."[4] Nadel's choices of setting, Tekdemir contends, are grounded in nostalgia: "Twenty-first century Istanbul is a sprawling metropolis; yet, Nadel's city is still confined to the limited geography that one encounters in nineteenth-century travelogues."[5] Tekdemir cites Nadel's acknowledgment in a 2003 interview with Turkish journalist Muhsin Ozturk that her emphasis on "historical neighborhoods" and on the city's cosmopolitan heritage is partly about marketing: "'if you are thinking of being published in distant countries such as Australia and [the] United States, then you choose these neighborhoods and themes to provide familiarity for them.'"[6] Hence, Tekdemir argues, Nadel's Istanbul appeals to British readers as an intelligible and relatable, yet reassuringly distanced and stylized, surrogate for their own urban environments: it "offers a geography onto which [...] fears of [...] uncontrollable chaos and of racial mixing as a consequence of modernity are projected, expressed, made legible; hence, purified."[7] Though not groundless, this is an over-schematic view of the likely effects of Nadel's books, scanting nuances of particular volumes and especially of the evolving series.[8] Yet while Tekdemir is not specific about how "Istanbul and the East End start to look alike"[9] for readers of Nadel's early novels, this critique does point to the way later İkmen books address the increasing extent to which the two territories *are* alike as environments being acted-upon by globalizing neoliberalism and its brands of populism. So, indeed, does a closer look at the first İkmen book, *Belshazzar's Daughter*.

Written, and set, in the early 1990s but not published until 1999, *Belshazzar's Daughter* quickly begins to address implications of an English writer focusing on Turkish settings and subjects. The novel opens with the brutal murder of an elderly Jewish man in the old and worn district of Balat. After a brief, enigmatic description of the crime scene, narrative focus shifts to an English teacher, Robert Cornelius, who works nearby and likes what he thinks of as the "Dickensian charm" of the area. Evoking the villainous thief-master—and the possible anti–Semitism—of *Oliver Twist*, Cornelius muses that "Fagin, especially, would have fitted in perfectly. Jews, old Jews, were the one and only commodity that Balat could boast of having in anything approaching abundance."[10] Tekdemir identifies a resemblance between Cornelius's view of the area's "picturesque filth" and the distasteful accounts published by 19th-century travelers E.C.C. Baillie and Edmondo de Amicis.[11] However, even as the English teacher functions as a vehicle to advance the narrative, his condescending assumptions are held up for critical inspection, and his profession and nationality highlight questions of culture and language. Having glimpsed a figure near the murder scene who resembles his Turkish-Russian girlfriend, Natalia Gulcu, but who flees when hailed, Cornelius withholds this information from the police once he learns of the murder, and he becomes both witness and suspect.

İkmen himself appears first at the end of the opening chapter when his Sergeant, Mehmet Süleyman, summons him to the murder scene, and his initial interview with Cornelius in the second chapter uses the Englishman's perspective to further establish his distinctiveness: "He was the oddest police-man Robert had ever seen, in the flesh at least. Dishevelled, red-eyed, reeking of both booze and cigarettes, he was like some sort of crime novel character, a refugee from the 1950s" (33). Thus, depicting her main investigator through the eyes of a suspect Englishman allows Nadel to use familiar tropes while implicitly acknowledging possible biases and limitations. İkmen's character-ization is refined steadily as the series goes on, and from the start his dissolute appearance disguises his resourcefulness, as Cornelius realizes when the Inspector begins to question him: İkmen's English is so "perfect" that it "irri-tate[s] him" with a "feeling of being bettered and outshone," a reaction that hints at Cornelius's own depths (33–34). İkmen gets his linguistic and intel-lectual resources partly from his family: his father, Timür, is a multilingual retired historian. İkmen's knowledge of English is also connected, of course, with his late-1970s London visit, which he recalls after reaching out for more information about Cornelius to his Scotland Yard contact, Inspector John Lloyd (117). İkmen's command of the language may disguise possibly the most problematic feature of Nadel's choice of setting for the series: the fact that all of the Turkish characters speak (to one another) and think in contemporary British English.

This translation and the inconsistencies it brings are exemplified when Sergeant Süleyman, less fluent in English than İkmen, fields Lloyd's return call about Cornelius, whose history includes accusations of assault from his period of teaching in East London: "Süleyman struggled to get it all down on paper. Mr. Cornelius had quite a past for a quiet English teacher, or so it seemed. He just hoped he'd got it all down properly and that Hackney really was spelt HAKNİ" (146). Nadel herself confronts difficulties of getting voice onto paper here, as the London borough appears in Süleyman's inner monologue first as itself, so to speak, in its standard English spelling, and then in his Turkish phonetic approximation. Yet in context Süleyman's version defamiliarizes the London place name as much as it suggests ignorance on his part—and "HAKNİ" should also serve to remind most Anglophone readers of their own unfamiliarity with Turkish orthography.[12] An additional challenge of translation comes when Lloyd's mention of "an accusation of racism against Cornelius" by a Jewish lawyer in London leaves the Turkish sergeant nonplussed: "'Racism?' The word was not immediately familiar to Süleyman, although what he felt upon hearing it unaccountably alarmed him" (146–47). Yet his familiarity with the concept of racism has already been shown. The Balat murder scene has included a swastika painted with the victim's blood (12), and Süleyman later notices that İkmen is shaken by the fact that "something hideous and, most importantly, racist had taken place on his patch, in his city" (85). The silent translation of the Turkish characters' conversations and thoughts into English, then, can sit awkwardly with scenes involving actual translation between the two languages. Arguably, nevertheless, the conversation between Süleyman and Lloyd in itself quite plausibly represents a routine process of communication across languages that is part of global police procedure.

The conversation closes with an exchange of admiring remarks on İkmen's individual methods, which Süleyman describes haltingly: "'Inspector İkmen looks to er...' He groped for the right word and he didn't find it. 'Psychological explain, you understand?'" Lloyd confirms his understanding by paraphrasing this description: "Oh, Çetin! Tearing around building biographies, getting to know the victim" (147). After the conversation with Lloyd, Süleyman receives another call, from Istanbul police commissioner Ardiç, who is impatient for progress on the Balat case and describes İkmen's procedure dismissively as "'[a]rsing around with life histories'" (148). The phrase is another notable example of the British idiom of Nadel's Turkish police— as are Süleyman's thoughts as he searches for the lab report Ardiç has demanded on İkmen's messy desk with its "tower block of files" (149). This likening of case files (containing human information) to the multi-storey apartment buildings that house many people both in Istanbul and in British cities is repeated later in the text (267), and it serves as a further subtle evocation of İkmen's interest both in people and in their environments. İkmen's detective practice is characterized as a form of populism. Consistently, he takes pains to understand those he deals with as individuals: both *Death by Design* and *Land of the Blind* dramatize this procedure. Effective as it is for characterization, the Turkish characters' demotic English—which is similar to that used by the central characters in Nadel's London series—would seem to help assimilate Istanbul to conventions of the contemporary British procedural. Nadel comments in the Kunzmann interview on the balance between authenticity and practicality in her handling of language: "Although I work in English I do try to translate at least the feeling of the Turkish context. Some characters are more traditional than others and pepper their speech with religious sayings and/or ancient forms of address[....] However[,] one has to be aware of pace and so I can't overload the text with such artefacts." Yet, the Turkish characters have to speak *some* distinctive, recognizable variety of English: there is no recognized degree-zero, neutral version of the language, and whatever idiom was used would carry associations. Further, in the ongoing context of Nadel's work, the Istanbul detectives' use of English is a two-way bridge, setting up, in particular, a view of London through Istanbul as well as vice-versa, and helping the series speak to British problems as well as Turkish ones.

In *Belshazzar's Daughter*, English characters are in themselves problems for the Turkish police: near the end, the English teacher Cornelius drunkenly attacks and kills a Balat rabbi (348–49). Cornelius is not the original murderer but has been deranged by the machinations of his girlfriend and her family, who believe themselves to be heirs of the Romanovs. The book's plot, which also involves a Nazi pedophile, sounds especially lurid in a brief summary. Yet in another of the text's implicitly self-reflexive moments İkmen remarks to Süleyman that "it is quite exotic enough having the Englishman 'involved' with the lovely Gulcu girl without throwing the disturbing Mr. Smits into the equation too" (138). The passing remark reinforces emphasis on the peculiarity of Englishness and on the procedural ordinariness of the Turkish protagonists. The exchange illustrates how Nadel's books are both overwrought and understated. They do indeed employ caricatures and exotic tropes. Violence can be horrific and ruthless, with sympathetic characters sacrificed. Crimes often result from obsessions involving sex, religion, money, and/or power. And dramatic revelations of hidden schemes and secret identities figure regularly. However, these twists do not simply fulfill the conventions of mystery plots; they also serve the subtler aspects of Nadel's narratives, where identity-secrets of both people and buildings repeatedly, as in both *Death by Design* and *Land of the Blind*, help to challenge simplistic, nativist kinds of populism. While it is possible that many of Nadel's readers seek suspense and shock and treat the material on setting and procedure as packaging, it is equally possible to regard the lurid material of individual cases as scaffolding for the more durable and distinctive attention to the evolving condition of their territories.

İkmen and his colleagues draw constantly on detailed, first-hand, and idiosyncratic yet usually fact-based local knowledge. The series certainly features landmarks and the stories underlying them, but it also repeatedly attends to specific and seemingly ordinary homes, buildings, and streets as central settings. Like the police characters' use of British English, this connection with what Martin Priestman identifies a "tradition of the strongly localized inspector" in British police fiction[13] could seem to anglicize the Istanbul series but actually supports its exploration of similarities between Turkish and English situations. A key component of localized procedurals is what Inga Bryden theorizes as "streetness," or the way specific and singular physical details, such as "exteriors of buildings" and "objects found," can offer "clue[s] to the hidden lives of others."[14] Bryden's remarks on the narrative potential of city spaces undergoing transition and reconstruction[15] also resonate with the fact that Nadel's protagonists are localized in places that are changing rapidly. City space itself can be an object of crime, as well as of contention, in Nadel's series, while hidden, neglected, and/or secret spaces frequently serve as metaphors for forgotten or overlooked possibilities with regard not only to individual cases but also to the larger condition of the city. Consistently, local matters and cases have wider implications: they are not cozily and insularly wrapped up: *Death by Design* and *Land of the Blind* are prime cases in point.

# Death by Design

While several earlier volumes have English connections, *Death by Design* puts İkmen in London and uses his now-established perspective as Nadel's main investigator to develop an unconventional view of the city's place in the world. Equally significant to Nadel's exploration of links between globalism and populism is the detailed plot that takes İkmen to the UK capital. The book's Prelude and opening chapter are set in Istanbul in a counterfeit goods factory that police raid after a tip about its grim conditions. Confronted by a grenade-brandishing young man who declares, "'I must be rid of you or my soul is damned!'" İkmen finds time for reflections that point to several of the book's main concerns:

> Surrounded by fake Prada, Gucci, and Louis Vuitton handbags, religious fundamentalism was not something İkmen had expected. But then he supposed that the slave labour that was used to make these things included all sorts of individuals [2].

Despite İkmen's efforts, the young man detonates the grenade, killing himself. The episode leaves İkmen injured and the police uncertain whether they are dealing with criminals or terrorists or an alliance between the two, and it sets up a focal question for the volume, and for later installments in the series, including *Land of the Blind*, as to whether overbearing religion or feral capitalism is the more fundamentally dangerous force. The opening chapter also introduces the book's focus on connections between globalization and exploitation, outlining the evolution of a traditional and relatively harmless "'knock-off' trade [...] not only in Turkey, but across the world," into "a multibillion-dollar industry [...] controlled largely by criminal gangs" trafficking both in counterfeit goods and in impoverished migrants whose labor produces them (4). In a pattern noted repeatedly in Nadel's books, luxury and misery exist in proximity, as the hellish factory "in the rundown district of Tarlabaşı" is "[j]ust seconds from the bright lights of the fashionable district of Beyoğlu" (4). Further, the physical juxtaposition underlines an ethical (rather, unethical) relation between luxury and misery. The counterfeit consumer objects revealed in the Tarlabaşı raid serve as items in an indictment of the globalized fake populism of so-called "must-have" designer brands— a populism almost as fake, as shoddily manufactured and illegitimately disseminated, as the knock-off items themselves. The title has more than one meaning, but it certainly fits *Death by Design*'s indictment of counterfeit fashions, and the book resonates with the more theoretical approach of Ackbar Abbas's 2012 article "Cloning Disappearance, Consuming Fakes," which questions the value both of "the *global commodity*—all those brand-name products destined to colonize the world's subconscious" through media representations—and of assumptions that the ability to consume designer goods is something everybody around the world wants and needs.[16]

The investigation into the mysterious forces behind the Tarlabaşı factory turns on a fragment of paper found in the wreckage with the letters "E, P, P, I, N, G" (19): "Süleyman wondered what it meant and whether it was actually a word at all. He didn't even know what language it was in" (20). The unexpected perspective on a familiar English place-name echoes Süleyman's encounter with Hackney/HAKNİ in *Belshazzar's Daughter*, as a detail that both hails English readers and reiterates the Turkish perspective of the series. After a London-trained forensic investigator recognizes the word, a supercilious British intelligence officer, Nightingale, explains its London provenance: "'Epping's at the far eastern end of the Central Line, where the underground system hits the edge of the countryside'" (21). The fragment of paper comes from a map of the "tube," and Nightingale adds that its conjunction with the "'boy [who] detonated himself after full jihadi battle cry'" suggests the danger of further terror attacks like those of 7 July 2005. Suppressing anger at the English agent's manner, Commissioner Ardiç—by this point in the series a much more sympathetic and nuanced figure than he appears in the first volume—acknowledges inwardly that "[l]ike Istanbul, London bore the battle scars of numerous terrorist attacks," and promises "full assistance and co-operation" (23). While the English minor character

Nightingale implies that Muslim Turks may be unreliable, the text itself emphasizes solidarity between Turkey and Britain, Istanbul and London, and İkmen's experience and knowledge equip him to render the assistance Ardiç promises.

In detailing the parameters of the London mission, Nadel's narrative elaborates on the nature and scope of globalization's underside. The Istanbul investigation links the Tarlabaşı factory to a man called Ahmet Ülker, a dual Turkish/UK citizen known to the Metropolitan Police as the owner of comparable factories in London that are under investigation for links with larger villainies. Inspector Patrick Riley, the Scotland Yard man on the case, briefs İkmen on the exacting nature of the undercover operation he is being asked (rather than ordered) to take on. Because the police "have no idea where Ülker's global influence begins or ends" (34), extreme secrecy will be required: İkmen's colleagues and family—including a son who is a doctor in London—will not know where he is, and the official story will be that he is working in counter-terrorism operations in eastern Turkey. His journey to London will itself be clandestine, as Riley explains in a passage that surveys trials undocumented migrants may face:

> We cannot risk your coming into Britain legally and then attempting to disappear amongst the ranks of the truly dispossessed. Those who traffic people are always on the lookout for police plants[....] Commissioner Ardiç tells me that you speak German and so the idea is that you travel to Germany and make contact with people traffickers in Berlin. The German police [...] will keep you under surveillance as far as they can but they, and we, cannot guarantee how the traffickers might bring you into Britain. It could be in a packed container full of hundreds of frightened and desperate people, it could be in a very leaky boat across the English Channel from France[....] Traffickers lose people all the time. I would be failing in my duty to you, Inspector İkmen, if I didn't tell you that you might not even make it to Britain[....] Think about it. Think about it very carefully before you give me your answer [35].

Riley's chapter-concluding injunction invites readers also to "think about it"—and to consider global migration as a process that consumes, or simply wastes, some human beings. Images, or imaginings, of hundreds of people bypassing the border controls of wealthy countries are often mobilized by anti-immigration populists, and passages like this could risk exaggerating the extent of what reputable news reports suggest is a relatively small-scale if recently increasing pattern of migration to Britain[17]; Nadel's framing and phrasing, however, clearly and yet quite subtly urge sympathy for "the truly dispossessed" among migrants.

İkmen's actual journey to England presents further variations on the ordeals Riley outlines, as he is transported in a hidden, extremely cramped truck compartment with two others, a couple he believes to be Somali who are collected soon after arrival in England and taken away to what İkmen's smuggler describes only as "jobs," whose possible nature leaves him uneasy (70–71). İkmen's own cover-story job implicates the ostensibly shiny side of globalized consumption: his migrant identity is Çetin Ertegrul, who has "recently been made redundant [...] as a security guard at the Akmerkez mall in Etiler" in Istanbul, "possibly because his employers felt that he was too old to be seen amongst their younger and trendier customers" (50–51). İkmen's in-person view of contemporary England and its people amplifies his pre-mission thoughts: "they were quite clearly much richer now than they had been. But as the truck was passed by a madly speeding Subaru complete with passengers making rude hand gestures out of the windows, he could see that money had probably not improved them" (72). "'Uncle, you're in the UK now, everything costs!'" explains his police contact, Ayşe Kudu, a Manchester officer who is undercover in London's Turkish community as his niece (74). Ayşe places İkmen in a guest house whose owner, Abdullah Yigit, has ties to the factory owner Ülker, and in due course Yigit introduces him at the factory, whose East End Hackney Wick location strikes İkmen as "semi-derelict" and recalls the dingy city of his first visit (121). The landlord notes with enthusiasm the area's impending transformation for the 2012 Olympics, and the text neatly implies a skeptical view of this enterprise by juxtaposing it with Yigit's demand for a "Job-finder's fee" of £250, to be paid from the two pounds an hour İkmen will receive for 12-hour security shifts (122–25). İkmen's under-cover job exposes deeper levels of exploitation: his security duties include keeping workers inside what proves to be "a carbon copy of Ülker's factory in Tarlabaşı," whose dire conditions are reiterated: "Row upon row of people bent over sewing machines[....] The noise was bad but the smell was worse. Just as in Istanbul, these people pissed and defecated where they sat, the women bled. Most of them seemed to be African" (151–52). Like the account of İkmen's undercover arrival in the UK, this scene may dramatize the scale of the misery it depicts, but the scenario is not entirely invented.[18] The hyper-bole works to underline the implication of western consumers in what goes on in such places, wherever they are located.

Fittingly, it is at the Hackney factory that İkmen first encounters the designer of the plot he is investigating, a small man "with a trim grey beard and a large white turban" who looks on "beatifically" as boxes of counterfeit medication are delivered and who is described by İkmen's co-worker Mustafa as "'a very holy man. Ayatollah Hadi Nourazar, from Iran'" (152–53). The London police identify Nourazar as an "agitator" whose fundamentalist and anti–Semitic rhetoric is so fierce that "the Iranian government aren't too keen on him" and who is particularly hostile to Muslims who reject extremism (155–56). The narrative goes on almost immediately, however, to reveal the renegade cleric's real agenda: while he is indeed conspiring with Ülker (whom he has met in Istanbul) to arrange a bombing in London, his ultimate motives are mercenary and material: "if he, Hadi Nourazar, brought enough death to enough infidels, then the world, not just the Iranian government, would have to respect him. And then of course there was the money[….] That, as nothing else about him, was real" (167–69). Weaponizing the fanaticism he foments in vulnerable followers, Nourazar seeks, in effect, to brand himself as a supplier of bespoke terror attacks. *Land of the Blind* will take up, and refine, the suggestion that money is a more fundamentally corrupting force than religion.

In parallel with İkmen's descent into the world of abused migrants, *Death by Design* also explores, or envisions, a London that is somewhat utopian: Nadel gives the city a Turkish-descended Muslim mayor, Haluk Üner, who pursues progressive social infrastructure programs while also taking firm measures against terrorism and crime—especially counterfeiting and associated networks of violence and exploitation. The narrative introduces Üner through a television interview that an off-duty Inspector Riley watches with approval both for the mayor's law-and-order measures and for his commitment to "several affordable housing schemes, in spite of the fact that economists were forecasting a recession" (65–66). A little later, İkmen (in his tiny rented room) watches television news and sees the mayor's response to tendentious media questioning about his heritage and religion: "'Yes, I am a Muslim and proud of it,' Haluk Üner said. 'My parents came here from Turkey back in the nineteen fifties. I am both British and Turkish and I am proud to call myself a Londoner too'" (82). İkmen's view of Üner's anti-counterfeit zeal is sympathetic but uneasy: "The fakers and their terrorist backers, if such parties really did exist, wouldn't put up with Üner […] destroying their goods and seizing their money[….] He had declared war on them on TV and probably via all sorts of other media too. İkmen could not help but feel a little fearful for Mr. Haluk Üner" (83).

One of the subtler threads *Death by Design* develops is a reversal or redirection of western myths of the mysterious and menacing Orient: it depicts a corrupted and endangered London that needs the intervention of principled and resourceful Easterners. Along with Üner and İkmen himself, another such figure is an elderly man, Abdurrahman Iqbal, whom the Istanbul police encounter living in a derelict house with other undocumented migrants. Iqbal has known "'Tariq, the boy who blew himself up in Tarlabaşi,'" and he explains to Süleyman how war in his native Afghanistan left the young man displaced, destitute, and vulnerable to recruitment by violent fundamentalists who promised to get him to London (116–17). Iqbal's own story illustrates that displacements and migrations are not just contemporary problems. He is an Indian Muslim unwillingly made a Pakistani citizen after the partition of the subcontinent following the end of British rule, and he no longer feels welcome in either country. However, he once "'worked as a driver to an English army

Captain'" who told him to "'regard his home as my home,'" and he seeks to take up this invitation and make his way to England to stay. While this aspiration seems doomed by time and change, Iqbal's Imperial experience makes him invaluable to the investigation: Tariq has left a diary in Arabic script that includes a significant reference which the elderly man decodes:

> "This says either Merk or Mark and then the other word could be Lene or Lana or Lena. I don't know. But there is something here in your Latin script."
> Süleyman leaned over his shoulder. "EC3?"
> "Yes." The old man looked grave now. "My friend Captain Jackson, the address I have for him from nineteen forty-seven is WC2. It means west city two. There are also east city codes. I think that EC3 is a district of London" [132].

Relayed to London itself, this postal decoding points to Mark Lane, E(ast)C(entral) 3, which Ayşe describes to İkmen as "'one of those City streets dedicated to commerce'" (146). The work of identifying an exact target, however, creates a kind of procedural suspense and allows for further commentary on east central London. Exploring the area with Ayşe—who indicates that, like the mayor, she identifies as "both British and Turkish" (176)—İkmen is struck by the juxtaposition of the medieval Tower of London and the modern City Hall just across the Thames that contains Üner's office. Ayşe comments on the mayor's habits: "'He is very fit but sometimes when he is under a lot of stress, you can see him outside City Hall having a cigarette. He's quite open about it. But I don't think he handles stress well.' She smiled. 'Poor man. Poor boyfriend or girlfriend of that man'" (177). The remarks echo earlier hints at Üner's vulnerability, and the area around Mark Lane itself presents further potential targets, both in the "standard selection of coffee bars and shops" that İkmen notes as present alike in "the City of London, [… in] Istanbul and almost everywhere that could be called urban across the globe" (184), and in a more distinctive building, Minster Court, a large 1980s office and retail complex whose design is evocative:

> "It looks a bit like Dracula's castle," İkmen said with a smile. "The pointed rooftops and the strange angles."
> Ayşe nodded. "One of the Met officers I know calls it the Fortress of Darkness" [185].

Without casting the building as a legitimate target, the exchange echoes İkmen's earlier reflections on the mysterious and possibly malign nature of London's financial centers, whose striking architecture could be seen as hiding in plain sight the opaque and possibly iniquitous transactions within.

The architecture of *Death by Design* is itself unconventional and perhaps risky. İkmen eventually learns at Ülker's factory that Nourazar is sending a fanatical disciple to make a suicide attack on the Underground; in the process İkmen is captured, and escapes with help of a factory worker he has befriended, an English-speaking Ethiopian who alerts Ayşe when the police search the building. The suspense in this stage of the narrative seems conventional, but the final phases are less so. İkmen's combined feel for "streetness" and rapport with people eventually pinpoints the Underground target: he smokes and talks with a veteran Underground worker who tries "to pump him for information" about the police closure of Tower Hill station, the nearest to Mark Lane, but ends up providing crucial facts: there is an Old Tower Hill station, disused since the 60s, whose "'proper name [was] Mark Lane'" (257). As in many of Nadel's Istanbul plots, re-emerging layers, both structural and historical, are key. In a further twist, however, the police arrive too late to prevent the explosion, which causes multiple fatalities—including Ayşe—and injuries, but whose impact Nadel's narrative perhaps underplays simply by continuing and adding further turns. Arguably, however, this move illustrates the way Nadel uses spectacular, dramatic situations and events partly as infrastructure for attention to less obviously vital matters, and it conveys the principle that the threat, or even the actuality, of terrorism should not paralyze ordinary life. İkmen himself escapes serious injury and rejects medical attention in favor of smoking; in a concession to verisimilitude, he vomits, but immediately lights another cigarette and then moves back "towards the Tower of London and the river" (264). The suggestion that İkmen is actually powered by cigarettes can be seen as homage to classic cinematic detectives, but in contemporary terms his smoking helps to characterize his personal kind of populism, since it is a habit that can be seen as antisocial yet also sociable, and in this connection, it is also linked to a further narrative twist. In his dazed-yet-clarified state, he once again contemplates "the oddly shaped glass building that Ayşe had told him was City Hall" (269) and in so doing sees the full design he is up against:

> Mr. Üner, the slick young mayor whose parents were Turkish immigrants, was in overall control. How wonderful, İkmen felt, that someone from such humble beginnings should end up as mayor of London. Working in a weird but fantastic building set in such a prestigious and lovely location. Now he looked at it, City Hall was situated in a small park. In that it was like his own place of work, behind Sultanahmet Park. But Mr. Üner made rather more use of his park than İkmen did of his. He went out jogging. But Ayşe had told him that Üner sometimes had to have a cigarette too. How weird modern life was! [271].

İkmen bursts into laughter followed by tears, and then, noticing a commotion at City Hall, suddenly understands what is going on: Üner himself is the ultimate target of Ülker and Nourazar. İkmen's affinity with the mayor comes not only from shared ethnicity but also from a shared ethic of populism—of getting out among people. İkmen alerts the London police; they confront Nourazar, who takes Üner hostage and escapes, as his zealous associates commit suicide, to the nearby home of one of his dead subordinates.

As "a block of old council flats where long concrete balconies provided access to apartments characterised by scuffed and time-worn doors" (307), the building aptly represents the public housing whose revival the mayor stands for. In a multi-directional confrontation, Nourazar denounces the mayor to the skeptical wife, Fatima, of his dead associate, as "'a homosexual,'" but Fatima takes Üner's side, praising his constructive agenda of parks and road safety. As the police close in, Üner himself calls the cleric's bluff, telling him he is "'as fake as Ülker's handbags'" (313), and Nourazar submits to arrest. In a hospital reunion with İkmen and Fatima, Üner rejects the suggestion that he needs heavier security and makes an adamant statement of progressive populist principles:

"I need to be out and about among Londoners. I have to know what they're thinking. Gives the police a headache but ..."

"Your prime minister doesn't do that," İkmen said.

"Nobody's prime minister does," Üner replied. "And that is what is wrong with this world, if you ask me. Nobody talks to the people any more, nobody cares about what they think. I tried to stop them getting ripped off by slave masters. I nearly lost my life because of it, but I see that as something to be proud of" [331].

The speech is an implicit retort to the claim from Ülker, under interrogation, that he is only providing people what they want, fake as his products may be (325), and the book as a whole suggests that safe public space is far more fundamentally popular than designer goods. The mayor goes on to rebuke himself for being slow to acknowledge that he is indeed gay, expressing wariness of the hero status his ordeal has conferred, and in effect warning of the role of celebrity culture in the spread of superficial, ersatz forms of populism.

As in some respects an anticipation of Sadiq Khan, the London mayor elected in 2016 who has proved to be a strong adversary of today's prominent right-wing populist politicians, Üner illustrates the insight and principles that make Nadel a significant writer. Üner, like Khan, represents a stable and stabilizing kind of hybridity, and an inclusive ideal of Englishness and of European-ness. Khan's precursor, the actual London mayor in office when *Death by Design* was published, was Boris Johnson, whose recent career Nadel's narrative implicitly but presciently repudiates. As mayor, Johnson was associated with moderate "One Nation" Toryism: a June 2019 article in the right-leaning periodical *Spectator* notes that he "backed an amnesty for illegal immigrants and suggested that people angry about immigration were partly motivated by racial difference." The same piece notes his metamorphosis by the 2016 EU Referendum campaign into "The Boris Johnson who repeatedly invoked the prospect of Turkish EU membership and Turkish immigration" as reasons for Britain to leave and "who later lied about having done so."[19] In a June 2019 *Guardian* opinion piece, Turkish journalist Elçin Poyrazlar cites Johnson's duplicity as an illustration of how "Brexit [has] brought to the UK the populist politics and distortions to which Turkey ha[s] already fallen victim."[20] While this formulation may overestimate Britain's previous freedom from manipulative politicians, it indicates how, in effect, Johnson's anti–European Union posturing has aligned his agenda with that of Turkey's increasingly autocratic leader.

Nadel's recent novels point to the ominous implications of such agendas for London and Istanbul alike.

## Land of the Blind

The London series that Nadel launched in 2012 with *A Private Business* extends her attention to clashes between inequitable urban developments and ordinary local kinds of diversity. The London protagonists, private investigators Lee Arnold and Mumtaz Hakim, are based in the city's East End, a territory that has particular affinities with İkmen's Istanbul as a place of layered and hybrid cultures, and as a site of particularly rapid contemporary change. *A Private Business* pointedly treats the Olympics as a sideshow to the quotidian concerns of ordinary residents of the area, while the fourth London volume, *Enough Rope* (2015), deals more centrally with the problematic effects of London's rising property values and the monetization of housing in areas such as Spitalfields, a district with an especially rich history of settlement by successive generations of migrants, including Mumtaz's Bangladeshi parents.[21] Lee, equally grounded in the area, reflects apprehensively on its vulnerability to wealthy and often-unseen property speculators.[22] In Nadel's works, gentrification is a common threat for London and Istanbul. While the London series continues to monitor the uneven development of the city in a general way, *Land of the Blind* (2015), Nadel's seventeenth Istanbul volume, offers a highly topical and specific take on the potential reshaping of Istanbul, and it also takes up *Death by Design*'s specific concern with consumer populism.

The main action takes place in late May and early June of 2013, as the government-mandated transformation of central Istanbul's Gezi Park into a shopping mall is blocked by strong popular protests. Events around Gezi are interwoven with multiple procedural plotlines. İkmen and colleagues investigate the death of a Greek archaeologist, Ariadne Savva, who sought to conserve artefacts of the city's Byzantine past, such as the remains of the Hippodrome where her body is found—and the piece of porphyry she is holding, a reddish stone that comes from somewhere else. The police also search for the baby she has recently given birth to. A person of interest in the case is influential property developer Ahmet Öden, who has clashed with Savva over his plans to demolish historic areas and displace their residents. Additional intrigue comes from Öden's obsession with a particular house whose owners, the Greek-descended Negroponte family, he pressures to sell. Further still, there is the cold case of a body discovered on the grounds of an elite school; possibly related, and initially most mysterious of all the narrative threads, is an untitled two-page opening section from the perspective of a man who has been buried alive. Central to the main plotlines are questions of which people the city—its heritage and especially its future—belongs to. The title *Land of the Blind* links past and present: it alludes to the mythical founding of the city by the Greek prince Byzas, who, advised by the oracle of Delphi, took advantage of previous comers' failure to recognize the advantages of its location; it also evokes the Gezi conflict—both the authorities' obliviousness to the value of the park and the literal, though usually temporary, visual impairment of protestors affected by tear gas.

The Gezi narrative—*or a* Gezi narrative matching accounts of the actual events from progressive Turkish and western observers—structures the novel. Numerous chapters begin with updates, often from the perspectives of Nadel's main series characters and their families and friends, on the widening ramifications of the protests and the increasing threat of violence. Early on, during a press conference about the case of the archaeologist, Police Commissioner Hürrem Teker (having just replaced the retired Ardiç) is confronted by a reporter with concerns about police actions at the park, and her reflections provide an overview of what is at stake:

> Angry at the government's decision to build on the last green space in the central Taksim area of the city, those opposed to the plan had been making their feelings apparent for some time. The encampment had taken the protest one stage further and now that the police were involved the situation was escalating. Hürrem knew that Gezi could potentially be a catalyst for unrest related to other issues people had with the government. Like the restrictions on the sale of alcohol [and the] opposition to a proposed extension to gay, lesbian and transgender rights.[23]

When the reporter reiterates that protestors "are being hurt [...] and all because they don't want yet another shopping mall in what is fast becoming a city of shopping malls," Teker inwardly registers her own views along with the procedural challenges of the situation: she "hate[s]" the narrow-minded and high-handed ruling party, "[b]ut for the moment they represented the state she had sworn to protect, even if some of her officers' zeal for the Gezi job had sickened her" (18). Teker's views align with accounts such as Turkish urban scholar Mehmet Bariş Kuymulu's essay "Reclaiming the Right to the City: Reflections on the Urban Uprisings in Turkey," written in June 2013 with the protests still in progress. Kuymulu observes that "destroying Gezi Park for a shopping mall was packaged as part of a larger project of 'urban transformation,'" which was facilitated by a 2012 law that "enabled the government to demolish and rebuild legally any building at risk in the event of an earthquake [...,] rendering the whole country legally ripe for gentrification."[24] Kuymulu contends that "the authoritarian neoliberal urbanism practiced at Gezi Park desired to transform use values embedded in an urban commons into exchange values through the construction of a shopping mall in the park's stead."[25] This agenda, combined with the escalation of governmental authoritarianism marked by violent response to the occupation of the park, galvanized a diverse coalition of resistance. Kuymulu concludes by expressing hope that the protests will in turn inspire wider activism in defense of the right to the city.

While *Land of the Blind* as a whole is clearly sympathetic to views such as Kuymulu's, the narrative incorporates debate about what the protests can accomplish. İkmen's and Süleyman's young colleague, Sergeant Ömer Mungun, tells his sister Peri, a nurse, that he "'can't condone'" police violence but feels that the protests are futile. Peri responds angrily: "'The people here don't want any more shopping malls[....] They have decided they want this park, why shouldn't they fight for it?'" (29). After his weak response—"'Because the State knows best?'"—she reminds him that they themselves, as non–Muslims from the eastern city of Mardin, are naturally aligned with various other constituencies at odds with the AKP (30). On her way to work a day or two later, Peri stops in the park to aid a victim of tear gas, a young woman "'with Muslims Against Capitalism.'" Another young woman, learning that Peri is a nurse, attempts to recruit her and rejects her explanation that she is needed at her hospital job. Peri's reaction further registers faultlines in Turkish society: "The girl, all dreadlocks and Goth gear, was beginning to irritate her. She spoke well, dressed and swore as she pleased. She probably came from one of those elite secular families the current government were so hacked off by." However, "the woman on the ground" (the recovering tear gas victim) intervenes more persuasively: "'We're all here together because we oppose the exploitation of our city. Doesn't matter if we're Muslims, Christians, secular people, Socialists, gay people, gypsies'" (80).[26] Peri elects to remain, and the encounter suggests how the Gezi movement was sustained partly by alliances negotiated from the ground up and by practical concern and solidarity as much as by radical rhetoric. Concerned for Peri's safety as the occupation continues, Ömer enlists İkmen to help him persuade her to leave. As he approaches, the Inspector is greeted warmly by two transsexuals, prompting Peri to appreciate the breadth both of the protest community and of İkmen's personal constituency: "Peri Mungun knew that Cetin İkmen had a reputation for being a man of the people but she hadn't realised that it meant people quite as diverse as these" (119). Meanwhile, İkmen and his wife Fatma have their own significant tensions concerning Gezi: unlike İkmen, Fatma is an observant Muslim and an AKP voter, but she points out to him that she also opposes the redevelopment: "'Just because some of the people who do want it are religious too, doesn't mean I have to agree with them'" (58). Her

226 Crime Fiction and National Identities in the Global Age

concern, and his, is with their youngest son Kemal's involvement in the protests. Later, when the protests have spread "to every open space across the city," Kemal returns home late at night with a wound from a plastic bullet, and İkmen reflects uneasily in terms that recall his apprehensive admiration of Haluk Üner's progressive program in *Death by Design*: "Gezi was an amazing phenomenon and he could only applaud its liberal, ecumenical spirit, but he feared for it and everyone associated with it" (241). Despite its festive spontaneity, Gezi is hard work.

*Land of the Blind* shows the Gezi protests as a clash of populisms. In debunking manipulative consumer populism, the novel echoes, and refines, *Death by Design*. In a mall, the consumer goods promoted may not be counterfeit, but the demand for them is a blend of real and synthetic, involving what Ackbar Abbas exposes as the dubious idea that global commodities such as designer clothes have particular intrinsic value. A park, in contrast, is public space freely available to be used and valued in diverse ways. The threat to Gezi has potential parallels in London, which as geographer Bradley L. Garrett points out is among many cities "being reshaped by the creation of privately owned public spaces ('Pops')," where "the rights of the citizens using them—our rights to the city itself—are curtailed."[27] Among examples of such London spaces Garrett mentions is "the area outside City Hall" itself, which plays a key role in *Death by Design*. Both in Nadel's narrative and in actuality, the Gezi protests can be seen as reclaiming not just public space but also populism itself as a force defined by genuine spontaneity and (like Üner's program) by grounding in the everyday use value of city space. Both Nadel books imply that constructive kinds of populism derive credibility and sustainability from the risk and effort, as well as the spontaneity, that ordinary people put into them.

If the diversity of opposition to the Gezi mall scheme is embodied in the range of protestors and motives Nadel's narrative includes, Ahmet Öden appears as a dominant embodiment of AKP ideology. When the developer's name comes up in the Ariadne Savva investigation, İkmen inwardly reviews his file: he "had become rich off the back of the government's Istanbul building boom. He was well known and admired by many. He was also despised by even more." Personally favoring the latter view, İkmen registers the awkward position it creates for him: "A lot of his colleagues were behind the redevelopment of the city. Some of them even said they saw it as a sacred duty to support what they called 'regeneration.' İkmen preferred to call it 'urban cleansing,' because when the developers moved in the traditional residents— gypsies, immigrants, prostitutes, transsexuals—moved out and he didn't like that. And what he disliked almost as much was the destruction of his city's history" (24–25). Öden's crass arrogance and its underlying insecurity are foregrounded in his first direct appearance in the text, where he rages after his architect's plans "for a radical new apartment block in Kadıköy" are recognized by his daughter's English nanny as a copy of The Shard, London's tallest building since its completion in 2012 (36–37). The episode implicitly mocks not only Öden but the UK structure as well, implying that its iconic status makes it, much like smaller objects of global prestige, likely to be knocked-off. The further implication is that both London and Istanbul are being shaped by questionable assumptions that high-profile architectural fashion is a measure of urban improvement. Öden's own history, summarized at this point, reinforces this idea yet also refines his characterization beyond caricature: having followed his father's example as an industrious manual worker, he found opportunity when the AKP came to power in 2002: "He'd worked on building sites for years, he was eloquent and pious, and so it wasn't hard for him to persuade people to invest. Also, then, he had wanted to build low-cost, decent housing for poor but observant people, like his parents" (37). These plans—which sound not altogether unlike Üner's—have been eclipsed by a combination of personal sadness and professional success. Öden's daughter has Down's syndrome, and the misfortune has "crystallised [… his] greedy side" and driven his career ambitions at the expense of his wife, driven to suicide by isolation and depression (38–39). Such indications of Öden's complexity and humanity (and even self-awareness) acknowledge that conservative populism does not necessarily arise from crudely evil intentions, yet also undermine the posture he strikes when he impatiently tells İkmen that he is not the bullying gentrifier described by the dead archaeologist's associates but "'a modern friend to the people'" who feeds the deserving poor while replacing worthless old buildings with desirable new ones (50–51).

Ahmet Öden's reflections on his life are followed directly by an exchange with his younger brother and employee, Semih, who mentions the Gezi situation: "'I think it will pass,' Ahmet said. 'People want to shop. Look at all the malls in this city. Of course they do. What use is a park?'" (39). Implying, or pretending, that ever-expanding retail facilities arise naturally in response to popular demand, these remarks echo the more purely villainous Ahmet Ülker's claim in *Death by Design* that his counterfeiting operations merely serve an existing market. After voicing his own less dismissive view of the protestors—"'Some of them look a bit crazy. But maybe they have a point'" (39)—Semih questions his brother's targeting of the Negroponte house, noting the availability of larger sites better suited to the luxury hotel Ahmet plans to build (40). The mystery of Ahmet's fixation on the house persists, as do his attempts to coerce the owners, who are the remaining members of a family victimized in the 1955 riots that saw Greek-descended Istanbul citizens killed and injured. When the developer confronts them with a bulldozer (in a scene that immediately follows Peri's decision to join the Gezi cause),

228 Crime Fiction and National Identities in the Global Age

the family call in İkmen, who has known them and the house since his childhood. Hakki Atasu, faithful Muslim retainer to the house's owner, Madam
Anastasia Negroponte, suggests to İkmen that Öden is both among those
who "'use religion as a weapon'" to advance neoliberal development schemes,
and yet is motivated as well by bigotry, targeting the Negroponte house
"because it is owned by Greeks" (94). These remarks help to keep Öden in
view as a suspect in the death of the Greek archaeologist Savva, with her zeal
for preserving the Byzantine past.

A major plot twist, however, revises Öden's profile as antagonist and
deepens the novel's exploration of what he represents. When his harassment
becomes intolerable, he is invited into the Negroponte house and is imprisoned, walled-in standing up, by Hakki and Yiannis Negroponte, Madam
Anastasia's son (or the man who has convinced her that he is her long-lost
son, separated from the family in the 1955 riots that killed his father). Öden
is the man buried alive whom the novel's opening section introduces, and
his ordeal is detailed in further brief installments. Making the developer victim as well as villain enacts a kind of revenge against neoliberal bullying but
also amplifies earlier reminders that conservative populism is a human creation. In the novel's final third, suspense over whether Öden will be found
combines both with tension over escalating dangers at Gezi and with further
revelations concerning the Negroponte house and Savva's death. With the
help of the archaeologist's colleague Professor Bozdağ, İkmen realizes that
the Negroponte house itself occupies the site of the porphyry-lined Red Room
"'where Byzantine empresses gave birth to future rulers'" (367). Öden has
known the house's history through his father, and it is in this room that he
has been imprisoned. Over Bozdağ's objections İkmen oversees the necessary
stone-cutting to extract the comatose developer. The Byzantine gives way to
the humane on the level of plot as well: complicated revelations proliferate
in the novel's final pages, as DNA testing proves the man calling himself Yiannis Negroponte an impostor, while Hakki Atasu turns out to be biologically
related to the Negropontes, who therefore favored his grandfather over
Öden's, provoking the developer's grudge. While both men are held accountable for their crime against Öden, who does not survive, the police fail to
solve Savva's death or find her baby. However, the reader is allowed to see
more, with a final section revealing that the archaeologist died accidentally
by falling after giving birth in the Red Room, while the child, fathered by
Yiannis, has been adopted by Hakki Atasu's humble son and his family. Meanwhile, with Gezi, too, much is left unresolved, although İkmen's investigation
of Öden's disappearance, plus Teker's help, has allowed him to avoid personal
implication as police are ordered to move in (346). İkmen and Süleyman are
left discussing the cases while watching Istanbul's Pride parade. The setting
in itself is hopeful, and openness and inclusiveness also speak when İkmen

notes developments since Ahmet Öden's demise: "'It's easy to judge conservative people and put them all in the same box[....] But look at Semih Öden—just made peace with Madam Negroponte, said he'd leave her alone, even wished her well'" (402). İkmen's awareness of his own possible biases helps to substantiate his characterization as a man of the people, one who genuinely appreciates diversity.

## Conclusion

Gezi Park remains in place, but so does Turkey's AKP government, which has used unrest since 2013 as a pretext for new authoritarian measures. *On the Bone* (2015), the İkmen novel following *Land of the Blind*, suggests the sinister reach of the regime in a plotline that also includes an especially neat illustration of the nuanced, progressive populism of Nadel's series. Commissioner Teker gets involved in the questioning of an arrogant American celebrity chef who is a suspect in the disappearance of an undercover police officer and in a possible case of gourmet cannibalism:

> "Word is that you shouted at her," Teker said.
> "Word? Whose word?"
> "Word," she reiterated. "As in popular opinion."
> He looked confused. It was great being able to flummox such an arrogant arsehole in his own language. And there wasn't a thing his minders could do about it. Not this time.[28]

Despite Teker's tactical victory here, the depraved chef does ultimately evade justice thanks to his connections with unspecified people of influence, leaving cannibalism as metaphor for feral capitalism's treatment of people. Recent volumes in both the Istanbul and the London series suggest that the unholy alliance of globalized capital and faux-populist authoritarianism is gaining strength. Yet, the ascendance of arrogant arseholes has been checked somewhat in 2019 with the victories of opposition candidates in the municipal elections of Ankara as well as—even after an AKP-contrived re-vote—Istanbul itself.

It may be in their distinctive kind of proceduralism that Nadel's books convey their strongest elements of hope. They express a consistent, quotidian kind of anti-elitism, as investigators regularly contend with self-serving officials, as well as with irresponsible or depraved wealthy suspects and witnesses. Correspondingly, the attention to painstaking and often-laborious police operations reaches out to readers who also must work for their living. The integrity of İkmen and Nadel's other protagonists resonates with Martin Priestman's observation that "in dovetailing various kinds of ability and commitment towards the knitting up of a constantly unravelling society, the police whodunnit expresses the fact that for many people of both sexes the strongest sense of community on offer is to be found in the world of work."²⁹ While sincere religious belief is respected in Nadel's books, more faith is placed in principled human action and interaction—and in vivid dramatization thereof. The fictive qualities of conservative and consumerist populism³⁰ arguably lend urgent importance to a figure such as İkmen, who possesses both broad cosmopolitan views and strong local loyalties, representing a fusion of globalism and populism.

## NOTES

1. Barbara Nadel, *Death by Design* (London: Headline, 2010), 33. Subsequent citations will appear parenthetically in the text.
2. Richard Kunzmann, "Barbara Nadel: Chatting about Her Newest Books and the Facts of Writing," *Richard Kunzmann's Blog: A Place for Crime and Thriller Enthusiasts*, July 5, 2009, https://richardkunzmann.wordpress.com/2009/07/05/barbara-nadel-chatting-about-her-newest-books-and-the-facts-of-writing/.
3. J. Sydney Jones, "Turkish Delight: İstanbul and Barbara Nadel's Inspector İkmen Series," *Scene of the Crime*, February 6, 2013, https://jsydneyjones.wordpress.com/2013/02/06/turkish-delight-istanbul-and-barbara-nadels-inspector-ikmen-series/.
4. Hande Tekdemir, "British Nostalgia for the Ottoman Past: The Legible Multiethnicity of Old Istanbul in the Works of Barbara Nadel and Jason Goodwin," in *Colonization or Globalization: Postcolonial Explorations of Imperial Expansion*, ed. Silvia Nagy-Zekmi and Chantal Zabus (Lanham, MD: Lexington Books, 2010), 26.
5. *Ibid.*, 30.
6. *Ibid.*, 33.
7. *Ibid.*, 35.
8. Another Turkish critic, Hatice Övgü Tüzü, presents a more balanced view: "Nadel certainly reiterates the image of Istanbul as a bridge between the East and the West, home of ethnic and cultural diversity, and the Imperial capital that is endowed with a mystical aura; yet, she also has a keen eye for the complexities of a dynamic city that is always in the making." Hatice Övgü Tüzün, "Orientalism Revisited: İstanbul as a Character in Barbara Nadel's Çetin İkmen Series," in *Images (IV)—Images of the Other: İstanbul-Vienna-Venice*, ed. Veronika Bernard (Zürich: LIT Verlag, 2015), 113.
9. Tekdemir, "British Nostalgia," 35.
10. Barbara Nadel, *Belshazzar's Daughter* (London: Headline, 1999), 3. Subsequent citations will appear parenthetically in the text.
11. Tekdemir, "British Nostalgia," 32.
12. Some, but only some, of the İkmen volumes include brief guides to Turkish pronunciation: see, e.g., *Pretty Dead Things* (London, Headline, 2007), 371–73.
13. Martin Priestman, *Crime Fiction: from Poe to the Present*, second edition (Liverpool: Liverpool University Press, 2013), 30.
14. Inga Bryden, "'There Are Different Ways of Making the Streets Tell': Narrative, Urban Space and Orientation," in *Writing The Modern City: Literature, Architecture, Modernity*, ed. Sarah Edwards and Jonathan Charley (Abingdon: Routledge, 2012), 217.
15. *Ibid.*, 218–19.
16. Ackbar Abbas, "Cloning Disappearance, Consuming Fakes," *Thamyris/Intersecting* 25 (2012), 144.
17. See, for example, Sarah Marsh and Alexandra Topping, "We Are All Migrants: Dover Divided by Boat Arrivals," *Guardian*, December 31, 2018, https://www.theguardian.com/uk-news/2018/dec/31/we-are-all-migrants-dover-divided-by-wave-of-boat-arrivals.
18. A 2017 *Independent* article reports a recent case of UK counterfeiters using slave labor: "One Leicester trading standards officer told of [...] a cluttered, fire risk of a workshop where [ ... ] he found three frightened undocumented immigrants sewing Henry Lloyd, Adi-

das and Ralph Lauren logos onto about 6,000 polo shirts." Adam Lusher, "'Counterfeit Street': the Trail of Misery Behind the Designer Knock-Off You Are Getting for Christmas," *Independent*, December 23, 2017, https://www.independent.co.uk/news/uk/crime/fake-designer-clothes-handbags-counterfeit-christmas-gifts-slavery-drug-dealing-organised-crime-a81125 81.html.

19. James Kirkup, "Rory Stewart Is a Reminder of What Boris Johnson Used to Be," *Spectator*, June 12, 2019, https://blogs.spectator.co.uk/2019/06/rory-stewart-is-a-reminder-of-what-boris-johnson-used-to-be/.

20. Elçin Poyrazlar, "How Brexit is playing into Erdoğan's hands in Turkey," *Guardian*, June 5, 2019, https://www.theguardian.com/commentisfree/2019/jun/05/brexit-erdogan-turkey-eu-democracy.

21. Barbara Nadel, *Enough Rope* (London: Quercus, 2015), 80.

22. *Ibid.*, 364–365.

23. Barbara Nadel, *Land of the Blind* (London: Headline, 2015), 17–18. Subsequent citations will appear parenthetically in the text.

24. Mehmet Bariş Kuymulu, "Reclaiming the Right to the City: Reflections on the Urban Uprisings in Turkey," *City* 17, no. 3 (2013), https://doi.org/10.1080/13604813.2013.815450, 275.

25. *Ibid.*, 276.

26. The word *gypsy* appears regularly in the novel and in the Istanbul series, notably in reference to Gonca Şekeroğlu, an artist who is Süleyman's lover. Her family has been displaced by redevelopment in Tarlabaşı, as Gonca reminds İkmen when they meet by chance, and previously (the narrative voice adds) "in the centuries old gypsy quarter of Sulukule" (135). Gonca then remarks that "'Roma are in Gezi in force'" (136), and her use of the more formal term for her people could represent an indictment of the prejudice that has driven their displacements and which *gypsy* may now be seen as fostering. Nadel's use of both terms (nearly) at once can be seen as illustrating the process by which language evolves.

27. Bradley L. Garrett, "Squares for Sale! Cashing Out on Public Space," in *The Right to the City: A Verso Report* (London: Verso, 2017), Chapter 6, ebook, versobooks.com.

28. Barbara Nadel, *On the Bone* (London: Headline, 2015), 235.

29. Priestman, *Crime Fiction*, 28.

30. On the damaging influence, for example, of self-mythologizing "characters" in British populist politics, see Nick Cohen, "Farage, Rees-Mogg, Claire Fox … Britain Is Seduced by Politicians Who Are 'Characters,' " *Guardian*, May 11,2019, https://www.theguardian.com/commentisfree/2019/may/11/farage-rees-mogg-claire-fox-britain-is-seduced-by-politicians-who-are-characters.

## Bibliography

Abbas, Ackbar. "Cloning Disappearance, Consuming Fakes." *Thamyris/Intersecting: Place, Sex & Race* 25 (2012): 141–159. EBSCOhost.

Bryden, Inga. "'There Are Different Ways of Making the Streets Tell': Narrative, Urban Space and Orientation." In *Writing the Modern City: Literature, Architecture, Modernity*, edited by Sarah Edwards and Jonathan Charley, 213–226. Abingdon: Routledge, 2012.

Cohen, Nick. "Farage, Rees-Mogg, Claire Fox … Britain Is Seduced by Politicians Who Are 'Characters.'" *Guardian*, May 11, 2019. https://www.theguardian.com/commentisfree/2019/may/11/farage-rees-mogg-claire-fox-britain-is-seduced-by-politicians-who-are-characters.

Garrett, Bradley L. "Squares for Sale! Cashing Out on Public Space." In *The Right to the City: A Verso Report*, Chapter 6. London: Verso, 2017. versobooks.com.

Jones, J. Sydney. "Turkish Delight: İstanbul and Barbara Nadel's Inspector İkmen Series." *Scene of the Crime*, February 6, 2013. https://jsydneyjones.wordpress.com/2013/02/06/turkish-delight-istanbul-and-barbara-nadels-inspector-ikmen-series/.

Kirkup, James. "Rory Stewart Is a Reminder of What Boris Johnson Used to Be." *Spectator*, June 12, 2019. https://blogs.spectator.co.uk/2019/06/rory-stewart-is-a-reminder-of-what-boris-johnson-used-to-be/.

Kunzmann, Richard. "Barbara Nadel: Chatting About Her Newest Books and the Facts of

Writing." *Richard Kunzmann's Blog: A Place for Crime and Thriller Enthusiasts,* July 5, 2009. https://richardkunzmann.wordpress.com/2009/07/05/barbara-nadel-chatting-about-her-newest-books-and-the-facts-of-writing/.

Kuymulu, Mehmet Bariş. "Reclaiming the Right to the City: Reflections on the Urban Uprisings in Turkey." *City* 17, no. 3 (2013). https://doi.org/10.1080/13604813.2013.815450, 275.

Lusher, Adam. "'Counterfeit Street': The Trail of Misery Behind the Designer Knock-Off You Are Getting for Christmas." *Independent,* December 23, 2017. https://www.independent.co.uk/news/uk/crime/fake-designer-clothes-handbags-counterfeit-christmas-gifts-slavery-drug-dealing-organised-crime-a8112581.html.

Marsh, Sarah, and Alexandra Topping. "We Are All Migrants: Dover Divided by Boat Arrivals." *Guardian,* December 31, 2018. https://www.theguardian.com/uk-news/2018/dec/31/we-are-all-migrants-dover-divided-by-wave-of-boat-arrivals.

Nadel, Barbara. *Belshazzar's Daughter.* London: Headline, 1999.

_____. *Death by Design.* London: Headline, 2010.

_____. *Enough Rope.* London: Quercus, 2015.

_____. *Land of the Blind.* London: Headline, 2015.

_____. *On the Bone.* London: Headline, 2015.

_____. *Pretty Dead Things.* London: Headline, 2007.

Poyrazlar, Elçin. "How Brexit is playing into Erdoğan's hands in Turkey." *Guardian,* June 5, 2019. https://www.theguardian.com/commentisfree/2019/jun/05/brexit-erdogan-turkey-eu-democracy.

Priestman, Martin. *Crime Fiction: from Poe to the Present,* second edition. Liverpool: Liverpool University Press, 2013. EBSCOhost.

Tekdemir, Hande. "British Nostalgia for the Ottoman Past: The Legible Multiethnicity of Old Istanbul in the Works of Barbara Nadel and Jason Goodwin." In *Colonization or Globalization: Postcolonial Explorations of Imperial Expansion,* edited by Silvia Nagy-Zekmi and Chantal Zabus, 25–39. Lanham, MD: Lexington Books, 2010.

Tüzün, Hatice Övgü. "Orientalism Revisited: İstanbul as a Character in Barbara Nadel's Çetin İkmen Series." In *Images (IV)—Images of the Other: İstanbul-Vienna-Venice,* edited by Veronika Bernard, 105–114. Zürich: LIT Verlag, 2015.

# The Global Hybridity
# of Sherlock Holmes

NEIL McCAW

Crime fiction has been a hybrid and malleable genre since its emergence as a cross-fertilization of a mélange of textual influences, including Gothic fiction, the Newgate Calendar, the novel of Sensation, the tabloid rhetoric of the "New" journalism, and the published crime statistics of law enforcement organizations such as the French *Sûreté Nationale*. And from the later 19th century, the mixedness and pliability of the genre came to be intrinsic to its wider, *global* popularity. For while crime and detective fiction had by this point begun to establish its own recognizable typology, tropes and formal conventions, the burgeoning intercontinental appetite for the genre required writers, translators, and adaptors to tailor their crime stories to the lived experiences and moral and ideological horizons of an ever expanding, increasingly diverse readership. While all-the-while remaining cognizant of the internationally familiar parameters of the genre, writers from around the world thus conceived plots, settings, and sensibilities more likely to chime with—and crucially more likely to appeal to—the characteristics of a range of native audiences.

Thereafter crime texts of all kinds became particular manifestations of cultural hybridity, an "exchange across a number of different national, transnational, imported and borrowed traditions."[1] Their inherent intermingling of nationalities and ethnicities was central to how the genre was able to address both international and local audiences in parallel, responding implicitly to global and regional sensibilities. Writers of crime and detective stories were able to fashion their settings, characters, and plots so as to be meaningfully relevant both to those readers with some degree of affiliation with the particular culture or nation depicted, as well as to those reading from the *outside* of these. Textual hybridity was as such facilitated by the inherent malleability of a genre that allowed itself to be adapted to fit the demands of a plethora of different cultures, and which was therein able to speak to a wide range of national and international audiences.

Perhaps the most longstanding example of the malleability and hybridity of crime and detective fiction is the case of the hero-detective "Sherlock Holmes." Because from the originary fictions of Arthur Conan Doyle at the end of the 19th century, to literally thousands of subsequent incarnations of the character across the whole range of media forms, Sherlock Holmes has been reworked more than any other cultural figure, and the international thirst for narratives featuring him seemingly remains unquenchable. The first global translations of Conan Doyle's works emerged during the 1890s, at the same time as early adaptations such as the stage skit *Under the Clock*, and since then Holmes has been recycled multifariously, with the Holmesian mythology played out across the continents of the world. There have been more than 1000 translations of Holmes works from 1887 to the present day,[2] and many thousands more pastiches, parodies, and adaptations. And each time Holmes appears the character receives a new inflection, melding the established features of the "brand" with aspects of the specific regional or national culture from which it emerges, making the cultural exportation of "Sherlock Holmes" an element of the wider process of globalization.

Indeed, it is possible to read global Sherlock Holmes translations, adaptations and reworkings as a case study in the nature of transnational reading and remediation, with the figure of Holmes at the heart of the broader ongoing interaction between national cultures. More specifically, to see the character as having been continually re-fashioned out of the tensions between the globalizing impulse to export cultural traditions and forms, and the localizing tendencies of specific cultures to assert their own identity and appropriate this "shared" culture in light of their own sensibilities and values. This is the process defined by Roland Robertson as "glocalization," when regional resistance to the homogenising thrust and impulses of globalisation manifests itself in the re-assertion of local identity, therein realigning the supposedly global text or cultural element to better fit "differentiated local and particular markets."[3] This global "product"—in this case the inherited figure of Sherlock Holmes—thus becomes partially regionalized. Which has resulted in Holmes evolving into a repeatedly exchanged cultural currency, traded between nations, ethnicities, and languages, and yet always seemingly *owned* by each of them.

The international evolution of the phenomenon of Sherlock Holmes—and specifically the glocalisation of the character for discrete regional audiences—is as such a complex, repeating, instance of cultural hybridity. Each time a new version, or synthesis, is achieved as the result of the interaction between the global and the local, Holmes is hybridized. But it is a particular kind of hybridity, not the one more usually detailed within post-colonial theory, seen as the "master trope"[4] of globalization. Kraidy among others has characterized this as embodying "unequal international media flows"[5] and a "democratic struggle and resistance against empire."[6] Whereas in the case of Sherlock Holmes, the process of transcultural communication is far less explicitly hierarchical than this, much more free-flowing and genuinely unpredictable. Each local culture is empowered—when recycling Sherlock Holmes for its own ends—to "transform and renew"[7] the character, rather than having someone else's version of it foisted upon them. There is little sign of Holmes regularly being deployed as part of a kind of totalizing cultural imperialism wherein the ideas, texts, and values of a dominating or colonizing nation are imposed on the lives of a subordinate or colonized one.

This postcolonial sense of a "Third Space" wherein native populations resist colonial dominance and subjectively assert themselves through hybrid cultural gestures and behaviors, is as a result inadequate as an estimation of the seemingly unrestricted free-for-all that is the cultural evolution of Sherlock Holmes as an international archetype. Holmes has always journeyed much more permeably into and out of a diverse collection of territories and has been almost limitlessly recalibrated. So, exploring hybridity in relation to Holmes texts requires a conceptualization that is both more nuanced and more compatible with the broader cultural fusing or melding of texts and identities that is evidenced by the global status of the Great Detective. Ultimately, we are talking about something more akin to what Bakhtin[8] has called "organic" hybridity, texts that are both diverse and contradictory. The international cultural presence of Sherlock Holmes needs to be viewed as the result of a set of "creative cultural practices,"[9] characterized by an innovative extension of pre-existing genres and texts that makes redundant all "notions of cultural authenticity."[10] In the analysis that follows, this sense of hybridity will be explored in relation to two specific 21st-century Sherlock Holmes franchises—Russia-1 and Central Partnership's *Sherlock Holmes* (2013), a Russian-language television series set in a nostalgic version of Victorian England, and HBO Asia's *Miss Sherlock* (2018–), a retelling of the Holmes legend set in a contemporary Tokyo. The discussion will explore how cultural hybridity manifests itself in these series and in particular the inherent interaction between the "native" cultures from which they emerged and the more global dimensions of the wider Sherlock Holmes legend.

## Sherlock Holmes *(2013)*

The Russian national fascination with the figure of Sherlock Holmes can be dated back to the late 19th century. Initially it was a feature of the wider emergence of detective fiction within Russian culture, with translations of writers such as Émile Gaboriau published from the 1870s onwards. But the character soon developed a profile of its own, and as such Holmes moved beyond being viewed solely as a manifestation of "the inexorable rise of the *detektiv*,"[11] becoming a cultural touchstone during a period in which Russia was striving to modernize and recover its infrastructure after the defeat to the British in the Crimean War (1853–56). Part of this wider process of modernization involved the country seeking to enshrine within Russian society a new, fairer application of the law for all citizens, introducing an independent judiciary along with fair and open trials.[12] Thus, when the first editions of Conan Doyle's Sherlock Holmes stories started to be published, beginning with a version of "The Adventure of the Speckled Band" in the popular magazine *The Star*[13] in December 1893, Russian readers were especially receptive to the idea of a super-heroic detective whose mission was to ensure justice for all, even if—ironically—this detective was at this time specifically *English* in origin. Perhaps, bearing in mind the status of Britain during the 19th century as the leading imperial nation, any potential awkwardness that might have been felt regarding the non–Russian national identity of the Great Detective was overcome by the fact that he was viewed as a personification of such lofty international pre-eminence.

From this point, Holmes stories became a regular feature of Russian popular magazines, including *Nature & People* and *The World of Adventure*, and the influential Panteleyeff publishers produced their own high-quality translation of all of the stories that Conan Doyle had written up to that point in their monthly magazine *The Herald of Foreign Literature*.[14] According to George Piliev, the wide-ranging popularity of these tales across all Russian social strata resulted in the word "Sherlock" becoming a familiar "synonym for ... detective."[15] Holmes, it was said, was believed by the Russian populace to belong "to everybody" as if he were "a supranational phenomenon ... a literary hero ... virtually real."[16] This deep-rooted national esteem was perhaps most poignantly represented by the appearance of the Holmes stories within the "Red Soldier's Library," a series of publications produced by the Russian state for the reading pleasure of its soldiers during and after the second world war. In the preface to this library, Sherlock Holmes is praised for being "heroically brave...[with a] remarkable strength of logical thought."[17] He is also claimed to be much more than just a literary character within the country at large—"they trust in Sherlock Holmes behind the Iron Curtain,"[18] it notes.

The 21st-century television series *Sherlock Holmes* (2013), produced by the Russian companies "Central Partnership" and "Rossiya 1," is the most recent in this long line of national articulations of the Holmes stories—of a figure who initially emerged from a foreign culture, but who has since been claimed as quasi-Russian. Created by Ruben Dishdishyan, and with a mostly

Russian production team (with the exception of English musical composer Gary Miller), the series was originally broadcast on the "Russia 1" television channel, with no global tie-in with any international broadcasting platform. This explains why the series was not produced with accompanying accessible foreign-language subtitles, and why even now—when it is viewable on other platforms, including *Soviet Movies Online*[19]—there are only limited subtitles available, in English and Spanish, and these are provided by an amateur, enthusiast group called "Spiritcc," rather than the production company itself.

Within the eight episodes of the series—the franchise was then abruptly ended by the untimely death of Andrei Panin, who played Dr. Watson—the reworking of the Holmes legend in terms of Russian culture is not explicit. Indeed, one of the only obvious instances where Russian national identity is even directly addressed is in the scene where the German Kaiser is shown celebrating Lodygin, the Russian inventor of the light bulb, who he says triumphed over the American Edison. Other than this, the Sherlock Holmes myth is repackaged as part of a much more subtle, complex interrelation of national identities. Instead of offering up explicit images of Russian-ness, the series apparently focuses on what it means to be English, or Western, while deploying varying representations of Englishness in order to define an ideal sense of collective identity, and the behaviors and mores that are to be lauded, as well as less desirable forms of identity, and the various values implicit in these.

The former of these is illustrated primarily through a prolonged, fabulously hackneyed caricature of Victorian London, teased out across the whole of the series. Individual scenes are situated against the backdrop of this Victoriana, an English urban landscape populated by friendly prostitutes, drunken but largely harmless sailors, knowing and helpful barmaids, and dubious looking though mostly benign street oiks, along with the occasionally nervous upper class-type who stumbles into the wrong part of town and falls under general suspicion as an outsider. This urban scene is also regularly punctuated by various stereotypical, Dickensian working-class pubs, with names such as "The Barrell House" and "The White Whale," locations that simultaneously imply a degree of social threat to some as well as a comforting "home base" for the clichéd lower orders for whom they are everyday landmarks. Inside these places, "authentic" straw-covered floors surround eccentric stage extras who offer various shades of character and color, such as itinerant vendors selling gutted fish and grubby street traders delivering the carcasses of pigs that they carry across their shoulders. These are venues that symbolize community cohesion and interrelation, made manifest by the loyal silence that greets any strangers who visit asking for information, or chasing down clues.

This contrived industrial poverty is a fundamentally sanitized one, with even the most apparently destitute characters sporting remarkably clean faces and well-kept beards, shepherding horses and cattle that are lithe and healthy and well-fed. At one point, in a bizarre mash-up of the charmingly exotic, a camel wanders across the screen to make its way along a cobbled London backstreet. It is Victorian London, but not as anyone really knew it, even leaving aside the fact that everyone is incongruously speaking Russian. The *Sherlock Holmes* series conjures up a particular version of the past, one tinged with warm nostalgia, an accentuation of the "heritage" aspects of this televisual Victorian city as an attempt at what Kate Mitchell calls a "positive and productive role in recalling the past."[20]

Hence each episode is conspicuously littered with national iconography: the most common of which being the image (and sounds) of Big Ben and the Houses of Parliament, which appear in every episode, as does the familiar recourse to the web of London streets and back alleys that serve as local touchstones locating the audience at the heart of the 19th-century British Empire. The River Thames is also key to this, appearing frequently throughout the episodes, portrayed as a vehicle for new clues, the ultimate resting place for various corpses, or else the means of escape or pursuit. It also provides an aspect of the scenic view of the Palace of Westminster, an ongoing reminder of overwhelmingly *English* flavor of the drama, and this is especially poignantly realized in the episode "Rock, Scissors, Paper," when the character Major Sholto rows Dr. Watson out onto the Thames in a small boat, and the two men reflect on their military excursions fighting for King and Country. The romanticized associations of an historical Englishness reach a climax in the episode "The Mistress of Lord Moulberry," when Sherlock Holmes boards a traditional English sailboat against the backdrop of the most celebrated of all national icons, the white cliffs of Dover.

The implicit nostalgia of this image of Englishness, embodied in such an idealized, heritage view of the nation, bears out Laurence Senelick's sense that "Anglophilia has been a potent undercurrent in Russian culture ever since Peter the Great." In particular, it accords with his view that this Anglophilia is at its core an "obsession with a mythical, cartoonish version of English etiquette—'merrie old England'—with its tea, self-deprecating humour and rigid protocols of politeness."[21] The longing evocation of "the Victorian" in each episode, through familiar archetypes and tropes, is in part a view of Englishness that has long since been popular within Russian culture. It has also been central to Russian reworkings of Sherlock Holmes, which almost always situate Holmes within his more familiar 19th-century context rather than any alternative historical period. From the most popular of all Russian versions of Holmes, the LenFilm produced series of films broadcast under the collective title *The Adventures of Sherlock Holmes and Dr. Watson* (1979–86), which conjures up its own mock–Victorian landscape, to less well-known Russian versions of the Holmes legend including the cartoon *Sherlock Holmes and Me* (1985), and the animated adaptations *The Murder of Lord Waterbrook* (2005) and six-part *Sherlock Holmes and the Little Black Men* (2012), Holmes has for most Russian viewers been fixed within the "original" context of English Victorian culture, usually a romanticized, wistful, almost sentimental recourse to a certain imagined past.

And this is profoundly ironic. For it suggests what is effectively an Anglophilic nostalgia on the part of a non–English production team, for an English Victorian time capsule. Whereas "nostalgia" is more usually understood to be a psychological or emotional "home-sickness" for aspects of one's own past experience or history. So, a series such as *Sherlock Holmes* poses the question as to whether it is possible to be nostalgic for a past that is not your own, or one that has seemingly played no part in your national-historical memory? *Sherlock Holmes* certainly seems to view aspects of a stereotypical 19th century with a degree of affinity and longing, and in so doing demands a reconsideration of precisely what it means to be nostalgic. We already understand that nostalgia does not have to be an evocation of an actual past, and often tends instead to be a selective evocation of an idealized version of our history, one that tends to be divorced from negative associations and rescued from the instability of social change. In which case, there is actually no reason at all that we could not be nostalgic for a history that we imagine but which primarily belongs to someone else.

So, just as there are many Shakespeare aficionados or Jane Austenites who think they long for an imagined version of the English Renaissance or Regency period despite the fact that their own family tree has no origins in England, it is surely equally feasible for Russian citizens to feel a degree of affinity for a romanticized version of the Victorian period? It is a form of nostalgia that feels closer to what Anne Herrmann has called "an excess of memory,"[22] wherein there is an overarching emotional connection to a perceived historical past, informed by a broader familiarity with this history through the lens of other cultural texts, wherein any gaps in knowledge are filled in through a mixture of individual psychology and life experience, creating an assumed form of empathy with that past. And in the case of the Russian affinity with the English Victorian era, any empathy with a version of Britain as the leading economic and military power in the world would hardly be surprising. It would not be too much of a stretch to speculate that some Russian people might feasibly imagine this image of 19th-century England embodies some of the characteristics their modern nation aspires to, or else might view the television series as offering an implied, displaced critique of what Russia has either not yet managed to achieve, or should not be striving to achieve, in the 21st century. Either way, in couching these debates in terms of a supposed English national identity, *Sherlock Holmes* allows a wider reflection on the nature of Russian national identity itself, while all the while displacing the potential poignancy and radicalism of this onto what is ostensibly no more than an examination of Englishness.

That said, whatever the underlying motivations of the particularly nostalgic view of national identity that is teased out within the series, it also has other things to say about the nature of Englishness at a moral and ideological level. The nostalgia is counterbalanced by an almost entirely negative portrayal of the sort of behavior and morality associated with 19th-century imperial Englishness in each episode. By implication, this also becomes a critique of so-called "Western" values and the impact of industrial capitalism and globalization. It is an ideologically loaded image of the nation characterized by debauchery, institutional corruption, and imperial chauvinism. This is evident from the very first episode, which centers on illicit immorality and corrupt class prejudice through the story of a sexually promiscuous rich young English woman who is being blackmailed on the basis of the salacious content of a number of indiscreet letters she has previously written to a lover—when all the time she is supposed to have been engaged to a fellow member of the British aristocracy. And while in its broad narrative outline it has much in common with original Sherlock Holmes stories such as "A Scandal in Bohemia" and "Charles Augustus Milverton"—as well of course as echoing one of the very first detective stories, Edgar Allan Poe's "The Purloined Letter"—nevertheless it has a much grubbier edge than any of these others. Whereas in the Conan Doyle tales the young women tend to be naïve more than calculating, foolish rather than entirely complicit, in the Russian version the Lady has fallen pregnant by her secret lover, and even attempted to perform an abortion on herself using a primitive folk remedy. Thus, she is never presented in a sympathetic light, and even when her behavior becomes known to her family, she continues to dupe her prospective husband and ends up marrying him, corrupting the assumed genetic purity of the English noble line by passing her illegitimate baby off as his own.

The immorality at the heart of English society is not just a matter of dubious sexual mores, however. For this is also a world in which violence and murder are rife, from the booby-trapped camera that blows a cameraman to pieces in the episode "Clowns"—prompting Watson to compare the victim to a soldier on the front line who has had his head "blown off by a shell"— to the brutal serial killing of multiple vulnerable women in "The Mistress of Lord Moulberry," and the graphic beheading of a hooded man in "The Musgrave Ritual." This is a London away from the trail of tourist landmarks that are featured elsewhere in these same episodes, a realm wherein kidnappers threaten to graphically maim and brutalize their victims, and where perhaps most tellingly, brutality and violence are carried out by both criminals and police alike. The official police force is shown throughout to be fundamentally self-interested and corrupt, beyond control and working outside any respectable sense of Victorian morality. It is part of the institutional corruption of the English state and a key player in the wider secret criminal enterprise that is on show. Even the otherwise honorable Inspector Lestrade is implicated in this behavior, turning a blind eye while most of the uniformed police officers in the series participate in corruption in one way or another, stealing jewelry, blackmailing, extorting, assaulting, and ultimately murdering. They are effectively employees of an underground criminal network, ensuring false convictions, carrying out violent assaults on prisoners and the public, and culminating in Lestrade being ordered by his "boss" to murder Sherlock Holmes himself.

This pervading corruption is at all time given a specific nationalistic context, associated with a heartless, imperialist English nationalism. The criminal police officers justify their illegal actions in terms of the supposed mass influx of foreigners, and Sholto, in a brutal riposte to advocates of the opening up of global markets, says: "Englishman tear off weaver's fingers in India so that they can't compete with our own products. How's that for civilisation?" His worldview is throughout rooted in an aggressive nationalism, "We are Anglo-Saxons! It is our duty and our burden," with his home wrapped in an imposingly-sized Union Flag, and littered with military memorabilia, imperial furniture, and ornate wall plaques commemorating English historical triumphs. He lives inside what is effectively a sanctum for an Englishness founded in the suppression of colonial Others, with his perception of the relationship between the police and the criminals couched in terms of the "Crusaders vs the Saracens." He has a self-anointed role within a supposedly sanctified, Christian, English campaign to purify national culture in the face of the diluting impact of "foreign natives." This is something reiterated by his celebration of the works of the effective "poet laureate of Empire," Rudyard Kipling, and in particular his view that East and West will never be able to live together in multi-cultural convergence—which is apparent in poems such as "The Ballad of East and West" (1889). In Sholto's case, however, this is not just rhetoric—the series includes flashbacks to past scenes of military conflict where he and fellow officers physically victimize native Afghans. It is a link between his crimes and his racialist ideology that permeates his claim that he "killed 68 Indians with my bare hands" because "they spawn like rats.... Either we conquer them, or they will conquer us.... We won't allow our culture, our beliefs, and our traditions … to be destroyed."

Across the higher echelons of English society this corrupt morality is represented within the series as "a coherent socio-cultural identity" fundamentally associated with modernity and "the West."[23] It is characterized by a pervading lack of decency and honor, with England seen as undergoing "a process of harmful Westernisation—or 'Westoxification'"[24] as industrial capitalism becomes further entrenched. The capital of this British Empire is defined by its organized law enforcement, capitalist commerce, and liberal moral standards, and each of these is shown to have debilitating social consequences. They are represented within *Sherlock Holmes* as symptomatic of the sort of inherent "emotionless rationalism, cynical secularism, self-centered individualism, and power-hungry colonialism"[25] typical of the Western, capitalist empire. Where there is also an accompanying absence of other values and features, such as "family, tradition, spirituality, morality, and hard work,"[26] those that might be usually associated with more traditional, less industrialized, less Western societies. As such, the series implies a distinctly Occidentalist sense of the English nation, in the sense of the cultural tendency to "look down on the West"[27] assuming anything non–Western "is bound to be better," and in particular viewing the Occident as "corrupt, degenerate, uncaring and hypocritical."[28]

Thus, rather than explicitly attempting to glocalize Sherlock Holmes in terms of a specifically Russian national identity, *Sherlock Holmes* offers a hybrid perspective on an apparently English national identity, exploring contradictory visions of the nation state. At certain points, it appears charmed and even seduced by a version of Victorian England—and the nation more generally—that is close to Ferdinand Tonnies' notion of *Gemeinschaft*. This is a community-based society typified by "such elements as family relationships, traditional folk customs, close-knit neighbourhood ties, and face-to-face contacts," often associated with an idealized sense of the historical past. Yet, elsewhere the series views the morality of Englishness as having been polluted by the negative impacts of modernization, focusing on those aspects of society that embody what Tonnies calls *Gesellschaft*—"rationality, formalised conventions, and limited-purpose contractual relationships."[29] The latter view of the nation is synonymous with the breakdown in communal links and the disintegration of society and common values that supposedly results from the shift from a feudal to an industrial economy. *Sherlock Holmes* is thus rooted in an essential opposition between the idealized, traditional, longstanding, pre-industrial and pre-globalized societies, and social formations in which the consequences of economic and cultural globalization are imagined to be almost entirely deleterious.

This means that although the series is not explicit in giving voice to an identifiably Russian identity, or to an explicit voice regarding the nature of contemporary Russian-ness, the way it favors supposedly more *authentic* national identities over the fractured, unharmonious visions of the modern (supposedly Western) body politic, says much by implication about prevailing views of contemporary Russian identity. For instance, the opposition between versions of the *gemeinschaft and gesellschaft* has become a common feature of 21st-century Russian political discourse, in which an idealized, traditional, organic, honorable sense of Russian-ness is regularly placed in opposition to the presumed decadence, individualistic selfishness, and moral laxity of the West. This is, for instance, a favored topic of the Russian president Vladimir Putin, whose rhetoric often concerns how "many of the Euroatlantic countries are actually rejecting their roots, including Christian values…. They are denying moral principles and all traditional identities: national, cultural, religious, and even sexual."[30] This is the language of a broader advancement of the cause of supposedly authentic native Russian identity that has been prevalent since the break-up of the Soviet Union, rooted in the fact that whereas ethnic Russians were once only around half of the population of the USSR, they are now "around four-fifths of the Russian Federation's people."[31] Ethnic Russians have as a consequence been "encouraged to identify"[32] with their nation state at a more essential level, and "to defend Russian culture" against the "homogenisation"[33] of economic and cultural globalization.

So, the national "internal identity crisis"[34] that is factored in to the portrayal of the Victorian English empire in the Russian *Sherlock Holmes* series can at one level be seen as a warning against the national division and loss of fellow feeling that are from an Occidental perspective seen as typical of "permissive and sinful"[35] Western culture. This explains why the integrity, justice, and order of Sherlock Holmes himself are in each episode pitted against the weight of the corrupt English establishment. The prevailing picture of a debauched Western/English morality serves as a Russian indictment of the capitalist, industrialized, "metropolitan life," a way of being that is seen to have "abandoned the organic links that individuals have to nature and community."[36] The morality of the English is portrayed as too consumed by superficialities and "commercial" values, a "mechanistic and materialistic outlook that stresses instrumental rationality and utilitarian values" and which marks it out as fundamentally different to other nations (such as Russia, presumably) that have held on to their own native "nationalistic and indigenist traditions."[37] The difference is, it is suggested, between those that are negatively changed by globalizing influences and those who refuse to lose sight of who they truly are.

# Miss Sherlock *(2018–)*

As with the Russian cultural interest in Sherlock Holmes, the Japanese fascination with the character can also be traced back as far as the last decade of the 19th century. Holmes rose to prominence in Japan at what was a particularly significant period in the history of the nation, at the time it was re-evaluating its own identity and position in the world, having up until recently—during its Early Modern, "Edo" period—been ruled by the isolationist military government of the Tokugawa family. These imperial rulers had demonstrated, since the earlier 17th century, an isolationist and non-interventionist attitude towards the West. However, when this family was replaced by the more outward-looking Meiji empire from 1868, there was an evident desire to modernize and internationalize the country. A new constitution was ratified, and the first democratically elected national legislature was formed, as part of an imperial mission to lift Japan out of its feudal past. This was to take place, it was decided, through a mixture of more systematic government and bureaucracy, industrialization, and a recourse to reason and law and order in order to facilitate this change. Japan committed to learning as much as possible about Western economies, societies, and cultures, and to use these models for their own modernization. One consequence of which was that Japanese people came to be introduced to, and quickly became obsessed by, the emergent European and American tradition of detective fiction. The genre embodied just the sort of contemporary sensibility for which they were striving, and as such 19th-century detective stories came to be associated with "the foundational influences of modern Japan,"[38] and as sites for "where these issues regarded as central to Japan's nation building and Westernisation process were explored."[39] Key to this was a growing fascination with the figure of the rational detective, a refraction of the evolving "modern" preoccupation with science, reason and progress across Japanese society and culture, as well as a representation of order and continuity at a time when citizens were anxious about the ground-breaking political, social and cultural changes taking place. The detective offered the potential of someone who could make sense of such disorienting change, who could understand, diagnose, and cure society's ills.

Thus, the first translations and reworkings of the Sherlock Holmes stories began to appear from 1894, beginning with an abridged version of "The Man with the Twisted Lip," titled "Kojiki Doraku." This was then followed by translated versions of *A Study in Scarlet*, and the first collection of short stories, *The Adventures of Sherlock Holmes*. At the same time, a discrete new genre of *niji sosaku* (secondary creation) Holmesian stories emerged, a range of pastiche or derived, rather than more literally translated, works that flourished long into the 20th century. Indeed, the trend towards Japanese Holmes pastiches has never really diminished, and has notably transcended social divisions and hierarchies, to the extent that one of the more prominent genres of Holmes pastiche has been animation, with series including *Sherlock Hound* (1984–), *Detective Conan/Case Closed* (1994–), and *Puppet Entertainment Sherlock Holmes* (2014–). There have also been a number of Manga graphic art/comic book series that feature or allude to Sherlock Holmes such as *Black Butler* (2006–), *Young Miss Holmes* (2007–), and *Sherlock Bones* (2012–). Each in their own way balances the generic features of the detective form with which the Japanese public has long since been fascinated, with the more glocal particularity of their own Japanese sense(s) of the character of the Great Detective.

The HBO Asia/Hulu Japan television series *Miss Sherlock* (2018–) is as such the latest addition to a longstanding, evolving national tradition. It is a contemporary manifestation of the Japanese obsession with Conan Doyle's Sherlock Holmes stories, originally conceived in the wake of the global success of BBC's *Sherlock*, which was itself watched by millions of viewers across Asia.[40] Originally only released on the broadcasting platforms of its producers, the series quickly garnered "so much attention (becoming a favourite of illegal streaming)" that HBO subsequently "decided to release it stateside"[41]— in the USA and across 19 countries in total. It thus became the first mainstream broadcast version of Holmes to feature a female actor in the role of "Sherlock"—in the series named Sara Shelly Futaba—an aspect of the series on which most media attention was initially almost obsessively focused, through its "two stunning leading ladies"[42] and the "unabashedly feminine" detective in "a killer pair of heels."[43]

But beyond its supposedly fresh take on gender politics, *Miss Sherlock* is at least as interesting for its nuanced reflection on the nature of Japanese national identity, with at its core a hybrid interaction between traditional and modern Japanese forms of what Charles Taylor has called the national "imaginary," an identity constructed through "images, stories, and legends."[44] The first strand of this Japanese imaginary embodies a "common understanding"[45] of a self-consciously traditional national identity that harks back to an ancient past, and the country's "Eastern" heritage. For instance, the episode "The Wakasugi Family Curse" opens in a bamboo/wood and screen Japanese house, and the camera systematically ranges across familiar architectural features such as the *amado* (the wooden storm shutters or doors), *shoji* (the screen doors made of wood and paper), and *engawa* (the passages that adjoin and link the various rooms). The episode then shifts to Sherlock herself enjoying a multiple-course Japanese buffet meal—"the irodori set"—with traditional *chawan* bowls. "Wato"—the series' Watson character—serves the meal dressed in what appears to be an authentic silk, pastel-colored kimono. Later the two young women both visit an ancient Japanese temple, to the accompaniment of ambient incidental music played on Japanese *Edo Furin* (wind chimes), overlaid with panoramic shots of indigenous housing and public buildings, and even a stereotypical pond full of Koi carp at the front of the Wakasugi family home.

In another episode, "The Missing Bride," even the otherwise rational, scientific, modern Sherlock appears to be seduced by this historically-sanctioned version of Japanese national identity, demonstrating an apparently "Oriental" dimension to her character by modeling a green silk kimono-type suit-jacket as she attends a tea ceremony at a Japanese tearoom. Then, when she returns to her home at 221B for the first time in the series, it becomes apparent that even this is situated within the familiar architecture of the traditional Japanese garden which surrounds it, implying an ancient, idealized sense of the centrality of the natural world. As the director Junichi Mori has stated: "I wanted to make it a new Sherlock Holmes by making a 221B that incorporates Japanese likeness rather than bringing it to London-like things…. I wanted an image like a museum."[46] The use of the word "museum" is significant here, and clearly loaded—referencing precisely the sense of a fixed, fossilized commemoration of a national past that is embodied in so much of the texture and geography of *Miss Sherlock* in its preserved, but also obviously highly selective, image of the nation. It is a geography that is intended to serve as a metaphor for the two sides of the "the head of a genius Sherlock, coexisting in harmony."[47]

Throughout the episodes of the first season of *Miss Sherlock* there is noticeable and ongoing recourse to a particular, longstanding, idealized aesthetic of Japanese-ness, an "ethnically standardised" and "culturally contained"[48] version of the nation and the national past that downplays ethnic differences and implies a unifying cultural homogeneity. It is a homogeneity that in numerous respects echoes the apparent stability of the underlying quintessential late-Victorian Englishness of Conan Doyle's originary stories, offering a sense of a stable nation that is especially reassuring within the context of hectic social change. Consequently, the "traditional, immutable core of culture" is maintained even in the face of "the shiny trappings of (post)modernity in a dizzying round of production, accumulation, and consumption."[49] And yet, while such a vision of the national imaginary offers continuity, the traditional, spiritual notion of Japan is also problematic; not just because it is fundamentally mythical—as with all such national imaginaries—but because it internalizes some of the most pervasive cultural stereotypes of "Oriental" Japanese culture. In particular, in celebrating the national "calm outlook (often represented as Oriental calmness, impersonality, unity with nature etc.),"[50] the national self-image becomes premised on "Orientalist representations" of Japan as "traditional, beautiful, spiritual, and emotional" to such an extent that its "exoticism of the Other" approaches the level of "self-Orientalism,"[51] an internalizing of many of the stereotypes that have historically been used negatively against the East.

The irony of this representation is compounded by the fact that this "reverse Orientalism"[52] runs counter to the 19th-century Meiji sense of detective fiction as an inherently modern cultural form. Whereas at that point the genre rose to prominence as the result of the wider belief that it was "thought necessary to import not only Western technology but also Western culture and Western way of life,"[53] and therein was viewed as synonymous with the wider process of modernization, in *Miss Sherlock* this logic is turned on its head. Instead, a well-known product of English national culture and global detective fiction is re-deployed in the name of an idealized Japanese *past*, a fundamental tension that is partially hinted at by series writer, Naokihiko Kitahara, who has noted the balancing-act he was engaged in while fashioning a series that both "cherished Conan Doyle's original book" while simultaneously striving for "a new story ... suitable for the current Tokyo."[54]

The hybridity of *Miss Sherlock* comes through the melding of this form of romantic nationalism and the resultant idealized sense of national heritage, with the more modern sense of the nation that co-exists alongside it. The latter consists of a contemporary Japanese sensibility that is explicitly related to the broader international process of globalization, the version of Japan with which the series actually begins, in the episode "The First Case." Here an unidentified young woman (who we later learn is "Wato," aka "Wato-San") sits on a plane reading an airmail letter in Japanese, while a Japanese steward notes that her flight is due to land shortly in Tokyo. Wato then looks out of the plane window, and as she does so the panning camera shot takes in the panoramic skyline of Tokyo in the daytime. The scene then cuts to the arrivals gate of the city international airport, with a parade of Asian travellers arriving, with various family and friends waiting at the arrival gate. Thus, within the first 10 minutes of the first episode of the series, the contemporary, international status of the setting has been firmly established.

The inherent modernity of this urban geographical location, reiterated via numerous scenes of Tokyo streets and cutting-edge architectural development, along with its antisocial flip-side, urban deprivation and graffiti, are part of a generic postmodern aesthetic that throughout is linked to an industrial landscape of roads, railways, and steel bridges—all used by the director as shorthand for the modern-day capital city. In the "Stella Maris" episode, for instance, the sheer scope of the urban setting is captured through a helicopter panning shot that takes in the full scope of the city from above, and across the first season of the series as a whole the identity of Tokyo as a character within the narratives becomes ever more prominent, with the repeated use of the familiar contemporary skyline and what the director Mori calls "the beauty"[55] of the wider urban environment. This reaches a climax during the final episode, "The Dock," in which the skyscraper skyline of Tokyo is the visual preface to the final dramatic scenes, and the potentially cataclysmic revelation that the city is in the grip of a viral epidemic which presents an existential threat to all of its 13 million inhabitants.

The metropolitan contemporaneity of this aesthetic is also matched by the characterization of Sherlock herself, moving the character beyond a more traditional focus on science and logic towards an apparently contemporary, consumerist, postmodern fascination with the transience and visual aspects of 21st-century culture. This is most explicitly embodied by Sherlock's own interest in art, beauty and fashion: "I can't think when my aesthetic sense is disturbed," she says at one point. The visual packaging of the character of Sherlock herself was so important to the producers of *Miss Sherlock* that they employed a well-known Japanese designer, Yuzumi Tomoki, to specifically oversee the lead-character's wardrobe, tasked with defining a new fashionable "Japanese interpretation"[56] of the legend. Sherlock is not just fashionable, but fundamentally *interested in* fashion and the fashion industry, as both a consumer and a devotee. She wears outlandish high-heeled, bejeweled shoes, vibrant designer coats designed by the likes of the French high fashion house Hermès and is, throughout the series, the well-dressed epitome of high-end, international *haute couture*. In the episode "The Missing Bride," this interest in fashion and beauty even extends into Sherlock manufacturing and distributing her own homemade cosmetic products, described by her landlady Mrs. H(atano) as "magical."

The fashioning of the particular form of contemporary Japanese identity evidenced by the series is as such reliant on the presumption that Japan is being reshaped by the broader processes of globalization, underpinning the emergent sense of the nation as a hotbed of commerce, technology, and 21st-century economic success. This—deliberately or unwittingly—resonates with the Meiji sense of the nation that emerged during the 19th century, wherein the nascent Japanese self-image was being founded in order, reason, science, logic, and the law, all of which were all seen as vital features of the country as a contemporary, developed nation.[57] Since the later 19th century, and especially after the calamity of the Second World War, this re-evaluation of the national self-image has also seen a shift towards a sense of Japan as less Eastern, instead as "on the side of the progressive and powerful West rather than on that of backward and oppressed East."[58] This amounts to a re-imagining across Japanese culture and politics that has resulted in the marginalization of some of the more romanticized, "Asian," elements of the conception of the nation; for some there are leftovers from the past, the legacy of a more feudal, backward, history of the nation.

That said, *Miss Sherlock* never represents these differing views of the nation as a binary choice. Instead the producers rework Sherlock Holmes, the most familiar of all Western detective characters/tropes, in terms of both historical and contemporary associations of Japanese-ness, confidently legitimizing both. Within the series as a whole the two models of national identity co-exist, despite appearing to suggest themselves as competing conceptions of the traditional and the modern. This implied equilibrium suggests that Japan need not necessarily choose one version of itself over the other, a form of harmonious hybridity that is seemingly conscious, as Naokihiko Kitahara, series writer, has indicated. He sees the series as dramatizing the Holmes stories in a "contemporary style,"[59] but still creating "a very Japanese Sherlock Holmes."[60] This allows a kind of balance between a self-Orientalizing Japanese-ness and the globalizing modernity of 21st-century industrial, scientific, technological Japan. It is neither "a total reversion to Sir Conan Doyle's most civilised characterisation"[61] nor a complete re-imagining of the legend, but rather an attempt to "inject Holmes's old white corpse with new [Japanese] energy"[62]—a hybrid sublation of differing Japanese national imaginaries.

## Conclusion

An awareness of the hybridity of international Sherlock Holmes texts, and especially adaptations, in all their "affiliations, cross-pollinations, echoes, and repetitions,"[63] offers fresh insight as to the prominence of this quasi-mythical figure within different cultures of the world. For while ideas of "the hybrid" have always been seen as synonymous with crime and detective fiction—which itself is a blend of numerous genres and literary influences which has regularly been translated and adapted across a range of cultural and linguistic contexts—hybridity is especially pertinent to the analysis of the vast legacy of Sherlock Holmes reworkings. Each new global version of the legend is an ingredient within an intertextual soup, a "rhizomic"[64] network of "glocal" texts connected in nebulous relations of differing types, including those of "variation, expansion, conquest, capture, [and] offshoot."[65] A consequence of which is that the figure of Sherlock Holmes has become a kaleidoscopically contested territory, with each new version an exploration of the "transnational"[66] cultural and linguistic borders between various nation-states. That does not identify Sherlock Holmes as part of what McLuhan called a "global village,"[67] but it does certainly confound the postcolonial view—articulated by Gayatri Spivak among others—that "in spite of the fact that the effects of globalisation can be felt all over the world ... the opposite is never true."[68] For while Doyle's Holmes stories might originally have migrated outwards from the industrialized West (viz. England) to the rest of the world, the resultant global presence of the character has—for the past century or so—repeatedly rebounded back to the "West" from other continents, meaning that it is now fairly routine for Holmes texts from all over the world to allude to, be influenced by, or become enmeshed in, each other. The obvious stylistic similarities between the Russian 2013 series *Sherlock Holmes* and Guy Ritchie's pair of films starring Robert Downey, Jr., such as the comparable quasi-stop-motion effect of their fight scenes, is one of a number of illustrations of the "antigenealogy"[69] of messy, often barely noticeable relations between transtextual articulations of the wider Holmes mythology.

The global hybridity of international Sherlock Holmes adaptations has as such to be viewed as a feature of a complex and multi-layered process within which each national imaginary shapes and is shaped by, particular senses of Holmes. It is a process that resembles fundamentally a range of comparable processes including métissage, mestizaje, syncretism, and brico-lage, but which is perhaps closest in nature to the underlying nature of Stuart Hall's "creolization," what he has called a "transculturation" arising "from the entanglement of different cultures in the same indigenous space or location."[70] The "indigenous space or location," in this instance, is each individual, dis-crete, native articulation of the figure of Sherlock Holmes, and the "entan-glement" Hall refers to is the hybridity that emerges out of the "variety of conflicting ideological positions [that] are given a voice and set in play."[71] Therein "Sherlock Holmes" functions as an intertextual mirror—reflecting back to the observing audience (whether they be Russian or Japanese, or else indeed Indian, Chinese, American, Czech, Turkish, etc.) a version of the detective that accords with, or can be accommodated into, their prevailing national and ethnic self-image. And as Holmes has become so culturally per-vasive across the world, every new adaptation will be informed by any number of other previous national and international manifestations of the character, articulations of the legend that haunt adaptors like spectral ectoplasm in a spirit photograph. Which means that the hybridity of Sherlock Holmes is now baked in, a by-product of the coming together of the desire to redefine Holmes locally and the pervasiveness of the legacy of the character within global popular culture.

NOTES

1. Brigid Maher, "The Mysterious Case of Theory and Practice: Crime Fiction in Col-laborative Translation," *The Journal of Specialised Translation* 22 (July 2014), 132–45: 134.

2. See "Sherlock Holmes," *Index Translationum*. Accessed January 15, 2019. http://www.unesco.org/xtrans/bsresult.aspx?a=&stxt=Sherlock+Holmes&sl=&l=&c=&pla=&pub=&tr=&e=&udc=&d=&from=&to=&tie=a.

3. Roland Robertson, "Globalisation or glocalisation?" *Journal of International Com-munication* 18, no. 2 (2012), 191–208: 194.

4. Marwan M. Kraidy, *Hybridity: Or the Cultural Logic of Globalization* (Philadelphia: Temple University Press, 2005), 23.

5. Kraidy, *Hybridity*, 148.

6. Marwan M. Kraidy, "Hybridity in Cultural Globalization," *Communication Theory* 12, no. 3 (2002), 316–339: 316.

7. Kraidy, "Hybridity in Cultural Globalization," 316.

8. Mikhail Bakhtin, *The Dialogic Imagination: Four Essays*, edited by Michael Holquist, translated by Caryl Emerson and Michael Holquist (Austin: University of Texas Press, 1981).

9. Stuart Hall, "Creolite and the Process of Creolization," in *Creolizing Europe: Legacies and Transformations*, edited by Encarnacion Gutierrez Rodriguez and Shirley Anne Tate (Liverpool: Liverpool University Press, 2015), 16.

10. Hall, "Creolite," 19.

11. Claire Whitehead, "Debating Detectives: The Influence of Publitsistika [polemical writing] on Nineteenth-Century Russian Crime Fiction," *The Modern Language Review* 107, no. 1 (2012), 230–58: 230.

12. Whitehead, "Debating," 231.

13. George Piliev, "Introduction," in *Sherlock Holmes in Russia, with an introduction by George Piliev*, edited and translated by Alex Auswaks (London: Robert Hale, 2008), Loc 16/2891.
14. Piliev, "Introduction," Loc 43.
15. Piliev, "Introduction," Loc 72.
16. Piliev, "Introduction," Loc 100.
17. A.D. Henriksen, "Sherlock Holmes in the Soviet Union," *The Sherlock Holmes Journal* 3, no. 2 (1965), 16–17: 16.
18. Henriksen, "Sherlock Holmes," 17.
19. *Soviet Movies Online.* Accessed January 1, 2019. https://sovietmoviesonline.com.
20. Kate Mitchell, *History and Cultural Memory in Neo-Victorian Fiction: Victorian Afterimages* (London: Palgrave Macmillan, 2010), 5.
21. "Curious Incidents: The Adventures of Sherlock Holmes in Russia." Accessed January 1, 2019. https://www.calvertjournal.com/articles/show/2817/sherlock-holmes-in-russia
22. Anne Herrmann, "Heimweh, or Homesickness." *The Yale Review* 95, no. 3 (2007), 23–32: 24.
23. Jukka Joukhi and Henna-Riikki Pennanen, "The Imagined West: Exploring Occidentalism." *Suomen Antropologi* 41, no. 2 (2016), 1–10: 2.
24. Joukhi and Pennanen, "The Imagined West," 4.
25. Joukhi and Pennanen, "The Imagined West," 4.
26. Karin Sarsenov, "The Literature Curriculum in Russia: Cultural Nationalism vs The Cultural Turn," *Culture Unbound: Journal of Current Cultural Research* 2 (2002), 495–513: 500.
27. Diana Lary, "Edward Said: Orientalism and Occidentalism." *Journal of the Canadian Historical Association* 17, no. 2 (2006), 3–15: 9.
28. Lary, "Edward Said," 10.
29. Arthur K. Davis, "Review Essay: Community and Society, Gemeinschaft and Gesellschaft by Ferdinand Tonnies and Charles P. Loomis." *Science and Society* 23, no. 3 (1959), 268–71: 269.
30. Speech by President Vladimir Putin at the Valdai International Discussion Forum in September 2013. Accessed January 2, 2019. http://russialist.org/transcript-putin-at-meeting-of-the-valdai-international-discussion-club-partial-transcript/.
31. Peter J.S. Duncan, "Contemporary Russian Identity Between East and West." *The Historical Journal* 48, no. 1 (2005), 277–94: 282.
32. Duncan, "Contemporary Russian Identity," 283.
33. Duncan, "Contemporary Russian Identity," 287.
34. Glen Chafetz, "The Struggle for National Identity in Post-Soviet Russia," *Political Science Quarterly* 111, no. 4 (1996–97), 661–88: 687.
35. Akeel Bilgrami, "Occidentalism, the Very Idea: An Essay on Enlightenment and Enchantment." *Critical Inquiry* 32 (2006), 381–411: 384.
36. Bilgrami, "Occidentalism," 384.
37. Bilgrami, "Occidentalism," 384.
38. Keith E. Webb, *Sherlock Holmes in Japan* (Bellvue, WA: NextChurch, 1998), 12.
39. Satoro Saito, "The Novel's Other: Detective Fiction and the Literary Project of Tsubouchi Shoyo," *The Journal of Japanese Studies* 36, no. 1 (2010), 33–63: 34.
40. See, for example, Paul French, "Sherlock Holmes and the Curious Case of Several Million Chinese Fans." *Blog of the Los Angeles Review of Books*, September 1, 2014. Accessed February 2, 2019. http://blog.lareviewofbooks.org/chinablog/sherlock-holmes-curious-case-several-million-chinese-fans/
41. Kristina Manette, "Why you should watch Japan's answer to Sherlock Holmes, now on HBO." *Polygon*, September 28, 2018. Accessed February 2, 2019. https://www.polygon.com/2018/9/28/17883722/miss-sherlock-hbo-japanese-holmes-tv-series
42. Manette, "Why."
43. Manette, "Why."
44. Charles Taylor, "Modern Social Imaginaries," *Public Culture* 14 (2002), 91–124: 106.
45. Taylor, "Modern Social Imaginaries," 106.

46. Hulu, "Production Note." Accessed January 24, 2019. https://www.happyon.jp/static/miss-sherlock/note/6.html.

47. Hulu. "Production Note." Accessed January 24, 2019. https://www.happyon.jp/static/miss-sherlock/note/6.html.

48. Marilyn Ivy, *Discourses of the Vanishing: Modernity, Phantasm, Japan* (Chicago: University of Chicago Press, 1995), 1.

49. Ivy, *Discourses*, 1.

50. H. Yoshioka, "Samurai and Self-colonization in Japan," in *The Decolonization of Imagination: Culture, Knowledge and Power*, edited by J. Nederveen and B. Parekh (London: Zed Books, 1995), 99–112: 101.

51. K. Iwabuchi, "Complicit Exoticism: Japan and Its Other." *The Australian Journal of Media & Culture* 8, no. 2 (1994), 49–82. Accessed January 23, 2019. http://wwwmcc.murdoch.edu.au/ReadingRoom/8.2/Iwabuchi.html.

52. Rebecca Suter, "Orientalism, Self-Orientalism, and Occidentalism in the Visual-Verbal Medium of Japanese Girls' Comics." *Literature and Aesthetics* 22, no. 2 (2012), 230–47: 238.

53. Tsutsumibayashi Megumi, "'There's a West Wind Coming': Sherlock Holmes in Meiji Japan," *Keio Communication Review* 37 (2015), 83–109: 83.

54. Hulu, "Production Note." Accessed January 24, 2019. https://www.happyon.jp/static/miss-sherlock/note/4.htm.

55. Hulu, "Production Note." Accessed January 24, 2019. https://www.happyon.jp/static/miss-sherlock/note/7.htm.

56. Hulu, "Production Note." Accessed January 24, 2019. https://www.happyon.jp/static/miss-sherlock/note/6.html.

57. Megumi, "There's a West Wind Coming," 85.

58. Suter, "Orientalism," 238.

59. Hulu, "Production Note." Accessed January 24, 2019. https://www.happyon.jp/static/miss-sherlock/note/4.html.

60. Manette, "Why."

61. Justin Charity, "Rehabbing the World's Greatest Detective: The Brilliant Reinvention of *Miss Sherlock.*" *The Ringer*, August 31, 2018. Accessed January 1, 2019. https://www.theringer.com/tv/2018/8/31/17804014/miss-sherlock-holmes-hbo-show-review.

62. Josephine Livingstone, "The Irreverent Joys of a Japanese Sherlock Holmes," *New Republic*, August 31, 2018. Accessed January 5, 2019. https://newrepublic.com/article/151011/irreverent-joys-japanese-sherlock-holmes

63. Rita Felski, "The Doxa of Difference" *Signs* 23, no. 1(1997), 1–21: 12.

64. This is the sub-heading of chapter 3 of Jan Nederveen Pieterse, *Globalization and Culture: Cultural Melange* (Lanham, MD: Rowman & Littlefield, 2003).

65. Gilles Deleuze and Felix Guattari, *Three Plateaus: Capitalism and Schizophrenia* (Minneapolis: University of Minnesota Press, 1987), 21.

66. Steven Vertovec, "Conceiving and Researching Transnationalism," *Ethnic and Racial Studies* 22, no. 2 (1999), 447–61: 447.

67. Kraidy, *Hybridity*, 15.

68. Gayatri Chakravorty Spivak, *Death of a Discipline* (New York: Columba University Press, 2003), 16.

69. Deleuze and Guattari, *Three Plateaus*, 21.

70. Stuart Hall, "Creolite," 15.

71. David Lodge, *After Bakhtin: Essays on Fiction and Criticism* (London: Routledge, 1990), 86.

## BIBLIOGRAPHY

Bakhtin, Mikhail. *The Dialogic Imagination: Four Essays*, edited by Michael Holquist, translated by Caryl Emerson and Michael Holquist, Austin: University of Texas Press, 1981.

Bilgrami, Akeel. "Occidentalism, the Very Idea: An Essay on Enlightenment and Enchantment." *Critical Inquiry* 32 (2006), 381–411.

Chafetz, Glen. "The Struggle for National Identity in Post-Soviet Russia." *Political Science Quarterly* 111, no. 4 (1996–97), 661–88.

Charity, Justin. "Rehabbing the World's Greatest Detective: The Brilliant Reinvention of *Miss Sherlock*." *The Ringer*, August 31, 2018. Accessed January 1, 2019. https://www.theringer.com/tv/2018/8/31/17804014/miss-sherlock-holmes-hbo-show-review.

"Curious Incidents: The Adventures of Sherlock Holmes in Russia." Accessed January 1, 2019. https://www.calvertjournal.com/articles/show/2817/sherlock-holmes-in-russia.

Davis, Arthur K. "Review Essay: Community and Society, Gemeinschaft and Gesellschaft by Ferdinand Tonnies and Charles P. Loomis." *Science and Society* 23, no. 3 (1959), 268–71.

Deleuze, Gilles, and Felix Guattari. *Three Plateaus: Capitalism and Schizophrenia*, Minneapolis: University of Minnesota Press, 1987.

Duncan, Peter J.S. "Contemporary Russian Identity Between East and West." *The Historical Journal* 48, no. 1 (2005), 277–94.

Felski, Rita. "The Doxa of Difference." *Signs* 23, no. 1 (1997), 1–21.

French, Paul. "Sherlock Holmes and the Curious Case of Several Million Chinese Fans." *Blog of the Los Angeles Review of Books,* September 1, 2014. Accessed February 2, 2019. http://blog.lareviewofbooks.org/chinablog/sherlock-holmes-curious-case-several-million-chinese-fans/

Hall, Stuart. "Creolite and the Process of Creolization." In *Creolizing Europe: Legacies and Transformations*, edited by Encarnacion Gutierrez Rodriguez and Shirley Anne Tate, Liverpool: Liverpool University Press, 2015.

Henriksen, A.D. "Sherlock Holmes in the Soviet Union." *The Sherlock Holmes Journal* 3, no. 2 (1965), 16–17.

Herrmann, Anne. "Heimweh, or Homesickness." *The Yale Review* 95, no. 3 (2007), 23–32.

Hulu. "Production Note." Accessed January 24, 2019. https://www.happyon.jp/static/miss-sherlock/note/4.htm.

Hulu. "Production Note." Accessed January 24, 2019. https://www.happyon.jp/static/miss-sherlock/note/6.html

Hulu. "Production Note." Accessed January 24, 2019. https://www.happyon.jp/static/miss-sherlock/note/7.htm

Ivy, Marilyn. *Discourses of the Vanishing: Modernity, Phantasm, Japan*. Chicago: University of Chicago Press, 1995.

Iwabuchi, K. "Complicit Exoticism: Japan and Its Other." *The Australian Journal of Media & Culture* 1994, 8(2), 49–82. Accessed January 23, 2019. http://wwwmcc.murdoch.edu.au/ReadingRoom/8.2/Iwabuchi.html.

Joukhi, Jukka, and Henna-Riikki Pennanen. "The Imagined West: Exploring Occidentalism." *Suomen Antropologi* 41, no. 2 (2016), 1–10.

Kraidy, Marwan M. "Hybridity in Cultural Globalization." *Communication Theory* 12, no. 3 (2002), 316–39.

Kraidy, Marwan M. *Hybridity: Or the Cultural Logic of Globalization*, Philadelphia: Temple University Press, 2005.

Lary, Diana. "Edward Said: Orientalism and Occidentalism." *Journal of the Canadian Historical Association* 17, no. 2 (2006), 3–15.

Livingstone, Josephine. "The Irreverent Joys of a Japanese Sherlock Holmes." *New Republic*, August 31, 2018. Accessed January 5, 2019. https://newrepublic.com/article/151011/irreverent-joys-japanese-sherlock-holmes.

Lodge, David. *After Bakhtin: Essays on Fiction and Criticism*. London: Routledge, 1990.

Maher, Brigid. "The Mysterious Case of Theory and Practice: Crime Fiction in Collaborative Translation." *The Journal of Specialised Translation* 22 (July 2014), 132–45.

Manette, Kristina. "Why you should watch Japan's answer to Sherlock Holmes, now on HBO." *Polygon*, September 28, 2018. Accessed February 19, 2019. https://www.polygon.com/2018/9/28/17883722/miss-sherlock-hbo-japanese-holmes-tv-series.

Megumi, Tsutsumibayashi. "'There's a West Wind Coming': Sherlock Holmes in Meiji Japan." *Keio Communication Review* 37 (2015), 83–109.

Mitchell, Kate. *History and Cultural Memory in Neo-Victorian Fiction: Victorian Afterimages*, London: Palgrave Macmillan, 2010.

Pieterse, Jan Nederveen. *Globalization and Culture: Cultural Melange*, Lanham, MD: Rowman & Littlefield, 2003
Piliev, George. "Introduction." In *Sherlock Holmes in Russia, with an introduction by George Piliev*, edited and translated by Alex Auswaks. London: Robert Hale, 2008.
Speech by President Vladimir Putin at the Valdai International Discussion Forum in September 2013. Accessed February 1, 2019. http://russialist.org/transcript-putin-at-meeting-of-the-valdai-international-discussion-club-partial-transcript/.
Robertson, Roland. "Globalisation or glocalisation?" *Journal of International Communication* 18, no. 2 (2012), 191–208.
Saito, Satoro. "The Novel's Other: Detective Fiction and the Literary Project of Tsubouchi Shoyo." *The Journal of Japanese Studies* 36, no. 1 (2010), 33–63.
Sarsenov, Karin. "The Literature Curriculum in Russia: Cultural Nationalism vs The Cultural Turn." *Culture Unbound: Journal of Current Cultural Research* 2 (2002), 495–513.
"Sherlock Holmes," *Index Translationum*. Accessed January 15, 2019. http://www.unesco.org/xtrans/bsresult.aspx?a=&stxt=Sherlock+Holmes&sl=&l=&c= &pla=&pub=&tr=&e= &udc=&d=&from=&to=&tie=a.
*Soviet Movies Online*. Accessed January 1, 2019. https://sovietmoviesonline.com.
Spivak, Gayatri Chakravorty. *Death of a Discipline.*, New York: Columba University Press, 2003.
Suter, Rebecca. "Orientalism, Self-Orientalism, and Occidentalism in the Visual-Verbal Medium of Japanese Girls' Comics." *Literature and Aesthetics* 22, no. 2 (2012), 230–47.
Taylor, Charles. "Modern Social Imaginaries." *Public Culture* 14 (2002), 91–124.
Vertovec, Steven. "Conceiving and Researching Transnationalism." *Ethnic and Racial Studies* 22, no. 2 (1999), 447–61.
Webb, Keith E. *Sherlock Holmes in Japan*, Bellvue, WA: NextChurch, 1998.
Whitehead, Claire. "Debating Detectives: The Influence of Publitsistika [polemical writing] on Nineteenth-Century Russian Crime Fiction." *The Modern Language Review* 107, no. 1 (2012), 230–58.
Yoshioka, H. "Samurai and Self-Colonization in Japan." In *The Decolonization of Imagination: Culture, Knowledge and Power*, edited by J. Nederveen Pieterse and B. Parekh, London: Zed Books, 1995, 99–112.

# About the Contributors

Somdatta **Bhattacharya** has a Ph.D. in English studies from Jadavpur University. She is an assistant professor in the Department of Humanities and Social Sciences, Indian Institute of Technology Kharagpur, West Bengal, India. Her research interests are rooted in areas such as the city in literature, social theories of space and spatiality, crime fiction, urban cultural studies, and South Asian popular culture.

Peter **Clandfield** teaches in the Department of English at MacEwan University in Edmonton, Alberta. His interests include contemporary English, Scottish, and Canadian fiction; literary and screen representations of urban development and redevelopment; questions of adaptation, remaking, and cultural recycling; and debates concerning surveillance, censorship, and freedom of expression.

Heath A. **Diehl** is a teaching professor in the Honors College and Department of English at Bowling Green State University. His areas of specialization include contemporary American and British fiction, dramatic literature, and trauma studies. His work focuses on how addiction is ideologically framed and consumed within Western cultural artifacts.

Jean **Gregorek** is an associate professor of English at Canisius College in Buffalo, where she specializes in postcolonial literature, cultural studies, and crime fiction. Her publications include an essay on Henning Mankell's Wallander novels in the journal *Genre* and on Tana French thrillers in the collection *Class and Culture in Crime Fiction*.

Colette **Guldimann** has a Ph.D. in English from Queen Mary, University of London, and is interested in transnational cultural crossings and cultural meanings. Her research focuses on interpretations of popular genres within postcolonial contexts, particularly crime fiction in Africa. Educated at the University of Cape Town, she teaches at the University of Pretoria, South Africa.

Alexandra **Hauke** studied English and American studies as well as Hispanic studies at the University of Vienna and at the University of Maryland at College Park. She is a lecturer in American studies at the University of Passau, Germany, where her research areas include Native American and First Nations' studies, Gothic and horror studies, crime and detective fiction, and contemporary American TV and film as well as American popular culture.

255

Julie H. **Kim** is a professor of English at Northeastern Illinois University in Chicago. Her primary fields of research include early modern British literature and detective fiction. She is the editor of *Race and Religion in the Postcolonial Detective Story, Murdering Miss Marple,* and *Class and Culture in Crime Fiction.*

Tim **Libretti** is a professor in the English Department and acting associate dean of the College of Arts and Sciences at Northeastern Illinois University in Chicago. He has published numerous book chapters and articles on U.S. working-class literature and culture; U.S. racial and ethnic literatures and cultures; the politics of race, class, gender, and sexuality; and a range of cultural studies issues.

Neil **McCaw** is a professor of Victorian literature and culture at the University of Winchester (UK). He has published widely on the Victorians, crime and detective culture, and in particular Sherlock Holmes. He is the academic director of the Arthur Conan Doyle Collection, Lancelyn Green Bequest, and is working on a multiple-volume collection of 19th-century crime fiction resources for Routledge.

Andrew Hock Soon **Ng** is an associate professor of literary studies and creative writing at Monash University, Malaysia. His research interests include Gothic and horror narratives, postcolonial writings, and postmodern literature. He has contributed articles to numerous peer-reviewed journals and collections of essays and is the author of *Women and Domestic Space in Contemporary Gothic Narratives.*

Somali **Saren** is a research scholar in the English and Foreign Languages University, Hyderabad (India). Her dissertation is "Postcolonial Crime Fiction: Exploring the Genealogy and Current Trends." She has published and presented various papers on the crime genre and postcolonial studies. Her other areas of interests include Global South studies, transnational and diaspora literature.

Janice **Shaw** is a lecturer at the University of New England (Australia) in crime fiction, children's literature, and film and gender studies. Her Ph.D. was based on a study of the discontinuous narrative in Australian fiction. She has published articles on crime fiction with a focus on P.D. James as well as the relationship between mathematics and the detective in literature, film and popular culture.

# Index